Mirror of the Indies

Library of the Indies

E. M. Beekman, General Editor

Translated by Frans van Rosevelt

Edited by E. M. Beekman

The University of Massachusetts

Press, Amherst, 1982

Mirror of the Indies
A History of Dutch Colonial Literature

Rob Nieuwenhuys

TO E. DU PERRON

"... and named it Mirror of the Indies,
because it tells not only of many
common affairs and of those described
by others but because it recounts
many noteworthy incidents and the
circumstances of noteworthy people
and events. These the Mirror of the
Indies sincerely relates, and without,
as they say, buttering anyone up."
Nicolaus de Graaff in his preface to his
Mirror of the Indies *(Oost-Indise
spiegel, 1703)*

Originally published by
Em. Querido's Uitgeverij, B. V., Amsterdam, Holland,
under the title *Oost-Indische Spiegel,*
copyright © 1972 by Rob Nieuwenhuys.
Copyright © 1982 by
The University of Massachusetts Press
Printed in the United States of America

Library of Congress Cataloging in Publication Data
Nieuwenhuys, Robert, 1908–
Mirror of the Indies.
(Library of the Indies)
Translation of: Oost-Indische Spiegel.
1. Dutch literature—Indonesia—History and criticism.
2. Indonesia in literature.   I. Beekman, E. M.,
1939– . II. Title. III. Series.
PT5911.N513   839.3′1′099598   82–4755
ISBN 0–87023–368–8   AACR2

The publisher and the editor gratefully acknowledge
the support of the Translations and Publications
Programs of the National Endowment for the
Humanities, the Foundation for the Promotion of the
Translation of Dutch Literary Works, and the Prince
Bernhard Fund, in making this publication possible.

Contents

Preface vii

Introduction xiii

Author's Introduction xxiv

I *The Period of the Lofty Company* 1
East Indies Voyages 1
Valentijn, Camphuis, Rumphius 22

II *Breakthrough of New Ideas* 33
Willem and Dirk van Hogendorp, Father and Son 33
The Era of Van der Capellen 42

III *Van Hoëvell and Junghuhn* 59
Wolter Robert, Baron van Hoëvell 59
Franz Wilhelm Junghuhn 67

IV *Eduard Douwes Dekker* 77

V *Four "Eccentrics"* 94
S. E. W. Roorda van Eysinga 94
H. N. van der Tuuk 100
A. M. Courier dit Dubekart 103
Alexander Cohen 106

VI *P. A. Daum* 111

VII   *The Indies World of Couperus*   123

VIII   *The Indies Maligned and Avenged*   134
Bas Veth and His Opponents   134
Creusesol   141
The Other World   145

IX   *The World Beyond*   154
The Ethical Movement   154
John Company   163

X   *The Netherlands East Indies*   167
The Young Dutch Wives   167
M. H. Székely-Lulofs   170

XI   *The Idea of Federation*   177
Noto Suroto   184

XII   *Between the Thirties and Forties*   189
Country of Origin   189
In Search of the Country of Origin   193
Critique and Reconstruction   204
Beyond Constraint   210
Willem Walraven: A Colonial Tragedy   213
Distant Thunder   221

XIII   *Best Forgotten*   225
"Asia Raya": The Japanese Occupation   225
"Indonesia Merdeka": A Free Indonesia   239
"Irian Barat"   248

XIV   *Not to be Forgotten*   255
Maria Dermoût   255
Beb Vuyk   267
Johan Fabricius   278
H. J. Friedericy   282
A. Alberts   290
Two Authors: Hella Haasse and Aya Zikken   298
Indonesia Revisited   307
Rob Nieuwenhuys/E. Breton de Nijs   323

Index   331

Preface

This volume is one of a series of literary works written by the Dutch about their lives in the former colony of the Dutch East Indies, now the Republic of Indonesia. This realm of more than three thousand islands is roughly one quarter the size of the continental United States. It consists of the four Greater Sunda Islands—Sumatra, larger than California; Java, about the size of New York State; Borneo (presently called Kalimantan), about the size of France; and Celebes (now called Sulawesi), about the size of North Dakota. East from Java is a string of smaller islands called the Lesser Sunda Islands, which includes Bali, Lombok, Sumba, Sumbawa, Flores, and Timor. Further east from the Lesser Sunda Islands lies New Guinea, now called Irian Barat, which is the second largest island in the world. Between New Guinea and Celebes there is a host of smaller islands, often known as the Moluccas, that includes a group once celebrated as the Spice Islands.

One of the most volcanic regions in the world, the Malay archipelago is tropical in climate and has a diverse population. Some 250 languages are spoken in Indonesia and it is remarkable that a population of such widely differing cultural and ethnic backgrounds adopted the Malay language as its *lingua franca* from about the fifteenth century, although that language was spoken at first only in parts of Sumatra and the Malay peninsula (now Malaysia).

Though the smallest of the Greater Sunda Islands, Java has always been the most densely populated, with about two-thirds of all Indonesians living there. In many ways a history of Indonesia is, first and foremost, the history of Java.

But in some ways Java's prominence is misleading because it belies the great diversity of this island realm. For instance, the destination of the first Europeans who sailed to Southeast Asia was not Java but the Moluccas. It was that "odiferous pistil" (as Motley called the clove), as well as nutmeg and mace, that drew the Portuguese to a group of small islands in the Ceram and Banda Seas in the early part of the sixteenth century. Pepper was another profitable commodity and attempts to obtain it brought the Portuguese into conflict with Atjeh, an Islamic sultanate in northern Sumatra, and with Javanese traders who, along with merchants from India, had been the traditional middlemen of the spice trade. The precedent of European intervention had been set, and was to continue for nearly four centuries.

Although subsequent history is complicated in its causes and effects, one may propose certain generalities. The Malay realm was essentially a littoral one. Even in Java, the interior was sparsely populated and virtually unknown to the foreign intruders coming from China, India, and Europe. Whoever ruled the seas controlled the archipelago, and for the next three centuries the key needed to unlock the riches of Indonesia was mastery of the Indian Ocean. The nations who thus succeeded were, in turn, Portugal, Holland, and England, and one can trace the shifting of power in the prominence and decline of their major cities in the Orient. Goa, Portugal's stronghold in India, gave way to Batavia in the Dutch East Indies, while Batavia was overshadowed by Singapore by the end of the nineteenth century. Although all three were relatively small nations, they were maritime giants. Their success was partly due to the internecine warfare between the countless city-states, principalities, and native autocrats. The Dutch were masters at playing one against the other.

Religion was a major factor in the fortunes of Indonesia. The Portuguese expansion was in part a result of Portugal's crusade against Islam, which was quite as ferocious and intransigent as the holy war of the Mohammedans. Islam may be considered a unifying force in the archipelago; it cut across all levels of society and provided a rallying point for resistance to foreign intrusion. Just as the Malay language had done linguistically, Islam proved to be a syncretizing force when there was no united front. One of the causes of Portugal's demise was its inflexible antagonism to Islam, and later the Dutch found resistance to their rule fueled by religious fervor as well as political dissatisfaction.

Holland ventured to reach the tropical antipodes not only because their nemesis, Philip II of Spain, annexed Portugal and forbade the Dutch entry to Lisbon. The United Netherlands was a nation of merchants, a brokerage house for northern Europe, and it wanted to get to the source of tropical wealth itself. Dutch navigators and traders knew the location of the fabled Indies, they were well acquainted with Portuguese achievements at sea, and counted among its members individuals who had worked for the Portuguese. Philip II simply accelerated a process that was inevitable.

At first, various individual enterprises outfitted ships and sent them to the Far East in a far from lucrative display of free enterprise. Nor was the first arrival of the Dutch in the archipelago auspicious, though it may have been symbolic of subsequent developments. In June 1596 a Dutch fleet of four ships anchored off the coast of Java. Senseless violence and a total disregard for local customs made the Dutch unwelcome on those shores.

During the seventeenth century the Dutch extended their influence in the archipelago by means of superior naval strength, use of armed intervention which was often ruthless, by shrewd politicking and exploitation of local differences. Their cause was helped by the lack of a cohesive force to withstand them. Yet the seventeenth century also saw a number of men who were eager to know the new realm, who investigated the language and the mores of the people they encountered, and who studied the flora and fauna. These were men who not only put the Indies on the map of trade routes, but who also charted riches of other than commercial value.

It soon became apparent to the Dutch that these separate ventures did little to promote welfare. In 1602 Johan van Oldenbarneveldt, the Advocate of the United Provinces, managed to negotiate a contract which in effect merged all these individual enterprises into one United East India Company, better known under its Dutch acronym as the VOC. The merger ensured a monopoly at home, and the Company set out to obtain a similar insurance in the Indies. This desire for exclusive rights to the production and marketing of spices and other commodities proved to be a double-edged sword.

The VOC succeeded because of its unrelenting naval vigilance in discouraging European competition, and because the Indies were a politically unstable region. And even though the Company was only interested in its balance sheet, it soon found itself burdened with an expanding empire and an indolent bureaucracy which, in the eighteenth century, became not only unwieldy but tolerant of graft and extortion. Furthermore, even though its profits were far below what they were rumored to be, the Company kept its dividends artificially high and was soon forced to borrow money to pay the interest on previous loans. When Holland's naval supremacy was seriously challenged by the British in 1780, a blockade kept the Company's ships from reaching Holland, and the discrepancy between capital and expenditures increased dramatically until the Company's deficit was so large it had to request state aid. In 1798, after nearly two centuries, the Company ceased to exist. Its debt of 140 million guilders was assumed by the state, and the commercial enterprise became a colonial empire.

At the beginning of the nineteenth century, Dutch influence was still determined by the littoral character of the region. Dutch presence in the archipelago can be said to have lasted three and a half centuries, but if one defines colonialism as the subjugation of an *entire* area, and dates it from the time when the last independent domain was conquered—in this case Atjeh in northern Sumatra—then the Dutch colonial empire lasted less than half a century. Effective government could only be claimed for the Moluccas, certain portions of Java (by no means the entire island), a southern portion of Celebes, and some coastal regions of Sumatra and Borneo. Yet it is also true that precisely because Indonesia was an insular realm, Holland never needed to muster a substantial army such as the one the British had to maintain in the large subcontinent of India. The extensive interiors of islands such as Sumatra, Borneo, or Celebes were not penetrated because, for the seaborne empire of commercial interests, exploration of such regions was unprofitable, hence not desirable.

The nature of Holland's involvement changed with the tenure of Herman Willem Daendels as Governor-General, just after the French revolution. Holland declared itself a democratic nation in 1795, allied itself with France—which meant a direct confrontation with England —and was practically a vassal state of France until 1810. Though reform, liberal programs, and the mandate of human rights were loudly proclaimed in Europe, they did not seem to apply to the Asian branch of the family of man. Daendels exemplified this double standard. He evinced reforms, either in fact or on paper, but did so in an imperious manner and with total disregard for native customs and law (known as *adat*). Stamford Raffles, who was the chief administrator of the British interim government from 1811 to 1816, expanded Daendels's innovations, which included tax reform and the introduction of the land-rent system, which was based on the assumption that all the land belonged to the colonial administration. By the time Holland regained its colonies in 1816, any resemblance to the erstwhile Company had vanished. In its place was a firmly established, paternalistic, colonial government which ruled by edict and regulation, supported a huge bureaucracy, and sought to make the colonies turn a profit as well as legislate its inhabitants' manner of living.

It is not surprising that for the remainder of the nineteenth century, a centralized authority instituted changes from above that were often in direct conflict with Javanese life and welfare. One such change, which was supposed to increase revenues and improve the life of the Javanese peasant, was the infamous "Cultivation System" *(Cultuur-stelsel)*. This system required the Javanese to grow cash crops, such as sugar cane or indigo, which, although profitable on the world market, were of little practical use to the Javanese. In effect it meant compulsory labor and the exploitation of the entire island as if it were a feudal estate. The system proved profitable for the Dutch, and because it introduced varied crops such as tea and tobacco to local agriculture, it indirectly improved the living standard of some of the people. It also fostered distrust of colonial authority, caused uprisings, and provided the impetus for liberal reform on the part of Dutch politicians in the Netherlands.

Along with the increased demand in the latter half of the nineteenth century for liberal reform came an expansion of direct control over other areas of the archipelago. One of the reasons for this was an unprecedented influx of private citizens from Holland. Expansion of trade required expansion of territory that was under direct control of Batavia to insure stability. Colonial policy improved education, agriculture, public hygiene, and expanded the transportation network. In Java a paternalistic policy was not offensive because its ruling class (the *prijaji*) had governed that way for centuries, but progressive politicians in The Hague demanded that the Indies be administered on a moral basis which favored the interests of the Indonesians rather than those of the Dutch government in Europe. This "ethical policy" became doctrine from about the turn of this century and followed on the heels of a renascence of scientific study of the Indies quite as enthusiastic as the one in the seventeenth century.

The first three decades of the present century were probably the most stable and prosperous in colonial history. This period was also the beginning of an emerging Indonesian national consciousness. Various nationalistic parties were formed, and the Indonesians demanded a far more representative role in the administration of their country. The example of Japan indicated to the Indonesians that European rulers were not invincible. The rapidity with which the Japanese conquered Southeast Asia during the Second World War only accelerated the process of decolonization. In 1945 Indonesia declared its independence, naming Sukarno the republic's first president. The Dutch did not accept this declaration and between 1945 and 1949 they conducted several unsuccessful military campaigns to re-establish control. In 1950, with a new constitution, Indonesia became a sovereign state.

I offer here only a cursory outline. The historical reality is far more complex and infinitely richer, but this sketch must suffice as a backdrop for the particular type of literature that is presented in this series.

This is a literature written by or about European colonialists in Southeast Asia prior to the Second World War. Though the literary techniques may be Western, the subject matter is unique. This genre is also a self-contained unit that cannot develop further because there are no new voices and because what was voiced no longer exists. Yet it is a literature that can still instruct because it delineates the historical and psychological confrontation of East and West, it depicts the uneasy alliance of these antithetical forces, and it shows by prior example the demise of Western imperialism.

These are political issues, but there is another aspect of this kind of literature that is of equal importance. It is a literature of lost causes, of a past irrevocably gone, of an era that today seems so utterly alien that it is novel once again.

Tempo dulu it was once called—time past. But now, after two world wars and several Asian wars, after the passage of nearly half a century, this phrase presents more than a wistful longing for the prerogatives of imperialism; it gives as well a poignant realization that an epoch is past that will never return. At its worst the documentation of this perception is sentimental indulgence, but at its best it is the poetry of a vanished era, of the fall of an empire, of the passing of an age when issues moral and political were firmer and clearer, and when the drama of the East was still palpable and not yet reduced to a topic for sociologists.

In many ways, this literature of Asian colonialism reminds one of the literature of the American South; of Faulkner, O'Connor, John Crowe Ransom, and Robert Penn Warren. For that too was a "colonial" literature that was quite as much aware of its own demise and yet, not defiantly but wistfully, determined to record its own passing. One finds in both the peculiar hybrid of antithetical cultures, the inevitable defeat of the more recent masters, a faith in more traditional virtues, and that peculiar offbeat detail often called "gothic" or "grotesque." In both literatures loneliness is a central theme. There were very few who knew how to turn their mordant isolation into a dispassionate awareness that all things must pass and fail.

E. M. Beekman

Introduction

Rob Nieuwenhuys, chronicler of the literature written by the Dutch about their lives in their former colony in Southeast Asia, was born in 1908 in Semarang, a large port on the northern coast of Java. His father was a Dutchman, a *totok;* his mother was of mixed blood, descending from a matrilineal line of Javanese from the city of Solo in central Java. In 1909 the Nieuwenhuys family moved to Batavia, where in 1912 the father advanced to the prestigious position of manager of the most famous and, at the time, largest hotel in the Indies: Hôtel des Indes. Nieuwenhuys received his secondary education in Surabaya and not until he was nineteen did he go to Holland for an extended period of time. At the University of Leyden he first studied the particular law of the Indies under Van Vollenhoven—an expert on *adat* (native) law, whose studies are still primary sources. Later he switched to the study of literature.

In 1935 Nieuwenhuys returned to Java where he taught in Semarang from 1935 to 1940. From 1940 to 1942 he was a lecturer in literature at the University of Batavia and was active in literary circles. He spent the next three years (until 1945) in Japanese concentration camps, separated from his wife and child. He did not report on these harrowing experiences until 1979.

After a year's furlough in Holland, Nieuwenhuys returned to the Indies in 1947, where he worked for the ministry of education until 1952. In that year, when Indonesia's independence had become an unalterable fact, he repatriated to the Netherlands where he did not settle in The Hague (which was the city most old-Indies hands retired to), but chose instead to live in Amsterdam. He returned to teaching until 1963, and from then until 1973 he was employed by the Royal Ethnological Society in Leyden where he established a documentation center for Indonesian history. In his retirement Nieuwenhuys has continued to produce works that, in one way or another, deal with the colonial Indies.

Nieuwenhuys is ideally suited for the task of fostering this particular genre of literature. He spent nearly four decades in the Indies as a child, a young man, and an adult. The Indies was part of his life from the very beginning, not as something extraordinary, but as a fact of daily life. His mother used native expertise and lore without the embarrassed self-consciousness of a European who would consider such things superstition. For instance, the *dukun* (Javanese medicineman) was consulted in case of illness, certain native rituals were observed for funerals and, just as it is described in his novel *Faded Portraits*, the house was purified with incense once a week. He learned Javanese as a child from his *babu* (or *ayah* in British India), Nènè Tidjah, who cared for him for the first seven years of his life. She imbued him with a sense of awe for tropical nature, an environment the Javanese consider to be spirited (*angker* in Javanese), and made him party to an existence where nothing is static or barren but alive with a fertile magic that does not recognize a barrier between the natural and the supernatural worlds. Her importance can be assessed by the fact that, even as a man in his seventies, Nieuwenhuys could still recollect her smell as clearly as when he was a child.

Though Nieuwenhuys was a product of both the Indies and Holland, he was always partial to his mother's homeland. In his father's country he acquired knowledge, and it was there that his intellect was formed. But this was a superstructure, for below the surface lingered the Java of his *babu* and his mother and this undercurrent nurtured his imagination, his emotions, and his passion. As was true of others from that era, Nieuwenhuys remained intellectually and emotionally a displaced person, a liminal man because he could never call himself a native of either region. In the Indies he would always remain an outsider to the Javanese community while, to echo what Kipling said of England, Holland for him could only be "the most wonderful foreign land I have ever been in." And if we consider those mutually exclusive regions metaphorically—the Indies as summer and Holland as winter—Henry Adams's characterization of his youth in New England provides an apt corollary: "Winter was always the effort to live; summer was tropical license . . . summer and country were always sensual living, while winter was compulsory learning. Summer was the multiplicity of nature; winter was school."

The present work is unique in Dutch letters. There was only one other published attempt to present an account of colonial literature (*Java in Our Art [Java in onze kunst]* by G. Brom, published in 1931). The considerable efforts by E. du Perron—only surpassed by Nieuwenhuys—ended with his premature death of a heart attack in 1940, at the time of the German invasion of Holland. With characteristic modesty, Nieuwenhuys felt that he was merely fulfilling Du Perron's wishes who had written him, recommending such a labor in the manner of a mandate.

Gerald Brom's *Java in Our Art* was favorably reviewed by Du Perron in 1931. Brom had realized that whatever had been written about the Indies should be seen as a separate genre within the overall tradition of Dutch literature. Until that time it had been judged only from what Du Perron called "a European sense of superiority," which automatically considered such writing suspect because it was not properly Dutch. As Du Perron put it: "the waringin trees are wrong because they don't sway as smugly as trees do in Holland, therefore nothing that one can experience in the Indies is really equal to the pleasure of a glass of beer [in Amsterdam]." Brom's work rectified this perspective. From the point of view of criticism, however, *Java in Our Art* falls short.

First of all, the tone of Brom's discourse is far different from Nieuwenhuys' and more akin to Du Perron's writings. It is polemical, argumentative, at times almost strident. Despite Du Perron's plaudits, the book's negative tone would appear to agree with the critical arrogance of the mother country, because its main objective apparently was not to discover what was superior as literature, but rather to denounce colonialism from a historical and sociological point of view. Brom's book seems to have been written with the blessing of Multatuli's spirit and such a benediction could only be applauded by Du Perron who, after all, considered himself Multatuli's caretaker. But it is a curious act of criticism when an author only refers to mediocrity and leaves out much that is superior. One comes away with a contradictory conclusion. First, there is surprise that anything was written at all and, second, there is wonder why there was so much of it.

The other antecedent for Nieuwenhuys' study is the work E. du Perron published during the last years of his life. Du Perron was ideally suited for such a task. The son of a wealthy patrician family in Java, he was born in 1899, spent the first two decades of his life in the Indies, and later became a respected member of the intellectual elite in Holland. A cosmopolitan, Du Perron had belonged to literary circles in Paris and Brussels, had established a reputation as a poet, novelist, and essayist, and was feared as a polemical journalist with a very sharp pen. After he finished his masterpiece entitled *Country of Origin* (1935, published in this series), he returned to Java in 1936. During the next four years he wrote a considerable amount of material on various aspects of intellectual life in the Indies, and became known as a vociferous apologist for Multatuli.

For two years he regularly commented on what was published in the Indies. These reviews and articles were collected in *Memo from the Indies (Indisch Memorandum)* and were published posthumously in book form in 1946. He wrote introductions to several books, for instance, to *Black Magic (Goena-Goena)* by P. A. Daum, one of the best novelists of the Indies who had been discussed by Brom in a strangely contradictory manner and whose work was practically unobtainable at the time. Nieuwenhuys was instrumental in having Daum's novels republished in the sixties.

In 1939 Du Perron published an anthology of colonial poetry written between 1600 and 1780: *John Company's Muse (De Muse van Jan Companjie)*. As was true of Brom's work, this was also a strange choice because poetry was the least appropriate medium for rendering the tropical experience. Du Perron admits as much when he says that his labor was primarily sociological and historical and that it had little to do with literary excellence. He argues that to ignore this verse from the two centuries of the Company's dominion in the Indies is "historically not responsible" because, "though they hardly possess literary value these versifiers . . . mirror their times better than what greater talents might possibly have done."

Du Perron wanted to follow *John Company's Muse* with another anthology of belles-lettres from the Indies to be entitled *From Kraspoekol to Saidjah (Van Kraspoekol tot Saidjah)*. "Kraspoekol" was the title of a tendentious novella by Willem van Hogendorp published in 1780 and critical of slavery. "Saidjah" refers to the celebrated tale from Multatuli's novel *Max Havelaar* published in 1860. This project was never realized because of Du Perron's death in 1940. He had written most of the introductions for the material he wanted to include and it is clear, once again, that literary worth was not a criterion. "Here again—as was true of *John Company's Muse*—the principal value is historical and sociological, though one will find a great deal more reading material . . . by storytellers who are often absorbing and enjoyable. Because they are rarely substantial from a literary standpoint, these writers have to compensate with experience and keenness of observation for their lack of either a superior interpretation of their subjects or a refined artistic ability." His choice of authors certainly corroborates his statement. Only Franz Junghuhn should have been an exception, but Du Perron neglects him as a writer so that he can emphasize Junghuhn's far less important role as a critic of religion and society.

It should be clear to the reader of *Mirror of the Indies* that Nieuwenhuys' major innovation was in examining this body of work as literature. In other words, unlike Du Perron and Brom, he made an aesthetic judgment, which resulted in a selection of what was the *best* writing. Nieuwenhuys redressed the balance by making aesthetic choices, but he did not ignore what was implicit in the work of Du Perron and Brom, which was the fact that there were other sources of literary excellence besides fiction and poetry. Hence Nieuwenhuys' "Mirror" reflects the work of superior imaginative talents, but it also finds evidence of literary skill from other sources, as Edmund Wilson did in *Patriotic Gore* (1962), his study of mostly nonfictional documents of the Civil War.

In this manner Nieuwenhuys was able to recover some predictable writers who had made use of the particular perspective of the Indies (such as Multatuli, Couperus, or Du Perron), but he also was able to display for the first time superior material from unlikely sources Brom ignored, such as the descriptions of tropical plants by the seventeenth-century botanist Rumphius (published in this series), the fascinating anecdotes by the historian Valentijn, the inspired descriptions of Java's grandiose nature by the scientist Junghuhn, the biting letters of the linguist Van der Tuuk, or the superb letters and stories of Willem Walraven. (Valentijn, Junghuhn, Van der Tuuk, and Walraven are all represented in the anthology of this series.)

Du Perron was the first to argue that these texts should not be considered strange marginalia of Dutch literature. Nieuwenhuys further removed them from those disreputable outskirts to their own domain where they no longer needed to apologize for their rightful place under the sun. Furthermore, *Mirror of the Indies* describes a particular genre—that of colonial literature—which also exists in both English and French. Together with material in Spanish, Portuguese, and German, a collection of this genre would represent a fascinating and instructive documentation of the manner in which European nations experienced a totally antithetical way of life. And finally, such an anthology of colonial or "tropical" literature would afford a welcome change from our present monoculture.

If similar works about colonial literature exist in other languages, one would hope that they are as agreeably written as *Mirror of the Indies*. Histories of literature are most often warehouses not known for a graceful display of their contents. Yet there is no law that legislates that works of scholarship must be dull. Nieuwenhuys' style is consistent with that of his other efforts. He writes a plain prose that might be called "natural." It is "artless" in its effect, though its composition can be just as demanding as its baroque, artfully contrived counterpart. One could describe it using Du Perron's phrase, as having a "parlando" style. This is an Italian musical direction to indicate that a passage is to be sung or played as if speaking or reciting. It is a style where the written word is molded by the spoken one. It so happens that, like the literature from the American South, a great deal of the literature from the Indies is modeled on the oral rhythms of storytelling. It is, therefore, fitting that a chronicle of this literature should have a similar delivery.

Except for Du Perron's eccentric selections in *John Company's Muse* and its never realized sequel, it has been Nieuwenhuys' anthologies that have given Dutch readers a chance to become acquainted with this uncommon literary currency. In his review of Brom's *Java in Our Art*, Du Perron speculated that it should be possible to compile an anthology of colonial literature, "if need be in two or three volumes," which, with proper emphasis, "might produce a masterpiece of sorts."

I doubt that if such an aberration did exist, it could ever find universal approval. The anthologist will always be reprimanded for inclusions as well as exclusions, and Nieuwenhuys performed this thankless task three times. By gradually expanding his material he finally produced a compilation that could serve as a parallel text for his literary history.

"Anthologies," Randall Jarrell correctly noted, "are, ideally, an essential species of criticism." Nieuwenhuys' first attempt, *Parting of Ways (Bij het scheiden van de markt*, 1960), presented fourteen authors Brom could not have known because they began writing during or after the war or, as in the case of Du Perron, published their major works after Brom's study. At least eight of them, however, are in the vanguard of Dutch colonial literature. His second anthology, published in 1965, *Gossip and Literature (Van roddelpraat en litteratuur)*, is much more of a critical gesture than Brom's. Of the sixteen authors included, all but one (Cohen) had published prior to Brom's study. Of the remaining fifteen, five were never mentioned by Brom, and three only cursorily. The host of inconsequential authors Brom paraded before his readers in order to mock was drastically cut by adhering to the simple expedient of choosing by standards of literary excellence. Nor will one find any of the dismal poetasters Du Perron had garnered. In 1962 Nieuwenhuys published a fine selection of Van der Tuuk's writings *A Pen Dipped in Bile (De pen in gal gedoopt)*, and in 1966 he produced his judicious selection of Junghuhn's writings, *Inexhaustible Nature (De onuitputtelijke natuur)*. In 1980 he published an expanded version with the same title, one that includes the stunning drawings Junghuhn made of the Javanese volcanoes he loved so much, as well as his precocious photographs from around 1860. By selecting from their work what was still fresh, imaginative, and of fine literary quality, Nieuwenhuys had "rescued" these two writers for future generations. In 1972 he published the present work, *Mirror of the Indies* (2d rev. ed., 1973, 3d rev. ed., 1978), where his superior discriminations were given a basis in fact, and in 1974 and 1975 Nieuwenhuys published his definitive anthology of Dutch colonial literature in four volumes. Expanded to include fifty-five authors and parallel with his literary history, Nieuwenhuys had fulfilled Du Perron's dreams, had outclassed Brom's work, and had once and for all claimed a private domain for Dutch colonial literature as a legitimate genre with its own character, its own literary tradition, and its own integrity. He had, in fact, distilled all his previous efforts—including the volume of essays *Between Two Fatherlands* (*Tussen twee vaderlanden*, 1967), articles in various journals, and his numerous introductions—into his life's critical summation.

The present translation of Nieuwenhuys' literary history, along with the other volumes in this series, constitutes yet another critical choice. Because this "Library of the Indies" is intended for a different audience, and because a foreign language inevitably demands certain restrictions, the imperatives of choice must be distinguished from Nieuwenhuys'.

Because most of the material is unknown to an American audience, the main concern has been to present what is the best rather than to be all-inclusive. What Nieuwenhuys had excised from Brom has been even further pruned. This was also necessary from the practical consideration that fairly large amounts of material would be impossible to translate, or would require so much explanatory commentary that the result would be ludicrous, as if straining a gnat. The major writers of colonial fiction are represented by what is their best effort. Where it would be impractical to publish individual works, generous selections were made which, accompanied by critical introductions, are collected in the anthology of this series. A case in point is Junghuhn. It would be absurd to translate his four-volume study of Java, and it would be unwise to publish the entire text of *Images of Light and Shadow* whose philosophical portions are of little interest today. In such a case, selection most definitely represents an act of criticism. The same is true for the exclusion of poets. The poetry written in the Indies was, for the most part, lamentably bad and, moreover, disproportionally difficult to translate. The quality did not warrant the effort. Nieuwenhuys of course wanted to be as inclusive as his Dutch audience might desire, but it seemed unnecessary in the present volume to continue to put forward what is minor for an audience unfamiliar with what is best. Hence several chapters were cut from the original text of *Mirror of the Indies*—chapters on pamphlets, magazines, theater, popular music, and dimmer literary lights. The criterion for what to keep and what to discard was always excellence. An attempt was also made to decide what would be of interest to a non-Dutch audience, and what could be clearly translated without irredeemable damage to the original.

Part of the appeal of this literature is a nostalgic one, a partiality long gone and irrevocably lost. This mixed feeling of want and longing is expressed in the Malay phrase *tempo dulu*. This was also the title of Nieuwenhuys' unique book of photographs with the subtitle "photographic documents from the old Indies" *(Tempo doeloe, Fotografische documenten uit het oude Indië)*. It is surprising that no one else in Holland had ever had the idea of commemorating the colonial past pictorially. Photographs are, after all, the most direct form of tribute our modern age knows. Nieuwenhuys was fascinated with photography for most of his life. His only novel (which is published in this series) is called *Faded Portraits (Vergeelde portretten)*, which is to indicate that the particular lives described in it are as peculiarly defamiliarized as are the faded photographs of a family album, tarnished with the blemishes of time. Among many other reasons, the nineteenth-century naturalist Junghuhn appealed to Nieuwenhuys because he was the first to use photography as an aid to his explorations in Java, and had even fabricated a timer that allowed him to make self-portraits.

Tempo doeloe is an almost perfect illustration for Susan Sontag's essays *On Photography*. These photographs taken between 1870 and 1910 "furnish evidence" that this chimerical society existed. One realizes how apt Nieuwenhuys' title was because, as Sontag agrees, "photographs actively promote nostalgia. Photography is an elegiac art, a twilight art. . . . All photographs are *memento mori*."

Most of these photographs were once mundane witnesses that these people actually existed in a particular place at a particular time, but now, nearly a century later, they have entered another dimension where that very banality has changed to idiosyncrasy. Mute and innocent, they stare back at us as if imploring that we will verify their existence. Just as the literature of those lives is far more dramatic and alien now than it must have seemed to them, so do these photographs seem mysterious because "what renders a photograph surreal is its irrefutable pathos as a message from time past."

These images are melancholy icons of what is in the process of becoming a mythical time. There is little evidence of joy. These metonymies of loneliness suggest the isolation people had to endure if they did not live in the few large cities. Those people, used to the intimate society of the Netherlands, suddenly found themselves adrift in an indifferent vastness. The eyes in these portraits often show fear, betraying an emotional agoraphobia that contradicts the vigor of the poses. And as if time were not sufficient to alter normalcy, what was for them a strange environment, made the grotesque quotidian. The book has such images as a baby in a pram that is virtually obliterated by excessive decorations of flowers and plants. Or an Eiffel Tower built of bamboo. There are also countless *tableaux vivants* which look hopelessly European and incongruous in the tropics. Then there is an elaborate bridal bed that seems menacing rather than inviting; the severed head of an elephant; a Javanese aristocrat in fifteen different poses and as many costumes, as if part of a bizarre kaleidoscope; officers in the colonial army dressed up as cowboys; bare-breasted dancers *(ronggengs)* who look dejected and ill at ease because, contrary to popular imagination, the Javanese are an extremely proper people. And what is probably the most chilling photograph depicts a formal portrait of a high Dutch official (resident) and a Javanese aristocrat of ancient nobility. Next to the alien extravagance of the Susuhunan, the resident looks vulnerable and sober despite his superior height and dress uniform. The pose is also odd to a Westerner because the native nobleman stands arm in arm with the European as if they were a bridal couple. Yet it is the slender, small, delicate Javanese who seems to concentrate a great deal of power in his person. It is a bizarre and menacing picture, an ominous pictorial oxymoron that symbolizes the futility of the hope that these two cultures would ever be a match. This photograph summarizes the nature of the literature this volume describes. It is the literature of a world that housed two manners of living. Though they may have reached out to each other now and then, they remained distinct and separate, even when they showed to the world at large this formal pose of alliance.

Notes

That his *mother* had native blood, was always a source of pride for Nieuwenhuys. See his own biographical statement in *Singel 262* (Amsterdam: Querido, 1954), p. 7; see also his lecture "De houding van de Nederlanders in Indonesië zoals deze weerspiegeld wordt in de toenmalige letterkunde," in *Bijdragen en Mededelingen betreffende de geschiedenis der Nederlanden* (Den Haag: Martinus Nijhoff, 1971), 86:68. He notes there that his mother and the *babu* Nènèh Tidjah lived together "in a completely Javanese magical world."

He wrote about his *experiences in the camps* in Rob Nieuwenhuys, *Een beetje oorlog* (Amsterdam: Querido, 1979).

That his *love for nature* was nurtured by Nèneh Tidjah, and that he easily recalled the way she smelled see Lisette Lewin, "Portretschrijver," *Vrij Nederland* 41 (12 July 1980): 7–8.

Kipling's comment on England from Charles Carrington, *Rudyard Kipling: His Life and Work* (London: Macmillan, 1955), p. 369.

The quote from Henry Adams is from *The Education of Henry Adams*, ed. Ernest Samuels (Boston: Houghton Mifflin, 1974), p. 9.

The complete title of *Mirror of the Indies* in Dutch is *Oost-Indische Spiegel. Wat Nederlandse schrijvers en dichters over Indonesië hebben geschreven, vanaf de eerste jaren der Compagnie tot op heden* (Amsterdam: Querido, 1972). The present translation is based on this edition, augmented with some of the revisions of the third, revised edition of 1978.

Gerard Brom, *Java in onze kunst* (Rotterdam: W. L. & J. Brusse N.V., 1931).

Du Perron's *review* is E. Du Perron, "Oost-Indische opbrengst," in *Verzameld Werk*, 7 vols. (Amsterdam: Van Oorschot, 1955–1959), 2:621–34.

Du Perron's writings on *Multatuli* fill the entire fourth volume of his collected works *(Verzameld Werk)*. All his other work on the Indies has been collected in volume 7.

Indisch Memorandum is in *Verzameld Werk*, 7:7–131. Du Perron's introduction to *Goena-Goena* is in *Verzameld Werk*, 7:135–38. Brom's contradictory evaluation of Daum is in *Java in onze kunst*, pp. 115–30, esp. pp. 118–27.

Du Perron's only published anthology is E. Du Perron, *De Muze van Jan Companjie. Overzichtelike Verzameling van Nederlands-Oost-Indiese Belletrie uit de Companjiestijd (1600–1780)* (Bandoeng: A. C. Nix, 1939).

The introduction to *De Muze van Jan Companjie* was reprinted in his *Verzameld Werk*, 7:169–71. The quote is on p. 170.

The fourteen introductions that were to be used for *Van Kraspoekol tot Saidjah* have been preserved and were printed in *Verzameld Werk*, 7:175–302. The quote is on p. 177.

Parlando. Du Perron collected his poetry under this title. See *Verzameld Werk*, 1:6–162.

Du Perron's remarks about anthologies in *Verzameld Werk*, 2:632. Jarrell's note on anthologies, Randall Jarrell, *Poetry and the Age* (New York: Random House, 1953), p. 155.

Nieuwenhuys' *anthologies* are the following: *Bij het scheiden van de markt. Een bloemlezing uit de Indische letterkunde van 1935 tot heden* (Amsterdam: Querido, 1960); *Van roddelpraat en litteratuur. Een keuze uit het werk van Nederlandse schrijvers uit het voormalige Nederlands-Indië* (Amsterdam: Querido, 1965); *Wie verre reizen doet. Nederlandse letterkunde over Indonesië van de Compagniestijd tot 1870* (Amsterdam: Querido, 1975); *In de Schommelstoel. Nederlandse letterkunde over Indonesië van 1870 tot 1935* (Amsterdam: Querido, 1975); *Het laat je niet los. Nederlandse letterkunde over Indonesië van 1935 tot heden. Mensen en landschappen* (Amsterdam: Querido, 1974); *Om nooit te vergeten. Nederlandse letterkunde over Indonesië van 1935 tot heden. Bezetting en revolutie* (Amsterdam: Querido, 1974). Nieuwenhuys also edited a collection of stories from the Indies in translation: *Memory and Agony. Dutch Stories from Indonesia,* ed. Rob Nieuwenhuys, trans. A. Dixon (Boston: Twayne Publishers, 1979). Nieuwenhuys' two "discoveries" are Herman Neubronner van der Tuuk, *De pen in gal gedoopt. Brieven en documenten verzameld en toegelicht,* ed. R. Nieuwenhuys (Amsterdam: Van Oorschot, 1962); Franz Wilhelm Junghuhn, *De onuitputtelijke natuur. Een keuze uit zijn geschriften,* ed. R. Nieuwenhuys and F. Jaquet (Amsterdam: Van Oorschot, 1966); and Franz Wilhelm Junghuhn, *Java's onuitputtelijke natuur. Reisverhalen, tekeningen en fotografieën,* ed. Rob Nieuwenhuys and Frits Jaquet (Alphen aan den Rijn: A. W. Sijthoff, 1980). His collection of essays is R. Nieuwenhuys, *Tussen twee vaderlanden* (Amsterdam: Van Oorschot, 1967).

Nieuwenhuys published his *book of photographs* under a pseudonym, E. Breton de Nijs, *Tempo doeloe. Fotografische documenten uit het oude Indië* (Amsterdam: Querido, 1962). He used the same pseudonym when he published his only novel, E. Breton de Nijs, *Vergeelde portretten uit een Indisch familiealbum* (Amsterdam: Querido, 1954).

Nieuwenhuys published another book of photographic documents about the Indies which, though it duplicates some of the material from *Tempo doeloe,* is essentially a new book with a great number of new discoveries. See Rob Nieuwenhuys, *Baren en oudgasten. Tempo doeloe—een verzonken wereld. Fotografische documenten uit het oude Indië 1870–1920* (Amsterdam: Querido, 1981).

Susan Sontag, *On Photography* (1977; reprint ed., New York: Farrar, Straus and Giroux, 1980). The quotes are on pp. 5, 15, 54.

Author's Introduction

Je n'aime pas la grande littérature.
Je n'aime que la conversation écrite.

Paul Léautaud, *Marly-le-Roy*

Anyone setting out to explore the literature of the Dutch Indies enters into an entirely different world. He will not feel quite at home at first and will start looking for something familiar. Everything will seem alien and strange. Not only the landscape, its people, and their relationship to one another will be different, but so will the forms of expression of its writers. Any explorer will find his own criteria next to useless. He may try to measure things by genre or style but he will soon realize that this leads nowhere, just as any attempt to organize things in this new environment on the basis of literary historical categories will also prove useless.

Only after he has gradually gotten used to this "new world" will he realize that his literary distinctions are irrelevant because the literature of the Indies, although written in the Dutch language, does not resemble literature as we know it. Anyone trying to discuss things in terms of, say, French Classicism, Baroque tragedy or Renaissance prose, will soon be talked out. If he should wish to use literary historical concepts such as Enlightenment, Romanticism or the New Realism, they will turn out not to apply. Should he wish to apply literary genres such as the story, the novella, or the novel, he will realize that these genres gradually merge with the memoir, diary, letter, serialized story, pamphlet, or broadside. For as it turns out, Indies literature contains both literary and nonliterary genres. It includes the novels by Daum, as well as the letters of Walraven or Van der Tuuk, the stories by Alberts, as well as Junghuhn's grand evocations of Indies mountain landscapes, replete with tables, longitudinal transverses,

altimetry, and climatological data. It also embraces Maria Dermoût's
The Ten Thousand Things, and the description of the minute world of
shells, sea animals, plants, and trees by Rumphius, as well as Multatuli's pamphlets on the freedom of labor, Johannes Olivier's satirical
pieces, and Du Perron's *Country of Origin*. The farther back in time
we go, the more we encounter nonliterary forms, to a point where we
come upon the first travel accounts. Needless to say, therefore, that
in a situation such as this, all literary criteria simply evaporate. Seventeenth-century Dutch "salts" (as De Haan is in the habit of calling
them in his great work *Priangan*), impressed as they were by all they
saw, heard, and experienced on their "adventyrous Voyages," could
often write a great deal better than educated scribblers, for all their
fancy words. Then we realize more than ever that it makes little
sense to rank writing according to genre or style, especially in a literature such as that of the Indies which has no literary tradition. This
lack is one of its most striking characteristics. This should not really
surprise anyone. Indies literature evolved in a society where a life of
letters was not the most likely activity. This is not to say that people
there did not feel the need to write; on the contrary. The critic Busken
Huet called the Indies the writer's milch cow. In fact, an enormous
amount has been written about the Indies and life in the Indies. Some
of it was written with amazement, some with hatred and love, with
bitterness, or with criticism and delight, all according to varied experience recorded in various ways, in journals, stories, novels, newspapers, and letters. Perhaps most important, in letters home, many of
them fascinating and stirring. It has indeed been said that the literature evolved from "the letter home." There is something to be said for
this but it does not quite tell the whole story. Some Indiesmen (as
they are called) certainly did write home about conditions and people
out in the Indies, but not all of them did. Many Europeans who had
been living in the Indies for years on end had become naturalized to a
point where they hardly felt any tie with the home country anymore.
They had developed new interests and were thoroughly changed. We
have this on the authority of one Rouffaer, a keen observer, who made
a trip through the Indies between 1885 and 1890. The findings in his
(unpublished) notes are confirmed by what the journalist W. L. Ritter
wrote in 1856 in the way of social criticism: "a European, no matter
where he may have been born, becomes an entirely different creature
in the Indies from what he would have been had he stayed home. Although a stranger in the land of his choice, he still identifies so closely
with everything around him that he truly can no longer be regarded as
a European ... he simply becomes a citizen of the Indies." An observation such as this is significant, especially because Ritter himself was

also subject to a process of acculturation which made a changed man of him too: "The European who goes to the Indies removes his old self, as it were, in order to assume a new self."

Essentially the same point was made in a variety of ways, in faded letters and in Indies novels, even later on, when communications with Holland had improved and the country had come closer. European society in the Indies—and maybe it is best to speak of a collection of several social groups—was and continued to be different from society in the mother country. The key to an understanding of Dutch literature in the Indies lies in our realization that this society had changed over the course of time and had in the process developed its own literary subjects, themes, and methods of publication. Only when we relate Indies literature to changes in society can we interpret it and begin to understand something about the position of the writer there. Without a social perspective, any description is doomed to be little more than a paraphrase or a commentary, and any treatment of its writers merely biographical.

The absence of a literary tradition and of a literary climate in the Indies is obvious from its social structure. It did not have any room for literary people because its top layer was not sufficiently diverse. Socially speaking, literary people never quite fit in anywhere, as authors such as Greshoff and Du Perron painfully discovered shortly before the war. In order to belong to society, one had to be "something," an official, planter, officer, housewife, governess, teacher, or a scientist if necessary, but not a literary person. To be sure, there were officials, planters, governesses, and so on, who also wrote, sometimes even literature, but if and when they did, they were really stepping out of bounds socially. Some of them drew their own conclusions from this and availed themselves of a pseudonym. The vast number of pseudonyms in Indies letters is as striking as the number of authors who began to write late in life, some of them very late indeed. Multatuli made a late debut and was already forty years old when he published *Max Havelaar*. Walraven, Friedericy, Alberts, Breton de Nijs, and Vincent Mahieu came out with their first work when they were more than forty years old, and Maria Dermoût was sixty-three when she made her literary debut. Living outside of a literary tradition has its advantages and disadvantages. The disadvantages seem obvious enough, certainly to authors left too much to their own devices, while the advantages seem less self-evident. Even so, life beyond the literary pale has its good side. Generally, it forces writers to lose their pretensions and to do without the constraints a life of letters imposes. The author's impulses too can have freer rein, he or she will feel less fettered, and the writing is likely to be more spontaneous. Literary currents and fashions certainly made their influence felt—although not that frequently—but their dictates were often foiled by the demands of the story. And storytelling in Indonesia, both among Indonesians and Dutchmen, has always been held in the highest esteem. A good storyteller, or someone who could recite well, was looked up to in a village community, sometimes even more so than the village chief. Anybody who could tell a "good story," as it was invariably called, also could greatly improve his chances for promotio. Considered something very worthwhile, storytelling was practiced with devotion everywhere. The very way in which people lived in the Indies contributed to it. Indonesia may not have had a literary tradition in the ordinary sense of the word but it most definitely did have a different and very strong tradition of storytelling. It could only exist, of course, against the background of the great adventure in the tropics, the solitude of the Indies and that of plantation life, as well as the Indies clubs, complete with "gossip corner" and easy chairs, and the Indies houses with their wide verandas in front and in back, with their terraces and patios. In the absence of any other distraction, especially in the early days but later on as well, people in the Indies possessed or were possessed by an irresistible urge to talk and to gossip, to "shoot the breeze" endlessly.

Rouffaer asked himself the question: "What do people in the Indies talk about? They talk about other people, or about conditions in the Indies, and all the time with a frankness bordering on the incredible." The same frankness made it possible to dramatize and to make minor or major changes in the circumstance or event that had given rise to the story in the first place, and this is how conversation gave birth to Indies literature.

Conversation, of course, could be about anything at all and might therefore lead anywhere. Its object could be information, praise, and veneration (i.e., "the sacred Indies"), but also criticism, grumbling, bellyaching, and gossip. It is amazing how much people complained and how much they criticized things in the Indies, how vehemently and, indeed, how frankly. It was not just Multatuli who did. He was far from alone and had plenty of precursors and followers. For example, the eloquent speeches which Van Hoëvell delivered in Parliament, two volumes of them, written before and after Multatuli's *Max Havelaar*, are one long complaint and accusation against government policy and its administrators in the colonies. People in the Indies, mostly members of a society without roots, come to think of it, were notorious for their protesting, grumbling, bellyaching, and gossip. All we can say is that there were some excellent bellyachers and gossips among Indies writers. Olivier was one, so was Daum, Bas

Veth another, so was Walraven and so were many others. Their fierce criticism and biting sarcasm often make for delightful reading.

There certainly was enough to bellyache and gossip about. It was a very heterogeneous society which perpetually split up into small groups, into little coteries and separate individuals. As an "old timer" wrote in 1897: "Everybody lives by and for himself here." What really prevented society from developing into something tight and homogeneous were the everlasting dividing lines between white and brown, between high and low, as well as short careers and frequent transfers, all resulting in merely superficial contact between people. In addition, they had no culture in common, there was little or no intellectual development, there were no close family ties, in short, no developed esprit de corps.

"The many-headed monster of gossip," as Daum called it, was free to roam the offices, houses, and clubs. If one is to believe Indies novels and other writings, people spent an awful lot of time talking, jawing, and gossiping, especially in the turn of the century Indies. We ought to make a distinction, of course, between stupid and venomous gossip, on the one hand, and detached, high-level gossip on the other. The latter variety required no mean talent. It presumed a curiosity and a perpetual and lively interest in all human affairs, unchecked by considerations moral or polite, in order to devote itself fully to the irresistible urge to meddle and pry into other people's most intimate secrets.

Good gossip requires a sound knowledge of human psychology, a keen sense of social differences, and an intuitive intelligence and imagination. A considerable part of Indies literature evolved from precisely this sort of enriched and ennobled gossip. This is not to say that all gossips are writers, they are only potentially so, nor does it follow that all writers are necessarily gossips but it would be hard to imagine a good gossip who was a poor storyteller. Such a typical talent was the late nineteenth-century author P. A. Daum. He wrote a score of Indies novels in which he revealed himself as an expert connoisseur of Indies situations and people, as well as an excellent storyteller.

Especially after World War I, the structure of Indies society changed. It became Europeanized and normalized, and a qualitatively improved upper layer came into being. The resulting changes in the way of life and manners did much to push the bellyaching and gossip into the background, although it did not disappear right away. It continued freely and unabated in the Indies daily press where often very personal attacks and polemics appeared written by journalists such as Wybrands, Thomas, Beretty, or Zentgraaff, much of it thanks to a grateful and cooperative reading public. It gradually disappeared from literature but its storytelling aspects remained. This aspect is characteristic of a great part of Indies literature. There is an unbroken line starting with the very first ship's journals and travel accounts that runs via Nicolaus de Graaff's *Mirror of the Indies* and Daum's novels straight on through to Du Perron, Walraven, Dermoût, Vuyk, Friedericy, and others. In short, it leads right up to the entire group that began writing after 1935 and which continued, ever renewing itself, to develop an intensive literary activity. What is most striking is that these postwar "Indies writers" have remained storytellers more than anything else.

Dutch Indies literature evolved from a different tradition than that in The Netherlands, and from a different stylistic tradition as well. Although its study requires different materials, it can still not be considered as entirely separate and distinct from Dutch literature. It is naturally a part of it. "Real art, the kind produced by Europeans out here in the colony," wrote Du Perron in a book review, "is moreover very soon regarded as belonging to the art of Holland, and rightly so." One could consider Indies literature as part of Dutch literature. It could then assume a position in a book about Netherlandic literature similar to that occupied by Flemish literature now, without any distinction being made. Flemish literature, however, conforms to the same principles of style and genre as Dutch literature. What is possible for Flemish literature appears to be much more difficult for Dutch Indies literature. In view of what has been said at the beginning of this introduction, this makes sense. The usual arrangement in various books about literature is irrelevant to the Indies. Some authors might well fit in but others would not. The least problematical would-be writers such as Multatuli, Huet, or Couperus, the same ones that were also influential in The Netherlands. Daum too might be fitted in still and placed with the naturalists, for example, although with some reservation. It would be possible to do the same with other writers, especially those who came after the war. It would be extremely difficult, however, to find a suitable slot for authors such as Valentijn, Rumphius, Junghuhn, Van Hoëvell, Van der Tuuk, Walraven, and others. Of course, it would be possible to create a separate category, as used for "Indies writers" and for "Dutch writers from Indonesia."

They would make a welcome addition to Dutch letters but it would be impossible to integrate Indies literature in its entirety. After all, it evolved from a completely different cultural and social situation and it manifests itself in different ways, with a slight preference for non-literary genres. It simply looks different and herein lies the justification for a treatment of Indies literature that is separate and distinct.

For practical reasons, the old Dutch spelling of Indonesian words and phrases has been kept. Not only is it appropriate to the age when these texts were written, but it also will aid a student of this literature in finding other sources pertaining to this genre. All such secondary literature will have this spelling, including dictionaries, atlasses, and other references. For those who would wish to follow the modern orthography of Bahasa Indonesia, the following changes should be noted:

The old spelling tj [tjemar] is now c [cemar]; dj [djeroek] is now j [jeruk]; ch [chas] is now kh [khas]; nj [njai] is now ny [nyai]; sj [sjak] is now sy [syak]; and oe [soedah] is now u [sudah]. Only the latter change was adopted in this series because the diphthong [oe] is not familiar to readers who do not know Dutch.

I
The Period of
the "Lofty Company"

1 East Indies Voyages

There have been two movements in our literature, wrote Busken
Huet, that of the "systematic humanists," and that of the poets, such
as the patricians Hooft and Huygens, who kept one ear cocked to the
vernacular, and provided abundant proof of knowing it very well
indeed. Their comedies especially prove their knack for common
speech. To be sure, they themselves regarded the use of the vernacular as little more than a diversion. No doubt they held their other
works, their letters included, in higher esteem. Hooft, Huygens, and
Vondel all share this attitude. We do, however, find the vernacular
used as the natural means of expression in many ship's logs and travel
accounts, which were particularly well liked in the seventeenth century. These accounts represented the popular literature of that period, the broad current below that of literature in the stricter sense.
Their function was comparable to that of medieval chapbooks.

Again it was Busken Huet, the insufficiently recognized pioneer of
Dutch literary history, who emphatically draws our attention to
these travel stories. It struck him that the writers of Dutch literary
histories and the compilers of anthologies had paid insufficient attention to these seventeenth-century chapbooks. These were printed
and reprinted in square format, with gothic letters and on poor quality paper. The printers were usually not too careful with the text,
which invariably showed signs of last minute corrections. They had
to supply, after all, an immediate and large demand. Large collections
of these editions are still to be found in several libraries in the Netherlands. The former Royal Batavian Society Library in Djakarta con-

tains one such collection. Most of them were never reprinted. The Linschoten Vereeniging did publish numerous journals, accounts, and diaries concerned with voyages to and in the Indies themselves, and other areas. Modeled after that of the English Hakluyt Society, it is an impressive series of expertly introduced, annotated, and illustrated texts, published to look as much like the originals as possible. Still, this series can hardly be called popular literature for today's reading public.

It would, in fact, be foolish to assert or pretend that many of these ship's and travel journals would suit a contemporary reader, not even if they were published in a more accessible way. The accounts are usually long, and contain too much in the way of pure fact and detail. The more readable parts, rarely lacking in any of them, are for that matter either "too enmeshed with the fantastic or the boring, or altogether buried underneath the same," according to an eighteenth-century publisher of such accounts. Because of their superabundance, they lack the tension that the modern writer creates by arranging the literary facts. If they should interest us for one reason or another, then they do so because of their subject matter, their occasional humor, or their apt figurative speech: "The ship resembled nothing so much as an iceberg, so that it was frightful to see for all on board. And the sails were frozen stiff as doors." They have a certain appeal also because of the dry manner in which shocking and often gruesome things are told. In that respect, they involuntarily create a literary effect familiar to the modern reader. For example, a man such as Nicolaus de Graaff, about whom we will hear more later, can coolly describe the impalement of a slave accused of having been "too forward" and of having committed murder: "A Malay slave has cruelly murdered his master's wife, with whom he had repeatedly committed adultery, and mortally wounded several others. Several days after his crime he was captured and executed in the following manner: The guilty one, while alive, was tied to a cross and had his right hand pinched off with a red-hot pair of tongs. Thereupon both arms and legs were smashed, and in that condition, still alive, he was impaled, that is to say: a long iron rod was inserted from below into his nether parts, and made to exit again behind his neck. In that manner they left him high upon a wheel, stuck onto that pin for as long as it took him to die. But the sufferer lived on for three more hours into the afternoon, and asked, since he was still alive upon the wheel, if he could possibly have a pipe of tobacco and a drink of water."

A seventeenth-century audience, incidentally, must have had a different attitude toward this kind of cruelty. We can rule out, in any case, that we are here dealing with a literary technique such as the dispassionate account of essentially cruel reality. There must be a different explanation for the popularity of these stories, and that leaves out present-day criteria. There is no doubt the seventeenth century too had its standards of quality. Not all travel stories enjoyed the same popularity, and it simply is not true that the stories with the most adventures were the most widely read.

One of the favorite accounts, never out of print until well into the eighteenth century, is that of the unfortunate voyage of one Skipper Bontekoe. To this day, it stands out as the most readable of all accounts and journals, and there is no doubt that its narrative style sets it apart. To assert this means applying a literary standard, of course, but it still does not explain quite why the travel genre was as popular as indeed it was in the seventeenth century. There were other reasons for its popularity. For one, these accounts were much more immediate than they could hope to be today. Many people then felt directly involved in the events described. For another, they also satisfied an immediate craving for information, for people were curious to learn about the yet unknown world. The known world had suddenly expanded, and this aroused not only hopes and expectations of wealth and riches but exerted, moreover, a great influence on the imaginative and adventurous spirit.

In 1584, the twenty-year-old boy from Holland, Jan Huygen van Linschoten, wrote to his parents: "My heart thinks day and night of nothing other than wanting to see strange countries." Van Linschoten was one of the first Dutchmen to sail to the East, albeit in Portuguese service. At the age of sixteen, he left his parents' house in Enkhuizen, with their consent, to be sure, and traveled to Spain, where his half brother lived. First he stayed in Seville and learned Spanish; a year later he went to Lisbon. From there he sailed to Portuguese India in 1583 with a fleet of about forty ships. After a good voyage out, lasting five months and thirteen days, he arrived at Goa. He stayed there for five years, and then returned. This time the voyage was anything but fortuitous but at least he survived. Upon his return, he began to write his famous *Itinerario* and his no less important *Travel Account of the Navigations of the Portuguese (Reysgheschrift vande navigatien der Portugaloysers)*, which for years were to be considered the authoritative texts on Asia and voyages hither. These books were reprinted and translated scores of times. An English and a German translation appeared in 1598, two Latin ones in 1599, and a French one, subsequently reprinted many times, in 1610. In 1885, the Hakluyt Society published a reprint of the English edition of 1598. After the establishment in the Netherlands of the Linschoten Society, all the works were published following the original Dutch text. The two first volumes in this series appeared in 1910, the final one in 1957.

The publication of the *Itinerario* in 1596 must have been a revelation to Van Linschoten's contemporaries. An unknown world was disclosed to them. Despite the fact that there were numerous stories about Dutchmen and foreigners who had accompanied the Portuguese to the Indies, there had not been anyone who had so extensively described these exotic parts. A marvelous world had been opened to them. Now they could read of different peoples and places, about different customs and dress, alien attitudes and strange climates, and they also read about the treasures and wealth that were there for the taking in the East, and about the frightful dangers and privations that had to be endured as well. And of course they read too—most important to the Dutch—Van Linschoten's opinion of the Portuguese. He criticized their lack of organization, their ignorance, their divisiveness and greed, and in so doing he attacked the myth of Portuguese indomitability. It may well be true, of course, as Van Linschoten's most recent biographer, the American Charles McKew Parr, suggests, that Van Linschoten was not altogether correct in his assessments, but the notion that enterprising competitors could gain a share in the wealth of the Indies was to prove correct all the same.

Van Linschoten's work, much more than a travel account, introduces a number of topics and facts which had hitherto been unknown in the Low Countries. His *Travel Account* contains a compilation and survey of all the sea routes to the Indies, which he culled from Spanish and Portuguese pilots' manuscripts.

It was Van Linschoten and Plancius, in many respects antagonistic toward one another, who made the first Dutch voyage to the Indies a possibility. Van Linschoten did so with his descriptive *Itinerario* and *Travel Account*, Plancius, the cosmographer and cartographer, did so by providing essential sea charts for explorations. Nobody left port without Plancius' charts and without that navigator's bible, the *Travel Account*. Countless contemporary ship's journals refer time and again to both his *Travel Account* and the *Itinerario*.

Still, even after everything Van Linschoten had revealed about the Portuguese in his *Itinerario*, the Dutch Republic, for the time being, avoided war. Apparently it had for too long endured the pressures of a strong and mighty Portuguese realm in Asia, and Van Linschoten's tarnished image of it was not quite believed by those in power. In any case, they did not base their decisions upon his information. Moreover, since Van Linschoten thought there existed a different route to the Indies, one that was some 2,000 miles shorter, they decided to find that route. It somehow had to exist, they believed. As we know now, their supposition was based on rumor and very limited information. Of course, the famous geographer Hakluyt had spoken of an ocean devoid of ice to the north of Asia. Tacitus too had mentioned "a slow and motionless ocean which girds the globe, where one hears the sound of the rising sun." Although Tacitus' allegation must have carried authority, especially in a time when the classics were esteemed, despite his fine phrasing, no such sea would ever be discovered.

Even so, they undertook three expeditions to the north. The first one still seemed somewhat promising. Van Linschoten went along as supercargo and had the job of writing up the journal for the trip. He went along on the second one as well, but it was a failure. The third voyage, during which Barentsz and Van Heemskerk wintered on Nova Zembla, turned into a disaster. It left us, however, with one of the most impressive journals, Gerrit de Veer's "truthful description of sailings so strange as never heard of in this world." The account, which was twice published in English in the nineteenth century, is not only impressive but also shocking and touching in its unadorned style. This account, however, only bears very indirectly on the voyages to the Indies.

Between the first and the second voyage looking for the Northeast Passage, ways of sailing south of the equator and past the Cape of Good Hope were investigated. One Cornelis de Houtman was sent to Portugal as some sort of spy, or so it has been alleged. More likely he went down as a merchant "in order to obtain information about aspects of East Indian and Moluccan trade," because the way hither was known well enough. Early in 1594 he was back in Amsterdam. Only then the real preparations were begun, which took almost a year. Even though the *Travel Account* and the *Itinerario* did not appear in print until 1596, it is clear that these works were consulted. It is known for a fact that De Houtman took the galley proofs along with him on the trip. Van Linschoten himself had been consulted too. It was he who determined that the route around the Cape be taken. The Dutch States General wished to avoid conflict with the Portuguese, and Van Linschoten's advice had therefore been to set course for Java, thinking the Portuguese were not trading there yet. Although he was wrong on that score, it is partially owing to his advice that the future colonial empire of the Dutch came to have its foundation on the island of Java. The scientist Plancius was also involved in all of the plans and discussions, and his maps and instructions accompanied the ships sailed by the mariners he had trained.

The first voyage in 1595 of four ships under the command of Cornelis de Houtman was, by and large, a failure. Its preparations had been adequate enough but its lack of success was owing to the general unfamiliarity with the situation on Java, where the Portuguese had in fact already made some inroads. Their "chief" proved anything but hospitable to the Dutch. We have several journals from this first voyage to the Indies; among them was one kept by the youthful attorney Frank van der Does (1569–1645) who had served as ensign on the trip. His journal, *Short Account, or Ship's Journey (Cort verhael ofte schypvaert . . .)*, is quite matter of fact as journals go, but at times the reader can sense the excitement between the lines. For example, here is Van der Does talking about a treacherous attack on one of the Dutch ships off Banten, west Java: "It filled us with great sadness to behold all those so treacherously murdered lying about. They had perished shamefully, suspecting nothing. The ship throughout resembled a slaughterhouse, all spattered with blood, as if animals had been killed therein. And similarly this ship was covered with human blood running out of the scuppers, the scene of a true massacre. That same day each of those killed was put over the side, not in a coffin but in the clothes they wore. We tied stones to their bodies, cast them overboard where they sank, a grievous sight to behold."

The second voyage, commanded by Jacob van Neck, an educated man, was a complete success. Van Neck is the author of an account that contains many readable and interesting passages. Especially praiseworthy is Van Neck's often quoted feeling for nature. On the return voyage, Van Neck ordered a respite along the Sumatran coast, where the sick were taken ashore, and they replenished the water supply. Van Neck himself went ashore "thinking the landscape agreeable." Having told us about their banquet out in the open, beneath shady trees, he continues: "The view of the verdant hills and beautiful valleys was extremely soothing. Beneath the umbrous trees a rivulet gently flowed; a little higher up, many tilled fields of diverse colors, and further up still, the mountains reaching through the clouds. Along the beach, gently lapped by the waves, many country people came bearing excellent fruit, which we purchased and conveyed to the ships gracefully anchored among the many happy isles." The passage is striking because there is no evidence at all in any of the other journals that the landscape of the tropics made much, if any, impression on the travelers of those days. Van Neck's is an interesting description in its own right but obviously not devoid of literary pretension, and conforms to the Renaissance genre of the arcadian idyll. Van Neck, of course, was no ordinary salt but an intellectual, a prominent man who went on to become mayor of Amsterdam.

An appendix to the second volume of *Priangan* by F. de Haan nicely traces the response to nature during the East India Company's period.

This essay, which De Haan himself calls "an excursion," with an abundance of quotes from contemporary works, reveals the extent to which the Dutchman's way of looking at the Indies remained limited by his native perspective. His appreciation of the landscape increased in proportion to its increased resemblance to the countryside of Holland. There were exceptions, of course. In the first place, Rijklof van Goens (1619–1682), like Van Neck, was a prominent man, who became a five-term ambassador to Mataram and, later on, governor-general of the Indies. Among his writings there is the travel journal concerning "the way from Semarang to the capital Mataram," straight through central Java. Van Goens' descriptive language is anything but concrete. His word choice, however, especially when describing the mountainous regions, reveals an immediate sensitivity lacking in literary overlay. Nowhere does a native Dutch perception obscure the landscape of the tropics. There is a clear explanation for this in that Van Goens was nine years old when his parents took him to the Indies, and he was thirty-six before he returned to the Netherlands. Tropical surroundings had shaped his image of nature from the start.

Another positive exception, according to De Haan, is Johannes Hofhout (1740–1807), otherwise unknown, who left us a description of a journey from Jacatra to the hospital in Tjipanas, some hundred kilometers into the interior. Hofhout was much less burdened by literary tradition than Van Neck, for example. He was just eighteen and a mere clerk, working for the Company. Very likely Hofhout's lack of literary training was a definite advantage here, because it allowed him to see things for himself, without resorting to literary cliché, which, particularly in the eighteenth century, had an unfortunate way of cropping up. This stood him in good stead, even though he does not altogether escape the enticements of poetic language. There are instances where the sun turns into a "golden torch," and where "the golden dawn withdraws the sable curtain of the night." There is an instance when, right in the middle of a story, his prose leaps into poetry but fortunately this poetic attack does not last long and is followed by a fragment such as this:

> On this plain, where everything seemed happy, the miserable lot of us made a halt, and with great difficulty we were laid onto the ground to ease our stiff, wracked and tortured bodies on the verdant grass. We were all strangers to one another, having come together in the dark, and we now beheld one another's face for the very first time. And as is wont among fellows in misery, we became acquainted right away. There, amidst all the imaginable beauties of

nature these parts had to offer, we were confronted with a horrible bunch of mortals either wracked by disease or struggling with death. Fresh air and a refreshing sip of mountain water rejuvenated our parched throats and slimy tongues, both half eaten away by the poisonous air and sulphuric water which kills off thousands of Europeans down in beautiful Batavia. I myself felt the surge of change and relished what seemed new life.

But to return to De Houtman's and Van Neck's voyages. Their "sailings" had scouted the terrain and set the course. With increasing regularity ever larger fleets sailed for the Indies with, as Busken Huet said, the reliability of a ferry service. The fact that this "ferry service" did not always operate too smoothly is evident from the great many popular books that preferably deal in storms, hurricanes, skirmishes with natives and the Portuguese, hunger, thirst, and sickness. No matter how regularly the ships went to and fro, by our standards certainly each voyage must have been an ordeal. Just think of the cramped space on board, the tensions among the crew, fights, the terrible food and drink, and especially the notorious scurvy. We do not require shipwreck on top of all that to dispel the notion that those voyages were anything like a scheduled ferry service. However, a popular book without shipwreck or a detailed account of its horrors would not have been worthy of the name, and needless to say, the number of accounts dealing with "disastrous voyages" is exceedingly great. No doubt they had an attraction all their own. One of the most colorful descriptions of a "disastrous voyage" which became particularly popular was the *Adventurous Voyage to the East Indies (Avonturelijcke reyse naer Oost-Indiën)* by Willem Ysbrantszoon Bontekoe. Before 1800 it was published at least seventy times. Its popularity is indicated also by the number of translations. Even as late as the nineteenth century, a German and a French translation appeared. There was also a translation into Javanese and one into Sundanese. An English one appeared as recently as 1929, and parts of the journal appear frequently in anthologies. The first complete edition since 1800 came out in 1915, edited by G. J. Hoogewerff, reprinted in 1930, and again in 1952. This last edition, entitled *Journals of the Memorable Voyages (Journalen van de gedenckwaerdige reysen)* is included in the series *Works of the Linschoten Society (Werken van de Linschoten-Vereeniging)*. It is also the best and most complete, and has an introduction, a bibliography, appendices, and an index.

Willem Ysbrantsz. Bontekoe was born on June 27, 1587, in Hoorn, the town in North Holland after which Cape Horn has been named. His father was also a skipper, as captains used to be called, but when his son was born he was not yet calling himself Bontekoe (literally "spotted cow"). Only later on did he and his three sons come to bear that name. As was the case with the family name of the Amsterdam Renaissance poet Brederode, or Breero, the family was named after their dwelling, which was adorned with a gable stone depicting a spotted cow, in this instance. The father died in 1607. The son sailed for the Levant as a thirty-year-old skipper. Even at that early age misfortune already dogged him. The *Bonte Koe* (for such was the ship's name too) was taken first by a Turkish pirate and then again by the Spaniards. There could not have been any doubts about Bontekoe's seamanship, however, for a year later he got the risky job of taking to the Indies in his ship *Nieu-Hoorn* a cargo of supplies and war materiel, including 180 barrels of gunpowder. The ship *Nieu-Hoorn* blew up in the Sunda Strait but Bontekoe escaped unharmed. He sailed from the Indies to China in a fleet commanded by Cornelis Reyersz. In October or November of 1625 he was back in Holland and settled in his home town of Hoorn. It is not known whether he made any other voyages, and his age and place of death are equally unknown. Twenty years after his return from the Indies "he spent his final years in contented retirement." Bontekoe was not a famous personality and he and his unlucky voyage would have been totally forgotten if a fragment of his journals had not fallen into the hands of the Hoorn printer Jan Deutel in 1645 or 1646. He writes that he has come into the possession of

> the description of this memorable East Indies voyage of Willem Ysbrantsz. Bontekoe, which seemed, as far as he was concerned, already doomed to oblivion. But I, reading the same, deemed it worthy to be preserved everlasting for us and our descendants. I begged him therefore to be allowed to print his description. To this he took but little fancy, deeming it on the one hand all but forgotten and staled by time, and on the other hand as unfit to print since he had not written it in a style and manner befitting that purpose. Finally, upon many kind requests and supplications from several of his best friends, he consented to the same.

The book appeared in either July or August of 1646, and became the best-read book of its kind in the seventeenth and eighteenth centuries. Few among us will have read Bontekoe's journal in its entirety but every Dutchman knows that he literally got blown into the air and yet survived. And everyone knows too how he sang little ditties in order to save his life, something we owe to Potgieter's anecdotal and historically unreliable *Chanties of Bontekoe (Liedekens van Bontekoe)*. Most people, however, cherish his name on account of the immortal juvenile classic *Cabin Boys of Bontekoe (De scheeps-jongens van Bontekoe)* by Johan Fabricius. This book has never gone out of print, no doubt partly owing to adult interest.

Bontekoe made three memorable voyages in all, the unfortunate voyage out, the trip from the Indies to China and back, and the voyage home. All three are described in the 1646 chapbook. Only the last two voyages are based on the original journal. It is hardly surprising that the first voyage is not, because there could not have been much left after the *Nieu-Hoorn* exploded at sea. The published work is in the main more readable than the original journals, even though it is less exact where facts and dates are concerned. From a literary standpoint there is nothing wrong with this, for if we compare Bontekoe's story to any other contemporary account, the liveliness of his style is striking. His style is workaday and free of cant and the merely anecdotal. There is nothing Bontekoe can not turn into a good story with frequently telling detail. Nothing much seems to have escaped him, and he relates everything in a matter-of-fact way. As the literary historian G. Kalff has observed, impression and expression almost overlap. It is perhaps for this reason that we are aware of the author's voice, which is usually lacking elsewhere. He gives the impression of addressing his audience as the story unfolds, and we have the impression of getting to know him better than the events he is relating to us. This personal tone makes him unique but we should keep in mind that the publisher has most likely intervened where punctuation and errors were involved. We do not know to what extent the text has been tampered with beyond that. We do know that the manuscript from which the *Memorable Voyages* was printed was itself a copy, and in any case not in Bontekoe's handwriting (see *De Nieuwe Taal-gids*, 1963).

Bontekoe must have been a guileless and good-humored man who, instead of giving orders and shouting commands, resorted to "gentle persuasion" which served his ends just as well. He can not have been ambitious or vain. The reasons he gave and his reluctance to allow his stories to be printed both support this. And he was anything but arrogant. On a number of occasions he confesses openly to having things no longer under control, and then invariably resorts to a quick prayer. This gives him new strength and, on occasion, new ideas. A case in point is the incident with the natives of Sumatra, the very one that inspired Potgieter to write his *Chanties of Bontekoe*. Following the *Nieu-Hoorn* disaster, after the lifeboats finally reached shore, it was decided that Bontekoe and four sailors would sail up river in a native craft to buy provisions. Among other things, they bought a buffalo, but the beast proved so wild that they did not dare take it into the boat with them. They decided that Bontekoe would return alone for help, leaving his four men behind in the village. Nobody, however, seemed willing to row him back downstream. "From among the lot of them I grabbed a couple by the arm and pushed them toward the canoe," Bontekoe writes (and we are citing a passage here that will also give an impression of his narrative style),

> just as if I were master there, though I was less than a slave. They looked frightful, real bullies, but they obeyed and two of them joined me in the canoe. One of them sat down in back, the other in front, each holding a paddle, and we pushed off. Each had a kris visible at his side, a kind of side arm like a dagger with a snaking blade. After we had gone a bit, the one from the rear came up to me, because I was seated in the middle, and indicated to me that he wanted money. I felt around in my pocket, took out a quarter, and gave it to him. The one in front, seeing that his mate had gotten something, also came up to me and made clear he wanted something too. Seeing that, I took yet another quarter from my pocket and gave it him. He stood and looked at it. He seemed to be in doubt whether to take it or whether to take me on, which they could easily have done, because I was unarmed and they, as I related, each carried a kris. There I was, a sheep between two wolves, fearing a thousand fears! God knows how I felt. We sailed downstream meanwhile, for the current was swift there. About halfway, they began to yell and to argue with me. There was every indication they were thinking of doing me in. Seeing that, I got so frightened that my heart trembled and shook for fear. I turned to God therefore and prayed for mercy, and for council what best to do in this circumstance. And it seemed that inwardly I was told I should sing, the which I did, even though I was afeard. I sang, and it resounded through the woods and trees, the banks being overgrown on either side with tall trees. And when they saw and heard how I burst into song, they burst into laughter, their mouths opening so wide I could look them in the throat, and so it seemed they thought I was not worried about them. But deep down inside I felt quite differently from the way they suspected. It was there I discovered that man can sing for fear and terror, and in this way our canoe gradually reached a point from where I could see our boat. It was then I stood upright and waved at our people standing about the boat. They, seeing me, right away came toward me along the bank, and I made clear to those two that they were to put me ashore, which they did.

I gestured to them to walk on ahead of me, because I was thinking: That way you will not stab me in the back, at least. And then we reached our crew.

What happened next was far more serious. When the buffalo was brought down the next day and proved still as wild as ever, Bontekoe ordered cutting its hind tendons with an ax. This angered the natives no end and they began to look really menacing. Then Bontekoe cried: "Men, everybody run for the boat, for if they cut us off, we're done for!" They ran, every one for himself ("We began to run, everyone heading for the boat"). They managed to escape but after a head count later on, "we discovered," writes Bontekoe, "that we had lost sixteen men, which grieved us sorely, and we lamented their loss but we thanked the Lord that not all of us had perished."

In Batavia, Bontekoe was received by none other than Governor-General Jan Pietersz. Coen, "and we told him the whole story, blow by blow." Coen laconically replied: "Never mind, you just had bad luck." He then served Spanish wines and drank a toast to Bontekoe's rescue. As we said earlier, Bontekoe then left Batavia to sail for China but gradually he became homesick, "finding truth in the proverb, tested by experience, that home is home, be it ever so homely." His return to Holland was nearly as disastrous as the voyage out, and it is very likely that Bontekoe decided then he had had enough. His name does not appear on a single muster roll after that.

A narrative style equally as guileless as that of the antiheroical Bontekoe belongs to Seyger van Regteren (1600–1645), a chaplain. His *Journal of a Voyage to and from the Indies (Journael, gehouden op de reyse ende wederkomste van Oost-Indien)* is characterized by a number of lively, personal incidents. It came out in 1639, six years after his safe return to his native town of Zwolle. One of his amusing stories happens in fact to deal with this safe return. His wife and little daughter were on board with him, and they appear throughout his journal. On entering the Texel roads of North Holland, with a storm coming on, the ship runs aground and threatens to founder in sight of the harbor. The women and children are taken on by the pilot and safely put ashore. Seyger van Regteren begs the ship's chief merchant to be taken ashore as well but the latter replies: "No, we had better stay together and see what deliverance our Lord will provide." Van Regteren, however, by his own confession, has nowhere near that kind of faith, and he writes: "But my heart felt greater yearning for my wife and child, and I seized my chance by jumping into a second pilot boat just then leaving for shore." However, his escape in this small ship is fraught "with such misery and peril as I had hitherto not experienced on my entire trip." Even so, he does reach wife and child again, and even the ship containing all their belongings manages to make port the next day. As was to be expected, he ends with a prayer: "Praise be to God, praise and honor forever more. Amen."

To be sure, compared to the total merchant fleet, the number of ships sailing annually from Dutch ports in order to trade thousands of miles away was relatively small in the seventeenth and eighteenth centuries. Even so, some thirty East Indiamen sailed every year. Considering that each ship kept a journal for every voyage, and that from the middle of the seventeenth century onwards publishers avidly hunted down these journals or stories taken from them, one can begin to get an idea of the flood of books and pamphlets that was released.

This kind of literature is so vast that a well-considered choice remains out of the question. One writer got to be better known than the next, this one saw different things than that one did, but they all aimed for the same thing: the description of the unknown, "for the edifying amusement of our compatriots," as Wouter Schouten, a lay reader, says in his *East-Indian Voyage (Oost-Indische voyagie, 1767)*. To that end neither he nor any of the others required fancy or literary language. They were not poets or authors, nor did they pretend to be. To be sure, there were some who felt obliged to use literary language but most of them employed a stylized or barely stylized version of the fairly uniform language of the common people. It goes without saying that these books are indispensable for learning the language of the seventeenth and eighteenth centuries. Their function at the time was to fill a gap between literature on the one hand and the uneducated on the other. Judging by the number of editions, to a lot of people these books had a social function in that they were something like "popular classics."

The primary goal of the authors, and this they achieved, was to inform their readers in pleasant and readable fashion about foreign and unknown lands, allowing them to participate in the seventeenth-century's single most important adventure, the discovery of other worlds. To them it must have been as interplanetary travel is to us. These stories dealt with strange countries, unknown seas, alien peoples, unknown and remote affairs and things, in short, with a new world seen from an exotic perspective. Their urgent wanderlust compelled them to go and explore it, and they were so taken up by it that their descriptions at times seem endless. But all of a sudden, right in the middle of such a description we are struck by a surprising and concrete use of language which makes the entire scene come alive to us, as in the case of the previously mentioned Wouter Schouten and his description of a storm:

The frenzied wind with its driving black clouds increased ever more. The ship was pummeled up and down between waves now reaching up to the sky and again toward the deep of the measureless ocean, to be gradually lifted up higher and higher toward the clouds, and all the while rolling so terribly that no one could either stand or move, and we spent this terrible night fearing for our very lives. A dismal dawn on Sunday, February 15th, came and went and we could still not see a single ship, nor even distinguish the sea from the dark clouds above and over it, all on account of the heavy fog and moisture laden air. Yet it seemed the roaring storm would abate and our limp hopes began to revive somewhat when, alas, after a brief while, because it was only eight in the morning, the wind picked up again and began to howl as never before. The seas, more turbulent than ever, now swamped the entire ship with immense torrents so that we were preparing to see and suffer nothing short of the sudden going under of each and everyone of us. Yes, the terrifying waves, which no one had ever seen as frightful as these, now began to hammer and pound the ship's taffrail and stern in such a manner as to make everying seem to break apart in bits and pieces.

It is hard to tell at times whether it is the events themselves or the narrative that is so striking. Possibly it is the shocking events or the wry chronicling of them that creates this effect, or their juxtaposition. In any case, one aspect of good writing is having a knack for details and the ability to insert them into the text precisely where they have their greatest impact.

In 1942, a facsimile edition appeared of Andries Stokram's *Short Description of the Unfortunate Return Trip of the Ship "Aernhem" (Korte beschryvinghe van de ongeluckige weer-om reys van het schip Aernhem)*. It had originally appeared in 1663. It tells the story of the horrors of sailing in an open boat for more than a week without food or drink after the *Aernhem* sank off Mauritius in January 1662. Here is a fragment by way of illustration:

January 17th, and wind and weather as before. Tossed a couple of men overboard, the same having drunk sea water which caused their insides to burn and gave them insufferable thirst. With nothing to seek shelter under, we sat in the sun during the day and in the cold at night. There we drank our own water, asking others if they could spare some of theirs. There were some who could not bring themselves to drink their own water. Some drank sea water which drove them crazy, whereupon they died shortly. Others, taking an example from that, preferred to suffer thirst as much as they could,

hoping God would look after us, help us land and send us rain to
slacken our thirst.

For all its clumsiness and sobriety, this is a touching and shocking
fragment. This is not the only fragment that is readable, however; the
entire, brief account is very much so. Stokram and a small group of
others stayed on Mauritius longer than anybody. The others had been
picked up successively by passing ships. When they were finally
taken on board a Dutch privateer, Stokram had been living for eight
months the way Robinson Crusoe would a century later, in an environment Daniel Defoe knew from descriptions such as Stokram's.
His stay on the pirate ship did not last long. Together with two others,
Stokram was put ashore again, this time on St. Helena. The description of this island is effective, neither too long nor too short, but well
considered, and without a single attempt at embellishment. The
island is situated, according to Stokram, "like a buoy in the Spanish
sea, . . . a very high and mountainous country, which is usually covered by clouds. The land itself is arid and ashen, as are the trees, present in great number. It looks and feels like a place half-burnt away,
similar to all those islands scorched by volcanic outpourings."

That it can be done differently and far worse is illustrated by an account, deservedly not reissued, of the same unfortunate voyage written by one Simon van Kerckhoven, lay reader on the *Aernhem*. Unlike Stokram's, his account is not in the diary format but even so is
more personal, in the sense that the author intrudes time and again
with all sorts of personal and moral observations; yet, his prose remains colorless, and after a couple of pages we know enough. He
lacks the very qualities Stokram possesses, an eye for detail and a
sense of proportion: proof, if proof were needed, that this nonliterary
genre too had its standards.

We now read these travel accounts from a different perspective
than their contemporaries did, and what arrests us today is not what
amazed them then. We marvel much less at the descriptions of remote kingdoms, jousts, festivities, morals, and customs, or a listing
of, for example, native fruits and gems, but we are all the more struck
by the horrors these voyages to the Indies involved. What really taxes
our credulity is that many of their authors, after voyages lasting years
on end and despite everything, shipped out again. And we would indeed be wrong to assume it was mere grasping for money that motivated them. If, however, we look at it from their point of view, the
reasons become clear enough. A stay of many years abroad with a way
of life utterly different from the one at home must surely have ren-

dered a great many of them unfit for ever adjusting again to life in the mother country. They must have had a great many conflicts with their old environment, and with their families. Having become strangers in their own country, they could not settle down, they became restive and ultimately left again. "Traveling," writes the eighteenth-century naval surgeon Pieter van Woensel, "makes one restless somehow, ill at ease, and discontent to stay. I know of some people who are in a bad way because of it. The only remedy for their disease is the one that aggravates it, travel itself." (Quoted from an article in *Tirade*, May 1959.)

The life of Nicolaus de Graaff, ship's surgeon, judging by the relatively few facts known about him, goes some way to illustrate the above. It is not known where or when he was born. We have his own word for it that he received his professional training in Alkmaar and there and then "got the urge to see the world, because of the wonderful tales I heard told every day." This is why he signed on with the East India Company, especially because he thought to acquire a good deal of practical experience during these travels "notorious for accidents, wounds, and injuries." He left home by the end of April 1639 and returned in August 1643. He probably married shortly thereafter. Only a few months later he was back at sea, again headed for the Indies. He returned in July 1646. On examining his chronology further, it appears that only after his fifth voyage (to Brazil that time) did he stay ashore longer than several months, for three years, to be exact. The "severe poverty, hunger, and misery" that he suffered during the last voyage more than likely influenced his decision. From then on, interrupted by a few months only, sometimes a year, he made short voyages to the North Sea, the Mediterranean (with Admiral de Ruyter), to Portugal, Denmark, and elsewhere. In 1668 he rejoined the Company and went to the Indies for a third time, staying away well over two and a half years. Then follows his longest period ever ashore, nearly four years. It almost seems as if he planned to settle down. He bought a house in Egmond-on-Sea and became an alderman there. But in 1676, one year later, he sailed away not to return until 1679. In 1681 he is deacon of the church council. A year later, he appears to be "sickly in bodily health." Even so, one and a half years after that he went traveling again, first to China, then to Batavia, thence to the Moluccas via Java's northern coast. In 1686 or early 1687 he was in Banten and Batavia again. In August 1687, he "returned safely, thanks to God's Mercy, to a safe haven." That safe haven was the Texel roadstead. There ended his sixteenth and final voyage. In between he had married twice, begat and lost children, and became deacon and later even burgomaster of Egmond. After 1687, well over sixty years old by then, he refrained from traveling.

Nicolaus de Graaff was "a remarkable man," as the publisher of his *Travels (Reisen)* somewhat vaguely characterizes him. He appears to have been a restless character, an inventive and experienced surgeon, and, moreover, a first-class storyteller. His writings have unequaled vigor. De Graaff has both an eye for detail and a sense of humor. He shows himself, for example, to be an expert in popular etymology. The Great Mogul of Aurangzib he calls the Orange Chief, the village of Sumenep on the island of Madura becomes Sewmynap, and Juggernaut, the Hindu God, he translates as Jug her Not. He is particularly good at understatement, as is already apparent from the excerpt quoted earlier. The manner in which he describes his surprisingly successful treatment of a patient is telling: "On Barbados we refreshed ourselves every day, and one time, going to the woods, we came upon an English boy of about fourteen or fifteen years old lying on the ground . . . who had tripped over a stone and fallen forward, thus breaking to pieces the brandy bottles he had been carrying between his shirt and body. He had injured his entire belly in such a way that his intestines had spilled out. After we lifted him, we cleansed his intestines from dirt and broken glass as thoroughly as time and place allowed, put them back into the abdominal cavity, and stitched the wound." In a hammock, the patient was taken to his master, who asked De Graaff to continue treating the boy. "Treated the youngster again, by taking out the stitches, removing the bowels again and placing them into a shallow bowl. Inspected them for cuts or injury from glass and then washed them off with lukewarm milk. We put them back carefully and then closed up with as many stitches as were needed. After the bandages were on, we gave him a fortifying drink, and the next morning a laxative, which was followed after several hours by a healthy stool, indicating that the bowels were uninjured and in their right place. Within the span of five weeks this young man was by and large restored to his former health with God's blessing."

De Graaff wrote accounts of all his sixteen voyages, more extensively about some than others. They were published for the first time in 1701 under the title already mentioned, *Travels,* . . . In 1704, a reprint came out "enlarged with the author's posthumous writings," indicating that De Graaff had died by then. The first edition of his book contained a curious, additional essay. Called *Mirror of the Indies (Oost-Indise spiegel),* it too was fortuitously reissued in 1930 by the Linschoten Vereeniging, and this over the objections of the editor, one Warnsinck, a navy captain. He considered the style of the *Mirror of the Indies* as "less polite" than that of the *Travels*, and its criticism of Batavian society, especially where the ladies are concerned, as somewhat too cutting. To think that such objections could ever be considered valid criteria! However, there are people who think differently about the *Mirror of the Indies*. Du Perron called it "the most exciting prose to come out of the era of the Company," and included a sizable part of it in his anthology *John Company's Muse (De Muze van Jan Companjie,* 1939). The essay is, in fact, pivotal to that anthology, not because of its length but simply because it is the best piece of writing in the book. It falls somewhere between an ordinary description of town and country, on the one hand (a common enough genre in those days) and a moral satire on the other, one written without hypocrisy or "buttering anyone up."

Following a brief, informative introduction to the city of Batavia and "the inhabitants of the same," De Graaff is increasingly in his element until he starts writing about the European way of life there. Then he really cuts loose, particularly about those "East Indies little ladies," and the way they go to church on Sunday, "all fancy and decked out. And there they sit in church by the hundreds, spruced up, proud and pearly like a shelf full of pretty dolls; the least among them looking more like a princess than a merchant's wife or daughter, a sight revolting to very Heaven!" His criticism, to give credit where credit is due, does not discriminate between white, brown, or black. His revulsion is all-encompassing and complete.

Warnsinck first depicts De Graaff as the type of popular ship's doctor ("the kind we still have even today in the merchant marine and navy," he adds), then as a "pleasant ship mate," and finally as "an agreeable partner." But his *Mirror of the Indies* reflects quite a different image and personality, sooner that of the church deacon which he was in fact to become, dressed in black with a lace bib, calling for repentance with the voice of a Savonarola.

He was stirring things up and he knew what he was doing: "and so I threw the shoe in among the lot of them, thinking that if the shoe fit, they could either put it on or leave it off, I did not care which." As it happened, the shoe did fit all of them, and not just the ladies either but all those servants of the Company intent on their own (prohibited) private trading. It was not just petty graft they were guilty of either. Their private dealings were in fact "unbelievably blatant and crude." De Graaff shows us that corruption was already general and widespread in the second half of the seventeenth century. The disease had spread among the upper and lower classes alike, but most infected were the lay preachers and chaplains, those "lying hypocrites." De Graaff himself was not without his shortcomings either, of course, but greed was not one of them. Money was neither the driving force behind nor the aim of his actions, and he retired only moderately well off. What really compelled him to go to sea time and again was the same restiveness that had prompted the likes of Jan Huygen van Linschoten, Wouter Schouten, and so many others.

Aernout van Overbeke was a wag, unlike the equally lively but basically devout and serious Nicolaus de Graaff. Both Van Overbeke's poetry and his *Humorous and Amusing Travel Account to the East Indies (Geestige en vermaeckelicke reys-beschryvinge naer Oost-Indien)*, published in 1672, belong to the burlesque genre. In the second half of the seventeenth century, the Netherlands too had several practitioners of this genre, which, influenced by France, found its most noteworthy exponent in Willem Godschalk van Focquenbroch (1640–1670). It demands a certain erudition and an intellectual effort because of the incessant application of "ribtickling stratagems." Van Overbeke was not just any old "salt," as De Haan would have it, but a man of literary acumen. He was several years younger than De Graaff but died much earlier, in 1674, two years after his return from a four-year stay in the Indies as a councilor of justice. His *Verses (Rijm-werken)*, which later on came to include his travelogue, were reprinted numerous times. The tenth edition appeared in 1719. His popularity likely depended on the easy, open, and cheerful way in which he wrote about things and about himself, which must have struck his contemporaries as "ribtickling" indeed. His travel account is not based on a diary, as most of them are, but written in the epistolary style instead. Van Overbeke's "letters" are helter-skelter, they allude to memories, contain allusions and double-entendres, they are larded with Latin quotations, and he never stops showing how witty he is. At times, he even strikes us as humorous by our own standards. When his ship was anchored in the roads off Batavia, an East India Company official came on board and noticed a package among Van Overbeke's luggage that did not carry the required Company seal. "That has not been registered," stated the official. "So what?" replied Van Overbeke, "just so it doesn't register with you," and it passed.

Occasionally he refers to his own existence, and then a human tone becomes audible. It appears that despite the laughs his life was not all that amusing. During a trip a shark was caught. When it was cut open, there was a large fish inside, which in turn contained a small flying fish.

The whole business looked like those Russian dolls that can contain as many as a hundred smaller ones, and it struck me that human life is miserable too, and that I have had my share of it. Those flying fishes are pretty and seem happy enough but [Van Overbeke adds], Messieurs, that is one grand *erreur*. They are, in fact, the most miserable little creatures in the world. Down there in the water a shark chases their tails, and up in the air they are picked off by sea birds. In toto: Upstairs or downstairs they lose out, just like me, whether I am in Amsterdam or in The Hague. I am either pursued by N. N. or chased by P. P. and I invariably resemble Icarus. Had I had Daedalus' insight, the sun would not have scorched my scalp in these tropics.

That kind of phrase, which reveals the writer in him, one will not find in the well-known writings of J. S. Stavorinus, whose travel accounts have been translated into French, German, and English. He served as a captain with the Zeeland Admiralty but joined the East India Company to satisfy his craving for travel, his publisher informs us. He wrote two books about his travels, which he made between 1768 and 1778 throughout the entire territory where the Company had its factories and depots. The first appeared in 1793, the second and best known in two volumes in 1797, entitled *Journey from Zeeland via the Cape and Batavia to Semarang, Macassar, Ambon, Suratte, etc. in the years 1774 to 1778 (Reize van Zeeland over de Kaap de Goede Hoop en Batavia naar Samarang, etc.)*. He did not write to convey his impressions to his readers but rather "with the intent of being useful," which reveals him as a true citizen of the eighteenth century. To inform his reader is uppermost in his mind. He describes the fish, the sea birds, he writes about many diseases and sums up the symptoms of scurvy and the possibly even more dreaded "diarrhea symptomatica." He provides directions on how to sail among reefs and ledges, and extensively describes cities and countries, listing their principal exports. He gives the number of ships, sugar mills, and houses; he tallies death rates, current prices, and so on. But Stavorinus, a versatile man, does more than just that. He also describes European society as he finds it abroad. In giving an account of their habits, he gives us the facts, of course, but at the same time he criticizes them, especially when he deals with women, and with the treatment of slaves. The society he describes a hundred years after De Graaff had done so had not basically changed. Stavorinus still sees a small mixed society where money and rank connote social distinction to an absurd degree, where private wealth contrasts sharply with the "dilapidated condition" of the Company itself. Despite all their wealth and glamour, Stavorinus finds that most Europeans seem "very melancholy," not surprising if we take into account the high death rate which at times depopulated entire towns. The Company lost annually one sixth of its servants, according to Stavorinus. Some ships reach the Indies with barely half their crews alive. Curiously enough he pays scant attention to the excessive corruption and greed of the Company's servants.

Not so Jacob Haafner (1755–1809), who also traveled far and wide, and perhaps more extensively than Stavorinus. He witnessed the Company's death agony and demise, and wrote about it. He has a lively and compelling manner. Haafner, whose name was spelled Hafner originally, was a German by birth who had joined his father, a surgeon, in the service of the Company. His father died on the voyage out, and he, still a child, had to continue wandering alone. He experienced the most dreadful things and witnessed inhuman cruelties. These traumatized him to such an extent that he became a "mortal enemy of oppression and coercion." "I condemn and loathe all manner of injustice and cruelty," he wrote in the Preface to his *Voyage from Madras to Ceylon (Reize van Madras naar Ceilon, 1806)*. "I respect all those, no matter what their nationality or religion, as my fellow men and brothers. Whosoever shares my conviction will not be offended but will, on the contrary, note with pleasure that I defend the oppressed Indians and intercede on their behalf, and that I aim to heap shame upon their oppressors." His target was chiefly the English but, as he says, the Dutch were just as bad. Wherever he came, it was the same story: the same decay, corruption, cruelty, arrogance, and avarice. "Making one's fortune! Indeed, there is not anybody who does not go East to make his fortune. That unhappy part of the world has become the prison yard of the Europeans. Scoundrels, wastrels, thugs, all those who because of their crimes or for other reasons have been banished from their birthplace, bankrupts and people like that, all of them scurry to the Indies as to a common prey, all of them desiring to make their fortunes there, and how do you think they seek to realize their aim? In no other way than to rob the Company they serve, or to oppress, plunder, and kill the poor Indians. Nine out of ten who return wealthy from India have certainly gotten their loot in exactly that fashion." *(Voyage from Madras to Ceylon, p. 11.)*

On one of his voyages, after a severe illness, he also ended up in the Dutch East Indies. He tells us about this in his *Adventures and Earlier Sea Voyages (Lotgevallen en vroegere zeereizen)*, posthumously published by his son in 1820. What he has to say about the way of life of the Europeans in Batavia corroborates both De Graaff and Stavorinus. He also tells us of torture and executions, and he too describes the impalement of a slave and his subsequent self-control, but unlike De Graaff, he goes further than just giving an objective account of the goings on. Haafner protests and accuses: "Control that desire for gold and blood among your famished vagabonds whom you are sending in droves to these unhappy shores. They are a plague which with every new visitation increasingly burdens the fate of the miserable slave, and which drives him finally to prefer certain death over an unbearable life."

Haafner too finds the women the worst and the most cruel, citing several examples. He too scoffs at their laziness and their "amorous inclination," but he is most incensed by the preachers and priests, those "damnable panderers of souls." He is angered by their sweet talk combined with so much arrogance, deceit, and grasping. "Many of them try by hook and by crook to be sent out to the west coast of Sumatra, pretending to want to baptize new converts and slave children but their real aim is illicit trade, even trading in slaves." He is as indignant as was De Graaff but he is no mere preacher of repentance; rather he protests in the name of something else, something quite different: Haafner protests in the name of justice, humanity, freedom, and equality. He is a true exponent of the Enlightenment.

2   *Valentijn, Camphuis, Rumphius*

For an age when poetry was considered the highest, if not the sole expression of literature, it is curious to discover how much better its prose is. Like poetry, prose was also subject to set rules, such as in the epistolary and several other genres, but it was still a great deal freer and more vital than a poetry that had generally degenerated all too much to a level of mere versifying. The writing of prose had taken on a dual purpose because it could also be made to function as the vehicle for subjects beyond the pale of literature, such as making speeches, writing history, and describing people, places, plants, animals, and many other things.

Such a writer of "serviceable prose" was François Valentijn, a minister. He was born on April 17, 1666, in the city of Dordrecht, where his father was an assistant head of the preparatory or Latin school. He died on August 6, 1721, in The Hague, where he had only been living for six months. He was buried in his and his father's native city "with six coaches beyond the ordinary number." To his contemporaries, Valentijn was a famous and celebrated man with an encyclopedic mind. His interests were numerous. Not only was he "a servant of God's Word" who had translated the Bible into Malay, he was also a lover of music and a passionate collector of such curiosa as shells, whelks, and marine plants. Valentijn's collector's urge also shows in his most important work, the history of the area where "The Lofty East India Company" held sway. In those days, its territory was considerably larger even than the 3,000-mile-long chain of islands making up the former Netherlands East Indies. Its depots and factories were located throughout Asia, in Tonkin, Cambodia, Siam, the Coromandel coast, Malacca, Ceylon, Japan, the Cape of Good Hope, Mauritius, etc. Valentijn lacked firsthand knowledge of some of these places. In fact, he was only familiar with the city of Batavia, various parts of east Java, and particularly the Moluccas. Of the latter, his favorite was the island of Ambon or Amboina. His far-flung treatises and descriptions depended to a large extent on other people's notes, observations, and stories. These sources he credits in a haphazard fashion. He relied on whatever material reached him, whether in print, in writing, or by word of mouth. For this reason some of his chapters are disproportionately short, others long. By our present standards, his *The Indies, Past and Present (Oud en Nieuw Oost-Indiën*, 1724–26) is a curiously constructed historical edifice lacking in balance and form, its plan nothing but a maze, yet impressive in its wealth of substance.

Valentijn spent many years working on his book. The idea for undertaking such a grand historical work "already dates from the year 1688, after his first voyage out to the East Indies," the literary magazine *Library of the Sages (Boekzaal der Geleerde Wereld)* stated in 1722. He had clearly been carrying around the notion from the start. He must have started collecting his material as early as 1705, when he went to the Indies for a second time. He did not begin the actual writing until later, after his return to the Netherlands in 1714. "Whenever I am asked," says Valentijn in his introduction, "what moved me to write this work? Nothing short of obtaining distinction in the eyes of the Educated World, to prove that I used my time to diligent purpose while I as yet had no secure position." The immense volume of his work shows that he had been diligent indeed. In 1724 the first volume appeared, then the second in the same year. In just four years, the entire work had been published. It was an edition in large folio, printed in two columns, consisting of five volumes bound in eight separate books. They contained about five thousand pages. In addition, the work was richly illustrated with so-called pictorial illustrations and a great many maps. The publication was a grandiose enterprise. It was generally regarded as the standard work, and remained so for at least a century. Indeed, even today certain facts can only be found in Valentijn and nowhere else. In the middle of the nineteenth century his work was still considered sufficiently informative on the colonies for a limited edition of his work to appear in three volumes between 1856 and 1858. The selections were made and edited by Professor S. Keyzer of the erstwhile Delft Academy, which trained officials bound for the Indies. An 1862 reprint in a handier format served for years as a guide for many government officials, especially those stationed in Ambon. However, this edition has drawn some sharp criticism on account of its slightly altered text and footnotes.

Gradually, the critical tide began to turn against the work itself. In 1839, Baron van Hoëvell, the well-known clergyman from Batavia, pronounced the work "first rate" and even used words such as "great" and "grandiose." Only thirty years later, in 1867, the Indies scholar Professor P. J. Veth (author of the well-known book entitled *Java*) mentioned Valentijn's work with only a few slighting words. He purposely avoided listing Valentijn as one of the authors on Java. Busken Huet had mixed feelings about Valentijn. With the turn of the century came the great denunciation. Dr. de Haan acted as chief prosecutor in *Rumphius Commemorative (Rumphius Gedenkboek*, 1902). In his article entitled "Rumphius and Valentijn as Historians of Ambon," he reveals how Valentijn "looted" Rumphius' unpublished manuscripts (which had come into his hands upon the latter's death), and how Valentijn had paraphrased Rumphius' factual but reliable account of Ambon's history in a manner De Haan characterized as "twaddle." De Haan had introduced damaging evidence, combined with humor, mockery, and irony, and effectively destroyed Valentijn's reputation. After De Haan was through with him, Valentijn could do no good by anyone. In heaping scorn upon him in his *Java in Our Art (Java in onze Kunst)*, Brom in fact does little more than parrot De Haan, without having checked the latter's arguments. Now, De Haan's arguments do cut ice, but it is odd for a historian not to examine the values of Valentijn's own contemporaries. He also failed to take into account seventeenth- and eighteenth-century notions about historiography, and their different opinions about originality and the use of other people's ideas and sources. *The Indies Past and Present (Oud en Nieuw-Oost-Indiën)* is a large-scale compilation, and that is how it should be valued. It is a collection of documents that attempts to comprise whatever had been written on the subject, and not just Valentijn's own writing. Valentijn, who was a vain man, doubtless must have regarded his work as an important accomplishment, and he did so because he and nobody else had collected and annotated this material. It is all very well for De Haan to call Valentijn's paraphrases from Rumphius and others nothing but "twaddle," but that was one of the ways in which Valentijn sought to make the material accessible. Judge Valentijn's method as one will, and grant that his subject got out of hand, it should be appreciated that Valentijn tried to give unity to his work in a way that happened to be more to the liking of Busken Huet than to De Haan. Time and again, by introducing his own experiences, by adding a personal comment or inserting a story, he tried to enliven both his descriptions of countries, people, and customs, and his accounts of historical facts. And the fact is that Valentijn can tell a good story when he wants to, and one with a good point at that. It is easy to find fault with much of what he does, but we still have to admit one thing: some of his pieces are true oases in the desert of eighteenth-century historical writing. His style is lively, unlike that of any of his contemporaries, often picturesque and colorful, and has a good dramatic sense, coupled with an underlying mirth. Where one would least expect to find it, in the midst of pages of summary and description, a lively detail or telling anecdote may suddenly surface, throwing everything into perspective. It is just this quality that enables us to forgive him a great deal, even his hypocrisy.

Valentijn is at his best when writing about his own experiences, such as in part four of "Outward and Homeward Bound" ("Uijt- en Thuisreize"), which Huet praised. The account itself is quite readable, and it becomes delightful when Valentijn describes a silly incident, such as the theft of a wig while landing on the Portuguese coast near St. Iago.

> We sailed to shore, our skipper having warned us to take heed and furthermore watch out, since the place was inhabited by nothing but bandits and born sneakthieves. . . . We saw one of these *fidalgos* (one of these born sneakthieves, I mean) display his talents to Monsieur Langele. As he and I, on account of the surf, were being carried ashore by two sailors, and he being put down, at the same instant a Portuguese fellow appeared from behind who deftly filched his handsome hat in one fine swoop, as well as his pretty blond wig, and with these he quickly commenced a foot race along the beach, heading straight for the coconut trees, with one of our sailors, brandishing a sabre, following closely upon his heels.
>
> On the way he lost the wig, which the sailor picked up, on account of which the thief won enough time to be lost out of sight in the woods, and the sailor returned without the hat to the depressed gentleman, who was, however, somewhat cheered by seeing his wig again, and who, for the duration of his stay ashore, had no more need to worry about taking his hat off at the proper moment, like us, which consoled him somewhat. He looked a bit out of sorts because he was the only one in our company who went uncovered. The great heat we felt there prevented us from following his example.

Later on, when they are received by the local Portuguese official, Valentijn begins to understand why the wig and hat needed to be stolen in the first place. It makes for a splendid tableau, incidentally, their reception with the official in his worn clothes, accompanied by "a big papist wearing his long, black and fairly old cassock and a broad-brimmed hat on his bald head." We can just picture these Dutchmen and Portuguese sitting across from one another on rickety chairs and benches, drinking again and again of "that horrible Madeira wine."

Valentijn spent the greater part of his career in the Indies as a minister on Ambon. Probably owing to the sources to which he had access, such as those of Rumphius and Ridjali, a native of the island, his description of Ambon is most elaborate. It is also his liveliest, because he made use of his own observations. He knows Ambon well and experienced a great deal there. Valentijn has a striking, inborn sense for the macabre, which seems curiously modern. His accounts of cruelties perpetrated on Ambon and on Ternate, gruesome enough in themselves, lack any emotion whatever in that they are told with twentieth-century understatement. His description of an execution is so fine that it should be included here, if only for its final phrase. The story follows immediately upon the description of "The Town of Ambon" (part 2, second book, chapter four):

The old hospital or infirmary standing at the end of the Burgerstraat near the river Way Tomo is also a handsome stone building, 90-feet wide and 24-feet high, not including the roof. It served as an infirmary in the past, for which purpose it was well suited, but ever since a new hospital was built, the surgeon has lived in the lower half of the structure and the upper story has been used as judge's chambers and for local government, the council for orphans, and the commissioner of marriages. It is also well suited to allow the judges to lean out of the upper story windows whenever anyone is executed, because across the street stands the scaffolding with a sturdy gallows and poles. A sturdy gallows, I say, because on the old gallows I have seen them hang a good-for-nothing who, as it happens, was hanged no less than three times. The executioner having climbed with him up the gallows, which were weak and made of wood, tumbled down with the criminal, gallows and all, the moment he pushed him off the ladder; there would have been trouble if the soldiers who on such occasions surround the scaffold had not closed ranks as completely as they did. The executioner, a stout fellow and not easily intimidated, untied the criminal on official orders, took him onto the scaffolding again and hanged him from one of the poles, but because the rope broke, down he came again. Now he thought himself to be a free man, but the fellow was very surprised to be reminded that he had been sentenced to hang until death followed, and the executioner hanged him a third time, so securely, in fact, that he remained an inhabitant of the air.

By way of an appendix, part 4 contains the "Levens der Opperland-voogden," biographies of the governors-general of the Indies. Valentijn here announces his intention to be as brief as possible (he does, after all, find it difficult to limit himself) concerning "the memorable accomplishments of these men." These brief biographies are little more than summaries of events, names, and dates. However, the closer Valentijn gets to his own period, the more intimately these lives are described, and the more he inserts hearsay and his own experience. Among these twenty governors there was one who did not seem to fit in. He was different from the others in personal and official habits also. This was Johannes Camphuis (1634–1695), a gentle man of few words who did not speak much because he had little to say to those around him. He expressed contempt for the nouveaux riches about him by merely ignoring them as much as possible, and in this he was oddly enough supported by the Lords Seventeen back in Holland. Valentijn recounts with relish that Camphuis' appointment to governor-general was actually the result of a miscalculation on the part of the other members of the Indies Council, who all paid a heavy price when their intrigue backfired.

Camphuis, who started out as a silversmith's apprentice to become governor-general, was, as they say, "a man of culture," a patron of the arts and sciences, fond of music and poetry. Even so, he is not mentioned here principally as an admirer and follower of the Renaissance poet Jan Baptista Houwaert but rather as the author of a well-written treatise concerning the founding of Jacatra (Djakarta). It was that historical essay that Valentijn promptly included in his *The Indies Past and Present*, with Camphuis' own consent. In addition to history, he was interested in plants and animals, in short, nature and nature studies. Camphuis owned a large collection of shells and molluscs which he or instructed others had found in the bay of Batavia and on the beaches of thousands of islands. As we know, Valentijn was a similar collector. He himself tells us that he was the founder in Dordrecht of Neptune's Cabinet, a society of collectors who there exchanged their "nun's turds, lobes, pimples, navels, sea gloves, and flea farts." Valentijn's collection was the largest and most beautiful of all, at least he says so himself. Still more extensive and more beautiful was the collection belonging to the famous naturalist Georg Everard Rumphius, the Pliny of the Indies, as he was called. He lived in the Moluccas, on the island of Ambon, and devoted his entire life to the collecting and studying of hitherto unknown varieties of herbs and plants, fish and shellfish, and minerals. He and Camphuis were friends, and probably carried on a regular correspondence. At least we are inclined to come to this conclusion when we note the tone of one of the few letters remaining, one from Camphuis addressed to Rumphius, and its reply. Camphuis writes that he has been looking for shells along the coast of the island of Edam to add to his ever-growing collection, that he has had others look for him elsewhere, and that he already has quite a collection put together. Rumphius' answer to him dates from June 29, 1665:

> I have been informed once again that Your Honor has caused his servants to look on the islands of Edam and Alkmaar for enough marine rarities such as molluscs and shells to rival those found on Ambon and the Moluccas, which confirms my former suspicion, assuring me that it is at least partially correct, since I have already received some forty different varieties gathered on the Batavian beaches by various friends. But whether these could really rival the Ambonese in beauty or splendor is a question which infringes too closely on the honor of Ambon's long-standing reign over the rarities of the sea. I have therefore caused, by Your Honor's leave, to have a contest performed, and have to this end commandeered about a hundred Ambonese champions, packed in the accompanying firkin, to challenge Batavia's boast, expecting to be informed in time of the positive outcome of this contest. If they should lose, they do not need to come back but may remain in your prison.

The tone of this letter typifies their relationship.

Rumphius (born in 1627 or 1628, died in 1702) was a German by birth who, after an adventurous life including several years spent as a prisoner of war in Portugal, entered the service of the Company. First he enlisted in the army but "finding himself ill suited for military matters" he later entered the civil service. For years he was an assistant merchant and merchant on the island of Ambon in the Moluccas. In addition to his official activities (the official documents provide clear evidence that he was an excellent and conscientious official), he devoted himself to describing plants, all manner of vegetation, and animals, as he told his superiors in a letter.

He had already amassed a great many notes, had begun writing in fact, and his collection of specimens was growing, when in 1670 he was stricken with blindness in his forty-second year. "The merchant Rumphius became blind several weeks ago," wrote the governor of Ambon to the government in Batavia in a letter dated May 9. It is not hard to imagine what this meant to Rumphius. For a while it seemed as if his entire world would collapse. He feels submerged, he writes, "in a long, sad night." At first too, there was some uncertainty on the part of Rumphius' superiors but finally Governor-General Maetsuyker decided to appoint him to a position with retention of rank and salary. Now more than ever before Rumphius attacked his studies. Anyone inclined to think of the high government officials as exclusively bent on financial gain will be forced to admit otherwise: Rumphius was granted every opportunity to devote himself to his studies. Even a copyist and a draughtsman were assigned to him, and later his son assisted him. The latter drew the well-known portrait of his father, seated at a table before plants and marine flora, with the typical stare and clawlike hands of the blind. Until his death in 1702, Rumphius lived on Ambon. During an earthquake a new disaster struck: his common-law wife Susanna (probably an Ambonese woman, after whom he had named a rare flower, *Flos Susannae*) and two of their children were killed when a wall collapsed. The minutes of Victoria Castle on Ambon read: "It was heart rending to see the man seated next to his dead and to hear his cries of woe, due to his fatal accident and to his blindness alike." Rumphius, however, forged on with his work, slowly but surely. In 1697 he completed his *Ambonese Herbal (Het Amboinsch Kruid-boek)*, and his *Ambon's Museum of Curiosities (D'Amboinsche Rariteitenkamer)* came out in 1705.

They are both most impressive works, one an herbal and the other a picture book of marine life. They are impressive both on account of their size and content but especially for their compelling manner of observation and description. Rumphius' way of looking at a hitherto unknown world reveals his marveling at the unknown and his joy of discovery. All those herbs, trees, leaves, shells, and crustaceans are a wondrous world whose marvels he has seen and known, and which as a blind man he can only conjure up again in his imagination. His fingers have become a new sense to him. His sense of touch activates his already amazing memory. Only in that way can he reach the lost world, by retrieving and describing it. Rumphius, who has been called "the blind seer," writes most descriptively. Particularly remarkable here is his sensitivity to color and shade, which is even more acute than his feeling for shape and form.

Two quotations from an immense mass of print will illustrate these characteristic qualities. In the first, Rumphius is describing a species of jellyfish, the *holothuria* or mizzen. The second quotation is a description of the starfish tree.

The *holothuria:* The body is an elongated bladder and sideways, on the back, a number of ridges are attached by their broad edge, their tips standing up like a stay sail or mizzen royal. Near the top, all these little sails are attached to one another by a seam running across, which can lower and raise all those sails when it senses the presence of wind and wishes to sail. The body is transparent in color, like a crystal flask filled with bluish green *aqua fortis*. The sails are crystalline white and the upper seam is tinged with some purple or violet, beautiful to behold, as if the entire creature were a precious jewel. When the sails are set, the body is nearly triangular with the head curved upwards, the backside extending from the stomach, which is bluer than the upper part of the body, as if the *aqua fortis* were stored there and the rest plain crystal. . . . On one side, I think the right one, and all around the back, a number of long, thin strands are suspended. These are a clear blue, with a hint of green. They are fragile enough to break off easily at the touch and will adhere to whatever strikes them.

The *starfish tree:* The leaves and flowers of this tree are as beautiful as its trunk, bark, and general appearance are ugly. It has, moreover, a way of growing curious enough to have inspired the classical poets, had they visited these parts, with a myth of some rare metamorphosis. The tree resembles a landlubber looking for someone he is in love with out in the sea, because it invariably stands rooted at the edge of the forest, not daring to advance by as much as one step onto the naked beach, and hovers above the same at such an angle as if it desires to fall forward at any moment. It is a large, wild tree with a trunk thicker than any other. As I said before, it never stands up straight but is forever inclined forward, and has coarse, rough, and ungainly bark, as ugly as a crocodile's back, black, thick, and hard, and here and there visible among the cracks, a yellowish substance, but in very scarce quantity. The leaves, however, are among the fairest in the world. The large, broad flower bearing clusters appear out of the branches as if newly born from their tips. On these the flowers appear, first as white buds on long stems, very much like apple blossoms but somewhat larger, their stems in the crucifer also, and fashioned out of nine or ten snow-white round leaves in the shape of a small rose. The center is filled with short stems bearing saffron buds. In their center these stems hide a small, round, rose-colored bud with a white strand on it. The scent of the flowers is lovely, reminiscent of white lilies, and lingers for a day and a night.

Rumphius names his finds in an individual manner suggestive of a number of associations. He derives them from Latin and Malay but often makes them up himself. They conjure up an image, arouse a feeling, and they are both concrete and evocative at the same time. At times they characterize Rumphius' own relationship to "these little marvels of nature."

Rumphius is not readily accessible because his costly folios are now kept under lock and key in the rare book rooms of major libraries. For this reason, a sample listing of his nomenclature seems in order: Dragon heads, white eyes, black mouths, hairy ears, fat lips, lobes and pustules, fingers and centipedes; Father Noah's shells, letter shells, smooth gapers, flops and spotted kittens, toads and knurls, oxheads, duck bills, horse's feet and mizzen, jellyboats, pimples and organ pipes; quadrants, perspectives, spectres and winged birdies, silver mouths, white spigots, moon eyes and sea navels, bellies, bumps, freckles, hams and buttocks, nipple cups, milk bowls, cots and Venus hearts, fly specks, shards and little fur coats (from the *Museum of Curiosities*, a description of marine life around Ambon); inkwell root, stinking amaranth, lord of the flies, scarlet cutlass, flame of the woods, Venus hair, long globules, the starfish tree, gray-branched root bier, queen's leaf, nymph's hair, red bells, black coral, bitter beach bush, earth's sash, Indian sea dawn, fish bark, memory weed, the tree of pointed flowers, heartfruit tree, wood of paradise, peacock's crest, longevity wood, devil's toadstool, the blue clitoris flower and the true appendage, the growing nest, sad herb, simple snake tongue and festive grass, small crawling grass, pleading grass, accusing grass; wild widow's mite, trout killer, and little cardamon, maiden herb, wondrously capacious bush, rambling green and water fern, water stone and bittersweet plant, fiery toadstool and marveling herb, burning fever bush, stone amaranth, fire root, spot root, bloody mash, root puss and deadweed; night lover, night tree, the blind-eyed tree and wood whispers (from the *Herbal*, a book about tropical flora).

The *Herbal* manuscript was very nearly lost. It survived thanks to Governor-General Camphuis, who had it copied in Batavia before forwarding it to Holland. His caution proved justified when the ship carrying the manuscript was attacked and sunk by the French. Camphuis also appointed Dr. Engelhard Kaempfer, a German surgeon working for the Company, to go to Japan and describe that country. To this work Camphuis later on added his own notes. The work appeared finally in 1729 and contributed a great deal to a better understanding of Japan, especially since it was translated into English. Camphuis' own love for Japan and its customs derives from his stay there as head of Deshima, that minute island in Nagasaki Bay where, as everyone knows, the Dutch were the only Westerners allowed to carry on trade.

Camphuis, like Rumphius, never returned to the Netherlands but remained in the Indies, one of those "staying on." Upon his "most honorable and reputatious" discharge, he retired to his country house near Jacatra and to the island of Edam, situated in the bay off Batavia. The island was a present from the Lords Seventeen in appreciation of his prudent government service, and it was there he had a house built in the Japanese style. Valentijn once came to visit him, on a Thursday, and it happened that Camphuis had made it a habit on that day of the week to offer his guests a Japanese meal, with bowls, chopsticks, and all. Valentijn, who really loved down-home Dutch cooking more than anything else, had a rough time of it. Camphuis, as Valentijn himself knew, was quietly amused by it all. He also showed his guests his shell and rock specimens. Exotic plants grew in his gardens, which also housed a private zoo full of Javanese animals. Among these were two rare apes, one snow white, the other pitch black. All this is history now, thanks to Valentijn.

II
Breakthrough of New Ideas

1 Willem and Dirk van Hogendorp, Father and Son

Following happy student days, Willem van Hogendorp married Caroline van Haren. He was a relatively carefree man of means, which must have given him all the more reason to feel deeply surprised when her parents did not appear too pleased with his proposal of marriage. They considered him too flighty and superficial, and most of all too much of a spoiled brat; in brief, the very opposite of the opinion they held of their daughter.

Two sons were born from this marriage, Dirk and Gijsbert Karel, both of whom were to make history. Gijsbert Karel's role in politics, that of helping to establish the Dutch monarchy following the Napoleonic period, is more generally known than that of his brother. The latter's role is related to Dutch colonial history. Their father, Willem, also had something to do with the Indies and even with literature. When he was thirty-seven and his fortune needed restoring, he went to the Indies, leaving wife and children behind. He carried the best letters of introduction possible, written by none other than the Prince of Orange, William V, and in no time at all he was appointed resident of Rembang, on the northeast coast of Java. In those days, this appointment amounted to a diplomatic position of sorts. Two years later, he became administrator of the Company's warehouses on the island of Onrust, in the bay of Batavia. This was a most lucrative job in that it offered every opportunity of avoiding Company monopoly and of increasing one's own take by trading privately. Willem even owned his ship, and he enriched himself in a most clever and brazen fashion, which goes to indicate that he was a powerful man indeed. By

1784, he thought to have accomplished his goal of replenishing his coffers, and decided to return to the Netherlands. One of his enemies is reputed to have said: "If there is a just God in heaven, that fellow will never reach the Cape of Good Hope." And indeed, he did not make it. His ship foundered, evil tongues alleged, because it had been too heavily laden with loot. This impression is one-sided, to be sure, coming from Governor-General Alting and his circle, Willem's enemies. It is true, of course, that Willem had come to the Indies for no purpose other than enriching himself, and he did so with every means at his disposal, and without much scruple. He would have been rather surprised, in fact, if people had made a fuss about it. He considered his dealings perfectly all right, or rather, as a birthright of his regent class and its powerful relations. For that matter, he was not a money maker in the sense that he knew nothing about anything except accruing wealth. On the contrary, he was most active in social and cultural affairs. He was one of the founders of the Batavian Society for Arts and Sciences, one of the most important scientific institutions in Southeast Asia. Willem reveals himself in all his social activities as a typical man of the Enlightenment. He was particularly interested in the practice of inoculation against smallpox and in improving the treatment of slaves. To these ends he used all his literary talents, insofar as he had any. In any case, he put his ideas in literary dress in order to attain his social aims "in the interest of humanity," quite in keeping with eighteenth-century notions. In January 1780, he wrote his wife: "From time to time I shall be publishing some moral pieces. . . ." By then he had already published "an edifying novel," written in a fortnight, he says, entitled *Sophronisba, or the Happy Mother Who Had Her Daughters Inoculated (Sophronisba, of de gelukkige moeder door de inëntinge van haare dochters).* The subtitle, of course, is what is important here. In his preface he directly addressed the "gentle mothers of Batavia! . . . Accept then this little work with the same gladness it is offered you; read it without prejudice and remember that your children's well-being may depend on the decisions you make upon reading this."

It is the story of a dear and loving couple, Lysander and Sophronisba. Lysander is very much in favor of smallpox inoculation, which in those days before Jenner's discovery of the cow virus was still done by transferring the infection from one human being to another. Sophronisba, however, is afraid of adverse consequences. She is supported in her refusal by an old doctor, her parents' former physician, who for purely silly and egotistical reasons declares himself opposed to the inoculation. Thereupon our good Lysander decides to take the responsibility upon himself, and he has both their daughters undergo the "operation." The subsequent eruption of the pox makes him ecstatic, and even compels him to write a sonnet! Next we get his blow-by-blow account of the symptoms, interspersed with figures, quotations, and the names of people advocating inoculation. Meanwhile, a smallpox epidemic breaks out, "dragging" adults and children alike "into the grave." The daughters of our sage and enlightened Lysander are cured, and from that moment on, invulnerable to "that most evil malady." The old doctor, however, loses his wife and his son, and one of his daughters becomes lame, the other blind. He is overcome by remorse for his stubbornness, and commits suicide. And what happens to Sophronisba, the mother? Well, she "testified to anyone who wished to hear how she had become a happy mother on account of her daughters' inoculation." There we have it: wisdom (and not the good) is rewarded, narrowmindedness (and not evil) is punished. These too are typical eighteenth-century values.

Apparently Willem van Hogendorp was very pleased with his edifying novel. His wife in Holland must have been less so, for Willem wrote her: "Of all the people who have written me about *Sophronisba*, you appear to be the only one who is not satisfied with it." Judging by our tastes, she is right. *Sophronisba* is a hackneyed and self-satisfied job but, printed in Batavia in 1779, it apparently did not go unnoticed. A great many parents had their children inoculated thereafter. The community was shocked, however, when a young girl died following the process. After this, Van Hogendorp gave a "speech concerning inoculation" to the residents of Batavia, referring to that death, and said: "Fight on with renewed vigor. I assure you that the Branch of Victory will not elude your grasp!" Apart from some verse, Willem van Hogendorp wrote a second "edifying novel," entitled *Kraspukol; Or the Dismal Consequences of Excessive Severity toward Slaves (Kraspoekol; of de droevige gevolgen van een te verregaande strengheid jegens de Slaaven)*, published in 1780 by Dominicus, the same Batavian printer of his first novel. The novel is lacking in everything that might have made it into a passable story, but Willem's aim can only have been an edifying and moral one. All else must have seemed to him extraneous to his task of spreading enlightenment. Being an "author" must have given him a feeling of self-importance, a feeling that, considering all the evidence, he was temperamentally inclined to. Perhaps his entire writing career, consisting of "moral pieces," or his social activities generally, should be viewed as the justification of his stay in the Indies. His ambition too, which he, like his contemporaries, regarded as a virtue, must have been a contributing factor. He had not intended, incidentally, that his novel be in any way regarded as a revolutionary statement from him. As its title reveals, he directed himself only against the excesses in the treatment of slaves, and he stayed well within socially acceptable boundaries. The question arises whether there was in fact sufficient cause for Willem van Hogendorp's plea for an improved treatment of slaves. That question is not so easy to answer. Everywhere one reads that slavery in the Dutch Indies bore a mild character, even in the writings of those opposed to it. We must not overlook the fact that the condition of the slaves, who were used exclusively as domestics, was much superior to that of the so-called freemen. The latter had all kinds of obligatory services and duties to perform which the slaves did not. There exists the great eighteenth-century example of Cornelis Chasteleyn, who willed his extensive estate Depok, between what is now Djakarta and Bogor, to his Christian slaves. There they formed their own community, which they maintained at least until the Japanese occupation in 1942.

There exist, however, examples of arbitrary treatment and abuse. Nicolaus de Graaff mentions some, as does, of course, Valentijn with his penchant for the cruel. One of his eye-witness reports deals with a European woman whom Governor-General Camphuis sentenced to having her nose and ears cut off in public because she had had a female slave eaten alive by ants! From a social viewpoint, publishing the novel *Kraspukol* had some merit, and was conducive to the spreading of enlightenment.

In any case, after smallpox inoculation, Willem van Hogendorp concerned himself with the subject of slavery. This concern could also be traced directly to Rousseau. It was not then regarded as what we would now call a socioeconomic problem, but rather as a moral issue, and as an aspect of a much larger trend, one that sought to humanize and soften morality generally. His novel takes the form of a moral fable, quite in keeping with the times. Its appeal to humanity is undoubtedly rooted in his moral consciousness but it does not go so far as to question the principle of slavery itself.

Raising that question on the basis of moral principles is left to his son Dirk some twenty years later. The son continues to work toward his father's goals, one could say. However, he judges the social phenomenon of slavery according to his moral principles and he rejects it. Unlike his father, he goes one step further and also rejects the social conditions that allowed slavery to exist in the first place. There is something paradoxical here. Dirk reworked his father's novel for the stage. This meant, on the one hand, that he identified with the work to some degree. On the other hand, he deviated from the original on some very crucial points, not by changing facts but by changing the novel's intention. His stage adaptation reveals the evolution of ideas over a span of twenty years' time, as well as the difference in ideas between father and son. In order to clarify this it will first be necessary to take a look at the father's novel and then to see what the son's adaptation is like.

Father Willem's plot runs as follows. Two female slaves, one of whom is called Tjampakka (the "tjampakka" is a fragrant Indonesian flower), complain about the harsh treatment of their mistress. They are overheard by their female supervisor, who immediately tells the mistress. Mistress Kraspukol (which means hit hard) awaits her chance to get even. For breaking a plate, fair Tjampakka is tied to a ladder in the backyard in order to be whipped. The master of the house, called Wedano, accidentally learns what is going on. He has her freed and he banishes cruel Kraspukol, his sister, to the outbuildings. She refuses this humiliation and moves to an adjoining property. There she plots her revenge. She buys a number of male and female slaves and has them tortured regularly, preferably in such a spot that her brother Wedano can not but overhear the cries and screams. The "woeful groans of the unfortunate," the novel informs us, "really began to annoy him to such a degree" that he threatened to have his sister arrested. One day, a slave requests of his mistress Kraspukol permission to marry a female slave reserved for him. Kraspukol refuses him. When, however, the female slave in question comes to her with an identical request, Kraspukol becomes enraged and has her "soundly trounced." The slave who sees his beloved thus tortured avenges himself on Kraspukol and her supervisor. He takes his kris, stabs Kraspukol in the chest and stabs her supervisor through the heart. Bearing the bloody corpus delicti in his arms, the slave goes to Wedano and confesses his crime. Noble and fair Tjampakka goes next door and finds Kraspukol dying. She dies in Tjampakka's arms, a repentant sinner. The slave who has committed the double murder is dragged before the courts and put on the rack. In the evening, Kraspukol is buried, and her name, according to the text, "is added to those of women who have themselves to blame for the sad consequences of an excessive severity toward slaves."

So much for Willem van Hogendorp's novel. His son Dirk's stage rendition contains, in the first place, a preface lacking in the original. It is a clear denunciation of the principle of slavery: "My aim is to portray slavery and the even more abominable trade in slaves as abhorrently and hatefully as possible, and in so doing to promote the goal of prohibiting the slave trade soonest possible in our dominions, hence, to put an end to slavery itself."

Even more interesting are Dirk's changes in his father's text. Naturally, the adaptation for the stage in itself required alterations, but quite aside from those, Dirk made a number of additions. For example, he inserted Wedano's monologue following his talk with Tjampakka (another addition), where she tells him about her miserable fate. Following this, Wedano utters the soliloquy: "Unnatural slavery, damned slave trade, when will you be banished from this earth?" More arresting still is the insertion of an entirely new scene, which involves the appearance of a number of important visitors, among them a nobleman called Champignon (i.e., "toadstool"). His stage directions state: "Arrogance, incompetence, and pride emanate from every word and action of this man." Through their conversation Dirk criticizes the spirit prevailing among the Company's servants, especially through Champignon's remarks. He started out as a cabin boy who made it to the top, and misses no opportunity to tell everyone that he got there by stealing from and cheating the Company in every way possible, and that he is now worth millions. "My conscience? Ha! Ha!" he exclaims, "I have a real good laugh whenever I hear the work 'conscience' mentioned here in the Indies." Turning to Wedano, he says: "You must have come here for the nuggets too, I take it? Ha! Ha!" Exactly like Dirk's own father seeking his fortune, we realize that here is a character who is equally adept at finding his way in this corrupt society.

There is no mention at all in Dirk's *Mémoires*, published much later in French, about an actual production of his play. Even so, *Kraspukol* was put on once in The Hague. To be sure, it never lasted beyond the first act. Demonstrators made the performance entirely impossible. We know this from an eye-witness account of an Englishman named Carleton who was a teacher of English in The Hague at the time. This is his story:

> Six months after the publication of this play, with his name to it, he attempted to have it represented on the stage at The Hague, on the 20th March 1801; but the East India Gentry, not thinking it proper to exhibit the most illustrious actions of themselves and their noble ancestors upon a stage to vulgar European spectators, went to the play provided with little half-penny whistles and trumpets, and kept up such a tremendous whistling and trumpeting from the very moment the curtain began to rise, that not a syllable of the play could be heard—and, if these Gentlemen could, they would also have extinguished the candles, to keep in darkness what they and their ancestors never intended for the light. In short, the play, after being thus interrupted the whole of the first act, was broken off before the second, when the manager was obliged to give up the entertainment.

However, what happened next was predictable enough: "The next day the ignorant part of the audience was so curious to know the secrets which these East India Gentlemen had been thus industrious to conceal that the bookseller (as he told me himself) sold infinitely more copies of the play that day, than all he had sold the whole of the preceding six months, and had he ten times more, they would not have answered the numerous demands."

It would be nice to know the names of those who sabotaged the performance. All we know is that they must have been some shady members of the "East Indian Gentry." The play was stopped even before Champignon and his cronies were to come on. This may well have been their very intention. Either they decided that no matter what, they would not be ridiculed on stage, or else it was the play's message, or Dirk's reputation that had been enough to bring about their demonstration. Probably all three reasons had incited their action because two years earlier Dirk's sensational *Account of the Present Condition of the Batavian Republic's Possessions and Trade in the East Indies (Berigt van den tegenwoordigen toestand der Bataafsche bezittingen in Oost-Indien en den handel op dezelve)* had been published. It was a well-reasoned polemic that subjected the situation in the Indies to sharp, at times biting criticism, and that especially exposed the conduct of the commissioners general and the government. He accused them to their faces of having squandered the revenues and of having neglected their administration, and that "only greed and lust for power motivated them."

The most influential commissioner general happened to be his archenemy S. C. Nederburgh, who probably inspired his caricature Champignon. The two men were involved in an irreconcilable feud that bore a deeply personal stamp. Dirk was, moreover, a so-called radical who desired changes well before the 1795 revolution, whereas, according to the historian Stapel, Nederburgh championed the status quo. In 1796, while Dirk governed Java's eastern coastal district as "Gezaghebber," he had written an "Address to the People of the Netherlands" ("Aanspraak aan het volk van Nederland"), and forwarded it, together with a personal letter dated July 2, to his brother Gijsbert Karel. On January 21, 1797, he sent a second "Address." A copy of it came into the hands of Nederburgh that same year. He had Dirk arrested and incarcerated, charging him, among other things, with fraud. Taking revenues for one's private use was, of course, a general practice among officials in those days. Meanwhile, Nederburgh had been collecting evidence against him, including allegedly false evidence from some Chinese. Dirk managed to escape by way of Bencoolen, Sumatra, and reached the mother country. On the way, he probably wrote his *Account*, which can be considered an updated version of his "Address," although it lacked the supporting evidence Dirk had collected, all of Dirk's papers having been taken from him in prison. Dirk, by the way, complained bitterly about this. His *Account*, greatly approved by his influential brother Gijsbert Karel, created a sensation. A second edition was called for that very same year.

For that reason it had become a threat to the "East Indian Gentry," and Dirk was now suspect, especially after the stage adaptation of his father's *Kraspukol* came out the following year. While the repercussions of the *Account* could still be kept within limits, the stage production was bound to reach a far wider audience. This was an unbearable strain, given the social fabric of those times—or so it was thought, for the importance of literature was then greatly overestimated. When a year later yet another performance was announced, they knew they had to stop it at any cost. It was simply unthinkable that the regents of the East India Company would allow themselves to be portrayed on stage as a bunch of unctuous and unconscionable incompetents and cowards. This is the background to the "Hague brawl" of March 20, 1801.

Kraspukol remains Dirk's sole literary venture, and, as in his father's case, it would be too much to assert that he was a great literary talent. However, it would be wrong to underestimate his political influence on the colonial history of the Netherlands. It simply will not do to evaluate Dirk van Hogendorp on either his literary or his political merits alone. He had both, and a great deal more besides. From early on, his was a captivating personality, albeit overshadowed by his brother's. Gijsbert Karel was honored with a statue, whereas his brother had to be content with an official portrait. During his stay in Indonesia from 1936 until August 1939, Du Perron did quite a lot of research on the Van Hogendorps, as a number of articles testify, but he was especially intrigued by Dirk. His intention was to write a novel about Dirk patterned on his previous novel *Scandal in Holland (Schandaal in Holland)*. While in Indonesia, he gathered what limited materials he could, and made notes. Back in Holland, he investigated everything he could find about Dirk in the Federal Archives (Algemeen Rijksarchief) in The Hague. There he came upon the correspondence between him and Gijsbert Karel, largely written in French. This find proved an important gauge for the brothers' relationship.

Gijsbert Karel shows himself as having been the successful man, intelligent, even keeled and certainly not insensitive, but much more of a conformist in his outlook than his more radical and spontaneous brother. Dirk admitted to having all too often judged subjectively

("During the course of my life, I have often judged others by my own standards," *Mémoires*, p. 137). In yet another way Dirk seems to have lived in his brother's shadow. The available facts bear out that for many years, during his whole life perhaps, he had felt the need to compete against his brother's real or imaginary superiority. This may well explain why he always felt the need to assert himself, as Paul van 't Veer has pointed out in an essay contained in his *Straight Talk (Geen blad voor de mond,* 1958). Du Perron was still working on a novel based on Dirk's life when his untimely death occurred in May 1940. Two parts of it were published posthumously in the October and November 1940 issues of *Greater Netherlands (Groot-Nederland).* Its title was to have been *Giving Account (Zich doen gelden).*

There is a great deal more to Dirk that lies beyond the pale of literature. Suffice it to say that although his career was not as successful as his brother's, he was no less an individual than his brother and definitely more interesting. It would also be wrong to measure his influence solely in terms of its immediate success. Dirk left his mark on Dutch colonial history by virtue of his sharp criticism of the Company, that "realm of violence and tyranny," as he called it. His ideas about the future of the colony were in part realized, even if much later. He did not live to see the changes in colonial rule. Only once did he seem to have a chance, in 1805, when the Batavian Republic came to be headed by Rutger Jan Schimmelpenninck, a proponent of political innovation in the colonies. Dirk fully expected to be appointed governor-general of the Indies, but the government decided otherwise. Two high officials were sent to Java in order to implement the new policies. Going by way of North America because the English held the South African cape, they never got beyond New York. They were recalled, for in their absence the Kingdom of Holland had been declared, supplanting the Republic. Napoleon required a strong man more than he needed new policies, and he directed General Daendels to go to the Indies. This finished Dirk's political aspirations. The opportunity to realize his political ideas would never come his way again. Afterwards, he held a number of important diplomatic posts in Europe, and Napoleon even appointed him general. Subsequent political changes ultimately put him out of commission, and he spent his final days as a voluntary exile in Brazil. There he lived on a small remote coffee and citrus plantation named Novo Sion, after the estate Sion near Delft where he had spent his childhood. A traveler coming across him tells us that his simple dwelling contained the life-size portrait of himself wearing a general's uniform, a memento of past glory.

2   *The Era of Van der Capellen*

We know from some of his letters that Dirk van Hogendorp never managed to put the Indies behind him, not even after his career there had ended. This abiding interest was not only transferred to his brother but, in all likelihood, to his children as well. It most certainly influenced his son from his first marriage, Carel Sirardus Willem, born in Bengal, India, in 1788. Following a military career, he went to the Indies in 1817 as an official second class, equipped with letters of recommendation from his influential uncle, Gijsbert Karel. By the time Dirk died a lonely man in Brazil on November 9, 1822, his son had already been promoted to resident of Buitenzorg near Batavia, and was on friendly terms with the governor-general, Baron van der Capellen.

The Colonial Treaty signed in London on August 13, 1814, signaled the end of the English interregnum over all colonies captured from the Dutch since 1803. King William I of the Netherlands then appointed a commission to see to the proper transfer of power. G. A. G. Ph. baron van der Capellen was one of the three men appointed to this commission, which was to be dissolved upon the completion of its task, leaving Van der Capellen alone in charge as governor-general of the Indies.

Van der Capellen was to prove himself one of the ablest governors-general ever, a statesman of vision and character as well as "a promoter of the arts and sciences." He is, in fact, the only one to stand comparison with his English predecessor, Sir Thomas Stamford Raffles. However, to use a fashionable phrase, Van der Capellen has been "left out of the picture" by historians. The reason for that is understood easily enough if we remember that he did not measure up to the standards of colonial historians of liberal persuasion, and it was precisely their interpretations and values that prevailed for the longest time. Be that as it may, to typify Van der Capellen as a "conservative" would be misleading, to say the least. In fact, he desired change more than anything else, significant change that would bring the Indies closer to independence and establish a government founded on humane principles. One might just as easily and with more justification call him a "progressive," but one would do best simply to accept the fact that he was his own man, a truly independent spirit.

Even in his own time, Van der Capellen was a controversial character who was admired and hated in turn. Some regarded him as a man without principle, others as a man of both character and principle. His friends admired him as a "noble spirit" and a great governor-general, whereas his enemies accused him of betraying his liberal ethics and resented his authoritarian and autocratic rule.

By the time Van der Capellen became governor-general in January 1819, his service record was already quite impressive. As early as 1809, before he turned thirty-one, King Louis Napoleon of Holland had appointed him minister of protocol and internal affairs. He resigned this post in 1810 in protest against Napoleon's annexation of Holland in that year. He refused the French Imperial Order of Reunion and went abroad for a time, only to return after the sovereignty of the Netherlands was restored. In September 1814, King William I appointed him, together with Elout and Buyskes, to the Commission General, the triumvirate charged with taking over the administration of the Indies from the English and developing it along modern lines. It was October 1815 when Van der Capellen could finally depart. This High Commission faced a number of very difficult problems in the East, one of which was the agrarian question, pivotal to colonial rule. Now they had to try and solve the agrarian problem in accordance with the politically liberal ideas of the early nineteenth century. The triumvirate was well schooled in these ideas, and it was precisely for this reason that the king had chosen them.

During the reign of Raffles, extensive tracts of land had been sold, and many promises and concessions had been made. When the High Commission assumed power, it was inundated with applications. Contrary to every expectation, however, and with only a few exceptions, these applications led nowhere. The Commission General, which according to its liberal principles was supposedly prepared to sell government land to private individuals, now found itself advised to exercise extreme caution in this matter by such able advisors as Muntinghe, who had also been an aide to Raffles. The Commission General's job was twofold: on the one hand it had to look after the financial interests of the state, and on the other hand its task was to look after the interests of the native peoples. Its high-sounding declaration of principles had in fact stressed that native interests were its prime concern, and any sale of lands had to be considered with that in mind. Short of reneging—and this was no longer really possible—the commission now found itself obliged to limit the very principle of economic freedom itself. The situation was most paradoxical.

The Commission General was dissolved in 1819. Elout and Buyskes returned to Holland, Van der Capellen stayed behind, stuck with an unsolved agrarian problem because the Commission General had been unable to make up its mind on the question. Left to himself, Van der Capellen began to pursue a policy that increasingly favored native interests. This invited a great deal of adverse criticism. He was accused of having abandoned his liberal principles and, following the departure of the Commission General, he had allegedly "succumbed to a reactionary spirit." Also, he was rumored to have paid too much attention to his advisors, especially to Van de Graaff, member of the Council for the Indies. The fact is, however, that through it all Van der Capellen remained uniquely himself. He was basically a liberal but the moment the economic application of this philosophy came into conflict with his humanitarian principles he opted for the latter. He thought about the subject somewhat as follows. Whenever one wishes to reach a certain goal, one should see if the way to reach it is, as he expressed it, "passable." And if that way "should be or become drenched with the blood of millions of Asiatic peoples then that is a way not to be taken."

When Van der Capellen arrived in the Indies in May 1816, he found a small European community there which since the liquidation of the Company in 1795 had been subject to all kinds of political changes and under the constant threat of foreign and domestic war. For years the Indies had been practically isolated from the mother country and left to its own devices. The result was that the European community had become estranged from Europe. It had gradually evolved a pattern all its own, that of a mixed, particularly Indonesian society, which continued to exist for a long time. One aspect, for example, was that concubinage, as well as mixed marriage, was a normal and socially sanctioned form of family life. The writings of De Haan and Stavorinus will attest to this with respect to the early years, as will those of Olivier for the period from the early nineteenth century on. This small society of about a thousand Europeans was very heterogeneous, one of its essential and permanent characteristics. Another characteristic was its general lack of what one would call education or culture, even though it had its amusements in receptions and parties, and such. De Haan calls it "a somewhat barbaric society."

Indeed, if we regard the Batavian Society for Arts and Sciences, founded in 1778, as the touchstone "by which every branch of arts and sciences can be judged," then the arts and sciences were in dismal straits in the beginning of the nineteenth century. A minister of the church wrote: "The decay of that institution during the most recent years of the Dutch presence in the Indies resulted also in the decay of letters generally." Between 1800 and 1813, hardly anything worthy of the name of either literary or scientific activity can be said to have taken place, neither within nor without the Batavian Society. According to the *Yearbook (Gedenkboek)* of 1878, the cause "lay probably in the difficult and tumultuous times," although that does not sound very convincing. Those were barren times indeed, producing just some occasional verse and some anemic amateur theater that soon expired. When in 1811 the English took over the control of Java from the Dutch, an English major by the name of W. Thorn observed: "There are no places of public amusement at Batavia; not a single theatre of any kind" (*Memoir of the Conquest of Java*, p. 249).

Especially during Daendels's previous government, general political uncertainty and relative impoverishment had cast a pall over the European community. People lived increasingly, as they put it, a "plantation" life, and some did in fact little more than vegetate. Indeed, the European was generally lampooned as a gross, indolent character stretched out in a chair and surrounded by a number of female slaves dressing or undressing, putting him to bed or fanning him. Only the English interregnum (1811–1816) introduced some cultural revival but this was largely limited to the top layer of society. Everyone else was left out and continued to enjoy the "plantation" life.

This should in no way detract from Lieutenant-Governor Raffles's important accomplishments. This Englishman personally took it upon himself to further social development through the revival of the arts and sciences, assisted by his celebrated wife, Olivia Fancourt. The languishing Batavian Society provided a suitable contact with the Dutch community. He renewed the society's directorship under new rules and regulations and he saw to it that it was properly housed. He participated in its activities by reading a number of his own papers, by getting the Dutch involved, and by attracting lecturers from England and elsewhere. A Dutch contemporary of Raffles says that "by his actions he aroused a creative spirit among the Dutch as well." For a number of Dutchmen, English rule under Raffles promised a much more tolerable existence.

However, under English rule, a revival of *Dutch* literary activity was hardly to be expected. Its renaissance, albeit modest, only occurred after Van der Capellen had replaced Raffles. The former was also an educated man with a style few governors could match. Raffles had stimulated and tried to upgrade life in the capital. Van der Capellen continued on a similar but carefully guarded course, and his directions remind one, inescapably perhaps, of those of a Dutch uncle. His punctuality, restraint, and moderation set an example, and in one of his speeches, a contemporary informs us, he declared himself to be "an enemy of anything even remotely licentious." Of course Van der Capellen was more than just a pious killjoy. He sought to find the causes for what dissoluteness he encountered, and as a typical product of the Enlightenment, he naturally thought they lay in the lack of proper education and training. As it happens, education had been one of the weak points of English rule.

Upon the restoration of Dutch rule in 1815, the Commission General sent to Java was accompanied by a large and competent staff, including one Dr. C. G. C. Reinwardt, in charge of education, sciences, and agriculture. Reinwardt was a German by birth and had studied medicine in Amsterdam. He was especially interested in flora and fauna, and it was he who founded the botanical gardens in Bogor, which have long since become world renowned, and for which he is most famous. But he directed his attention first and foremost to the areas of education and health. He was a many-sided man, and Van der Capellen supported him wholeheartedly. During the era of the Company, nobody had really bothered much with education, and therefore everything had to be started from scratch. New schools were established, such as a military academy, and "excellent institutions for the rearing of girls from six to sixteen." Girls had never received any education at all, and these schools represented a hitherto unknown opportunity for the numerous offspring of mixed and common-law marriages. Needless to say, this was part of an attempt to influence and educate society from "without," as it were. Reinwardt returned to The Netherlands in 1822. The year before he had made a tour, the account of which was posthumously published in 1858, bearing the title *Voyage to the Eastern Parts of the Indies Archipelago (Reise naar het oostelijk gedeelte van den Indischen archipel)*. The book contains an extensive biography of Reinwardt. Van der Capellen had the great good luck to find a successor to his educational duties in the energetic and idealistic person of J. van der Vinne, who also involved himself with the activities of the Batavian Society. Dr. C. L. Blume assumed Reinwardt's duties in medicine and the natural sciences in 1822, and he too made frequent trips to study flora and fauna and to become acquainted with the country and the people. The fight against such endemic diseases as cholera and smallpox also dates back to Van der Capellen's early days. Thanks to him, Dr. Blume was able to extend smallpox vaccination programs to a considerable degree. As the man in charge of the country, but more so on account of his own personality, Van der Capellen became the center of what we would nowadays call an intellectual elite. This was a small group, to be sure, when we consider the modest list of members of the Batavian Society and the recurrence of certain names such as Reinwardt, Blume, Norsfield (an American), Van der Vinne, C. S. W. van Hogendorp, M. W. Muntinghe, Van de Graaff, Meylan, Joh. Olivier, G. M. Nagel, J. I. van Sevenhoven, Ph. Roorda van Eysinga, and a few others. These men sang Van der Capellen's praises without exception, often in what we would now consider excessive terms. Nonetheless, neither this praise nor his personal charm and "unequaled interest" quite explains the influence of this exceptional governor. This is sooner explained in terms of the spread of the ideas of the Enlightenment, in the Indies as elsewhere. Van der Capellen was such an enlightened man, who entered into his diary: "Obtaining the maximum goods for the minimum prices is no longer our object but . . . providing the population with prosperity and raising it up from humiliation and contempt is our goal." He belongs to the new breed of governor who dares to put his liberal reputation at stake by writing to the minister of foreign affairs: "When I observe that in the Netherlands liberalism is interpreted to mean protecting European landowners at the expense of the native population, which is so dear to my heart, then I feel compelled to declare myself an antiliberal in the extreme." What is even more telling is that he took his ethical principles seriously and acted on them.

In 1818, uprisings had broken out in the Moluccas. Van der Capellen sent out his assistants Van de Graaff and Meylan, and their extensive report proved alarming. In 1824 he went personally, accompanied by a large staff, including the two illustrators Bik and Payen. We know quite a lot about this trip from Van der Capellen's own journal and because Johannes Olivier, who traveled in the same entourage, described the same trip also in his *Travels in the Moluccan Archipelago (Reizen in den Molukschen Archipel,* 1834). Van der Capellen was deeply shocked by what he encountered, and took immediate action on his own responsibility. He caused improvements to be made, and right away eased the population's tax burden. To the king in Holland he forwarded a report proposing to liquidate the system of forced labor, and to abandon the requirement of growing just one crop, the so-called monopoly system. During his stay in the Moluccas, in April 1824, he gave an address to the population of the Moluccas in both Malay and Dutch. The address is couched in a fine and nearly impassioned prose:

> Peoples of Amboina, of Ley Timor, of Hitu, of Oma, of Honima, of Nusa Laut, of Ceram, of Buru, of Ambelau, Manipa, Bonoa and Goram, and of the islands hereabouts. When leaving our fatherland and our king eight years ago, in order to govern in his name the extensive lands amidst these seas, we were bidden by him to look especially into your situation. Now we find ourselves in your midst and this arrival alone must be proof to all of you of the interest we feel in your well-being and in the well-being of your children. We wanted to convince ourselves with our own eyes to see if the reports prepared for us on our own orders are indeed correct, and to ascertain if our opinion of your situation were true. We would have wished this to have been otherwise but to our deep dismay we have

found your plight more lamentable than we could have imagined. You are poor even though providence has blessed your fields with abundance; you are dependent on other peoples because you do not taste the fruits of your own labor and industry; your days are full of disquiet because the rule of peace, law, and justice is absent; you hate and deny the legally instituted sway of your chiefs descended from your ancient families because their interests are not your interests. You hide from the rule of law because you can not value its powers to protect you. You are carrying on dangerous and detrimental smuggling because the advantages of safe and free trade are unknown to you; you dislike labor because you associate it always with force and obligation; you are the victims of the rapacity of foreign peoples who would certainly fear your strength and courage if you knew how to unite and defend your goods and chattels, your wives and children. Manyfold and great are your disasters!

Following this, Van der Capellen outlines the many measures he has taken, and concludes, promising new laws.

Where have we heard this before? It reminds us of another address by a white official to native chiefs. It is strikingly similar, of course, both in tone and cadence, to Havelaar's address to the chiefs of Lebak in the later, epochal novel *Max Havelaar* by Douwes Dekker. Douwes Dekker did in fact read Van der Capellen's address, quoted here in part only. He writes in his *Max Havelaar* (1859): "One should try to get hold of what Baron Van der Capellen already wrote on the subject in 1825. The writings of this true philanthropist are to be found in the *Indies Gazette [Indisch Staatsblad]* of that year."

Multatuli, Douwes Dekker's pseudonym, is referring in fact to the *Batavian Courant (Bataviasche Courant)* of 1824, which carried Van der Capellen's speech in its August 7 and 14 issues of the same year he made his trip to the Moluccas. The oratory and the sentiment, the style, more than the content of this proclamation must have strongly appealed to Multatuli. Its text must have served him as the example of his own "official" address to the chiefs of Lebak, although there is evidence that the Bible and the Koran influenced his fiction too.

The question remains whether the address was written by Van der Capellen himself or by his close collaborator and friend Van de Graaff, or by both. It does in any case clearly reflect Van der Capellen's ideas and his frame of mind. Elsewhere he writes in his diary: "At long last, because of my decisions, there now exist regulations which in essence proscribe every torment, and not just those in existence now; they also call for all limitations of individual freedom to be abolished, canceled, and prohibited."

"Individual freedom" indeed! The government in Holland, so attached to its liberal policies and its profit making replied "that the Banda islands can in no way be regarded as fit for a system of free agriculture." Van der Capellen must have been fuming. He had failed as a governor-general, for the one thing he had neglected to do was to keep his king's and his ministers' interests at heart. He had too deeply cherished his administration, he had been too independent, not sufficiently humble, and more than anything else, he had not toed the liberal line. He had preferred practical need over mere doctrine. To the very last, Van der Capellen had refused to sacrifice the interests of the native population to the requirements of the European landowners, and he certainly refused to do so under the guise of liberal principles. For this he was scorned by his king and his ministers, and reviled by liberal historians afterwards. He bore their scorn with dignity and without yielding. "My heart bleeds," he wrote, "whenever I think of Java, and I cannot help but think of that fine country all the time!"

Olivier tells us that Van der Capellen "brought happiness" to the population during his ten-year stay (from 1816 until 1826) in the Indies. This could only have been true in a very limited sense. His task was simply too vast, a number of the lesser officials too uncooperative, and money and manpower insufficient. The fact remains that he took numerous measures in the interest of the people and that he strongly resisted pressure groups in the Netherlands and in the Indies that demanded the allocation of lands to private investors. Van der Capellen categorically refused to give in to this demand because inspection tours and reports had convinced him that most private investors and planters were really nothing more than "parasitic plants, which in their dark and crooked ways manage to get a stranglehold on the native population, choke it, and stifle its growth."

He was probably able to do more for the European community but even there one gets the impression that the results remained limited to its top layer. The community as such seems to have remained unchanged but with a difference. To be sure, in a city the size of Batavia things had changed but Olivier tells us in so many words that this was mere hypocrisy, "pulling a more sober and more inscrutable mug." For the rest, the community continued "to regard manners and morals as useless because they often stand in the way of making one's fortune." True enough, Olivier's description of the European way of life generalizes—it is definitely one-sided, incomplete, and unfair—but it is also as revealing as a good caricature can be. Those pages among his writings where he is obviously getting even with a mentality he abhors are also among the best he ever wrote. For example:

It happens at times that those anxious to be sent home fake some sort of liver ailment, perpetually keep their hand to their side and grimace with pain. I have known others who invariably wish to seem deeply concerned about the future of the country, whereas only the future of their bank account was uppermost in their minds. The latter category either sat or lay in their carriages, chins propped up in their hands with a pious look on their faces. Wherever they went, they exuded morality and gentility. One might almost have mistaken them for demi-gods, like the old Roman senators bestriding the Forum, if it had not been common knowledge that these Tartuffes, the moment they got indoors, would compensate themselves many times over for their pious performance in public by throwing an orgy that would have made old Bacchus or the White Friars blush with shame.

Even so, Olivier concedes that there were good, "disinterested" officials as well, such as H. W. Muntinghe, an earlier advisor of Raffles, and J. I. van Sevenhoven, who had not arrived until after the departure of the English in 1817. These were deserving of every respect in his opinion, "but far and away the majority of Europeans here avoids and detests these men as if they were dangerous creatures." What made them dangerous and hated was that they lent their support to policies that no longer regarded Dutch interests as central. They most certainly did not kowtow to the private interests of all those bureaucrats and burghers who had come to the Indies with the obvious intent of enriching themselves as soon as possible. And, according to Olivier, that was precisely what "the great majority" were after.

The new generation of top-level administrators now focused its attention on long-neglected areas such as topography and ethnography. The Batavian Society increasingly issued an impressive number of publications on flora, fauna, geology, climatology, as well as customs, social conditions, and languages. What is even more telling is that they generally reveal a changed and new way of looking at the tropical landscape and its people. Countryside and population are no longer the backdrop for the Company's officials' wheelings and dealings. Whereas the merchant had rarely ventured away from the coast, the government official, following Van der Capellen's example in exploring the entire archipelago, now penetrated the interior. The natural world about them no longer looked forbidding, and although they never ceased to marvel at it, they also came to know it. Their acquaintance developed from the overly descriptive to one that at times came to border on reverence, as exemplified by Franz Junghuhn in the latter half of the century.

Even more important perhaps, the attitude toward the "native" during these first decades of the nineteenth century changed perceptibly. The native ceased to be an oddly decked-out stage character inspiring enmity, and gradually became a human being. He hailed from a different world, to be sure, but he was nonetheless a human being with common virtues and vices. He was still measured by European standards but now he was no longer the enemy. In keeping with the ideas of the times, he became in fact a "noble savage," a citizen entitled to protection who was, according to Olivier, "to be regarded as being in many respects superior to his European overlord." A remark like that typifies the dramatically new attitude that also influenced the administrations of Raffles and Van der Capellen.

One can not help but notice that the period of cultural revival under Raffles, and especially under Van der Capellen, was particularly strong in the sciences, despite the fact that some have called it "the golden age of Indies literature." Actually, the arts, and literature especially, were only modestly represented. This is hardly surprising, and characteristic rather of a period when the acquisition of learning had absolute priority. Science and not literature was the preoccupation of the Enlightenment; at least literature had no autonomous existence and was relevant only to the extent that it was useful. It is this principle that kept vague and indistinct the borderline between the literary and nonliterary genre, between fiction and nonfiction, as for example between a travel account and a novel. Therefore, whenever Olivier is talking about "literature," he automatically includes descriptions of voyages and expeditions. He remarks that "the predominant spirit of the new literature is clearly seen to extend and increase our knowledge of the physical world." "Travel accounts," he goes on to say, "are a *pleasant means* to the attainment of a very *useful goal* in that they provide *entertaining* literature which expands our *knowledge* of foreign lands and peoples." It should be clear from the italicized words that usefulness and entertainment, play and study are paired and linked, and not considered the separate categories they are nowadays. In an analogous case, C. S. W. van Hogendorp first wrote a bulky *Consideration of the Dutch Possessions in the East Indies (Beschouwing der Nederlandsche bezittingen in Oost-Indië)*, which originally appeared in French, before going on to write several "nouvelles." Yet all his writings shared the same purpose, "making the Indies somewhat better known." He chose the novel form solely "to reach another category of readers," those who might have shied away from "the more serious travel account that includes all sorts of statistics." He hopes to "be useful," and "to please" at the same time. Of course, every nineteenth-century, strictly literary author and his nineteenth-century descendant followed the same reasoning. No eighteenth-century author, not even one we have come to regard as a strictly literary writer, would have spoken differently. Literature aimed at targets beyond its own pale and continued to do so for quite some time afterwards. In fact, we find traces of this in the literary magazine *The Guide (De Gids)* and in the opinions of the nineteenth-century Dutch author E. J. Potgieter. Even Multatuli, when praised for his style, pointed out that his true aims lay beyond literature. That same quality in his writing makes him one of our most important authors today, and it is a quality of a kind all too often lacking in C. S. W. van Hogendorp's "nouvelles," in the so-called sketches by G. H. Nagel, and in the "songs" by Philippus Pieter Roorda van Eysinga. Olivier, who never pretended to write literature, let alone "fiction," is a better writer than the whole lot of them, especially when the subject is close to his heart. There are scores of pages in many of his books that contain nothing but fact, which are often repetitious (indicative of the working journalist he was for some years), but every once in a while something happens in his writing. His long sentences tighten up, they become more concentrated, quicker, and they are more to the point. His satire of the European community in the Indies is no longer an attempt to provide us with useful knowledge but reflects rather a hurt and angry sensibility that is at times rancorous, but he is a better writer because of it.

Johannes Olivier (1789–1858) was born in Utrecht. From what he tells us he did not have an easy childhood. His mother died when he was two years old, his father remarried a year later, and only English was spoken at home from then on. His stepmother died young as well. His father went abroad, leaving his sister to take care of the boy. The aunt was gentle enough but altogether too permissive, and Olivier grew up to be a spoiled and undisciplined boy. After the father died there was no more money. Young Olivier must have had literary aspirations from an early age but the notion that he could make a living as an author proved an illusion. At wits' end, he left for the Indies in 1817. There he got promoted fairly rapidly and became secretary to two future councilors of the Indies, Muntinghe and Van Sevenhoven, respectively. In 1823, however, he was fired from his civil-service job "for excessive consumption of strong drink" and was transferred to the colonial navy, where he became a scrivener. Later on, in one of his books, he was to quote the English actor Quin, who was in the habit of saying "Life would stink in my nose if I did not steep it in claret." In 1826, the same year when King William I recalled Van der Capellen, Olivier was sent back to the Netherlands on account of "grave insubordination" toward a navy colonel he had had a fight with while intoxicated. Back in Holland, he went to live in the town of Kampen but he could not get the Indies out of his mind. From 1835 until 1837, he edited a magazine which he had entitled *The Oriental (De Oosterling)* and which was devoted to Indies interests. He repeatedly asked to be sent back. The comments on these applications all recognize his ability and his writing talent. Finally, much less rambunctious, he was permitted to return to the Indies in 1839 as an English translator. He died in 1858 as the head of the government printing office in Batavia.

His list of publications in the *New Dutch Biographical Dictionary (Nieuw Nederlandsch Biografisch Woordenboek)* is impressive and includes translations from French and English. His chief work is the three-volume *Travels by Land and by Sea in the Netherlands Indies (Land- en zeetogten in Nederland's Indië, 1827–30)*. Then there is *Annotations from a Trip in the East Indies (Aantekeningen gehouden op eene reize in Oost-Indië, 1827)*, which had been serialized earlier in the magazine *Cybele,* an eighteenth-century Dutch version of the *National Geographic.*

Olivier's work shows a thorough understanding of the Indies and its peoples that is ahead of its time and that puts him squarely in Van der Capellen's camp. His books do not emphasize the European world but the autochthonous society instead. He attempts to come close to and understand the native born, and what is more telling, he shows appreciation and fondness for them. He recommends ways in which European officials and officers ought to approach the population that are progressive by any standard: "Nothing is more important than for a European to deal with the native in the right way. As has been stated before, it is absolutely essential to remain affable, always friendly and never short-tempered or insulting. A friendly attitude is an official's *duty.* . . . A European's positive attitude, if it is to be effective, has to be rooted in a spontaneous feeling of sympathy, love of mankind, and the desire to do as much good for the population as is possible. . . ." Olivier berates most Europeans in the Indies for their feeling of superiority and their "arrogant stupidity." "There is as it were a veil between the natives and their European masters on account of which the essential character of the former remains almost entirely unknown to the latter." Professor van Vollenhoven, the renowned scholar of native or *adat* law, might well have said something similar to his students a hundred years later. Olivier's writings aim at something that lies beyond the ken of literature and is concerned with informing his "curious compatriots." Even so, its alert and personal tone is still far superior to many travel accounts of this type, with the possible exception perhaps of those written by Ph. P. Roorda van Eysinga, to whom Olivier dedicated one of his books "with personal respect and friendship."

Philippus Pieter Roorda van Eysinga (1796–1856) started his career as an officer. He fought at Waterloo and marched into Paris with the victorious allied armies. With plenty of money in his pockets, the nineteen-year-old subaltern painted the town. He was surprised that the Parisians in the streets ignored him and his smart uniform. In 1816 he was garrisoned at Antwerp for a year, attended its academy of fine arts, and became acquainted with "a young poet whose fiery imagination sparked his interest in poetry." In 1819 he left for the Indies.

Ph. P. Roorda van Eysinga described the *Various Travels and Adventures (Verschillende reizen en lotgevallen)* in the Indies of himself and of his father, the clergyman Sytze Roorda van Eysinga, in four volumes. His own adventures begin on page 187 of the second volume, and take up the next two volumes as well. The four volumes appeared between 1830 and 1832 and, with the exception of his father's career, they concern only his first stay in the Indies up to the year 1830.

Ph. P. Roorda van Eysinga is today known especially for his linguistic work, particularly in Malay and Javanese. As he tells us himself, the moment he set foot in the Indies, he became fascinated with languages. Already on his second day in the new country, he conceived the idea of compiling a Malay-Dutch dictionary. He had discovered, to his great surprise, that nobody had ever bothered to write one. Roorda did a great deal of spadework, which received Van der Capellen's gratitude and praise because he considered a knowledge of native languages indispensable to his officials. However, during his lifetime, when great advances in linguistics had taken place, he was sharply criticized, especially for his bold pronouncements and opinions about the Javanese language. A. B. Cohen Stuart, an established linguist, commented: "If I were to give my honest opinion about it, I would have to use language which might well obviate any forgiveness for the errors in my own work." He writes well about his own adventures. He may strike us as somewhat conceited perhaps—he was, after all, just thirty-five when his book appeared—but that does not mar his style. His political opinions are enlightened and similar to those of Van der Capellen. He makes short shrift of Dutch prejudice against the Javanese which portrayed them as lazy, treacherous, cruel, and disloyal. Such an attitude he considered "a disgrace to our country," and he feels compelled, he tells us, "to come to the defense of Javanese honor." He argues for the kind of relationship between Dutch authorities and the Javanese and their chiefs that sounds similar to Olivier's suggestions. What also sets him apart from his contemporaries is his outright admiration for the Javanese. He finds them a beautiful people, especially their women. He sounds forthright and progressive in everything he says until he comes to discuss Van der Capellen's anything but progressive successor, Du Bus de Gisignies. There he becomes circumspect, and says he does not want to judge Du Bus's administration. Elsewhere, however, his vanity tempts him to confide to his readers that the tightfisted Du Bus never thought of cutting his own salary.

Roorda's *Various Travels and Adventures* are still exciting reading, his ideas sound and clearly stated. One of its best sections is possibly the one where he gives us an eye-witness account of the way slaves were transported aboard ship, which he saw on returning from Rio de Janeiro. This clearly shocked him and without circumspection he indignantly blames his fellow Christians for allowing this sort of thing to go on. The moment Roorda turns to poetry, however, he loses us completely. He wrote a poem "in eight cantos," consisting of some two hundred pages. The very boastfulness of its title already rings hollow, *Netherlands Fame and Glory in the East Indies (Nederlands roem in Oost-Indië*, 1831). It was composed in the Indies and meant to praise the administration of the Dutch, especially Van der Capellen's, but this imitation of Bilderdijk does not even come close to Helmer's paean *The Dutch Nation (Hollandse natie)*.

C. S. W. van Hogendorp, the son of Dirk, also traveled in the Indies. He was resident of Buitenzorg and Batavia respectively and he too reveals himself as a proponent of benign government, protecting the native population from European depredation, and he also praises Van der Capellen. His *Review of the Dutch Possessions (Beschouwing der Nederlandsche bezittingen)*, smacks altogether too much of those "Testimonials of Transfer" succeeding residents so proudly bequeathed to one another. Van Hogendorp goes into all kinds of detail about such things as the cost of groceries, trade balances, etc. The book does contain some fairly readable sections, but one can not help wondering if those are not partly owing to Olivier's translation from the original French. Left to his own Dutch and his own literary devices, he wrote a number of "original tales." He brought out as *Tableaux of Javanese Morals (Tafereelen van Javaansche zeden*, 1837) a compilation of four of these, which had earlier been serialized.

Van Hogendorp wrote them in his spare time upon returning to the Netherlands, where he had established himself as a stockbroker. He had elected to use the medium of literature in order to reach a wider public but his chosen medium did of course remain subservient to his need to write about morals, customs, and politics. His tableaux are a bit of a mishmash and anything but lively. Some of his dialogues and monologues are really lectures on Javanese wedding ceremonies and such. In order to instruct and delight his readers, Van Hogendorp goes to some curious lengths indeed. For example, he wants to inform his reader painlessly about the situation on Java, and proceeds on the premise that Javanese society is a static one. He then superimposes events from his own time on Java's long history, as in the case of his first story, "Radeen Ningrat," which derives its plot from a Malay chronicle from the seventeenth century. In so doing, and quite contrary to his intention, he creates the impression of greatly appreciating the period of the East India Company, while in fact, he intended to praise Van der Capellen's era. His narrative use of Javanese sources results in an anachronistic hodgepodge that portrays every native priest as "a fanatic," and which calls local religion "superstition." His second story, a small novel in fact, is also based on Javanese history but as our enlightened Van Hogendorp informs us, he has cleansed it of its "fables." That is really all one can say about it. His third is a *Paul et Virginie* sort of romance, set in Java, and a forerunner of Multatuli's "Saidjah and Adinda," his story within the story of *Max Havelaar*. The tragic biography of "Corporal Rampok" (literally "Corporal Pillage") might possibly have been a good story. Van Hogendorp claims to have come across the notes of a young man who was told the story by an original participant. However, Van Hogendorp chose to make this story into an edifying tale about people addicted to what he calls "poppy juice," opium. Still, what is most telling about these "nouvelles," about the period, and about Van Hogendorp himself, is the interest they all show in the Javanese world.

The author G. H. Nagel is a fair representative of the European community. Born in 1795, he was the son of a Latin schoolmaster from the town of Tiel. This parentage probably goes some way to explain the liberal use of Latin quotations in his literary labors. Precisely when he arrived in the Indies the records do not show, probably some time around 1821. He came as a second-class clerk in the civil medical service. It was there he met Dr. Blume, who took him along in 1824 on a trek through Java which lasted a year. This trip Nagel described in his "Journal of a Trip through Java" ("Dagverhaal eener reize door Java"), which came to be included in the first volume of his *Sketches from My Javanese Portfolio (Schetsen uit myne Javaansche portefeuille*, 1828). It was dedicated to Johannes Olivier with the usual flourishes of respect and friendship. The journal is an anemic account by someone who seems to have nothing to say. After reading

Nagel, one doubly appreciates the travelogues of Olivier and Roorda. In April 1826, Nagel returned to the Netherlands for two years' furlough, later extended by another two. He was then fired. Later on, he went back to the Indies for two more years. Finally back in the Netherlands, he got around to publishing what he had all the while committed to paper in the Indies. He tells us he wrote exclusively to ward off the "taedium vitae," which, according to him, plagued every European living in the Indies. What commends his modesty is that he had to be persuaded to publish at all. To him, writing was nothing more than "relaxation." There is in fact little more to his writing than an occasional, passable anecdote, a morning stroll in verse, and a poem contrasting a "bad njey" (*njai* is the native housekeeper) with a good one, accompanied by the inevitable and uplifting moral that "some njeys are good, and some njeys are moot." Nagel seems to represent the average Dutchman in the Indies whose horizon was about as limited as that of the average settler. Hence the relative popularity of his books, because his *Sketches* were followed by a sequel, and then by another. There are scarcely any ideas in Nagel's works, and if he ever had any, his modesty must have prevented him from putting them down in writing. Anyway, he himself says something to that effect. All he has to offer is some mild prejudice about the Chinese, the Jews, and the Indos (people of mixed parentage), whom he likes to place in ridiculous situations. He does pull off a nice caricature of an old-timer (modeled after a known Batavian character), who has himself stroked and fanned by a number of female slaves. He can depict interesting glimpses of life in the Indies, as in his "Junket from Weltevreden to Batavia" ("Toertje van Weltevreden naar Batavia"), but his humor rarely rises above that of the local planters' club. In all probability his readership held him back from being more than the average transient in the Indies, although the potential must have been there. As historical and "social" documents of sorts, Nagel's sketches are irreplaceable, the more so perhaps because they are representative of a common attitude.

The one thing all these writers from between 1820 and 1830 have in common—and this holds true for Olivier, Ph. P. Roorda van Eysinga, Van Hogendorp, and Nagel—is that they did not begin to write until after their return to the Netherlands. Their experience lay in the Indies, and it provided their material. Whichever way one looks at it, the Indies of Van der Capellen molded them. Another thing they have in common is that they all left shortly after Van der Capellen was replaced by Commissioner-General Du Bus de Gisignies. Du Bus, a Belgian by birth, had a much different personality from that of Van der Capellen, and he was much more the kind of official to carry out the

directives of his king and ministers. He had been ordered to econo-
mize, and the king had given him carte blanche for the time of three
years in which to do so. Du Bus saved expenses with a vengeance and
drastically slashed the budgets for education, the arts, and the sciences. In 1826, Muntinghe stepped down as councilor of the Indies.
Van de Graaff, Van der Capellen's closest assistant, left on November
2, only to suffer shipwreck on the voyage back. Dr. Blume left in the
same year.

Both Van de Graaff and Van Hogendorp had some bitter things to
say about Du Bus, especially Van Hogendorp in his *Review* (p. xviii).
He departed in 1827. Shortly upon the arrival of the new commissioner-general in the Indies on February 3, 1826, Olivier was sent
from the Moluccas to the island of Java in order to be returned to the
Netherlands from there. He wrote: "The transfer of power to this Belgian official was soon followed by great changes everywhere. . . . A
new constellation rose on the political horizon of Java, accompanied
by dark clouds which soon increased from day to day and seemed bent
on smothering all prosperity on that lovely island" (*Travels by Land
and by Sea*, 3:394–95). Nagel left a few months later, in April 1826, on
a two-year furlough and was dismissed following its extension. Roorda van Eysinga, whose linguistic studies strongly tied him to Java, remained for a while longer. His attitude toward Du Bus remained cool
and reserved but he speaks vehemently about "various individuals"
who ingratiated themselves with the new commissioner-general by
"slighting their previous benefactor." In the middle of 1830, Roorda
returned to the Netherlands also.

Yet the Indies continued to hold all of them in her spell, and after
several years, they all returned, one after the other. However, they
were never to experience another era such as that of Van der Capellen,
and they talked about it with nostalgia.

III
Van Hoëvell and Junghuhn

1   *Wolter Robert, Baron van Hoëvell*

In 1830, Du Bus de Gisignies was in turn replaced by Van den Bosch. This was not just another official but a man who, in collaboration with J. C. Baud, introduced an entirely new agricultural policy, the so-called culture system. Once implemented, this system, based upon the obligatory cultivation of prescribed crops, had a positive effect on the agricultural development of the Indies. It benefited the population by and large. On the whole, however, the interests of the impoverished Netherlands prevailed and again became the focal point of all endeavor. Whichever way one looks at the value of this system of agriculture based on forced labor—and recently voices have been raised in its defense—to the Indies it meant turning back the clock. Once again the colony was ruled as a conquered territory owing tribute. No doubt Van den Bosch and Baud were capable men but the government pursued a policy that was out to profit the mother country. It is not surprising therefore that such things as education and the arts and sciences were neglected. It should be pointed out of course that *nothing* was spent on educating the native population. S. L. van der Wal informs us in his *Educational Policies in the Dutch East Indies (Het onderwijsbeleid in Nederlands-Indië*, 1963, pp. 119–20) that in 1830 the Resident of Banjumas requested thirty guilders per month for native schools. After a year and a half of waiting, this request was denied. But also for educating the Europeans, so little money was made available as to seriously impair their chances for any kind of development, let alone any degree of polish.

When W. R. Baron van Hoëvell (1812–1879) arrived in Batavia as a twenty-five-year-old minister of the church, he was immediately struck by "its desolation and lack of spirit." He was a nephew of Van der Capellen. His mother was the daughter of Robert Jasper van der Capellen, who as a "patriot" (a republican) had opposed the House of Orange prior to the Batavian Revolution of 1795. This Robert Jasper had a brother, called Alexander Philip, who was the father of the governor-general of the Indies after Raffles. All of them, including young Baron van Hoëvell, were intellectual descendants of the Enlightenment. It is not surprising therefore that Van Hoëvell thought that the cause for the absence of anything resembling culture lay in the general lack of education. The educational system was not just poor, it was totally inadequate. We are speaking here of grammar schools, because secondary education was simply nonexistent. The number of schools was limited and even some fairly sizable towns lacked schools altogether. Hundreds of Indo-European (Eurasian) children went without any education whatever. Their common language was Malay, and they used Dutch only to address "real" Europeans and in a way calculated to make them the butt of jokes among these European ladies and gentlemen. The neglect of any educational system worthy of the name victimized especially all those "stayerson," those thousands of Eurasian half-castes or "liplaps," as they were called, who made up far and away the majority of European society. Not only were they effectively prevented from getting on in life, but the "higher-ups" too were suffering the consequences. The latter were obliged to send their children back to Europe at a very early age, often at great financial sacrifice. Other drawbacks were that families were torn asunder and that everyone suffered the consequences of estrangement. In short, the educational policies of the government, or rather the lack of them, created a situation that was detrimental to society as a whole, with the inevitable attendant complications, tensions, and tragedies. Tensions grew but found no outlet. Then, in 1830, the minister for the colonies, J. C. Baud, decreed that certain positions could henceforth be occupied only by someone educated in Europe.

This measure hurt the Eurasian group more than any other. It was discriminatory, of course; at least that seemed evident from its phrasing, which suggested that only imported European males could qualify for jobs "whose dealings unfailingly reveal the desire to instill among the natives a high regard for their rulers through noble, just, and proper behavior." The wording of this document alone is astonishing, to say the least, especially if one recalls what men such as Olivier, Roorda van Eysinga, and others had written about these self-same Europeans. The Education Commission in Batavia protested the measure but the minister persisted. Van Hoëvell wrote: "The actions and regulations of this statesman were not the result of a temporary whim or fancy but rather the consequences of a rockbound and rigid system. They were strictly enforced and with an iron will." An earlier request to institute secondary schooling in the colony had simply been changed to one that was the very opposite of the commission's suggestions. Baud's reply was that there were indeed plans to improve the training of Indies officials but that this training was to take place in the Netherlands. This is why the Delft Academy was established in 1842. Successful attendance meant eligibility for the higher positions. Even the job of clerk third grade required having spent at least some years at Delft. To the Eurasians, largely less well off and unable to send their children to Holland, this requirement was tantamount to sentencing them to remain forever locked in relative squalor and social immobility. Baud's measures were clearly designed to exclude this group, which he himself chose to call "bastards of Europeans."

Van Hoëvell's assignment in Batavia was that of "minister to the Malay community," which consisted largely of Eurasians. He came to know these people and their grievances, which, the truth be told, were also shared by a number of Europeans and high officials. His parishioners must have expected a great deal from him, including improvement of their social position. Van Hoëvell realized that his duties were to serve them, but he also knew that he was powerless to do anything for the time being. His opportunity did not present itself until 1848. That year of revolution did not quite mean a changeover in the Netherlands but it did result in the fall of the cabinet and proposals for constitutional amendments. On May 14, 1848, the overland mail, then the fastest, brought the tidings that "spread general joy," the news that Baud had resigned. Following this, a number of high officials, Van Hoëvell among them, took the initiative to use the upcoming reviews of the constitution to press the wishes of those in the Indies. They asked first of all for educational improvements and "elimination of the clause which excluded people born and bred in the Indies from becoming civil servants." On May 22, 1848, a meeting was held in the club "De Harmonie," which was very well attended, also by Eurasians. By popular acclamation Van Hoëvell was elected to become its president. It was then decided to forward to the king their petition that the most offensive laws be rescinded. It was a request reasonable in every respect, and couched in very moderate and respectful language. Thereupon Van Hoëvell closed the meeting and left. There were a great many, however, who thought that the petition to His Majesty had not gone quite far enough, and following Van Hoëvell's departure, they adopted two additional petitions to be forwarded. From all accounts this meeting must have been rather boisterous, although the doors of "De Harmonie" were closed by nine that evening. There were no disturbances elsewhere. Even so, those in power were greatly troubled and disturbed by this sudden eruption of public opinion, still known to history as the "May Movement of '48." Now the culprits needed to be found. The following month, as Van Hoëvell was traveling on business in Banten, western Java, the rumor reached him that the resident of Batavia had been trying by hook and by crook to obtain damaging evidence against anybody suspected of having incited Batavia's inhabitants to riot. Van Hoëvell was supposed to be one of them. The government charged the church council to investigate. It so happens that one of the council's members was also president of the Indies Council, hence very much a member of the government. On July 4, without so much as a hearing, Van Hoëvell was dismissed. His alibi was foolproof, however, and his dismissal was changed to a declaration of censure, whereupon Van Hoëvell asked for a voluntary discharge and left for the Netherlands. His position in the Indies would have been untenable. He had been branded as "suspect" and that meant that he would have been ignored and avoided in his strongly hierarchical little world of officials.

The series of events described above is not only relevant to his subsequent writings, but lies at their very core. He wrote a pamphlet dealing with these events, but also based one of his novellas on them. It is called "The Suspects" ("De suspecten"), written in 1858, and was included in his volume *About Life in the Indies (Uit het Indische leven,* 1860). It is one of his best works, and has remained relevant to this day. At once recognizable is the pattern it describes of an authoritarian society. Using his biographical data with a hint at the "May Movement of '48," Van Hoëvell suggests an analogy with the French Jacobins who persecuted their opponents through a system of intimidation and social ostracism. A Jacobin law of 1793 made anyone suspect who "had dealings with former nobility, priests, counterrevolutionaries, aristocrats, and moderates." To Van Hoëvell, the parallel between "former nobility, etc." on the one hand, and simple liberals and those favoring constitutional government on the other, was obvious. It did not take much, either in the Netherlands or in the Indies, to get oneself branded as a "suspect." His story concerns a man who has long kept silent but whose conscience finally compels him to put down the truth in writing. The veracity of his book will, he hopes, deal a blow to the old colonial system, but the moment the book appears, he finds himself bereft of all former sympathy, honor, and respect. People avoid him because they are afraid of being themselves called suspects by "having dealings with colonial liberals, opponents of the minister for the colonies, with any antagonists whatever, or anyone showing the slightest interest in them." In short, the Jacobin strictures of 1793 are applied to the colonial conditions of 1848.

The sequel to these events which casts a glaring light on some aspects of Indies life can be told briefly enough. After Van Hoëvell had been back in the Netherlands for three months, he received a letter containing a copy of the secret correspondence between the government and the church council. For obvious reasons the sender remained anonymous. Van Hoëvell sent the minister of the colonies a report of what had taken place, including no less than forty different copies of those documents in his possession. The king cleared his name completely. Meanwhile, he had become acquainted with the statesman Thorbecke, who just then happened to need an Indies specialist. Van Hoëvell managed to get himself elected to the House of Representatives, and remained a member for a dozen years, during which time he steadfastly looked after the interests of the Javanese. He proved himself neither a wholehearted politician nor a liberal but was principally a man of ethical persuasion and moral goals. After his eleven years' stay in the Indies, he wrote in 1848: "All my labors and research . . . were sooner aimed at the moral than the physical interests of the country. Both are so narrowly related, however, and the system of government is so all pervasive, that it is capable of stifling all progress, even life itself. Whoever wishes to cure a disease, first has to remove the causes, and that is why I strayed into the study of politics, at least to the extent that governmental addiction to secrecy allows itself to be studied."

As a member of the House, he bent the colonial policies of the liberal party to his own inclination, and on the strength of his moral convictions the party attacked the system of forced agriculture, occasional hypocrisy in practice notwithstanding. Van Hoëvell found himself often strongly opposed by all sorts of interest groups within and without his own party, but he was nonetheless able to leave his personal mark on policies pertaining to the Indies.

On stepping down in 1862 as a member of the Chamber of Deputies, he wrote that he considered his task completed, since the reforms he had wanted had by this time become basic government policy. The House listened when Van Hoëvell spoke, the opposition included. His speeches were always lucid and adapted to the limited knowledge about the Indies of the other members. Whenever he spoke about the agricultural system, he had to first make clear to them what this odious system was all about, of which, indeed, many were ignorant. Often by simply lecturing or shaming the House he taught them to understand problems to which they really were outsiders. His rhetoric and conviction impressed them. Anyone looking through his *Parliamentary Speeches (Parlementaire redevoeringen,* 1862–1866) today will find little that is politically relevant but will be struck by Van Hoëvell's persuasiveness. His speeches are logical and to the point. They are written, moreover, in a stylized but vital language that shows continuous adaptation to the spoken language. His speech concerning the culture system of December 8, 1851, has often been called his *apologia pro vita sua.* Its logic, clarity, and word choice are exemplary and this explains its persuasive power. A textual study of some of Van Hoëvell's *Parliamentary Speeches* would show the degree to which his politics were a natural extension of his ethical principles, and how little he was taken in by liberal dogma. It would also reveal how he could first intuit the sensibilities and motivations of his opponents and put himself in their shoes, only to refute their position in the end. Anyone studying Van Hoëvell's style would do well to also consider how he makes use of conscious understatement, for example, by soft pedaling emotionally charged words, by adding subordinate and major clauses, and so on, only to reveal his true emotion in the right place, so as to underscore his argument at the right moment.

Except perhaps for his novella "The Suspects," it appears that, as in the case of his precursors, his power lies not in literature so much as in his effective rhetoric. The stories in his volume *About Life in the Indies* are essentially debates dressed up as stories. Some of them accompany his other writings in literary disguise, as it were, while others are basically descriptive, but they all share either his social or moral criticism. His essay on "The Pedati" (a primitive native cart with two massive discs for wheels) turns into an indictment of the frivolity of the numerous "overly smart ladies and gentlemen" in the Indies. They stand in sharp contrast to the Javanese who have been using this vehicle for over five centuries. The story of "The Japanese Stonecutter," which Multatuli must have read in *Netherlands Indies Magazine (Tijdschrift voor Neerland's Indië)* of 1842 and later on included in his *Max Havelaar,* attacks the desire for ever greater riches in the Indies. Its obvious moral is that one should be content with one's lot. His "Slave Auction" ("Eene slaven-vendutie") complements his *The Emancipation of Slaves in the Netherlands Indies (De emancipatie der slaven in Neerlands-Indië,* 1848) and his speeches on the subject of slavery in the House of December 23, 1851. The story provides Van Hoëvell with an opportunity to illustrate his argument with descriptions and scenes which he allows one of his characters to call "immoral" and "disgusting." Similarly, his "The Privilege of a European Education" is in fact inseparable from his plea for improved education. It is directed against the need for many parents to send their children to Holland at an early age, which renders real family life in the Indies impossible. His other stories deal with more abuses, such as the arrogance of higher officials, extortion by native chiefs, leasing of bird-nest harvesting, the disproportion of heavy forced labor, and much more.

Van Hoëvell, still close to the preceding generation, was also inclined to burden literature with a task really beyond its province. His choosing to write literature at all was determined by its effectiveness and its capacity to reach a wider audience. His principal aim was to inform that audience about conditions in the Indies, especially after he had come to realize, as he once mentioned in the House, that the "most frightful enemy" was Dutch ignorance of the colonies.

As a legacy of the eighteenth century, the first half of the nineteenth century was much more a period of travel, exploration, and discovery than subsequent decades were to be. People believed that if one only knew the facts as well as possible and if only one would get at the heart of them, then understanding and harmony would naturally follow. Van Hoëvell's optimism ran very much along those lines. He was a minister of the church in Batavia, and although he read, heard, and studied a lot, he must have always considered it a loss and a shortcoming that there were things he had not personally experienced. In 1847, about a year before his departure for the Netherlands, he made a trip which he reported on as *Journey through Java, Madura, and Bali (Reise over Java, Madura en Bali).* He had started writing it while still in the Indies when his problems with its government were reaching a critical stage. This explains the vehement tone of its first part. He forwarded the manuscript to P. J. Veth, an expert on the Indies in Holland. By the time part one was published, Van Hoëvell himself had already returned to Holland. There he continued writing about his trip. The work was first to consist of two, then three volumes. As it turns out, he only wrote two, which appeared respectively in 1849 and 1851. The account concerning his trip to Bali began to appear in 1854 but was never completed. Paul van 't Veer is right in saying in a recent essay about Van Hoëvell that this travelogue is one of the best to have come out of the Indies.

It is more readable than his novellas, and it is also much more than a mere travelogue or a description of people and places. It is the continuous account of someone who not only describes events and conditions but who also knows how to put them in a larger perspective. Neither physical fear nor the fear of losing face prevents the narrator from stating unpleasantries if need be, and there is an ongoing polemic against certain individuals and established opinion. This makes his first book, especially part one, so lively. He can lash out in indignation when, for example, he hears it said that the Europeans exert a moral influence, and he responds: "Do you want me to tell you? Your moral influence . . . consists of your bayonets and cannon."

A similar, maybe even sharper tone is heard in his pamphlet *An Epidemic in Java (Eene epidemie op Java,* 1849), which he wrote after having witnessed a cholera epidemic. It appeared under the pseudonym Jeronymus, which he had used previously for several of his stories. Neither this particular experience nor his reaction to it was something he could ever hope to publish in his own *Netherlands Indies Magazine.* The government had already been keeping a close eye on it for years and there had been trouble before. Professor Veth tells us in his "Disclosure in Colonial Affairs" ("De openbaarheid in koloniale aangelegenheden," *De Gids* 2 [1848]: 72) that nearly every issue of the journal caused friction between Van Hoëvell and the government's secretary general, who was apparently in charge of supervision. The first issue of the *Netherlands Indies Magazine* must have been prepared right after Van Hoëvell's arrival in the Indies in 1837 because it appeared as early as April of that year. Gradually it evolved into a widely read periodical that, after covering mostly scientific subjects, the arts, and odds and ends, began to concern itself with politics. It became the magazine for all those who did not want to depend on what the government saw fit to dispense in the way of information. Following Batavia's "May Movement of '48," publication was stopped, but continued in the Netherlands. There, especially after the political changes of 1848, he felt less constrained and this stood the magazine in good stead. It is an indispensable source for Indies history of the times. He stepped down as editor at the same time he resigned from the House in 1862, but the magazine existed until the end of 1902. Veth, who continued to correspond with Van Hoëvell up to his death, informs us that in the end little was left of Van Hoëvell's cheerful vitality: "Disaster upon disaster, blow upon blow, and misery upon misery hounded him in his final years." In 1873, following the death of his son-in-law, he wrote Veth: "Time is supposed to heal all wounds but I will never recover from this. Something has broken inside of me." Three years later, his two eldest sons died, also in the Indies. He must have welcomed death as a release, Veth adds. According to his wishes, he was interred in all simplicity on February 12, 1879. "Van Hoëvell was one of the most endearing men I have ever known," another friend said of him.

2   *Franz Wilhelm Junghuhn*

Franz Wilhelm Junghuhn (1809–1864) was anything but endearing, nor was he a man principally motivated by a moral ethos as Van Hoëvell had been. He was not stung into writing by a social conscience either. Even so, Junghuhn was a fascinating character, a man with the power to entice and, in the larger sense, an important writer.

The most striking characteristic of his words and actions was his independence. That enabled him to become a great naturalist as well as one of the first militant freethinkers. Multatuli, a freethinker himself, mentions his name just once, unfortunately, and that is in his *Ideas (Ideeën)*, but he does call him a "brother" there. Junghuhn was Van Hoëvell's counterpart in more than one respect, having an entirely different background and an entirely different slant on life. He rejected the notion of Christian revelation and that of a transcendental godhead. He formulated his creed as follows: "We believe in the existence of an invisible, great, and reasonable spirit inhabiting nature, and call it God. In order to understand God, one first has to understand nature and study her laws with every scientific means possible. I belong to a high-vaulted church, the roof of which is strewn with stars, the church of the naturalists who worship God and seek to know Him through his works."

His naturalist research, which was his life's work, is thus closely related to his philosophy and was nothing less than an act of faith. For example, in the midst of Java's natural grandeur, spending the night in a village hut, he surveyed his instruments spread out on a bench once more before going to sleep: "In front of me I had put on display the symbols of my faith: a terrestrial and a celestial globe, a sextant, artificial horizon, telescope, chronometer, thermometer, psychometer, a compass, magnet, microscope, Nicholson's airometer, a triangular prism, portable camera obscura, a daguerreotype camera, a small chest for doing chemical tests, and other such tools of applied science."

Anyone regarding nature and its study in this light will regard the natural experience and nature itself on a decidedly higher level. Compared to Junghuhn's observations and descriptions of nature, all others pale. He goes well beyond noting, as Van Hoëvell did, the "beauty and loveliness of the landscape," or "splendid, although rugged and wild, natural vistas." Junghuhn unfailingly prefers his landscapes rugged and wild, and majestic—majestic in her great silences and majestic in her forces; and alive too. He often describes nature in terms of animal shapes or human emotions. A motionless volcanic lake can momentarily be stirred by such passions as to destroy overnight what it took years to grow, much the same way man will let his emotions destroy his own happiness. This seems to come close to a personal confession. But there is more to nature than this recognition of an affinity: its spectacle is so all encompassing that it almost defies description. He does so nonetheless, and despite the fact that he was German-born and learned the Dutch language only later in life. Indeed, like someone who can suddenly cause a stone to spark, Junghuhn time and again manages to convey his sense of joy, elation, and relief while looking down some "labyrinthine landscape" that looks "torn" and "gutted." Similarly, he conveys being overtaken by a thunderstorm in the jungle or out in the open, or finding himself in the elephant grass, looking down on an ice cold, moonlit night into a bottomless canyon, its trees topped by a silvery sheen, with no sound audible other than that of the caprimulgus, a small nightbird "whose regular tapping resounded like clashing blows on an anvil throughout the valley below." Profounder observations he finds more difficult to put into words: "Where does one find the words to describe so much beauty? Mine are inadequate where beauty is mostly felt and observed." Junghuhn observed constantly, jotting down his observations right away with pencil into tiny notebooks. His rule was, he says, "to immediately commit to paper all natural objects and views before their impression could be erased by new objects." This explains why some of his descriptions can be overly detailed but the attendant emotion always comes across in fresh images and words. Even while only describing a natural phenomenon or listing varieties of plant and animal life, including their Latin names, or taking down temperatures, or measuring longitude and latitude, he still betrays the fact that these are his sole means of decoding nature's secrets. Junghuhn tells us nature is also indifferent and "pitiless," and not just majestic or powerful. It also destroys the life it creates in an unending cycle, as he illustrates in his account of nocturnal fights between turtles, wild dogs, crocodiles, and tigers, which concludes with vultures circing high above the battlefield the morning afterwards. That description is as unforgettable as that of the population's orgy of vengeance one night on a tiger they have killed.

Typical are those passages where natural description and philosophy are so interwoven as to sum up Junghuhn's own basic philosophy, that of the brotherhood of every living thing on earth. Seated near the edge of a mountain lake one night, the lake's surface without a ripple, the deadly calm interrupted only by the cries of a flying fox or galeopithecus, Junghuhn writes: "Filled with wonder I looked on, and it seemed to me I sensed the relationship and sympathy binding all living creatures ... as I got up from my rocky promontory, I said good night to the moon, the stars, the lake, the ducks, the forest with its millions of flowers, buds, and fruits, the galeopithecus, and all the other animals. Good night. To nature fair and inexhaustible, animated by God's breath, good night!

The same book from which we have quoted so far, and wherein nearly every single page testifies to the "unceasing revelation of God" was curiously enough to become a manifesto for freethinkers and atheists alike. The anonymous publication of *Images of Light and Shadow from Java's Interior (Lichten schaduwbeelden uit de binnenlanden van Java,* 1854) was a bombshell. In the first place, it created a lot of bad feeling which impeded but could not prevent its appearance in the Netherlands. In the Indies, the book was what we would now call a best seller. A critic wrote that "many people felt confirmed in their stand against Christianity, while the book threw others into doubt." The book was attacked by the Indies preacher J. F. G. Brumund, about whom more later, who launched a pamphlet called *Several Remarks Concerning Images of Light and Shadow Written by the Brothers Night and Day (Eenige opmerkingen over licht- en schaduwbeelden van de gebroeders Dag en Nacht,* 1856), which appeared in Batavia. Junghuhn's book was prohibited in Austria and in several German states and principalities because of its alleged "denigrations and vilifications of Christianity."

In the Netherlands, its appearance not only gave new impetus to changes already well under way, but it also led to the foundation of an actual movement. Without quite completing his book, Junghuhn had to break off his European furlough and return to Java. The first edition of his book announced a sequel, which was never written. Instead, the monthly *The Dawn (De Dageraad)* began to appear, which, though not edited by Junghuhn, advanced views similar to his. One may well ask what kind of book this was, going through several editions in just a few years. It was neither a novel, a story, nor a travelogue, but in fact a philosophical tract in allegorical form. In it, Junghuhn introduces four brothers called Night, Day, Dawn, and Dusk. Each develops his own philosophy as the tale progresses. They are making a trip through Java and, alternated by an account of their experiences and by some splendid descriptions of nature, they reveal their respective philosophies. Night represents orthodox Christianity; Day, who gets to do most of the talking, represents Junghuhn's own philosophy, which might best be described as deism tinged with pantheism, and which he himself calls "Natural Religion." Dawn and Dusk represent true atheism, and they are godless in that they do not believe in the existence of a Supreme Being or God. The conversations between Day and Night allow Junghuhn ample opportunity to attack Christianity: "I openly declare that up to now Christianity has done nothing but propagate ignorance and superstition, and has misled the spirit to pursue nothing but tyranny and greed." Right away, the very vehemence of Junghuhn's language makes one suspect whether there might not be some private experience underneath it all. That "spirit," which pursues nothing but "tyranny and greed," really makes one wonder. For an answer to a question such as this we usually look at a person's childhood, in this instance to Junghuhn's education and his relationship with his parents. Although he generally wears his heart on his sleeve, Junghuhn is uncommonly reticent on that score; clearly we are dealing with an old grudge here that he kept well hidden.

There is only one passage in his work that hints at some youthful conflict. In *Images of Light and Shadow*, his character Brother Day is made to say: "Is it my fault then that my parents were Christians and not Jews, and that I inherited my father's short temper and my mother's sensitivity?" For the longest time, this was our only clue. In 1909, however, celebrating the centennial of Junghuhn's birth, Max C. P. Schmidt put out a very detailed biography using a wealth of family documents and family stories. To tell the truth, Schmidt gives us a great many facts but does not do much with them. Schmidt's own father and Junghuhn were first cousins, even though the former was seventeen years younger. Their families knew each other well. Max Schmidt paints a rather sketchy portrait of Junghuhn's early years, using family memoirs and his father's recollections. Elsewhere in his book, however, and in a different context, we find increasingly new details which allow us to reconstruct and clarify a great deal more.

We do not necessarily have to picture Junghuhn's father as the proverbial Prussian to know that he was stern, self-willed, and irascible. A man, moreover, who longed for culture and adventure but who acted and thought according to handed-down patterns. Those same patterns were also applied to his son's education, for whom he, and not his son, had chosen the study of medicine. Himself a village surgeon and barber, he wanted his son to realize his own higher ambitions, while at the same time he wanted to cast him in his own mold. He desired his son to become a powerful figure who would live according to the strong bourgeois traditions of religion, authority, and obedience. He had him tutored for university entrance by, of all people, a theologian. Naturally, the scheme backfired. The boy came away hating Christianity, authority, and obedience. The obituary notice of Junghuhn, written by his brother-in-law H. Rochussen, which appeared in *Netherlands Indies Magazine* in 1866, strongly confirms this. Both father and son were excitable people and their clashes were numerous. There were scenes involving beatings with a stick, running away from home, several times no less, and an attempted suicide near the precipitous ruins of ducal Mansfeld castle. Max Schmidt, who gives us anything but a one-sided account of Junghuhn senior, tells us the following about the attempted suicide. After the severely wounded young Junghuhn had been discovered, they naturally warned the boy's father, who was a physician, after all. He was just pulling on his boots when they told him the victim was his own son. With a shrug of resignation, he then took his boots off again and threw them into a corner. Years later, when discussing his son's attempt to kill himself, he still could not understand how his son, a student of medicine, could have been so stupid as to shoot himself in the back of his head. With a meaningful gesture he pointed to his forehead, saying *"That's* where he should have aimed!," his face reddening with excitement. By contrast, Junghuhn's mother was weak, sentimental, and overly affectionate. This too went against his grain. Once, the twenty-year-old Junghuhn slit open the chest and belly of a live cat in order "to study the circulation of the blood."

It is not known what transpired between father and son after the latter tried to commit suicide. The father got his way to the extent that young Franz did continue to study medicine, albeit in faraway Berlin and not in Halle, situated near his birthplace. He traveled meanwhile, and would for weeks on end wander through Brunswick, Thuringia, and especially the Harz mountains. At the same time his first articles began to appear about mushrooms "out of the botanical twilight zone." His medical studies unfinished, he got drafted into the army. There he fought a duel, and although he himself was the one to get wounded and not his opponent, Junghuhn was sentenced, incredibly enough, to ten years imprisonment. He would not begin serving this sentence until the Prussian government had fully exploited his services as a physician, and it was not until Christmas Day of 1831 that he was actually arrested and sent to the infamous citadel of Ehrenbreitstein. Just what this imprisonment meant to a man with such immense love and veneration of nature, his memoirs tell us. Called "Flight to Africa ("Flucht nach Afrika") and written in 1834, this moving testimony is part of Schmidt's biography:

Imagine an immense, infinite, and empty space where neither a pebble nor a speck of dust could hope to strike a friendly ray of sunshine, where everything is impenetrably dark. Imagine that, and you will begin to get an idea what a prisoner's life is like. One day drags by as slowly as the next, very slowly and without a sound.

Nothing interrupts this eternal monotony. Morosely you rise in the morning, only to long for the coming of night again and a few hours of sleep. When evening comes and night does return, a new torment begins. You lie down with apprehension, afraid to wake up the next morning, fearful of the terrible loneliness that morning will bring, and that feeling in turn robs you of your night's rest. It is a blessing indeed if a diadem spider strays onto your barren walls and breaks the silence with its gentle ticking sound, like a clock. At the start of a new day, the eye searches the bare walls in vain for a new distraction, a bulge, or an irregular grain of sand perhaps. You try to get to see something through the window bars but the view is blocked by a treacherous wall, erected there by mistrust itself. I enjoyed each sound, each change, and every movement I could detect rekindled my spirits by interrupting the monotony. I even longed for the arrival of the guard, a stupefied, ugly clod who showed himself three times a day. The rattle of keys and the creaking of the door were music to my ears. Alone in that place I often thought about the phantom world conjured up by our divines and the fire and brimstone they like to scare and fool people with. I am surprised they do not portray hell as a limitless desert devoid of life, just as silent as it is infinite. If I could choose between two evils, I would opt for hellfire and its devils, anything but such a monstrous, empty wasteland.

Junghuhn's captivity lasted twenty months, till he managed to escape and flee across Germany to France. He made it all the way down to Toulon, then crossed the Mediterranean and enlisted in the French Foreign Legion. The terror of that particular experience is described in "Flight to Africa" also. After five months, he was sent on leave. Shaking with fever, he boarded a warship that took him back to France. In Paris, he met a Dutch botanist who informed him of the possibility of signing on as a colonial health officer for the Dutch East Indies through its recruiting offices in Harderwijk. On June 30, 1835, he departed from Hellevoetsluis on board the sailing ship *Jacob Cats*, and on October 12 the ship came into the roads of Batavia. Junghuhn was to spend the next thirteen years in Java. These would turn out to be his most important years, decisive for his outlook and development, during which time an unknown physician was to turn himself into a naturalist of stature. His medical career never really amounted to much. Among his family papers, Max Schmidt came across a list onto which Junghuhn had carefully entered every date and place of his stay. It turns out that he actually served no more than three years and seven months out of those thirteen years as a health officer in Batavia, Buitenzorg, Semarang, and Djokjakarta. The rest of the time he must have spent traveling about.

Junghuhn always managed to find people willing to support and help him in his naturalistic studies, which he regarded as his rightful calling. The first among these benefactors was the naturalist Dr. Fritze, chief of medical services, who took him along on his numerous tours of inspection and who laid the foundation for Junghuhn's future scientific career. Following Fritze's death in 1839, Junghuhn had no trouble finding different supporters. Junghuhn was an impressive figure even though he was a troublemaker and caused difficulties wherever he went. He was, all told, a full-blooded romantic, a man of conflicts with a divided personality. He described this duality of soul in himself with a quotation from Goethe's *Faust:* "Zwei Seelen, wohnen, ach! in meiner Brust." Of course, his ability, independence, and imagination made him stand out head and shoulders above the other officials. Especially in such a narrow society as that of the Indies, one could expect rumors and stories about a man who did not quite fit in. There exists a very telling anecdote about an encounter between Junghuhn, the outsider, and J. J. Rochussen, governor-general of the Indies. Junghuhn, it appears, had just published some less than respectful comments about several Javanese princes in the *Netherlands Indies Magazine.* His remarks had angered the government, which stood in a most delicate relationship to these same princes, and Junghuhn was called to account for himself. Rochussen was mad as a hatter and threatened to have Junghuhn thrown out of the country. Junghuhn kept silent through the entire tirade, while Rochussen got angrier and angrier, and told Junghuhn that he had been hearing other complaints about him as well, and that he always arrived far too late at the office. Junghuhn is then supposed to have said: "I admit, your Excellency, that I am often late to work but then again, I am always the first to leave." The rest of the interview was much less stormy, and it argues well for Rochussen and Junghuhn alike that the whole dressing down ended with the governor-general's promise to put Junghuhn up for membership with the Commission for Natural Sciences, the very thing Junghuhn had wanted all along.

The job on that commission gave him every opportunity to travel. There was hardly a place on Java Junghuhn did not visit. He was especially taken by the grandeur and the ruggedness of Java's mountains. For weeks on end he would tramp around, camping in villages or outdoors, wrapped in a blanket next to the campfire, the only European among Javanese bearers and guides. This wandering did make him melancholy at times: "Without a place I can call my own, without anyone really missing me on this entire island, I just keep on roaming along all by myself." But while musing thus, the tops of the Tjiremai and Tamponas mountains break through the clouds, and then he feels "elated" again, knowing that nature's grandeur more than makes up for the lack of human companionship. A nomadic existence like this ultimately had to wear down even someone as powerful as Junghuhn. In 1848, he realized that his health had taken a beating and his bodily strength had weakened. "I was exhausted," he writes. In June 1848, he once again ascended the Tangkuban Prahu Mountain (literally "upside down" or capsized boat), where he had a cabin built on the highest western ridge of the crater. There he withdrew in order to regain his strength. Friends sought him out and urged him to take a vacation in Europe. That decision finally taken, he still found it difficult to leave the country which he said had become his "second fatherland." Yet he sailed on August 28, 1848, but typically spent the voyage making notes which would later appear as *Return from Java to Europe (Terugreis van Java naar Europa*, 1851). It deals with an account of the trip made by the so-called overland mail route, that is to say, crossing overland from Suez to Cairo (the Suez Canal not being opened until 1869) and on to Europe. An Austrian ship took him as far as Trieste, and from there he crossed the Alps, where he felt at home again. He was most delighted with the trees: "How beautiful they all looked after fourteen years' absence." While he recognized the plants, shrubs, trees, and geological formations, there is nary a word about people. He considered the populace good natured but stupid, allowing themselves to be led by a bunch of "fat, arrogant, and intolerant priests." From Munich, the train took him to the center of Holland, and there his account abruptly ends. He felt disinclined to write about that section of the trip from the German-Dutch border to Leiden because only in Holland had he encountered "such a bigoted lot of people," and writing about them would only infuriate his readership. Better to be silent, he thought, and he wished his dear readers farewell.

Even so, he settled down in Leiden because he could use the university's library and he commenced to work on his notes with the same alacrity as he had taken them. From 1852 until 1854, four volumes appeared of his standard work, which was immediately followed by a revised, second edition entitled *Java's Shape, Flora and Internal Structure (Java, deszelfs gedaante, bekleeding en inwendige structuur)*. The work was "embellished" with maps and drawings, outlines of mountains and landscapes, all masterfully executed. Minister of Colonies Pahud also commissioned him to draw a *Map of the Island of Java (Kaart van het eiland Java*, 1855), and his book about Java has a companion volume of colored lithographs done after Junghuhn's own drawings called *Atlas of Views, containing Eleven Picturesque Scenes (Atlas van platen, bevattende elf pittoreske gezichten)*. To Junghuhn, an artistically appealing landscape meant "a question of fantasy, subject to a number of interpretations." "My landscapes," he wrote, "are essentially lifelike." They show cloud formations that look like "clenched fists," side views of geological strata, the shape of branches, and the structures of leaves. They have been drawn exactly as he observed them either with a magnifying glass or with a powerful telescope. Junghuhn's landscapes are meant to illustrate his scientific purpose of natural observation, and his introductions to the plates clearly reveal his working method. For example, a lithograph showing the mountain Gunung Gedeh is accompanied by the instruction that the spectator should imagine himself in the same forest as described in volume one of *Java's Shape*. However, in order to get any view at all, the dense jungle has been omitted and only the flowering leptospermum floribundum has been allowed to remain, he tells us. Although Junghuhn himself considered his drawings "lifelike," they do strike us as decidedly unreal because their details are not integrated with the whole. They resemble landscapes of an alien world, and that may well explain why they are so fascinating. The only extensive commentary written by Junghuhn on the lithographs is to be found in the German edition of 1853, entitled *Landschafts-Ansichten von Java*.

In 1852, Junghuhn married Louisa Koch, a lieutenant colonel's daughter. He had meanwhile become a Dutch citizen. During his furlough, which lasted an incredible seven years, he again made extensive trips (to Tyrol, Switzerland, Italy, the Pyrenees, Sweden, and the Caucasus), sometimes accompanied by his wife, sometimes alone. There is no evidence anywhere that he ever revisited his ancestral village of Mansfeld. We do know, however, that he did, and also that he went alone. Schmidt's father met him sometime during those years, and Junghuhn struck him as rather odd. "He could not take to life in this small rural town anymore," was the elder Schmidt's conclusion.

In 1855, Junghuhn finally returned to Java, but this time he had been specifically assigned to investigate the possibility of growing the cinchona bark to produce quinine for the treatment of malaria. With uncanny exactitude, using his knowledge of the climate, vegetation, etc., he pinpointed the best location for the cultivation of quinine, on the plains of Lembang in western Java. There exists a great deal of disagreement, however, about his choice of the quinine variety and its proper method of cultivation, and in connection with this he became a controversial figure. The curious thing is that Junghuhn became famous primarily for establishing quinine plantations, and only to a lesser degree for his naturalistic research. His popular fame therefore is based on the fact that he is regarded as one of the "builders of Empire" who has "wrought great things." All his biographers agree, however, that Junghuhn was well past his scientific prime by the time he got involved with quinine. This restless explorer had already become a retired planter who had withdrawn with his wife and child to the secluded Preanger area. He no longer undertook vast journeys but lived quietly amidst his family and his mountains, near his beloved Tangkuban Prahu, about which he said once that the mountain possessed "a human heart where peace abides." In 1864 he died of a liver ailment. His friend Groneman, a physician, and his brother-in-law Rochussen were present at his death. When Junghuhn knew that his end was near, he asked Groneman, on whose word we have this: "Would you open the windows, please? I want to say farewell to my beloved mountains, I want to see my forest for the last time and inhale once more the pure mountain air."

IV
Edward Douwes Dekker

Eduard Douwes Dekker (1820–1887) arrived in Batavia on January 4, 1839, when he was barely nineteen years old. In September 1852 he left for the Netherlands on sick leave. He spent altogether nearly fourteen consecutive years in the Indies, working at various jobs in various places, on Java as well as in the so-called outlying districts. Although communication in those days was difficult, it is still curious that the name Douwes Dekker does not appear in any of the Indies periodicals of those days, especially since we know that he had literary ambitions at an early age.

Before his departure for the Indies, he had already written poetry. His earliest poem, written in 1838, is called "My Skates" ("Mijn Schaatsen") and has no fewer than seventeen stanzas of seven lines each. Another early piece is a farewell poem addressed to his friend A. C. Kruseman and inscribed in the latter's *album amicorum*. It also appears that he wrote prose as well as poetry. After he had just arrived in the Indies, he wrote some conventional romantic prose and a no less conventional poem to Caroline Versteegh, a girl Dekker had fallen madly in love with and for whose sake he even became a Catholic.

After Dekker was transferred as a controller to the town of Natal on the west coast of Sumatra, around the same time he had broken off his engagement, he continued to write. None of it ever got published. Dekker however kept some of those writings and in later works and letters he frequently quoted from them. It is evident that he had already read a great deal when he was young, and he naturally read the *Netherlands Indies Magazine* and *The Transcriber (De Kopiïst)*, for these were then the only publications in the Indies. In his novel *Max Havelaar*, Multatuli (Dekker's pseudonym) tells us that he told the parable of the Japanese stonecutter to Si Upi Keteh, the native chief's daughter whom he was then living with. That must have been around

1843, for "The Japanese Stonecutter" ("De Japanse Steenhouwer"), Van Hoëvell's story, was published under his pseudonym Jeronymus in the April 1842 issue of his *Magazine*. Dekker wrote a long unpublished essay sometime around 1843 called "Digging Once Again" ("Nog eens Graven"). It was apparently meant for the *Magazine* but for reasons unknown was never published. Its title obviously refers to a piece entitled "Digging" ("Graven") by Van Hoëvell, which appeared in the August 1842 issue of the *Magazine*. The fact that Dekker also read *The Transcriber* and even subscribed to it is clear from a remark in *Max Havelaar*.

Dekker must have been fairly happy in Natal, at least before he became unfortunately involved in a never fully solved case of embezzled funds. At any rate, it freed him from a clerical job with the accounting office for which he neither was nor felt suited. Above all, Natal was a place where he could learn to forget Caroline Versteegh. Understandably, he regretted having to leave Natal, as he explained in a poem of six (originally twelve) stanzas, which ends:

> I searched out death, but Natal gave me life
> Rekindled hope, and so gave birth to joy.
> Dear place, so bountiful in all but strife
> Too soon I will no longer tread your soil.
> My last farewell and silent prayers now hear
> As they ascend to God, to keep you hale
> I must go forth to dwell beyond your pale
> Leaving you nought, nought but a silent tear.

This is obviously traditional, romantic stuff, complete with tears and eyes cast up to heaven.

Early in January 1844, Controller Second Class E. Douwes Dekker, stationed in Natal, was dismissed by General Michiels, the civilian and military governor of Sumatra's west coast. The reason was Dekker's mismanagement of finances. His salary was no longer paid out, which it had not been for three months anyway. He was recalled to the principal town of Padang, where the governor could keep an eye on him. There Douwes Dekker, abysmally poor, suffered the unkindest cut of all by being practically ostracized. The small European community centered around the governor treated him as an outcast. In order to get away from and master this tortuous situation, Dekker seized the means most readily available to him, writing. First of all, he continued work on a prose text already started in Natal, "Scattered Pages from an Old Man's Diary" ("Losse bladen uit het dagboek van een oud man"). More important to him, and for our understanding of his mental state at the time, is his play "The Outcast" ("De eerloze").

This he wrote in Padang, and it contains two interwoven themes, that of his dejection and hurt pride, and that of his relationship with Caroline. By writing "The Outcast," the manuscript of which has been lost, Dekker managed to take an objective look at his own situation. The play sustained him in an otherwise impossible predicament, and this explains his attachment to it. He reworked it again in 1859, and finally, in 1864, twenty years after it had been composed, the play came out under the new title of *The Bride Above (De bruid daarboven)*. Despite its changes, it did remain one of Dekker's juvenilia and, in literary terms, a romantic melodrama.

In September 1844, Douwes Dekker left for Batavia to stay with a friend while awaiting the outcome of his case. There he met S. van Deventer Jszn., head of the government printing office and editor of the state newspaper, the *Java Courant*. Van Deventer invited him to contribute to his paper, and its January 1 edition of 1845 contained Dekker's New Year's Day poem of one hundred lines, ending:

> Perhaps this year will bring us misery or distress,
> Perhaps each day will be a source of happiness . . .
> No matter: Our destiny will lead us quite away . . .
> To Heaven, which will then repay whatever life did us gainsay,
> There we'll cheerfully mock our former lot,
> On high with God!

There is absolutely nothing here that even remotely suggests that Dekker would one day develop into a writer characterized by his radically original use of language.

Recent Dekker/Multatuli scholarship has strongly emphasized his humanistic, social, and cultural significance, as well as his revolutionary impact. Too little attention has been paid, however, to his stylistic talents, which had a deep and lasting influence on a large segment of the Dutch people. His contemporaries regarded his use of language as unique. Wrote an unknown correspondent in 1876: "his language outshines anything that has hitherto appeared." Between the time he wrote his traditionally romantic poems and his novel *Max Havelaar* (under the pseudonym of Multatuli), he developed not only intellectually but in a literary sense as well.

After all, Dekker was writing well before he made his literary debut as Multatuli. It appears that up till then he had already written quite a lot, even though while still "à pure perte," completely at sea, as he himself characterized that phase. To consider Douwes Dekker's development also as a process of literary emancipation is to ask ourselves how on earth he managed to rid himself of the conventional language he still meekly used in 1845 and even later. It will not do to seek the answer by vaguely invoking the undoubtedly deep influences that shocking experiences had had on him. Admittedly by 1845 he had already "borne much," as his pseudonym implies. Certainly he had suffered disappointment, degradation, and injustice, but surely none of this had contributed much of anything to his *literary* development as such.

The year 1845 was to be an important year for Douwes Dekker. During the first several months of 1845, he made the acquaintance of Willem van der Hucht, on whose tea plantation, Parakan Salak, he was a guest for some time. This plantation did so well that Willem's brother, Jan Pieter, decided to join him in the Indies. He left from the Netherlands with quite a large party, including the three Van Wijn-bergen girls. They arrived during the early part of August, and Dekker went to meet their boat. He and one of the girls, Everdine (or Tine), fell in love at first sight. Both of them were to regard August 18 as the most decisive date in their lives. The event compelled Dekker to settle his still uncertain official position, especially since he was only on half pay. On September 13, he was assigned as a temporary official to the assistant resident of Krawang (west Java), whose administration was in a shambles. On September 26, Tine and he were officially engaged at Parakan Salak, where she had gone to stay with the Van der Hucht family. She stayed there, while Douwes Dekker went to his post at Purwakarta. They were literally mountains apart. To this physical separation we owe a correspondence of which, unfortunately, only Dekker's letters to Tine have been preserved.

Any writer, any would-be writer, tries to find those means of expression best suited to her or him, and searches for a form of writing that can best carry "the imprint of the soul," as it were. In Douwes Dekker's case, his medium of expression was sooner forced upon him than discovered. The correspondence that circumstances dictated he and Tine engage in freed Dekker from the literary conventionality which had hitherto always insinuated itself between him and his language. Their correspondence liberated him because the epistolary genre did not require him to stick to a "poetic" use of language. His letters most closely followed his natural way of talking, the very form in which to address Tine most directly. One of his first letters (dated October 2–11, 1845) already states that he wants to "talk" with Everdine, and that he wants their letter writing to be a continuation of their talks together. Several letters later, when Tine has apparently not reacted to his question, he writes: "Do tell me if you like my way of writing; I know that I have a tendency to jumble things a bit, and the reason is that I want to talk rather than converse with you, with serious things mixed in." He would like her to write him the same way and to be spontaneous also: "You know what I would like, a couple of pages written on different days with just anything that comes to mind in them. And please do not worry if it should all turn out to be a bit of a hodgepodge, because I would be the last person to mind. . . . The reason I am making this request is that it would tell me exactly what has been on your mind since I wrote you last."

Close reading of Dekker's letters to Tine will reveal his ultimate purpose. He clearly wishes to conquer and prepare a fiancée who is somewhat reserved by nature and bridled by her upbringing. Also, he wishes to change her and introduce her to his ideas, while at the same time wanting to persuade her to confide in him by making all sorts of confessions of his own. He tells her about his own vanity, but also about his chivalrous aspects, about his relationship with "that poor child" in Purwakarta that was so unhappy and how he kissed her and arranged to meet her below her window. He tells her about his relationship with his former fiancée Caroline, and each and every time he asks what Tine thinks about it all: "Write me truly if this bothers you in any way." Intermittently, he declares his love for her again and again, "Everdine, you are so dear to me." Gradually, he goes one step further. The letter of October 14, 1845, is particularly important: "Dearest Everdine, my own, do be entirely frank, write me whatever you think, wish, or feel; I deserve no less, after all, my angel, you belong to me as I belong to you." Then he states his notions about love and marriage:

> I think that in general people are too easily embarrassed before marriage. . . . Ever since August 18, I have been considering you as someone I have a right to and who has the same right to me. I pity all those who require public approval before they can belong to one another. Our situation is different . . . but just suppose there might be people who would stand in our way, or who would want to make our life miserable, say, then I know I would come over to Parakan Salak to take you with me, either as my girl friend, my bride, my wife, or as anything you care to name, but I would take you with me as *mine* in any case, without waiting for any formality whatever. And you would want me to, wouldn't you? I think you would, because you would trust in my love, wouldn't you, totally?

Several letters later: "Nothing should ever come between us, neither custom nor shame, because we must at all times have the courage to tell each other things." And in the same letter: "People usually do not talk about this sort of thing, one rarely bothers young ladies with this kind of subject, and hence, for reasons of false modesty, if you ask me, people altogether avoid what in my opinion is most important and most divine."

Gradually, it seems, Dekker is nearing his goal, because in a later letter, apparently with reference to Tine's reply to the one just quoted, we read: "Each time I love you more and more, my angel, because you have so entirely managed to overcome that little girl's modesty . . . and don't hide yourself behind so-called good manners." In one of the very last letters, on the point of joining her at Parakan Salak, he writes still: "Our engagement has been precisely what I think it should have been, a slow approximation of marriage, and we have by now come close enough to one another to take the final step which will bridge any distance remaining between us. . . ." Their correspondence has indeed well served its purpose of "slow approximation." Dekker especially owes a great deal to it. In the final analysis, he owes his authorship to it.

These engagement letters contain one more important statement, one in which Dekker, as he is writing these letters, discovers that he is an author: "No profession would suit me better than a writer's. . . . If I had enough money to be moderately well off, I really think I would never again bother doing anything else, certainly none of those things that never appealed to me anyway." He was still a good fifteen years away from publishing *Max Havelaar*.

Be that as it may, the epistolary genre enabled Dekker to exercise a manner of writing that prefigures his later style. Even so, he could not at the time (1845) quite dissociate himself from nineteenth-century mannerisms. The spoken language he did explore, of course, and this meant the first stage in his development as a writer leading up to the many free forms he would later learn to master with such great virtuosity.

By the time the engagement letters break off, Dekker's experiment with "direct language" is still not at an end. The process eludes us for several years. By 1851, however, Dekker writes several letters from Menado to his old school friend Kruseman. In these Dekker reveals himself as a full-fledged writer, no longer a victim of convention. He writes a "living Dutch" which was to distinguish him from all his contemporaries.

Those years spent in Menado (north Celebes), from April 1849 until 1852, were possibly Dekker's happiest years. He got on well with his boss and there were few tensions other than those within himself. ("By God, how do I come by this violent heart and wild imagination?") Most important, while writing in Menado, he found the very form that served as the exact "reflection of his moods." The letters he then wrote went on for pages, and those addressed to his brother and to Kruseman that have been preserved are, in the final analysis, all essays in the literal sense of that word, attempts and exercises at writing. While writing to Kruseman, we notice how he is actually practicing his future style of writing, "so as to get through to people," he adds. At the same time, he could show Kruseman, who was to become a publisher, what the latter might learn to expect from him: nothing other than a way of writing which would be altogether novel in the Netherlands, an untrammeled way of expressing oneself, rooted in his romantic conviction that first impulses are also the best.

He wrote down whatever came to mind, and in the order it occurred to him. This had the effect of creating an impression of total spontaneity and honesty. "Dear Kruseman," he writes in a twenty-four-page letter of minuscule handwriting, "accept my *manner* of writing for what it is. Don't expect me to complete every sentence or elucidate every point or opinion. . . . And do try and put up with my parenthetical remarks, —with the parenthesis within a parenthesis, for that matter—, and don't wait for me to continue necessarily where I left off. Life is best described in parentheses, mine is, at any rate." It is easy to see that the later author of the *Ideas (Ideeën)* is already very much with us. Like his *Ideas*, which are seemingly without form, these bizarre letters still constitute an entity in themselves. The unifying force is their authentic and deeply personal tone, and this characteristic gives Dekker every right to assert to Kruseman "I am my style."

Clearly, Dekker often interrupts himself in this letter to Kruseman. He does so to improve his own style as he goes along, by repeatedly correcting an inclination he has discovered in himself, that of reverting to a traditional way of writing. One example will suffice. He is writing to Kruseman: "It is evening now. A nocturnal butterfly is circling the lamp. My wife just caught the creature, very carefully, so as not to damage it. She is taking it outside, into the free and open air; she still walks with difficulty, because she has been very, very ill. She does all this in order that the cat not injure the creature," and without using so much as a period or completing the sentence, he then adds: "what terrible language this is, *in order that . . . not injure!*"

In any case, nothing came of the writing career, even if it had been concurrent with a bureaucratic one, which Dekker had imagined for himself. It would take another ten years for that to happen.

On May 14, 1860, the Amsterdam printer and publisher J. de Ruyter brought out the book that, according to Van Hoëvell, sent a tremor through the country: *Max Havelaar*, the first work by the totally un-

known author Eduard Douwes Dekker, who called himself Multatuli, a Latin jumble meaning "I have suffered a great deal." Quite a
history had preceded the book's appearance, and a great deal more
was to follow. The so-called Lebak Affair was what preceded it all. It
concerned a quarrel between Assistant Resident Douwes Dekker and
his superiors, a seemingly typical wrangle among officials like so
many before and after in the Indies. Thanks to Multatuli, however,
this affair achieved a notoriety way out of proportion to the case. The
book *Max Havelaar* turned into an indictment of everything and everyone proper and careful, of the Drystubbles and Slimerings of this
world. At the same time, it became a plea for all the errant Havelaars
and romantic idealists par excellence, such as Multatuli himself.
Faced with an already complicated governmental situation, Dekker
chose to act according to Western ideas of "justice and humanity."
He failed to consider, or rather willfully ignored, the indigenous social and cultural Javanese traditions. In so doing, he misjudged an institutional conflict. The Indonesian historian Sartono Kartodirdjo
wrote about the incident in his book *The Peasants' Revolt of Banten
in 1888:* "Here we meet with a lack of understanding of the background of Javanese patrimonial-bureaucratic structure."

In order to get some understanding of what took place in Lebak and
what Multatuli tells us about it, it is necessary to know something
about administrative organization in the Indies. The island of Java
was subdivided into residencies, comparable to provinces but with an
entirely different administrative structure. Each residency consisted
of departments or regencies. A residency, headed by the resident, was
governed by two parallel bodies, one Dutch, the other Indonesian. A
regency was headed by the regent, the highest Indonesian official, as
well as by a Dutch assistant resident. The latter was assisted by a
Dutch controller. A regent was assisted by a *patih*, who was in turn
assisted by district chiefs or *demangs* (also called *wedanas* elsewhere), and then followed the village heads or *lurahs*, and so on. The
nonadministrative official was the *djaksa*, in charge of police affairs.
What we ought especially to keep in mind is that there were distinct
administrative bodies governing side by side, one Indonesian, the
other European. In principle at least, the Indonesians were self-
governing, but under a European supervisor, who had more or less
general control. In practice, Dutch involvement went much deeper,
as is evident from the actions of Max Havelaar, in the book of the
same name, and other European officials.

Douwes Dekker was an assistant resident of Lebak, part of the residency of Banten, on the extreme western tip of Java. Its capital was
Serang, where the resident lived. The capital of the Lebak district was

Rangkasbitung. Lebak was situated in the area furthest south of the residency of Banten. The countryside was sparsely populated, ill suited for large plantations, and for that reason it was not a part of the "culture system." Toward the south it was wild, mountainous, and isolated. It was generally considered to be out in the sticks.

The sequence of events in Lebak is as follows: on January 22, 1856, Assistant Resident E. Douwes Dekker accepts his post at the Lebak department. On February 24, he forwards a written complaint against the regent, i.e., his Indonesian colleague and equal in rank, based almost entirely on research in the archives. In it, he accuses the regent of having abused his authority. Dekker also states that he suspects him of extortion. He proposes to have the regent removed "as quickly as possible" to the residential capital in order to prevent any witnesses from being unduly influenced during the investigation. The resident, Brest van Kempen, who was without any doubt a competent man, shows himself surprised and taken aback by Dekker's accusation. On February 26, two days after receiving it, he goes to Lebak in order to discuss the affair with his assistant resident, and to obtain further information and proof. Douwes Dekker, however, refuses to furnish either, and tells his chief that he wishes to be responsible in seeing the whole proceeding through. The resident, in turn, refuses Dekker's proposal, and rightly so, one is inclined to think. After all, he can not or does not wish to transfer his authority to an assistant resident he hardly knows, and certainly not in an important case like this. On February 29, Resident Brest van Kempen writes a memorandum explaining the situation to the governor-general. Dekker is informed about this. The advisory Council of the Indies disapproves of Douwes Dekker's actions and suggests that he be dismissed. Governor-General Duymaer van Twist accepts their advice only in part. He too censures Dekker's handling of the affair. He knows Dekker personally, and changes his proposed dismissal to a transfer. His decision is forwarded to Douwes Dekker and also contains a cabinet memorandum addressed to Dekker personally of which not even the resident receives a copy. Apparently because of this personal note, which disapproves of his official conduct, Douwes Dekker, it is now generally assumed, asks to be dismissed. His request is granted on April 4. On April 20, Assistant Resident Douwes Dekker leaves Rangkasbitung, and following his invitation, stays with the resident in Serang for a couple of days before leaving for Batavia. The entire drama takes less than three months. From that point on, Dekker becomes the jobless civilian who vainly tries to get a hearing, who writes petitions and letters, and who finally, and most important, writes his book *Max Havelaar* in Brussels from September through October 1859, showing his final and strongest card in his attempts to be rehabilitated.

To Multatuli, rehabilitation meant seeing justice done. This never happened, and his subsequent poverty forced him to live by his pen. It compelled him to become, in his own words, "un homme des lettres," a notion already familiar to him. Poverty and humiliation were the price he paid to become the writer who could turn into Multatuli. For a while it looked as though all this still would be exchanged for official rehabilitation and a significant promotion in rank. The well-known writer and conservative member of Parliament Jacob van Lennep came across the manuscript of *Max Havelaar*. He pronounced it "a masterpiece" to his friend Van Hasselt, "within limits, of course, or rather, those limitations which would be detrimental in an ordinary novel are precisely what give this work an extraordinary quality, and add something surprising and more shocking to its story. It is d——d nice, I don't know what else to tell you." And he concludes: "I would not be surprised at all if I could not work out something to his advantage, if he should give me carte blanche to go ahead."

Earlier, rumor that Douwes Dekker was writing a book against the government had reached Rochussen, the minister for the colonies. After several people had already put pressure on him, he declared himself willing to reinstate Dekker but "of course only if he refrains from writing" (letter of November 21, 1859, to Van Lennep). Dekker was now faced with a dilemma: "If I were not in debt, I'd prefer to be a writer, but the way things are, I am compelled to give higher priority to a job in the Indies for the sake of the money" (to his brother Jan, November 20, 1859). And on the same day he wrote to Tine: "I have thought it over, and I'm inclined to accept Rochussen's proposal but my conditions are: 1. The position of resident on Java, especially Passaruang in order to repay my debts (this district provided its resident a high percentage of its agricultural profits); 2. Restoration of time served, to count toward a pension; 3. A generous cash advance, and a medal in the Order of the Netherlands Lion. But I do not want to openly state these terms but wait rather to see what he will do." When rumors about an impending revolt in the Indies reached Holland, it was Van Lennep in particular who recommended that Douwes Dekker be sent out in a position of responsibility to help quell the revolt. Meanwhile, however, Dekker had upped the ante and demanded to be reinstated at no less a rank than that of councilor of the Indies. His Excellency Rochussen was surprised and annoyed: "Mr. Dekker mentioned something about becoming councilor of the Indies. I find that he can not possibly be serious." The rest of this letter to Van Lennep, dated December 9, 1859, concerns his absolute refusal to give in to Dekker's demands. That refusal definitely caused Douwes Dekker to become the author Multatuli. Did Douwes Dekker perhaps make such extreme demands in order to become Multatuli? It might seem so, especially if we remember that he had announced his literary ambitions many years back. When the die had been cast, Van Lennep did everything possible to find Dekker a publisher, and indeed managed to do just that. Van Lennep's involvement in the actual publication is somewhat murky and clearly ambiguous. He had already written Rochussen in a letter of December 11, 1859: "I would have much preferred to see the man working abroad than to have him here, stung into speaking his mind." We, like the critic Veth before us, get the uncomfortable impression that Van Lennep tried to curtail the political impact of *Max Havelaar* the moment its publication had become inevitable. In the first place, he asked Multatuli to sign over his copyright to him in order to get the novel published, whereas his power of attorney would have sufficed. He furthermore went through the manuscript, and made some changes which were not all improvements but which apparently served some other purpose. To be sure, he did all of this in consultation with Douwes Dekker, but he generally behaved as if he owned the manuscript. Van Lennep handled everything concerning the publication of the book. On May 5, 1860, he sent Multatuli three finished copies of the book, for which the latter politely thanked him. To Tine, he was exultant. His expectations were high indeed, especially following the extensive review of his book by no less a critic than the influential Veth in the July issue of *The Guide*. "But I am hoping to make a much greater impact," he wrote Tine. Several weeks later, when the book's reception proved disappointing, everything moved far too slowly, and nothing particular happened, Dekker showed his dissatisfaction with the book's high price and the way the publisher was marketing it.

Multatuli wanted more than anything to be read by everybody, he wanted to create "a stir," but Van Lennep, with his nineteenth-century aristocratic notions, clearly wished to limit the book to a small circle of men of letters. A conflict was inevitable, and Dekker even started a lawsuit against Van Lennep. He lost his suit on technical grounds. Meanwhile, the first edition of 1,300 copies had been sold out and a second was planned with Multatuli unable to interfere. It was not until after the book had gone from one publisher to the next, and finally ended up with Funke in 1874, that he regained control, and then only because of the latter's good will. We would find conditions such as these hard to imagine nowadays and would consider them nothing short of "theft of intellectual property."

Multatuli did not make use of the events in Lebak by writing a report, an account, a pamphlet, or brochure; he made them into a novel, creating a work of fiction. In keeping with the practice of his time, and in order to reach the widest audience possible, he "poetized and embellished" the facts, in his own words. The subsequent story is one where imagination and reality are mixed, although reality is never lost sight of. To convert his reader to his own point of view, he used every literary means at his disposal, such as conflicting characters and situations, contrasts and similarities, changes in point of view and of chronology, the use of irony, and so on. The method of his undisputed success in doing this is traced in the dissertation by A. L. Sötemann entitled *The Structure of Max Havelaar (De structuur van Max Havelaar,* 1966). It demonstrates how Multatuli managed to convince his readers of the righteousness of his cause, the propriety of his administration, while making them accept his self-contradictory character at the same time. This he did so well in fact that Sötemann characterizes *Max Havelaar* as an autohagiography.

The novel's title is self-explanatory. Max Havelaar, the assistant resident, is the central character, but its subtitle "The Coffee Auctions of the Netherlands Trading Company" requires some explanation.

The Netherlands Trading Company, founded by King William I in 1824, held the Dutch monopoly of selling at auction the products from the tropics. The trading company symbolized a political system existing exclusively to benefit the Netherlands, not the Indies and its people. Especially around 1860, its auctions had come under general scrutiny, and Multatuli is therefore hinting at existing conditions. Several cases of fraud and malpractice had been reported for which the auction brokers were especially to blame. For this reason, Multatuli begins his novel by introducing a coffee broker called Drystubble, representative of a loathesome sort of Dutchman, although he may have had a particular broker in mind.

Max Havelaar is dedicated to E[verdine] H[ubertine] v[an] W[ijnbergen], to Dekker's wife Tine. An "unpublished play" precedes the novel and serves as a device of sorts. The name Lothario is derived from Goethe's *Wilhelm Meisters Lehrjahre,* and he is a character who epitomizes nobility of soul and spirit. In the final sentence of this "unpublished play," the judge invokes Lessing's patriarch in *Nathan der Weise,* in which a Jew has raised a Christian child as a Jewess, and even though he thus has saved her from death, he has to be sentenced because he is a Jew. Lessing's "Tut nichts, der Jude wird verbrannt" ("Never mind, the Jew is to be burnt at the stake") parallels Dekker's "Lothario has got to hang."

The novel proper begins with the memorable phrase: "I am a coffee broker and reside at No. 37, Lauriergracht." That is how Drystubble introduces himself. He functions in the novel as the counterpart to the character Havelaar, who is the noble idealist, poetic spirit, and martyr to his ideals. Drystubble, on the other hand, is calculating, materialistic, and a self-assured hypocrite without the slightest feeling for poetry. Drystubble is the sole narrator during the first four chapters. He informs us how much he likes his profession of being a broker in coffee, and expounds upon his opinions about education, religion, and poetry: "I have nothing against poetry. If people wish to put words in a row, that is all right by me." Also, he goes on about the stage, about virtue and its rewards (the story about Lucas, the warehouse clerk), and so on.

Chapter two deals with his meeting with Mufflerman, which is what Drystubble calls Havelaar because he can not afford an overcoat and wears a muffler instead. Mufflerman, it turns out, is a former classmate of Drystubble's and none other of course than Assistant Resident Max Havelaar, lately dismissed and back in Holland. Multatuli tells the story about the Greek in order to underline their differences in character. The next day, Mufflerman drops off a package containing all sorts of articles which he has written over the years. The articles deal with various subjects, illustrating Havelaar's wide range of interests and the fact that he is well read. An enclosed letter asks for Drystubble's assistance in seeing the contents of the package published.

Chapter four lists the subject matter of every article contained in Mufflerman's package. Drystubble's son Frits and "young Stern," a German apprentice in Drystubble's office, both come across Mufflerman at a book auction. He has a job carrying in the books that are to be sold. He is seen accidentally dropping a whole stack of a ladies' magazine, for which reason he is fired ("he was lazy, pedantic, and sickly"). Later, while inspecting the package of papers Mufflerman had given him, Drystubble runs across a couple of articles dealing with the cultivation of coffee. These interest him, and he decides that "young Stern, . . . who is somewhat touched by poetry" anyway, should make a book out of the articles. They even draw up a contract of sorts. The resulting compilation is in fact the essence of the novel *Max Havelaar*. Chapters five through nine take place on Java. Multatuli's well-known "portrait of Havelaar" is in chapter six, and the address to the chiefs of Lebak occurs in chapter eight. Chapters ten and eleven are again situated in the Netherlands and provide yet another opportunity for listening to Drystubble. Chapter nine contains the sermon by Pastor Humbug, and chapter ten has Drystubble's comical commentary on Heine's poem "Auf Flügeln des Gesanges." Subsequent chapters take us back to Java again and continue to describe the events in the district of Lebak, together with a lot of digressions. The history of the Japanese stonecutter is in chapter eleven, and the history of Saïd-jah and Adinda in chapter twelve. These are followed by the subsequent events in Lebak which end in the famous peroration directed against the king of the Netherlands. Here Multatuli himself takes over and his characters Drystubble and Havelaar fall silent.

The publication of *Max Havelaar* may not have had the results Douwes Dekker hoped for. He was not made councilor of the Indies, nor resident, he was not rehabilitated, and he did not even get a pension. Still, the book had more impact than he could have realized at first. The impact was caused more by his utterly novel use of language than by his public grievances and accusations. Multatuli performed the feats of renewing the Dutch language and of liberating it from conventions that had for years stifled it. There is no doubt that many of his readers felt this way. All of a sudden a new writer had appeared on the scene, for in 1860 nobody could even begin to guess at the literary developments that had actually preceded the appearance of *Max Havelaar.* Van Lennep's reaction exemplifies the general reaction to the book. What had shocked him, and most people, was not the novel's *social* protest so much (as it had Van Hoëvell) but its surprising form and style. Everything else was secondary. The critic Busken Huet too was primarily struck by Multatuli's stylistic sensibilities: "Whenever he gets going, Multatuli reveals this talent to such an extent that his work, regardless of the argument, acquires its own raison d'être, and one loves and admires him even if one disagrees." Clearly, Huet dissociates himself from Dekker's ideas but he too is repeatedly taken by surprise by Multatuli's way of expressing himself, by what Huet calls his "style." We must remember too that Huet's definition of style meant a great deal more than "fine writing." For his part, Multatuli did not make such a distinction between style and content. He found the distinction useless, considering what its aims had been. Ten Brink tells us how he would run off in a huff and yell: "I don't want to hear about fine writing, I detest all that fine writing stuff!" Other times, he would complain that although people praised him for his "style," they still left him and his family in debt and poverty. His complaints on this score, stinging and ironical, took on a variety of forms. Several times they became parables, such as the one of the impresario looking for artists, the one about the alchemist, or the one about the mother who complained that people either could not or did not want to see her child on account of the pretty dress she wore. Multatuli vents his spleen also in such acerbic dialogues as the one between Dimanche and Don Juan, and especially in the "fairy tale" of Chresos in Boetia, which one can find in his *Amatory Letters (Minnebrieven)*. It is clear why he was so embittered but the fact remains that his resentment stemmed from a basic misunderstanding between him and his public.

His readers interpreted his message differently from the way he had intended, and understandably so. For reasons political and purely sentimental, a great deal had already appeared in the popular press concerning abuses in the Indies. Veth had already mentioned some writers in his *Guide* article, who had in no uncertain terms signaled administrative abuses before *Max Havelaar* appeared. Van Hoëvell, as head of the opposition, had already for years been attacking similar abuses, but the principal fact remains that hitherto nobody had done so in such an appealing and lively manner as Multatuli. It would do Multatuli a grave injustice therefore to judge him solely in terms of his idealism, his courage, and his martyrdom, without taking his style into account. To do so would be to deny the general significance which the act of writing has to an author, especially to an author such as Multatuli. More than anything else—and it is a point which can not be stressed enough—it was Multatuli's desire to write which brought him onto the literary scene. It would be equally hard to separate his social and cultural influence from his ability to make his language reflect, in his own words, each and every impression of the human heart.

There is no doubt that Multatuli had tremendous influence in many ways. He aroused and activated potential forces among his fellow citizens, and the more one studies the intellectual history of the Netherlands, the more one realizes the deep and lasting influences of his ideas. He caused an intellectual revolution, especially among the Dutch middle class, and taught it to see for itself, and in so doing changed the social conditions of his time.

Many critics have pointed out that Multatuli's ideas lacked originality and were without exception traceable to his own reading. Be that as it may, they were after all the ideas of his era, he did make them accessible to a great many people largely by virtue of his own, inimicable style. And it was only because of that that they were read and understood, which was precisely what Multatuli wanted. "Yes indeed, I desire to be read," he wrote, and people did read him, even in the Indies. They read him and followed his example.

In 1869, Multatuli had good reason to complain when he found out that his publisher had sent only twenty copies of his *Max Havelaar* to the Indies. The excuse was that books just did not sell out there. Even so, a great many more copies reached the Indies by way of private booksellers and such. The anecdote exists about the one copy of his book on the shelves of the social club in Batavia which was simply read to pieces, but that is deceptive. Multatuli, the author, had served his apprenticeship as an assistant resident. After 1860, a new generation of colonial officials graduated from the academy in Delft who had read *Max Havelaar*, and could recite large sections of it. Increasingly, a large number of people sharing Multatuli's convictions entered into the administration of the Indies, bringing with them a positive attitude about their task vis-à-vis the native population. Their influence on the political course of events was to prove unmistakable. One G. P. Rouffaer, who traveled through the Indies during the 1880s and who was convinced that the Havelaar affair could only be settled in situ, wrote: "Havelaar's influence on the administrative officials has generally been immense," and he then added a list of names of officials who qualified to be called "Multatulians" in his opinion. His list is an impressive one, considering the relatively small number of officials in those days. Rouffaer then lists on the next several pages the most outstanding examples of Multatuli's influence on the same administrators. They prove symptomatic of the influence Multatuli exerted. However, the fact that he was capable of exerting any influence at all, he owes to his language. For example, there exists a pamphlet written by the official L. Vitalis called *The Introduction, Effectiveness and Shortcomings of the Cultivation System on Java (De invoering, werking en gebreken van het stelsel van kultures op Java*, 1851). This pamphlet was really a much better documented and more devastating accusation of governmental mismanagement than Multatuli's *Max Havelaar*, but Vitalis never had anywhere near the impact Multatuli had simply because his argument was not nearly as persuasive.

The same man who made undeniably grave political errors more than made up for them once he had become a writer. Multatuli presents us with a paradox. The same Assistant Resident Douwes Dekker, romantic and individualistic visionary who got himself off on the wrong tangent by misjudging a sociocultural situation in Banten, was also the one who was to exert a lasting influence on government policy. This is a paradox that can be neither solved nor denied. The thesis holds therefore that Douwes Dekker failed as an administrator in Lebak, and succeeded in becoming one of the most influential and important authors. By the same token, his authorship has nothing whatever to do with that aspect of his personality that had gotten him into political trouble.

The novel *Max Havelaar* made Douwes Dekker into the writer Multatuli. The book became his touchstone and ethical standard. His attitude to all social problems seems either derived from *Max Havelaar* or from one of its basic themes. It is pivotal to his work, also because his stay in the Indies was decisive in the development of his authorship.

V
Four "Eccentrics"

"He is a man of a somewhat eccentric but deeply moral character"—The Resident of Menado about E. Douwes Dekker.

1   S. E. W. Roorda van Eysinga

In a letter of April 20, 1872, Roorda wrote to Multatuli: "My style of writing has not gotten me anywhere, and my ideas and abilities have up to now gotten me even less far. Only my "Malediction" ["Vloekzang"] will live on." In his *Collected Works* (*Verzamelde stukken*, 2d ed., published posthumously in 1889, p. 26) he stated the wish to have the following carved on his tombstone: "Here lies the poet who wrote the 'Malediction: The Final Day of the Hollanders on Java.' " Nothing ever came of that. One may well ask what this "Malediction" was, which the otherwise modest poet rated so highly among his own works. The truth is that it was a fairly bombastic piece of work:

Malediction: The Final Days
of the Hollanders on Java by Sentot

Would you keep us down much longer then,
Harden your hearts with gold some more?
Deaf to demands of right and reason,
Taunt gentleness with force still, as before?

Let the buffalo then be our symbol,
Who, tired of taunt, will put to rout
And throw off his cruelest rider and
Gore him; his hooves will stamp him out.

May flame of war scorch your fields then,
And vengeance roll through vale and hill,
Smoke rise up from house and mansion,
The air ring with the shout to kill.

Our ears will gladden at the sound
Your women's cries to hear,

We'll crowd around in joyful witness
And look on tyranny's low bier.

Then shall we slaughter all your children,
Ours, slake their thirst in the red flood,
Repaid be all the debts of ages past,
Usury cleansed with human blood.

And when the dark shroud of the night
Has covered over the smoldering ground,
And jackals lick, and chew and tear
The lukewarm corpses strewn around,

Then shall we take your daughters hence.
We'll feast ourselves on each young maid
On their white bosoms rest
From the work of war and hate.

And when her shame shall be complete
And we of all our kisses tired
And each is sated to his fill
The heart of vengeance, all that we had desired,

Then shall we feast:
First toast your Greed!
A second toast to Jesus Christ!
The final drink to Holland's Creed!

And when the sun climbs in the East,
Each Javanese to his Mohammed prays,
Earth's gentlest folk will yield up thanks
For chasing off these Christian strays.

Multatuli made the "Malediction" known. In a note to the 1875 revised edition of *Max Havelaar*, he compared it and preferred it to Camille's speech in Pierre Corneille's tragedy *Horace*. Earlier, in 1871, he had written Roorda that he thought the poem was "great." "I know of nothing quite as powerful," he added, "or as realistic! A poet, seer, and prophet, all in one" (in a letter of January 3, 1871). Roorda must have been overwhelmed by such praise, especially since it came from a writer he had been admiring for years and had just begun corresponding with. Although he at first weakly defended himself and seemed a bit uncomfortable on account of Multatuli's fulsome praise ("no matter how vain I may be, I still don't deserve the kind of compliment a young girl gets"), he did *in the long run* begin to believe in Multatuli's judgment, simply because he had always had great faith in all his pronouncements. As their correspondence progressed, however, Roorda became increasingly more critical of himself. For example, he simply did not accept what Multatuli wrote him on May 6, 1871: "I know of no one who writes as well as you do." In his reply of May 16, he confessed that his deepest desire was to be a great writer, but four days later he wrote: "Your friendship for me keeps you from seeing my shortcomings. I am an amateur, a dabbler. Lots of promise, but promising little of anything. So much for know-how. Ever since I was banished, my style of writing has only made matters worse. . . . I am a failed soldier, a failed engineer, a failed publisher, and my marriage aside, a failed human being!"

None of this smacks exactly of his overestimating himself, and that makes it even harder to explain why Roorda to the very last made an exception of his poem "Malediction," which he thought would immortalize him. It is quite possible that apart from Multatuli's praise, the prevailing romantic notions of writing poetry blurred his judgment. After all, to him and his contemporaries, poetry was an inspiration welling up from the human breast. Roorda had indeed felt inspired when writing his poem (he was seething with outrage, he wrote, about the terrible things that had been inflicted on the native population). For the rest, he had trusted to his first impulse, which had generated his "Malediction" in one mighty gush.

In 1866, he wrote a brief article entitled "My Banishment and My 'Malediction' " ("Mijne verbanning en mijn vloekzang") concerning the origin of the poem, but we should really see "the history of the malediction" in the context of his personal circumstances before and after. For that reason some biographical facts are in order. S. E. W. (Sicco) Roorda van Eysinga, according to Wertheim's article in *Bijdragen tot de Taal-, Land- en Volkenkunde* of 1960, was the half brother of Ph. P. Roorda van Eysinga and nearly thirty years younger. S. E. W. Roorda was born in Batavia in 1825 from their mutual father's second marriage to a fourteen-year-old woman. Like his brother, Sicco was educated to become an officer. He left for the Indies as a second lieutenant in the army's corps of engineers. He turned out to be totally unfit for military life. He contradicted his superiors, refused to follow orders, and did scores of things that are intolerable in a military man. In short, he proved a troublesome and useless officer. After eleven years of service, including one forced transfer, he finally requested a discharge, which was granted. Following a short stint as fellow editor of the *Batavian Commercial Daily (Bataviaasch Handelsblad)*, for which he had written before, Roorda became an administrator of a coffee plantation in central Java. There he replaced the owner, who was on vacation on Europe. Thanks to Roorda's "benevolent changes," which he instituted for the benefit of the population (the compliment came from Resident Bekking), he received every assistance possible from the government. He even managed to increase production. After a disagreement with the owner, who was critical of Roorda's expenses, the latter either left or was fired, and entered government service. He was appointed "supervisor of measurements for irrigation and shipping canals" in the historically infamous territory of Grobogan. In 1860, this station still showed signs everywhere of the terrible famine from 1849. Instead of former rice fields and inhabitants, Roorda saw nothing but impenetrable swamps and bamboo forests, inhabited only by animals. He wrote that it was a landscape of "fearful loneliness." When passing through nearby towns he sometimes saw more graves than houses: "Those mounds were so many silent accusations of my own people. All those graves lacked was a marker saying 'Died for Profit.' " While working there, Roorda had learned about the famine of eleven years ago, and this had made him "seethe with indignation." Then, in 1860, famine threatened again. "One can easily imagine how I felt on that December first (the anniversary of the composition of his "Malediction"), when another hideous famine stared us in the face." The poem, by the way, had been composed in fairly prosaic surroundings. While undressing in the bathroom, Roorda tells us, "The 'Malediction' just welled up ffom my enraged heart. It seems I must have been yelling and screaming a lot at the time, because my roommate's servant ran to his master saying: 'I am afraid Mr. Roorda is having trouble with his supervisor because there is a lot of noise and grumbling going on in the bathroom.' " Later on, Roorda declared (in a letter to Multatuli on March 13, 1882) that the poem's composition was inspired by *Max Havelaar.*

Roorda explained that his "Malediction" was not meant to be an incitement to riot but a warning to his compatriots to avoid the fate that had struck the English three years earlier. Roorda is referring to the great mutiny which had resulted in the massacre of a great many English men, women, and children. The events in British India, about which an extensive literature exists, were regarded as handwriting on the wall and caused apprehension among the European population in the Netherlands Indies. There, the native uprising known as the Java War (1825–1830) was still a fresh memory which Roorda himself must have shared. The "Sentot," which he made into both the author and narrator of his "Malediction" was the renowned and implacable leader Sentot who fought with Prince Diponegoro against the Dutch.

When the *Batavian Commercial Daily* refused publication of the poem, Roorda sent it to his brother in the Netherlands, who advised him not to publish it. Roorda then resigned himself to this, but he never hid the fact that he was the poem's author. On the contrary, he took great pride in it and read the poem repeatedly on numerous public occasions. This he did, we may imagine, with the accompaniment of appropriate gestures and vocal stress, in private as well as on public occasions when the resident was among the audience. The fact that he could do so freely only goes to show the extent to which emotional outbursts, regarded as a virtue by the romantics, were acceptable in those otherwise authoritarian times.

The notion that the colonial regime of the Dutch might just possibly come to an end seemed less improbable at the time than one would now think. Roorda was far from being the only one to give public expression to it. The fact is that a feeling of apprehension prevailed generally. It is amazing to read what private individuals and officials wrote, or were permitted to write, in some dailies. They spoke a language that would strike us as seditious. Its fervent tone suited the romantic age, and was customary in the fight against the system of enforced labor. That fight was waged with great fierceness during the 1860s, both within the government and without, particularly by the liberal party of the opposition. Roorda, to be sure, did belong to those opposing the so-called culture system, but he certainly was no liberal. His political sentiments went way beyond that, but his tumultuous articles and indictments created much less of a sensation than one might think. It was not his "Malediction" that got him banished from the Netherlands Indies but rather a small indiscretion contained in a pamphlet he had written to do homage to one Resident Nieuwenhuizen. What he had done was to tamper with the Pandora's box of Indies politics, namely to discuss the position of native princes, particularly in their relationship to European leaseholders of their lands. The manner in which his banishment came about, and the part some highly placed officials had in it, proved an altogether sordid affair.

Roorda departed for the Netherlands with a dishonorable discharge and without a pension. His son in the Indies supported him financially and for the rest he made do by writing. Numerous articles of his appeared in a great number of Dutch and Indies dailies and weeklies. Even his unsigned pieces betray his very personal style which is reminiscent of Multatuli's but, in his own words, "not as finely wrought."

In 1870 he began to correspond with Multatuli. Their friendship was to last almost until the very end. Multatuli died on February 19, 1887, and the last letter is dated August 22, 1886. Most of the letters were written between 1870 and 1875, however. From then on, increasingly longer silences occur. Multatuli especially proved tardy in his replies, his revulsion of anything having to do with writing often getting the better of him. "That goddamned pen," he exclaimed once.

The tenor of their letters remains friendly throughout but their attitude toward the world at large becomes more bitter. Multatuli's letters particularly are often somber and he complains about lack of recognition and understanding, about illness and aging, and especially
about the interminable necessity to keep on writing. Both of them invariably end their letters saying: "I have got to get on with writing for
a living. This will have to be it for now."

Toward the end, a third figure comes upon the scene. It is the Lu-
theran pastor, politician, and early Socialist F. Domela Nieuwenhuis.
We notice how Roorda's sympathy for socialism gradually increases,
a creed abhorred by Multatuli. With amazing energy Roorda starts
writing for Nieuwenhuis's periodical *Justice for All (Recht voor Al-
len)*. Following Roorda's death, Nieuwenhuis was able to compile a
book of over three hundred pages from just two years' writing. One of
Roorda's contributions to *Justice for All* was his famous exposé of the
life of King William III, whom he consistently referred to as "The Gorilla King." Roorda's less than flattering portrait of his sovereign, by
the way, turns out to be very similar to the image that emerges from
the diary of A. W. P. Weitzel, former minister of defense. The diary
did not appear until 1968 and was then published in part by Paul van 't
Veer entitled *But your Majesty . . . (Maar Majesteit . . .)*. Domela
Nieuwenhuis and Roorda van Eysinga knew each other's work and
had met several times. Following his imprisonment, Domela Nieuwenhuis stayed with Roorda, who was then living in Clarens, Switzerland. Upon Roorda's death on October 23, 1887, Domela Nieuwenhuis wrote his obituary. His memoirs, called *From Christian to
Anarchist (Van christen tot anarchist,* 1910), reveal his fondness for
Roorda. Their relationship with one another is evident from their as
yet unpublished correspondence. It would be wrong to say that Domela Nieuwenhuis had usurped Multatuli's place, but he is obviously no longer the only friend. It is a curious fact that the correspondence with Domela Nieuwenhuis is more intimate, "cosier" as it
were, and deals much less with affairs and opinions than the correspondence with Multatuli does. This is especially true after Nieuwenhuis's son came to live with Roorda in Clarens. Their correspondence, or what is left of it, also shows us that Multatuli could for
the longest time keep his fellow letter writers waiting for an answer.
Roorda in particular was often kept waiting: "I don't think Multatuli
is angry with you, unless it is because you failed to stop by last October. He hardly writes at all. This must certainly seem inconsistent of
somebody who always complains about a lack of response. I think
there is an explanation for his haughty announcement, and that is
that genius is most often tyrannical. He too was spoilt by praise and

he is now given to pronounce oracles. He considers it a sign of great statecraft to declare himself infallible (certainly most inconsistent with his writing, which reveals a minimum of interest in politics). His character is less great than his spirit but that is really something we had better leave to the Drystubbles to argue about. After all, we owe our ideas, our everything to him, and it would be peevish of us to demand that fortune had sent us an even greater human being." A month and a half later, Multatuli died in exile at Nieder-Ingelheim, Germany.

2   H. N. van der Tuuk

Somewhere in his correspondence with Multatuli, Roorda tells him he has copied "whole pages of Van der Tuuk's private letters" for a publisher. They were never published, however, and today the epistolary exchange between Van der Tuuk and Roorda is unfortunately lost. Apparently he was considered a great letter writer early on. It is evident from what little we know of Van der Tuuk's letters that he liked Roorda even better than Multatuli.

Van der Tuuk (1824–1894) was not a literary man in the sense that he wrote literature—he did not even leave us a malediction. All we have are his published polemics and his private, unpublished letters. Man of letters or not, he could write as none other, and often with biting sarcasm and derision. On top of that, he was also very well read, which included being well versed in literature. Upon his death, his bamboo house in Bali was found to contain a choice library which included the complete works of Shakespeare, Breero, and Starter, and, of course, all of Multatuli's works. It seemed at times as if Multatuli, Roorda, and Van der Tuuk all belonged to the same family. They had a lot in common, such as their dislike of Christianity, Dutch provinciality, and anything smacking of passivity. All three of them were troublesome, rebellious characters and centrifugal forces that did not know their own strength. When the going got rough, however, they all revealed themselves as *honnêtes hommes* and upside-down moralists.

Apart from being a troublesome fellow, Van der Tuuk was an eminent linguist, famous in his lifetime for his fantastic knowledge and his curious way of life. He was inclined to be crude and disrespectful when overturning sacred cows, shocking people, or fighting taboos, particularly those taboos that permeated science, society, morality, and the use of language. He detested dilettantism among his colleagues, and was also opposed to the enforced labor system of agriculture (the "culture system") and the politicians supporting or condoning it. He hated, furthermore, any abuse of power, hated hypocrisy, inflated oratory, and Christian morality. Whereas his dislikes and his own taboos clearly mark him as a representative of his own time, he strikes us as our contemporary by virtue of his lively manner of writing, his humor "sharper than a shark's tooth," and his stinging irony. He is one of us for the same reason Multatuli is, for his direct and natural way of addressing his readers. Van der Tuuk sometimes does Multatuli one better in sheer lack of decorum. Whereas Multatuli, by his own admission, needed to cover himself in his robe at least, instead of Buffon in his laces, Van der Tuuk literally and figuratively walked around as naked as the Balinese he lived among, wearing nothing but a sarong.

Many who knew Van der Tuuk mention his "odd ways," his unconventional and ill-mannered behavior, but others, those who really knew him best, praise his readiness to help and his graciousness. One of his friends detected his unsuspected characteristic of having "gentle and simple manners toward older and younger women." According to yet another witness, he was overly sensitive and easily moved to tears. To the outside world, he showed his "other face," which resembled that of his well-known photograph from which his "curiously piggy eyes" stare at us out of a clearly cantankerous and sour looking face. His "sensitivity" shows on occasion but it is always tempered by his irony.

Another unmistakable characteristic which suits his overall character is his susceptibility to depression, which could overtake him totally. It surfaces time and again in letters from his student days ("Why is it that this evening, of all evenings, moves me so?") but especially during his years spent in the Batak region of North Sumatra, following his nearly total mental breakdown in 1850 in Batavia. He could then only overcome his "indescribable listlessness" through "constant excitement." This may well explain his aggressiveness that, especially later in life, also strikes a tone of hopelessness.

Van der Tuuk was born in 1824 in Malacca, on the tip of the Malay peninsula, then still a colony of the Netherlands. He spent his childhood in Surabaja. When he was about twelve or thirteen years old, he was sent to Holland to attend school. He went to high school in Veendam, among other places, and in 1840, when he had just turned sixteen, he registered as a student at the University of Groningen. His father had meant him to study law but Van der Tuuk never took a degree. He had become increasingly interested in Oriental languages and went to study at Leiden. Despite the fact that Van der Tuuk's atheism is already apparent from the letters he wrote then, two of his professors recommended him for a position with the Bible Society as its "representative to the Batak regions." Van der Tuuk lived there from 1851 until 1857 and made the hitherto unknown Toba Batak language accessible. He considered it essential to deal intimately with the Bataks in order to learn their language. In so doing, he discovered a great many wrongs the government had either remained ignorant of or was indifferent to. Van der Tuuk did not fail to take to task the policies of the government and those of the Bible Society. He refused to consider linguistic problems as different and separate from a country's social and cultural conditions. From 1857 until 1868, he was back in the Netherlands for further study and to try to write down his material. Right away he got himself involved in all kinds of controversies, among them a scholarly quarrel he picked with the then very important linguist of Indonesian languages (especially Javanese), Taco Roorda of the Delft Academy. Van der Tuuk pursued him to the last, inspired by a motto he got from his admired Shakespeare: "Lay on, Macduff, and damned be him that first cries, 'Hold, enough!' " During those same years he became acquainted with Multatuli, becoming his critical admirer. He admired Multatuli's courage and independence and shared many of his opinions, but he was altogether too sober to be taken in by Multatuli's prophetic and messianic stance: "He wants to take Jesus' place but I do not think our times can accommodate a second Jesus; the first one is more than enough as it is" (from an undated letter written in 1888).

In 1868, Van der Tuuk went to the Indies again. From 1870 onwards he lived in Bali, somewhere in a village, living as a Balinese among the Balinese. It took him remarkably little time to learn the language, and he mastered it so well that one of Bali's princes remarked: "There is only one man on the entire island of Bali who knows and understands the Balinese language, and that man is Tuan Dertik [Mr. van der Tuuk]." Van der Tuuk began to compile a Kawi-Balinese dictionary which grew into a colossal, seemingly endless work. New information kept reaching him nearly every day. His dictionary never seemed to get finished ("such a mess of variants, enough to drive you mad; I am half crazy with misery," he wrote in August of 1888).

His strength greatly diminished during the final four or five years of his life. Like a sick tiger he had retreated to his bamboo house, growling and lashing out now and then at the shapes around him. He even attacked Multatuli when he was no longer living. "There is a great deal in his work that is simply unpalatable and written only to fill up a couple of pages and to line his purse. Now and then he is really full of shit" (in a letter from early 1888). Two years later he wrote: "I'm very disappointed in Multatuli. His notes are not worth reading and I am glad he is dead" (letter from March 28, 1890).

Still, Van der Tuuk had a lot in common with Multatuli. In the first place, he too wrote the way he was, although he was different. His handwriting, in contrast to Multatuli's, was terribly sloppy, his spelling extremely erratic and subjective, but what they did have in common was that they both used the spoken language as their model. Even more perhaps than from Multatuli, we get the immediate sensation of actually listening to Van der Tuuk as we read him, speaking excitedly, being angry, hopeless, bitter, or depressed. We seem to share every change of his mood. There is absolutely no distance between him and his language. In this respect we could say that Van der Tuuk went even further than Multatuli because he lacked the latter's reserve. Often Multatuli still betrays a certain degree of prudery. Not so Van der Tuuk. His totally uninhibited word choice was remarkable for a period of provincialism and puritanism. It also gave adequate expression to his contempt for the hypocritical morality of a nineteenth-century society stuck somewhere in a corner of Europe called Holland. "That crappy, uptight little country, where I felt put upon by the victims of Dutch gin and Dutch religion." He said that he considered it a blessing not to live there.

Van der Tuuk died in the night of August 16, 1894, in Surabaja's Military Hospital from the effects of dysentery and neglect suffered on Bali. His Balinese housekeeper, his *njai*, had stayed behind. He had also had to leave behind all those "trifles" he had nonetheless grown attached to, such as his dogs, his chickens, and his donkeys. Nearly a hundred letters and thousands of notes have been preserved. He once wrote to the secretary of the Bible Society that too much bile had begun to adhere to his pen. Indeed, there is much bile in his writings.

3   A. M. Courier dit Dubekart

In 1872, the publisher Van Dorp in Semarang published a peculiar book. Its title page informs us that it was "printed at the expense and responsibility of and published by the author." It was called *Facts of Brata-Yuda or Conditions in the Netherlands Indies (Feiten van Brata-Yoeda of Nederlandsch-Indische toestanden)*, and written by A. M. Courier dit Dubekart. He lived from 1839 to 1885. His book was nothing like the usual "pleasant diversion" which tried at the same time to convey some information about conditions in the Indies. Rather, it was meant to present the reader with nothing but straight facts, as the title of the work emphasizes. In fact, he tells us right off that he is not a writer, which is exactly what Multatuli did. Informing us of his dislike of writing, he then states that events had forced him to commit his facts to paper. His book, resembling a 700-page pamphlet, is actually a collection of letters to the editor of the *Surabaja Courant (Soerabaja-Courant)*. Its subjects range from shady dealings, corruption, and slander to suppression, the abuse of power, and outright assassination. The author had earlier fallen victim to an attempt to "bring to light these misdeeds in the name of justice," but was convicted of slander and sentenced to six months in jail. There he conceived of his book. He collected his newspaper articles, then added a few dealing with conditions in prison, and prefaced the lot with an autobiographical sketch. He certainly lived an eventful life, one rather characteristic of the romantic and extremely individualistic Courier dit Dubekart.

His conflict with society was total. Hindsight shows that nothing less could have been expected. Born in 1839 in Kapelle, he wanted to join the navy, as his father and his three brothers had done, because "even as a young lad I yearned to see foreign countries and peoples." The navy rejected him for poor eyesight. Following many quarrels at home, he took his chances by leaving for Australia to join the gold diggers. He was then sixteen years old. That existence proved too strenuous and hard for the still frail boy, and from there he ended up in Batavia, where he worked for a shipping company. It did not take him long to notice that European society in Batavia was characterized by "lots of bluff, impudence, nepotism, and spinelessness," and that in order to succeed "a flexible conscience" was required. Unable to maintain himself in this society, he departed for Java's interior, "compelled by irresistible forces." His boss in Batavia tried to restrain him but "my pigheadedness triumphed," he tells us. He headed for Kediri and Blitar in eastern Java and there he began his checkered career as an employee of a sugar refinery and tobacco plantation, supervisor and law clerk, shopkeeper, itinerant attorney, and so on. At the same time, his real conflicts began with his superiors, and with officials and other people. He clashed with society in the Indies, and society in a small outpost in the Indies clashed with him because he would not abide by its rules. Many were put off by his odd behavior and by his intimate relationships with the Javanese. What other European would dress up as a Javanese in order to live the life of a Javanese cart driver? And what European (his wife came from the island of Nias) would allow his children to grow up like "natives" without any schooling whatever, because he considered it worthless? His son, who later on became a planter, learned to read and write while tending water buffaloes.

He was at odds with everybody, and everybody was at odds with him. It seemed at times as if he was doomed to spend the rest of his life writing petitions, making public accusations, and demanding that justice be done, for that was the kind of man Courier dit Dubekart was. He wanted to inform the public about each and every thing, forgetting that not every detail was significant, and for that reason he often missed the mark. A book of 700 pages crammed with grievances, accusations, and proof simply does not work any longer.

More than once Courier dit Dubekart was compared to Multatuli, even before his book appeared. After Multatuli himself had mentioned *Facts of Brata Yuda* in volume four of his *Ideas,* no review failed to point out their similarity. The literary critic S. Kalff heard about Courier through Multatuli. In 1891, twenty years after the publication of *Facts,* he wrote a series of newspaper articles called "Multatuli and Brata-Yuda." The poet and critic Albert Verwey rediscovered Courier in 1919 without Kalff's intercession, apparently ignorant of the latter's articles, and called him "a younger contemporary of Multatuli."

A comparison with Multatuli would of course have been obvious, even if Multatuli had not written about Courier. Anyone reading *Facts* will be struck by ideas, phrases, and even a certain pathos reminiscent of Multatuli, as well as a similar source of inspiration and the same craving for martyrdom. The curious fact remains, however, that the character Brata Yuda informs us halfway through his book of never having read Multatuli. He even gets the name wrong and spells it Multatul*ie*. Not until August 1870, finally nearing the end of his work, does he inform us in a footnote of having at long last come across a copy of *Max Havelaar,* "just a few days ago." Half a year later, his preface contains numerous and unmistakable allusions to *Max Havelaar.* For example, Courier ironically states that he will *not* dedicate his book "to our honored and beloved king." He will also see to it that there are plenty of copies of his book available in the Netherlands. That way the king will be able to get himself a copy "in the event His Majesty should be interested in his overseas subjects."

Nineteenth-century literature is full of references to "conditions in the Indies," which are, or are considered to be, typical of its social make-up. It is impossible to be objective about these assertions, because we do not know how prevalent certain situations actually were. All we have to go on is what the literature of the time considered worth noting. What it did consider noteworthy were all sorts of

problems, *perkaras*, so-called, and the Indies seemed somehow ideally suited for *perkaras*. There is not a memoir that does not have its
particular *perkara*. It seems at times as if everybody in those days had
his or her private irritation. They were always writing about dismissal, about injustice, about injured feelings, and invariably their conflicts were related to some private pique or grievance. This is typical,
of course, of any small, heterogeneous, and very hierarchical society
such as European society in the Indies. A case in point is the Lebak affair, where personal ambition also played a part. Douwes Dekker was
not motivated solely by idealism, nor Brest van Kempen exclusively
by patriotism. Something similar applies to Courier dit Dubekart. If
one arranges the events in his *Facts of Brata-Yuda* chronologically,
one gets the distinct impression that purely personal and general motivations crisscross one another and overlap. Also, we get the impression that initially noble sentiments did not attain their full value until later, when they could be used to justify a certain course of action.
Regardless, Courier dit Dubekart's presence on the literary scene of
his time is refreshing.

The similarities with Multatuli are obvious but there remains one
important difference: Multatuli managed to elevate his private grievance to an accusation against injustice *generally*, whereas Courier dit
Dubekart ultimately never rose above being just another cause célèbre of the Indies. It may very well be that this difference is rooted in
their different abilities as writers.

4   Alexander Cohen

Once again it was Multatuli who, although much later, figured in
shaping a political and literary career. Apparently he inspired rebel-
liousness as well as a freely flowing pen. It would be difficult to say
which has been more important. In the first volume of his autobiography *In Revolt (In opstand)*, which did not appear until 1932, Alexander Cohen (1864–1963) talks about the unforgettable memories of his
youth. How, when his father told him to pray, he made believe by putting *Max Mavelaar* on top of his prayer book. He must have been sixteen or seventeen at the time. On September 1, 1882, just eighteen
years old, he enlisted in the colonial army and sailed for the Indies
with a sense of "enchantment," as he called it, which lasted the entire voyage out. "Farewell, my fatherland!"

A somber and joyless childhood had preceded this flight from the
parental home in Leeuwarden, for it would be hard to call it anything
other than a flight. When he was nine, his mother died of tuberculo-

sis, "consumption" in those days, "a quiet, beautiful, gentle, and dear woman." Alexander Cohen can only remember her as sickly, and the only image he retained of her was the one of her on her deathbed. This left just his father, an orthodox Jew and a figure he struggled with, "a hard man, full of systems and principles. Everything that went wrong, the misery at home, it all had its cause in his ideas and his misapprehensions about education." He wanted his children to grow up to become useful members of society. For that reason he took away their freedom, forbade all games and toys, and held back their pocket money. As far as Alexander Cohen's brothers were concerned, the system worked. They became "decent through and through," he tells us. But it made him into a "rebel and nonconformist." He hated his father and, because of him, hated any authoritarian system whatsoever. He became and was to remain, in his own image, "an unmanageable, wild animal leaping up against the bars of his cage, an animal that lashed out and bit people." Punishment, such as beatings, "going to bed without supper, or a diet of rye bread and water," proved pointless. Whatever he did not receive he stole. He ran away, twice even, but he was caught and returned. Increasingly it became a man-to-man struggle. There were, however, a few bright moments, such as the atmosphere during the Passover Seder. Most of all, he fondly remembered a few individuals, such as the cantor of the Leeuwarden synagogue who never failed to stroke him over the head when it was his turn to say kaddish. He especially remembered the man's voice, "a wonderful voice which exulted, complained, and cried all according to the occasion." There was also his mother's family from Rotterdam, especially her youngest sister, Tante Netje. "Charming, gracious Tante Netje!" She was "a bright spirit who was essentially melancholic but a true goddess," who always took him under her protection. He was extremely sensitive to any friendly gesture. She too died young, and had sensed her own early death. In a letter to her sister she wrote: "You'll be hearing from me on only two more occasions, upon my lying-in, and upon my death."

Following the events described so far, Cohen's decision "to go as a soldier" to the Indies seems anticlimactic. He did not rebel at the idea but welcomed it with a sense of relief. In leaving Holland, he must have thought he would leave the past behind as well, but the past was to catch up with him everywhere. His hard youth had left him permanently rebellious, recalcitrant, and aggressive.

While on board ship, things went reasonably well, as they did during the first few weeks as an army clerk, but then he fell seriously ill. He was well again after several months' care in a clinic at Sindanglaja. He was then to be sent into the jungle and welcomed the prospect:

"Right in the middle of the jungle? So much the better! The wilder and more rugged the landscape, the better I'll like it." Before he went, however, he had a run-in with his superiors. His first few months on Sumatra, in Lahat, were pleasant enough, for that matter, "pure, passive joy," but then the trouble started with an insignificant incident about his not saluting properly. "It was a pathetic little incident," he tells us, "but its consequences gradually dragged me down in a whirling maelstrom of unpleasant mishaps. Not that I am now complaining about these things, or ever did; I most certainly do not regret them. After all, everything on earth has its price. And no price is too high for those rare and precious commodities called self-respect and independence of mind."

The price he paid was an army record "with more black marks than any in the entire East Indies army." In Palembang, he was court-martialed to six months of military detention, and sentenced to serve one year, then another, for having thrice committed "insubordination involving the use of words." The third insubordination involved an incident where his captain had pronounced as "excellent" the stinking soup and rotten meat the men were about to be fed. Cohen yelled at him "Oh, come off it, how on earth could somebody like you pretend to have any taste left at all? You've still got the taste of gin in your mouth!"

He served his sentence of two and a half years in the well-known prison of Fort Pontjol in Semarang. Here all sorts of punishments rained down on him, such as solitary detention, and corporal punishments such as being beaten with rattan. Flogging was the least harsh of them. But he made friends he was to remember as fondly as he did the cantor of his youth. He liked them because they were human beings and humane, and not representatives of an abstract system. One of these friends, on leaving Pontjol, gave him his copy of *Max Havelaar.*

On Christmas Day 1886, he had served his sentence and because they considered him "totally unmanageable," he was sent back to Holland. Following these hard times, he returned to Leeuwarden only to hear his father tell him: "The best thing you could do is to leave as soon as possible." In Amsterdam he got a job proofreading for *Justice for All,* Domela Nieuwenhuis's paper. Nieuwenhuis was in prison at the time but the two met shortly thereafter. A few weeks later, as King William III rode past in his coach through The Hague, Cohen shouted: "Down with the Gorilla King! Long live socialism, long live Domela Nieuwenhuis!" He had the great misfortune of doing so with a plainclothes policeman standing right next to him. In fact, Cohen did not consider it altogether unfortunate, because during the legal proceedings that followed, he tells us, he got the opportunity to speak out on a number of things. For one, his trial gave him the opportunity to make greater publicity for Roorda van Eysinga's lampoon *The Gorilla King.* For another, he could make direct fun of the king and the judicial system too. His own defense during the trial was published as recently as 1967 as *One, Two, Three, String the Reds up in a Tree! (Hop, hop, hop, hangt de socialisten op).* At the time, this sarcastic defense attained great popularity, having been published in its entirety in *Justice for All,* while parts of it appeared in a great many dailies. All this he owed, he said, to "the great naiveté of those in power." Even so, he was once again sentenced to six months in prison.

After getting himself involved in the Socialist movement, he converted to anarchism, only to become a monarchist later on, but through it all he remained a "reactionary" in his own words, that is to say, someone "opposing nearly everything." When he was ninety-nine years old, Alexander Cohen died in Toulon, France, in fairly dismal circumstances. He longed for death, he wrote one of his friends, especially after his wife's death in 1959. Only once, in 1905, did he go back to the Indies. He went at the request of the French government to study medical facilities for the native population and stopped by at Fort Pontjol. His book *From Anarchist to Monarchist (Van anarchist tot monarchist)* contains an account of that trip. A manuscript copy of his report in French is still extant and will eventually find its way into the Literary Museum in The Hague.

Cohen's autobiographical works (*In Revolt,* 1931 and *From Anarchist to Monarchist,* 1936) are fascinating. His writing is an excellent, uncluttered Dutch, lacking any cant or bombast. His humor, irony, and sarcasm are sufficiently effective to make his autobiography a model of written memoirs, especially because most of them run afoul of self-aggrandizement. His irony and his making fun of himself make for a particularly effective antidote against this. Cohen added the following epigraph by Prudhon to his *From Anarchist to Monarchist:* "Irony and true liberty deliver me from the ambition of power, from the servitude to factions, from respect for routine, from pedantic science . . . and from *adoring myself.*"

Especially when comparing Cohen's memoirs with those of Domela Nieuwenhuis (*From Christian to Anarchist*), one realizes what good writing can be like and how superior Cohen's is.

We know that Cohen read Multatuli as a youth, and also that Multatuli meant a great deal to him. In his *Remarks from a Reactionary (Uitingen van een reactionnair)* Cohen refers to Multatuli on several occasions. One of these is: "The free man I have remained up to now owes his ideological liberation to Multatuli." He also translated some of Multatuli's work for the *Mercure de France* while he was, once again, in prison. It is difficult to assess Multatuli's stylistic influence on Alexander Cohen. For one thing, he himself never referred to it, but once put a question mark next to a critical statement which asserted that he wrote with "Multatulian fervor." Cohen had as much reason to claim what Multatuli said about himself: "I am my style."

VI
P. A. Daum

P. A. Daum (1850–1898) long ago ceased being unknown in Dutch literature. A number of his novels, all of which he wrote under the name of Maurits, have been reprinted and praised by the critics, and he has assumed his place in literary histories and textbooks. In the Indies of the eighties and nineties, he was a well-known and popular figure, especially as the editor of *The Indies Fatherland (Het Indisch Vaderland)* and the *Batavian News (Bataviaasch Nieuwsblad)* later on. Although he was anything but a forgotten author in his own time, he gradually got pushed aside by newer literary currents. Indeed, some people such as the columnist Henri Borel, writing for *The Fatherland*, and the poet Jan Prins continued to support him despite the adverse tide, but the new vogue drowned out their voices. Then, in 1931, Brom's *Java in Our Art (Java in onze kunst)* appeared. However much one may disagree with Brom's interpretations, the fact remains that he recognized Daum's qualities, devoting an entire chapter to him. The great rediscovery became a fact shortly thereafter when the literary magazine *Forum* came out in support of Daum. This created a snowball effect, which was of course checked by the war but which regained its momentum shortly thereafter.

In his review of *Java in Our Art*, which appeared in *The Guide (De Gids)* of 1933, Du Perron agreed with Brom's assessment of Daum. In addition, he ranked Daum with the novelist Willem Elsschot (1882–1960) for his gift of telling a story clearly and effortlessly. Du Perron especially praised Daum's similar "disenchanted but unflagging curiosity." It should come as no surprise that writers such as Du Perron and Ter Braak would be attracted to the intensive and skeptical interest Daum took in life around him and to his obvious dislike of pompous or fancy writing. Reading Du Perron or Ter Braak, one notices right away why they appreciated Daum's particular talent.

At the same time, they were prepared to take in the bargain the inevitable aspects of such a talent, Daum's sloppiness and much that smacked of serialization. The moment we compare Daum, or Maurits if one prefers, to his predecessors, his distinguishing characteristics become clear. These are marked by his style, his use of dialogue, his portrayal of characters, and his relationship to both literature and reality. It was clear that Daum aimed for something different and for something new. Shortly before he started writing *From Sugar into Tobacco (Uit de suiker in de tabak)*, a sort of "from the fat into the fire" story, which was to appear as a serial, he wrote a long article in his newspaper of September 15, 1883, dealing with "Indies novels." His strategy was one he had used before and was to use afterwards. He starts his article by launching an attack on Indies novel writing and he pronounces it "god-awful." He then enumerates his objections and proceeds to outline the "new approach." "Nobody can see better than I the shortcomings of this conventional genre, which is marked by the most incredible dilettantism," he writes, "because some ten years ago I cranked out nothing but cheap little romances myself." Those little romances, which caused Daum to blush by his own admission, are all listed in his bibliography in the September 1939 issue of *Greater Netherlands (Groot Nederland)*. They are indeed "terribly awful," written in a style best described as being in a "romantic rut." They also have exactly the same shortcomings Daum was to criticize in 1883. His indictment of these "Indies novels" in fact marks his coming to terms with himself and not just with literature.

After his first couple of years in the Indies he was a changed man. "Life in the Indies is so curiously less restrained," again in Daum's own words, and it meant a practical existence which had "worn off some of his idealism," and changed him into someone prepared to go through life "soberly, and with both eyes wide open." This sobriety and realistic turn of mind were to remain characteristic of him. Even so, the interaction between sobriety and his sensitivity, to which everyone attests, gave Daum a lively personality. He once wrote "I hope I am not a sentimental person," and he was not. Still, he could be moved easily, as his daughter tells us, but his distrust of any show of feeling protected him from sentimentality. In his novels too, one observes time and again this inclination to ward off emotion by keeping an even tone of voice while stressing story line, facts, and events.

Daum is admittedly not free of banality, not because he was a banal person but rather because of his dislike of the abstract and the profound. Whenever he expresses himself too carelessly or fails to pay sufficient attention to the use of words, we can trace the cause to his stated aversion to "word preening" and "resounding phraseology." His errors and shortcomings, in other words, stem from his virtues. His chief virtue as a writer is that he never strains. He possessed emotions and sensitivity aplenty but delivered himself of these with the least possible emphasis and invariably with a touch of irony. For precisely that reason he manages on a number of occasions to create moving suspense, as in his description of Geber's suicide in *Ups and Downs*, or in Abu Bakar's death in the novel of the same name. He does the same in *Done In (Nummer elf)*, which in its seemingly nonchalant ending suggests a great Indies tragedy: "Poor Lena got a fine, polished slab of marble on her grave with a touching inscription on it. Only now and then a visitor to the cemetery would point out to another that there lay yet another lady who had been 'done in.' Soon everything was forgotten, however. In the Indies the trees are always green."

Daum had received a traditional Catholic upbringing. While quite young he had married a Catholic girl. The waning of his religious belief was accelerated in the Indies. When in 1883 he headed his own paper, *The Indies Fatherland*, he openly declared his atheism in a long article, dated February 15 of the same year. This editorial deals mercilessly with the faith of his youth, which is now dead to him. He ridicules the Eucharist, talks about the "fanatical faith of millions," and the "childish notion of immortality." At the same time, he realized the need to erect a new philosophy "on the ashes of a vain, self-important, and selfish faith." He is aiming to build "a rational system" in the face of heavy opposition from tradition and prejudice. For the time being, all he can do is to delineate an area, using such points of reference as existence, reality, empirical history, and natural law "which causes birth, growth, development, and decline." Death, not eternity, follows. One of his characters in his novel *Indies People in Holland (Indische menschen in Holland)* comes face to face with death. Daum writes about him: "He was not concerned with any after life. He thought he would dissolve into *nothingness* when he died. He would live on only through his descendants, returning himself to dust and ashes. Looking at it that way, it did not frighten him to think of death." This reflection no doubt contains a great deal of Daum's own expectations.

As a journalist, he began to favor social conditions that were "adjusted to the demands of reality." Averse to imaginary and general conditions, he accepted the world for what it was. Espousing a kind of social pragmatism, therefore, he added: "There is no other possible way of making things better. After all, what have all those high-

minded phrases and slogans people in Holland are so fond of ever resulted in? In nothing, my friends, nothing at all." He formulated his
political creed in much the same way as he had his personal religion,
and directed it against the sentimental aspects of colonial policies: "I
simply refuse to tell 'Little Nell' stories, when in fact I take pen in
hand in order to describe the misery that afflicts an *entire* population
as a result of a repressive and pathetic government."

As a writer too he felt the need at about the same time to state his
point of view. As we have seen, he did so by repudiating his literary
past in order to avow his conversion to *realism* and to *naturalism*. His
philosophy is all of a piece and based on the premise that a firm grasp
on reality is the basis for all science, religion, and art. In this conviction, Daum reveals himself a typical product of his time. Life in the
Indies also contributed to his development in that its radically different social structure and cultural pattern had made an entirely different man out of him.

In his article dealing with "Indies novels," Daum sums up his
manifold grievances as follows. Despite every attempt to depict life
in the Indies, authors have not even begun to approximate its reality.
In the first place, their dialogue is conventional, sometimes childish-
ly stilted, or altogether so wooden as to have nothing in common
with natural conversation. Their portrayal of people in the Indies is
equally lacking in verisimilitude: "Whoever has lived in the Indies
and is familiar with the way people live, with the habits and speech
patterns of officials and private citizens, whether full-blood European
or native born, whether from the interior or from the city, that person
will spot right away everything that is wrong with their sketches."
Because every novel written in the Indies had to appeal largely to a
Dutch readership in Holland, everything that might have been typical or true in it was sacrificed to the tastes and wishes of people doting
on literature back in the Netherlands, and we know altogether too
well what these tastes were like around 1880. "It is really a pity,"
Daum says, "to look, for example, at the attempt to superimpose on a
Dutch novel a fat, native lady, speaking something resembling translated Malay, for authenticity's sake." His principal objection, however, is that "people are portrayed as being either exclusively benign
or totally rotten. Only rarely does European literature introduce a
character which is recognizably human as a composite of the qualities of good and evil." Daum's objection sounds like an echo of Zola's
prescription: "And therefore there are more abstract characters, more
of the absolute, but not real people." The similarity is no mere coincidence, for Daum possessed a fine set of Zola's complete works,
which, he assures us, he had read without exception.

Zola, as we know, did exert a great deal of influence on most of the younger authors of the 1880s. Even though the majority of them were gradually to drift away from naturalism, all of them continued to remember Zola as the master of their youth "without whose teaching," Couperus writes, "we never would have seen and known what life really is, stripped of its woolly wraps and with all the romantic sentiments of our parents and grandparents disdainfully pushed aside." On Daum too, Zola must have had a purifying and fulfilling effect, and following the changes in his total personality, his literary perspectives changed radically also.

Zola probably never had the faintest suspicion that a Dutch journalist out in the hot Indies was working up a sweat trying to refute before his newspaper audience the general notion that naturalism was "a display of filth." Daum was to come to Zola's defense time and again, and in each instance he would stress the need for the "new direction." He wrote about *Germinal*, about *Le Rêve*, *La Terre*, *Le Docteur Pascal*, and other works, and sometimes he himself translated selections of Zola and ran them serially in his newspaper.

Curiously enough, Daum's summary of naturalism nowhere mentions Zola's classification of facts, a method adapted from his study of biology and physiology, and the very method that strikes us today as characteristic of naturalism. Daum probably does not refer to it because he did not consider those scientific methods of writing novels essential to naturalism. Most likely he considered its characteristic to be its ability to render reality as it manifested itself, a natural phenomenon without preconceptions or moral tendencies. It was a view which might have qualified sooner as "realism." Although this certainly does not give the impression of following Zola's prescription of collecting "documents humains," Daum nevertheless did precisely that. For example, *The Indies Fatherland* informed its readership that a promised novel dealing with Indonesian-Chinese relationships was not forthcoming because Daum had been unable to gather enough information. Daum seems to have been in the habit of writing preliminary studies but there are several reasons why it seems unlikely that he did so in Zola's systematic and "scientific" fashion. For one thing, Daum's criticism nowhere refers to a "scientific goal" or anything like it.

His easy (sometimes too easy) manner of writing also betrays the lack of any specific construction. A contemporary critic of Daum especially admired the true amateur in him, "not an author who wields the pen to make a living," and his absence of literary dogma. Daum himself regarded his writing of serialized novels as secondary. He was fond of saying that he had taken up writing them in order to get inexpensive copy for his paper. Although we have to take this with a grain of salt (for Daum did have artistic pride in sufficient measure), it is typical nevertheless. So is the well-known anecdote that Daum did not start writing his serials until his typesetters began clamoring for copy, and that he did so straddling his work table. Many of these stories originated with him, and his family, seeing through the whole charade, called it "Papa's flirtation with his talent." This particular method of writing was an exception, to be sure, but it and several other remarks prove that he was devoid of the reverence for his own writing so indispensable to other writers. He himself realized that his lack compelled him to write what he called "unfettered novels." His sense of journalistic self-preservation, or something like it, made him persist in this particular mode of writing because he felt that his serials would have been much less readable if he had written them any other way.

By talking with plantation owners, and on account of his general familiarity with their world, Daum was able to depict people and circumstances in his first novel in such a way that they struck one as very familiar. Although the book has some soggy patches, it does give the impression that its entire perspective is that of Zola's "sense of reality." A thorough knowledge of people and situations in the Indies was fundamental to Daum's novels. His interests and his powers of observation, combined with his editorship of an important Indies newspaper, qualified him better than most. He drew from life, so faithfully, in fact, that his preface to the second printing of his book had to state emphatically that any similarity to living persons was purely coincidental. Even so, all his attempts to mislead his readers through vague descriptions and fictitious names and such backfired. Indies society proved too small and too keen on gossip to be fooled, and several of Daum's characters could be identified, if erroneously at times. Although the reading public could make mistakes, Daum on the other hand could make his portraits unmistakably lifelike. The amorous Mrs. de Bas, for example, a seeming caricature in his *From Sugar into Tobacco*, was in fact a character very much drawn from life.

The promotion in 1884 of the current secretary-general to councilor of the Indies was sharply criticized by Daum in a long editorial: "No doubt he only rose to the top because he was altogether lacking in substance," he commented, using the words of Multatuli. Shortly thereafter, his *How He Became Councilor of the Indies (Hoe hij Raad van Indië werd)* began to appear in serialized form. Not surprisingly, its main character, the mediocre Comptroller Kees van den Broek who makes it to councilor, was recognized by many.

Abu Bakar has been called an improbable tale but actually this book is largely based on the biography of a real person. Daum knew "Abu Bakar" very well. He often went to visit him in the native village, where he listened to all kinds of details of his marvelous life which he then either jotted down or remembered in order to use later on for his novel.

Some of his material for *Ups and Downs* Daum derived from the unwritten history of the Pamanukan and Tjiasem estates, an area so extensive it nearly comprised a country within a country. In 1872, the *tuan tanah* (lord of the land) Pieter William Hofland died on his estate Tenger Agung, known for its splendid parties. Hofland himself was known for liberally throwing dimes from his carriage along the road from Batavia to Subang beyond the ferry crossing of the Tjitarum river. When Daum's book appeared, there were still plenty of people alive who recognized Hofland in the character of Uhlstra. Fewer still had any trouble recognizing that Henri could be none other than the younger Hofland. He was like the character in *Ups and Downs*, who passed himself off as a Javanese prince and who could indeed afford to live like one. However, much wealth makes wit waver, and the Depression of 1885 did the rest. The heavy mortgage on the estate was foreclosed and the land came under the control of the bank. This started the decline of the once fabulously wealthy Hofland family, a decline that steadily gained momentum until well into the twentieth century. By then, the family had largely lost its social position, some of its members having ended up living in the native villages.

Daum did not finish this serialized novel until 1890, and he could not possibly have been familiar with this total decline of the family's fortunes. For that reason, the second part of his novel evidences a curious prescience, which to somebody who knew the Indies as well as he did may not have been too difficult. In addition, *Ups and Downs* chronicles not just the history of one family but that of a combination of several Indies lives. For that reason, the reader thinks himself involuntarily transported to one of those enormous Buitenzorg estates or immense *besarans* (manors). We know enough to understand Daum's method of writing, which his daughter confirmed when she wrote "whatever he encountered he combined, and his fantasy did the rest."

Daum and his wife often visited the kind of old-fashioned sugar factory or tobacco plantation described in *From Sugar into Tobacco*. For example, the sort of Indies party lasting several days, which we find described in *Ups and Downs*, Daum knew from his stays on the estate of the well-known Ament family. Similarly, Ketjil's trip in *Black Magic (Goena-Goena)* on horseback and in palanquin to the southern coast of Java to obtain the sea cow's tears was a trip Daum himself had made and reported in his paper. He did indeed work from life.

Daum learned a great deal from Zola but he still went his own way in writing his novels which, as noted earlier, he wrote under the pseudonym of Maurits. There were some things Daum's writing lacked, and had to be lacking in, if indeed he wanted his serials to be read. He could not afford to clutter his writing with detail or to keep a slow and frequently interrupted pace, creating a special atmosphere. Writing in serialized form kept him from the temptation to use "word painting," which is the original sin of all Dutch prose writers, stemming from their basic ignorance of the difference between writing and painting. The rare instance when Daum did indulge in anything resembling a "private view," the sort of thing poets of the Eighties Movement had a penchant for, may be due to his French example.

We know for a fact that Daum hated "word painting" because his newspaper articles tell us so. Far removed as he was from the literary scene in Holland, Daum never believed that naturalism should lead to artistic expansiveness. All he wanted to do was sketch "reality" and "life" without having to be preoccupied with stylistics or morality.

Daum was first and foremost a storyteller, deriving his story from the world around him and writing it down without bothering about any style whatever. And when Daum gets going, we listen because his story has momentum without ever giving the impression of being a finished puzzle, as is all too often the case with the lesser naturalistic writers. Daum too has his shortcomings, to be sure, quite a few in fact, but they are of a different kind and do not interfere with the quality of his writing. To this very day, his novels have preserved their liveliness and spontaneity despite some old-fashioned words and phrases. For that reason Daum can be republished today without any editing or excision. If we were to reprint a true representative of the Eighties Movement such as Netscher, for example, then we would realize how dated such a text has become, principally on account of a definite and set style.

The discovery that Daum's novels were nothing other than serials bound together—none too difficult because Daum did not even bother to smooth over the transitions—once tempted a critic to try to make a distinction between the novelist and the writer of stories in serial form. He declared Daum to be a writer of serials, and Daum even shows the defects, but there is obviously more to him. Only after first recognizing his qualities can we discuss his shortcomings, which indeed stem in part from his use of the serial format. It is amazing that Daum still had enough drive, time, and vitality left on top of his normal workload to write down his "stories," as he called them, and it is especially amazing how he managed, up to a point at least, to preserve his talent in the process. Up to a point, because it is obvious that Daum, by necessity perhaps, could act irresponsibly toward his own work, something he felt he could permit himself as long as he called himself an amateur novelist.

When reading Daum, we invariably sense that he was racing against the clock when he wrote, and that he never bothered to work out his story on paper beforehand. He collected his facts and only conceived of the broad outlines of the story. Only later would he work things out, while writing or dictating it to one of his children. Zaalberg, his assistant editor and later successor, has this to say: "It was announced beforehand in the paper when the serialized publication of *Ups and Downs* was to begin. On the day its first installment was to appear, Daum came to the office a little later than usual. Some current business was taken care of first, it was getting close to noon, and there still wasn't any copy to start our serial with. When I reminded him of it, it came out that he had forgotten all about the date. Only then did he start and write the first installment, just enough for the edition of that day. And that is how the book progressed on a day-to-day basis without any noticeable hiatus," Zaalberg continues, "the whole thing already completely worked out in his mind." This may well be true for *Ups and Downs*, at least for its first part, but the second volume and other books do not give that impression. There it seems as if the internal planning had been incomplete, and as if Daum had quite lost himself after having been surprised by his paper's deadline. There are stretches of superficiality and chapters devoid of feeling, which merely coast along on a certain flair. It can only be partly true what a contemporary critic said, that Daum wrote for the joy of it. To be sure, there must have been times when wielding the pen gave him intense pleasure but times also when he must have written with unconquerable indifference and revulsion. That is why it could happen that Daum's excellent first volume of *Ups and Downs* had such a poor sequel. Without any embarrassment or qualm he also concocted the very recipe of virtue and evil personified he had earlier reviled. His otherwise realistic dialogue becomes stagey, rigid, and clichélike, while a conventional style of writing reasserts itself.

All this is counterbalanced by many pages where he clearly gave his all, as they say, without worrying the language, which then seemingly ceases to exist altogether, making room for "just the action itself." Unwittingly transported by this action, it is as if we become part of these Indies lives, as if these characters come alive again, dwelling in their own world. No matter what his faults, Daum always knew what he was talking about. This makes him the historian par excellence of "tempo dulu," a period so drastically different from anything happening in Holland, which for that reason brought into being radically different people. He was not a psychologist but he could penetrate the minds and hearts of people in the Indies; without any training in sociology, he could nevertheless conjure up and call to mind a society utterly authentic in all its ramifications. He once wrote that he wanted to go through life with both eyes open. Maybe this explains the position his narrator occupies in his novels, as well as his own remarkable powers of observation. His books contain unforgettable characters and scenes, such as the Eurasian woman Roos or the skinny and sparse Dutch-born Lugtens, forever looking "for a fourth hand at bridge." Most memorable is his funeral, where the cortège consists of a single rented carriage wherein his housekeeper sits holding a small basket of flowers. This is all the more touching because it reveals what is not revealed anywhere else in the story, his utter desolation as a European in the Indies. The loyalty of his *njai* is the only thing of value left from a bankrupt existence.

Daum has the ability to formulate his observations in striking ways. Sometimes he uses a brief dialogue to explain a situation, then again a single remark can suffice to conjure up an entire world. For example, the young Comptroller Kees van den Broek from *How He Became Councilor of the Indies* has died. He is going to be buried, and Daum writes: "The funeral certainly deserved to be called stately. Two golden parasols, four top hats, and three pointed, gold-braided collars—a junior official could really not ask for more on such an occasion. Careful statistics computed by all ladies present reveal the total number of carriages following the coffin to have been forty-two, mostly privately owned; six of these were broughams." It is hard to be more effectively devastating than that. Daum was capable of biting mockery but never without a smile. He had a sharp eye for spotting foolishness in the official hierarchy, which, as in this case, could take on grotesque and lugubrious forms. He was capable of criticizing the backwaters in the Indies, notorious for their gossip, superficiality, and boredom, but when he asked himself if he were really annoyed by it all, his answer had to be "Oh, not really."

Daum can also create an atmosphere with a minimum of means. His atmosphere, however, does not include nuances, such as the gradations from light to dark or from green to gray, for example. He presents us rather with clear and translucent images altogether lacking in haze or indistinction. In that sense, they could be considered utterly without atmosphere, but anyone raised in the Indies or anyone who can sense what the past must have been like and who knows life in the Indies from stories, books, photographs, and pictures relives all this on reading Daum. The numerous visits, the ever-recurring house parties with dancing and card playing (playing omber without end), which all served to break the monotony of everyday life, all these things Daum describes as if one were physically present. He totally captures those immense houses in the Indies with their gigantic rooms and verandas, their marble floors and high, white walls, and especially the indefinable sense of space these evoked. One can simply see and smell the kind of little room where "Mama Tjang' lies dying in *Ups and Downs.*

Rarely does Daum describe nature. His landscapes are largely populated by people and things such as houses, gardens, a dusty road, but always with people present. Sometimes there is a tropical night devoid of people, or an avenue lined with tamarind trees at evening, rice fields vibrating with heat, or nature desiccated in the rainless, eastern monsoon season, but little more. Literally every page of his is otherwise crowded with people placed against the backdrop of Indies society, which not only determines their thinking and their behavior but their fate as well. The tragedy of the Ulhstra family, a fabulously wealthy family of plantation owners from western Java in *Ups and Downs,* is a typical Indies drama replete with the forces that hasten its decline.

Toward the end of volume one of *Ups and Downs,* Daum gives us the following social comment on life in the Indies: "Meanwhile, Indies society, ever in flux, changed; some people left with fortunes; others came to try and make theirs; from the world of the officials the sick went away and the healthy came in; the endless replacing of the retiring by newcomers continued. Not too many stayed on; the unlucky and the bad ones slid down the social scale, ending up in the native townships and slums, while the 'not exactly fortunate' stayed put at a certain level, unable to go up, and unwilling to go down." The picture he paints is quite different from the legendary Indies where fortunes were made. Apart from the fabulous careers, which were as conspicuous as they were rare, there was also a great deal of decay and ruin in the Indies. Weeds, walls green with mildew, floors powdery with age, weathered glass, and the figure of a disillusioned, cynical person left behind somewhere, forgotten by her or his fellow Europeans. It is precisely this kind of desolate Indies decay that obsesses Daum. Then too he is at his best as a writer, as when he writes about the slow decline of Van Brakel who gradually slides down toward the periphery of European society in *H. van Brakel, Engineer (H. van Brakel, Ing. B.O.W.).* Similarly, when he portrays the desolation of one as disillusioned as James van Tuyll, the chief character of Daum's first novel, *From Sugar into Tobacco,* who stays behind somewhere all alone on an isolated plantation, left with the bitter aftertaste of a failed life, and who can yet find the following, fitting words to describe his predicament:

Years have passed now. The two initially small enterprises have expanded and are now yielding profits. When our tobacco firm was totally ruined, my income from it also stopped. On the other hand, I was given the job to supervise things, which I did well enough, and that was ample compensation right there. As long as you succeed, people are not too down on you! I still continue to send Helen what she has coming to her every three months. I still think of her with a resigned sadness. She never gives me a sign of life, but then, neither do I. I'm quite alone here; my nearest neighbors live quite some distance away, and I live a lonely sort of life. Don't get into town much. At first my neighbors would drop by once in a while; they're about twenty miles away, but because I never returned their visits they stayed away and stopped inviting me to their house parties. I ride out in the morning and come home at night, sometimes not until the next day. I do get by, but I am no longer thinking of making a fortune. If I had stayed in the sugar business, then of course no number of creditors could have prevented my becoming a millionaire. My chance to make a fortune died the moment I got into the tobacco business. May it rest in peace. I really lack the desire and vitality to try and play at Lazarus now. Sometimes, in the afternoon, when I'm drinking tea and looking down from the front veranda over those endless fields that are now being worked, the feeling of desolation gets to me and it is then I realize how little it takes to make a life aimless.

VII
The Indies World of Couperus

Talking with André de Ridder in 1916, Couperus is supposed to have said: "I can't claim any Indonesian blood in my family but there is an Indies tradition. . . ." What are we to think of the first part of his remark, or how are we to understand it? Because Indonesian blood did run in the family, and Couperus must have known that. All one needs to do is check in the genealogical magazine *The Netherlands Lion (De Nederlandsche Leeuw)* of 1908 to see that his nieces were Eurasian girls with an Indonesian mother. He introduces them in his work, in fact. Couperus's remark to De Ridder is all the more curious because Couperus never felt the need to deny the existence of his Indies blood. On the contrary, he was just the man who would have welcomed a few drops of the "exotic." In his books, he smiles at the embarrassment of other members of his family such as Aunt Ruijvenaar or Aunt Floor when they begin to talk about the family. He himself could only have found them picturesque. Much more important than his ancestry, however, is his family's Indies tradition. As he said in his *Collected Works (Verzameld Werk*, 12:337): "I was a child born in Holland but within the Indies tradition in mind and spirit." That tradition was that of the class of higher officials in the Indies. The family belonged to the top layer of Indies society for whom it was customary to go and live in Holland after a career in the Indies, and Holland meant invariably The Hague. There, the members of this extensive family would come together again and be united. They lived not as a typical family of The Hague but as an Indies coterie, keeping the Indies constantly in the background because their interests continued to lie there. They lived Indonesian style, as one big happy family, partly because they felt themselves to be different, partly because they were estranged, as they say, but also because Dutch society excluded them. Literature is full of the often repeated complaint of Indies people on furlough and pensioners in Holland that they bore some mark, some Indonesian *tjap* or brand, that made them stand out. As Creusesol put it: "Join us, Indies man . . . come live *with* us, *among* us if you like, but *part* of us you'll never be" (*Holland Bound* [*Naar Holland*, p. 224]). Just how these Indies people, the officials, the officers, the planters, and especially those married to women of Indonesian blood sometimes continued to live in The Hague we can read in Daum's *Indies People in Holland (Indische menschen in Holland)*. The longer they stayed in Holland, the more they adapted, especially if they belonged to society. However, books such as Couperus's *The Books of the Small Souls* (*De boeken der kleine zielen,* 1901–1903) and *Of Old People and the Things that Pass* (*Van oude menschen, de dingen die voorbijgaan,* 1906) show us to what extent family life of the higher Indies officials in The Hague retained the patrimonial charcteristics so typical of an Indies way of life. The belief in fate as the great compelling force in life Couperus no doubt derived from the "philosophy" of the period. However, this belief also ties in very well with a culture that tried either to invoke or ward off the constant machinations of fate through prayers, charms, and sacrifices.

It has been said, and for good reason, that Couperus dissociated himself from his family in writing his great novels set in The Hague. This is only partially true. In the first place, it is questionable whether Couperus used just his own family as a model, and we have to consider further Couperus's personal ambivalence as an artistic spectator. Despite having taken some distance from them, he remained one of the family who never severed his ties. He was even an exemplary member of his clan, and behaved "like a dear," to use a typical Indies expression, according to his family. The author Beb Vuyk considered the families described in Couperus's novels set in The Hague "to have more in common with the Indies than with The Hague." "Despite the different background of Hague houses and gray skies," she wrote, "his family portraits retain the pattern of the Indies." And rightly so, we should add, for Couperus himself stresses the relationship of the non-Dutch aspects of his personality with his Indies descent and tradition: "I consider myself to be warmer, sunnier, and more Eastern than my compatriots in Holland are . . . the real Dutch part of me, I'm afraid, is a little taken aback by this."

"I was nine years old," Couperus wrote, "when I, born in Holland, left for the Indies." He was the youngest of a large family, the "last child in a long line," his sister tells us. His two oldest brothers had passed the higher civil-service examinations in Delft, which meant they were eligible for government jobs in the Indies. The father, a councilor of the Superior Court who had already retired a few years earlier, decided to return to the Indies with the entire family. They established themselves in Batavia, now Djakarta, and moved into a comfortable house facing the city's great central square. The five years during which the family lived there certainly influenced young Couperus greatly. He felt much happier there than he had in Holland. For one, he found it light and sunny. "When I was small," writes Couperus, "I rejoiced in the fact that the sun shone, for the sun had been something odd and hidden, back in Holland, even in summer. This permanent sunshine was something divine. A child is never bothered by the heat and I worshipped the sun. It was a god to me. The sun in that blue sky struck me as God Himself, certainly as His eye."

But Couperus did miss out on all those things that are usually associated with a youth spent in the Indies, such as the familiarity with ghosts and spirits. For that his parents were too European and he had probably come too late. His memoirs mention his Dutch nurse Caroline, but he was never cared for by a native Indonesian woman. This would have opened an entirely different world to him, as in the case of so many children born and raised in the Indies. For that reason, a great deal of magic, to which he certainly would have been most receptive, forever eluded him. Later on, when he lived in Italy, he realized what he had missed as a child in the Indies: "Now that I am in love with Italy, I know that however much the sun in the Indies delighted me, that although the Indies restored the South to me from which I had been mysteriously banished, I had all along been pining in the Indies for the Latin South. . . . The Indies did not have the memory of temples and gods, of palaces and endless roads lined with sepulchers, of arenas, processions, and celebrations. . . ." What would Couperus have said, however, if he had not spent five years living just in Batavia, a colonial center with obvious Western pretensions, but had instead spent those years somewhere in the Javanese principalities containing a thousand memories of Hindu-Javanese history, of old Javanese legends, of temples and monuments, of ruins and landscapes, of ancient tales, of music and dance, what then? Would he still have said that only Italy could offer a perfectly happy childhood?

In any event, he was happier in the Indies than he had been in Holland. "I thought Holland horrible," he wrote, "and I'm sure any child from the Indies feels the same way." School was the worst of all, and he says with typical Indies prejudice: "I thought the boys smelled funny, and I didn't think they washed themselves enough. . . . I looked down on the lot of them, and I thought they were childish, dull, and boring."

Couperus's work contains a great many more reminiscences about the Indies which appear in books and serials. On the occasion of a family reunion in the first volume of *The Books of the Small Souls*, Constance and Gerrit reminisce about their childhood in Buitenzorg, now Bogor, and talk about the river, with its huge boulders and children playing on them. These were in fact things that hail back to his mother's youth. The central event in *Of Old People*, the murder, takes place somewhere on Java during a dark night and a tropical rainstorm, in a guest house with next to it the wild, roaring, swollen river into which the corpse is thrown. It is an unforgettable scene. In the serialized "Children's Souvenirs" ("Kindersouvenirs"), written on the Riviera to the accompaniment of a howling mistral wind, he tells us about himself and his wife when they were children in the Indies at a costume party, himself dressed up as a page, his future wife as a marquise. This souvenir is followed by childhood memories of hers and one of his, both effortlessly told in a jesting and chatty sort of way but in a tone altogether unforgettable, told quietly, in a half whisper.

Couperus was in the Indies on three different occasions, the first time, of course, from his ninth till his fifteenth year. He was there a second time when he was thirty-six years old and a well-known writer, and for the last time just one year before he died, and then only as a passing tourist. His second stay began in the year 1899. In 1891 he had married Elisabeth Baud, who was born in the Indies and who had spent her youth there. They had come back because they were both drawn to the country, as well as the family. Apparently, Couperus was not thinking about writing a book about the Indies at the time. "I think it would be hard," he told an Indies newspaper critic, "to portray such heterogeneous types as these, such complicated circumstances, and such a curious society." And yet, during this same stay, which lasted about one year, the only Indies novel Couperus ever wrote came into being, *The Hidden Force (De stille kracht)*. During their visit to the Indies, Couperus and his wife stayed longest with his older sister and her husband, the Resident De la Valette, first in the town of Tegal, and later in Pasuruan, both on Java. There, in Pasuruan, he wrote *The Hidden Force*, the greater part of it, anyway. Back in Holland, he completed it in 1900. *The Hidden Force* contains much to remind us of Couperus's stay in Tegal and Pasuruan. Even so, we do have to be careful in identifying anyone or anything in Couperus's work. Someone who knew him quite well wrote, following his death in 1923, "Louis would literally put the nose of one person above the mouth of another." He did the same with events and circumstances.

How Couperus came by his theme of the secret, hidden force

(which is not, by the way, the basic theme of his novel), is not known. He probably did not have to go out of his way looking for it, but it must have suggested itself in the form of stories of supernatural events which were to remain inexplicable. The Indies have always been buzzing with that sort of tale. The familiar occult manifestations of stones raining down or of objects or things spitting betel juice are fairly well documented. Those occurring in *The Hidden Force* are based on authentic information, which Couperus obtained, according to the paper *Batavian News* (*Bataviaasch Nieuwsblad* of October 8, 1921), from the secret dossiers of the secretary general at Buitenzorg. It so happens that a similar case of stones raining down had occurred in Sumedang some ten years earlier. One Dr. Baudisch wrote a little book about such phenomena and he described that particular incident extensively. At the time, the government had ordered an investigation. The report, which also mentions an overnight stay in a haunted house similar to that in *The Hidden Force*, had since been kept in the archives in Buitenzorg. This Couperus consulted. In *The Hidden Force*, reference is made to the fact that the report, including the resident's findings, "had since been kept in the government's secret archives."

Anyone who remembers the old Pangéran, the ideal regent from *The Hidden Force*, may be reminded of the regent of Sumedang, Aria Suria Atmadja, who also bore the exalted title of Pangéran and for whom a statue has been erected. It has been said that the younger regent of Couperus's "Labuwangi" district, Sunario, was descended from the illustrious Adiningrat family of regents, who had been sultans on the island of Madura during the time of the East India Company. Most regent families in eastern Java were indeed of Madurese descent. Among them were descendants of Tjakra Adiningrat, who was elected in 1745 to become sultan and regent of Bangkalan, one of the three Madurese sultanates. Here we even see Couperus appropriating the name of a well-known Javanese-Madurese family, but it so happens that the regents of Pasuran were not descended from that family at all. This is precisely how Couperus worked. His character Leonie van Oudijck, the resident's wife who dwells in a perverted world of "pink fantasies," was instantly recognized by the family as the adulterous wife of grandfather Dr. Abraham Jan Daniel Steenstra Toussaint, "first surgeon of the City of Batavia." Her real name was Elisabeth Wilhelmina Petronella Couperus and, separated from her husband, she lived in Paris, where she died in 1889. Couperus's wife, his distant cousin, had in fact been named after her.

The educated Eva Eldersma is the life of Labuwangi society. She is the character who stages plays, gives receptions, and organizes picnics. She resembles Couperus's sister Trudy, much praised by him and others for these qualities. In the novel, she functions frequently as Couperus's spokeswoman. It is essentially his attitude she expresses when she comments on the Indies: "Still, she continued to sense something alien she could not put her finger on, something mysterious and darkly secret." Here is another instance of Couperus putting someone else's nose over another's mouth.

The Hidden Force is an excellent, intelligent, and clever book. Its composition is clever, and its intelligence shows in its understanding of Indies situations, especially those in government circles. Couperus owed this understanding, which exceeds merely being informed, to his brother-in-law De la Valette. Without his inside information, Couperus could never have written a book such as *The Hidden Force*, as he indeed openly admits. Because of all the things De la Valette told him, Couperus could imagine how a resident as head of a district government would act and feel if he had Van Oudijck's character. Van Oudijck is central to the novel, let there be no mistake about that, and "the hidden force" is not. One would certainly be wrong to consider the subject of the occult as its central theme. The mystical and mysterious properties with which Couperus foreshadows and shrouds everything time and again are primarily literary props. They serve mostly to conjure up the atmosphere of dread and fatality which is characteristic of Couperus. He experienced the world of the Indies in a way that was a projection of his own sensibilities. The powers of mystery were a means to focus this projection. Mood and atmosphere permeate the book, as in the description of the pompous residential house at dusk, inhospitable to family life ("always waiting for the next reception"), of the dark yard with the holy banyan trees, of the avenue along the Patjaram estate lined with the pinelike tjemara trees, the crescent moon above and the foliage "like tattered plush and unraveled velvet lumped against the clouds like cotton puffs." Couperus evokes, and the verb is most apt in his case, a scene such as that of a quietly breathing and fragrant courtyard at evening, with deep black shadows and flecks of light on the road or out on the yard. These evocations are charged with an atmosphere which Couperus time and again tries to describe with words such as "dark," "mysterious," "mystical," "incomprehensible." He does so either because he was ignorant of the word *angker*, or because he was reluctant to use it. However, the Javanese word *angker*, which is untranslatable but means something approximating "being magically possessed," is really the very word that describes the qualities Couperus is attempting to suggest. He certainly senses as much, even though he was an outsider and a European. The hidden force also serves to propel the action and to dramatically bring about intrigue and reversal. Still, the depiction of the characters is central, especially that of the main character, Resident van Oudijck. *The Hidden Force* is definitely not a "story about spiritualism and magic" or one about "shivers and ghosts," and even less "a third-rate serial," as Van Deyssel claimed it was in his *Bimonthly Magazine (Tweemaandelijksch tijdschrift)*. He certainly did not understand anything about the book. A critic of the Semarang daily newspaper *De Locomotief* was quick to point out the error of his ways in no uncertain terms: "Your criticism is an embarrassment to you, a disgrace to your magazine, and a disgrace to literature." That same critic also put his finger on the novel's essence when he added: *"The Hidden Force* is about the tragedy of the resident."

Quite so. Couperus added another dimension to the story, however, that of the resident as the colonial ruler in an alien land. Couperus had no need to portray the colonial as a brute or a usurper. He had no part in the ethical movement but was an artist who refused to take sides because to do otherwise would have meant to diminish "the fullness of life" itself. His portrayal of Van Oudijck is that of an upright ruler, a man who lives for his work and works only to further the welfare of his district, who looks after the interests of its people and protects them from the depradations of "private interest." Van Oudijck acts this way because he wants to do the right thing by his own convictions and not because he is following a particular set of instructions. He personifies the conscientious and upright Dutch government official in being honest, just, and patient, a man who knows his job and whose need for power and authority are entirely satisfied by the office he holds. "No other outfit can hold a candle to the civil service," Couperus has him think. He is the typical civil servant from the glorious days of the Indies civil service, which reigned autocratically with nearly absolute powers based on the principles of strictness and justice. Van Oudijck is a competent official of integrity, of the type who, ever mindful of the interests of the population, brooks no meddling with Dutch authority, which he regards as unassailable. Notions about self-government or democracy are alien to him. He is demanding of those working under him, but he can be jovial, and he lacks the arrogance of the high officials in the capital. He has a great deal of tact as well. He quells a revolt, for example, not through a show of force but through talking, through persuading and convincing people. This satisfies him deeply. He does, however, remain true to type in that he is an imported Hollander, a level-headed man who remains deaf and dumb in many ways.

He believed neither in the force beyond things, nor in the force within things themselves. He did *not* believe in a taciturn Fate, and he did *not* believe in silent gradualness. He only believed in what he could see with his own eyes: in the harvest, the roads, districts, and villages, in the welfare of his domain. This unclouded clarity of his simple male nature and his practical sense of life and of duty had only this one weakness: his tenderness, deep and female in its sentiment, which he felt toward his domestic circle; to his family, which he could only see as a blind man, unable to perceive their true nature, which he could only perceive according to his own pre-conceived notions and only in the way he *wanted* his wife and children to be.

His wife, "with the indolent grace of all Indies-born women," lives a life of perverted sensibilities and of a perverted love. She is carrying on an affair with Theo, Van Oudijck's son by a former marriage. His daughter Doddy falls victim to Addy de Luce, the great seducer, but Van Oudijck *sees* nothing and puts the anonymous letters in a desk drawer. He does have ideas and principles but he lives right past life's "hidden force." About the supernatural he senses absolutely nothing and he denies its existence: "because he did not believe in the hidden force, in life within life, and in all that teemed and tossed like volcanic fires within the mountains, like so many plots behind a throne, and because he did not believe in the mysticism of the visible world, life could catch him unprepared and weak precisely where it least conformed to his logical expectation of it."

The tension between this ever-present hidden force and the resident's total unreceptiveness to it is what controls the novel. The rhythmically returning theme is that of the tragedy of the European in a colonial world who is defenseless precisely because of his lack of faith in and disbelief of superstition. Couperus masterfully elaborates on this theme after having already introduced it in the first few pages of his novel, the theme of two separate worlds that never meet. Resident van Oudijck is shown going out for his evening stroll. He walks through the Lange Laan, past the club, all the time followed by a servant carrying a *tjali api* (rope torch), and heads for the pier. Legs apart, he stands looking out across the water. Before him, there is nothing but the sea, the wind, and the stench of fish. He steadies his footing, expands his chest, raises his military head, and sniffs in stench and wind alike. But the servant who guards him is worried:

"So strange, those Hollanders. . . . What could he be thinking now.
. . . Why does he act this way. . . . And why precisely here, at this
hour . . . with the sea spirits about now. . . . There are crocodiles below the water, and every crocodile is a spirit. . . . Over there they
have made a sacrifice to them, banana, rice and dried meat, and a
hard-boiled egg placed on a tiny bamboo raft below the base of the
light house. . . . What might the Kandjeng Tuan want here now. . . .
This place is not fit . . . tjelaka (calamity). . . . And his searching eyes
scanned up and down the broad back of his master, who just stood
there and stared. . . . What was he looking at? What did he see coming on the wind? . . . So strange, those Hollanders, strange . . ."

As Couperus continues to unfold his plot, the story slowly progresses, a story of love, hate, envy, and melancholy. As it progresses,
Couperus time and again causes us to sense the mystery. Each time
something incomprehensible and threatening occurs, something
that foreshadows the catastrophe we know to be inevitable. Repeatedly but in fine doses the hidden force is "served up," at first through
a single word or a single sentence, later, with increasing frequency
and emphasis, to culminate in the hail of stones and the spitting of
betel juice. With the introduction of the theme, the hidden force is al-
luded to for the very first time (the resident's stroll to the shore), and
fleetingly indicated by a pebble of unknown origin clattering onto the
tile floor. Then, several conversations obliquely refer to this "mystery." The first real confrontation comes during the seance with the
shifting table, which leaves a deep impression on everyone present.
When the company returns home that night, the hadji appears for the
first time. He seems to be crossing the yard but remains invisible. He
is to appear three more times at regular intervals. Following chapter
four, which in particular portrays Van Oudijck's character and his relationship to the "mystery of things visible," the threat comes closer.
From now on, it dominates every page. The climax begins with Babu
Urip's story about the souls of the little children crying in the trees,
and the one about the kuntianaks (she-devils who steal children)
roaming the gardens with bleeding hearts in their breasts. The catastrophe is reached in the scene of the stones raining down and the betel
juice being spat, just when Léonie van Oudijck is applying a beauty
ointment in the bathroom. Hysterical with fear, she runs totally
naked into the garden toward the swimming pool.

Soon after that more manifestations occur, such as the breaking of
a mirror, of a drinking glass, the staining of the bedsheets. The resident orders an investigation but without the slightest result. He then

has himself, together with four officials and his secretary, locked in the bathroom: "They never discussed what had happened but their night together was frightful." Following this experiment, the resident takes measures. He visits the regent and the regent's mother and has a brief talk with both of them. His words have a "great and threatening import." From then on, all mysterious events cease. Apparently the resident has triumphed but in reality he has lost, because he has lost all certainty. Just as in a classical tragedy—and it is once again obvious how closely Couperus patterned his novel after one—the reversal or peripeteia begins. The events have brought out Van Oudijck's vulnerable spot. He now becomes suspicious, restless, and unsure of himself. He ages rapidly and even becomes superstitious. Even so, he is unable to understand what has happened and can therefore not accept it. He loses everything. His wife leaves him and departs for Europe. Even she, the phlegmatic Léonie van Oudijck, appears to be infected. The resident requests an audience with the governor-general. He leaves for Buitenzorg and never returns to "Labuwangi."

He withdraws far into the interior, to live in a small village together with a Sundanese housekeeper. There the educated woman of "Labuwangi," Eva Eldersma, visits him for the last time before she permanently leaves for Holland. The essence of the book, that of the resident's tragedy, is once again revealed and compressed in what Van Oudijck tells Eva Eldersma:

> "But you see, that which happened . . . that . . . that is something I never understood . . . and it is that which has brought me here. All that, all those things which went on in the face of life, action, and logic . . . all that—here he hit his fist on the table—all that damned nonsense which . . . took place nonetheless . . . that is what did it. . . . That is what led up to my having to leave there, that is what led to the fact that I was as if struck dumb, like an idiot, a lunatic; —right in the midst of ordinary life, with all my logic and practicality, this life that suddenly seemed to me to be based on the wrong values, like a complete abstraction; —because right through it all events took place that belonged to another world, events that eluded me, me and everybody else. That and that alone is what caused it. I was no longer myself. I no longer knew what to think, what to do, or what exactly I had done. Everything in me faltered."

A discussion of Couperus's final book dealing with the Indies must inevitably be anticlimactic. *Eastward (Oostwaarts,* 1923) is little more than a serialized travel journal. It is the account of a tourist asked by the *Hague Post (Haagsche Post)* to make another jaunt through the Indies with an occasional nod to his hosts and sponsor.

The journal also corroborates the traditional European view of the Indies in describing them as prosperous and bursting with energy and, as a matter of course, closely and firmly tied to the Netherlands. Even though he prophesied somewhere that "the autonomy of Indonesia is only a question of time" (and such a prophesy came easily enough), this journal considers, or rather talks about Indonesian nationalism in the same disapproving terms as were then current among Europeans.

VIII
The Indies
Maligned and Avenged

1   Bas Veth and His Opponents

Inevitably Couperus's refinement and artistry collided with the colonial world, the end of which he had already foretold in *The Hidden Force*. Nor could he penetrate the "Oriental Indies," not for all his psychological intuition. His attitude remained ambivalent and complicated.

The attitude of Bas Veth (1860–1922) was anything but complicated. He hated the Indies, particularly the colonial Indies inhabited by Europeans, and in his general hatred he simply rejected everything, including "the other Indies." As a tradesman who had always lived in cities such as Macassar and Surabaja, he never developed an eye for them. He never even saw those "other Indies" where the native population lived but went right by them, on purpose as it were, as if to keep his ties to the Indies as loose as possible. The title of his book, *Life in the Dutch East Indies* (*Het leven in Nederlandsch-Indië*, 1900), seems innocent enough, but at the turn of the century it caused the blood of many people in the Indies to boil. A contemporary accused him of having "dipped his pen in vitriolic acid." Indeed, no book on the Indies so unreasonable and so rancorous as this has ever appeared before or since. To be sure, readers in the Indies had been a bit spoiled perhaps. Travelers who had visited the country and who had enjoyed typical Indies hospitality everywhere had invariably had pleasant things to say of the place.

The small book written by the Frenchman Chailley-Bert, *Java et ses Habitants* (1900), although critical in places, had reinforced the Indies reader's notion of living in a "splendid place" where life was beautiful. Earlier, Justus van Maurik, author of amusing sketches and a cigar dealer looking for a market in the Indies, had produced a cheerful and superficial travel account, written in part out of deference and in part because that was all he was capable of producing. His book of more than 500 pages, richly illustrated and expensively published, he entitled *Impressions of a Newcomer* (*Indrukken van een "totok,"* 1897). It was obvious he had appropriated all of the Indies prejudices during his brief stay there: the imperfect speech of Eurasians amused him, and he portrayed the native Indonesians as a childlike people. He repeated all the club and barroom stories and larded them with his own banal humor. In his unsuspecting, naive way he repeated a story about the *njai*, the housekeeper, whom he called "part of the furniture," according to tropical custom. In any case, he had put his Indies reader in a mild and generous mood toward himself. No wonder then that Justus van Maurik's trip had been a great success about which people talked for years.

Bas Veth did the exact opposite of Justus van Maurik. He too was a merchant, albeit in "mixed goods," but he did not have one good word to say about the same people in the Indies whom Justus van Maurik had found so generous and so hospitable. Bas Veth was not critical of the Eurasian but of the Hollander who had adapted himself to life in the Indies. He typified him as an "unbridled bourgeois indulging in the grossest excesses." He saw him as the product of a colonial society in which he could act out his lowest fantasies:

> The Dutchman in the Indies uses his prerogative of money, social position, and white skin to the hilt. We then realize the terrible power of the instrument called *colony*. Back in Europe, the same fellow would have remained the same fat bourgeois but at least held in check by something he likes to call "decency," which keeps him in line. . . . But once in the colony, the bourgeois turns into an Indiesman, and that is a curious variant of the human race. Wherever you find him, his essential characteristics stand out, whether in the Indies, on board ship, or back in Europe. He instantly gives himself away by his long-winded talk about petty things, by his way of telling the same story thrice to the same person, by the uncouth way he lies around in his lazy chair, pants rolled up and barefoot, and by the coarse way he behaves toward his native servants. He tends to corpulence and flabbiness. On the whole, he has a big belly and looks swollen. A description of his general characteristics would be incomplete without mentioning his unsavory dinginess. His expansiveness is nothing short of talking rot. He is a fierce swiller of "rijsttafel," the word "eating" would be too weak. He can stuff away plates heaped with the messy stuff until, finally, he

seeks out his lair where he'll lie digesting like a boa constrictor until five in the afternoon.

In his rancor, Veth comes up with some nice neologisms. In addition, his descriptions, sarcastic and otherwise, are often right on target but he begins to pall after a while in his own "long-winded talk about petty things," the very thing he accused his enemies of. In this respect, he is very much like his fellow countrymen in the Indies. Like them, his sole preoccupation is with the European living there. His limited vision then makes this entire quarrel between Veth and his seething opponents into something of a family feud. As in a difference of opinion on a question of taste between two cousins, one praises what the other despises; what the one calls pleasant, the other pronounces as vulgar, and what one considers outgoing, the other regards as ill-mannered and forward, and so on, ad infinitum. Essentially, however, both inhabit the same small world visited only occasionally by a few anonymous Indonesians. Neither party has any awareness of the world beyond. Of course, Bas Veth favors better treatment of the houseboy, the maid, and the *njai* because he thinks it unbecoming to yell or shout "goddammit" at them. Bas Veth, we begin to realize, was better educated, he was interested in literature and crazy about Heine, and pined to hear classical music. In the Indies, he discovered a dearth of lectures, concerts, and exhibits, and "polite conversation." Over and over, Bas Veth uses words such as "polite," "idealistic," "beautiful," "pure," "fair," and "healthy," and by his own admission, he found those words useless in the Indies. He was a typical late nineteenth-century idealist, an aesthete who wrongly ended up in Indies trading. Trading in the Indies of course meant "dickering with Chinamen about a secret contract, the kind of shady deal favoring him over other creditors, those idiots!"

Bas Veth was eighteen years old when he arrived in the Indies as an apprentice to a trading firm in Macassar. He was twenty-two or twenty-three when he wrote a small book called *Several Articles of Trade on the Macassar Market (Eenige handelsproducten van de Maccassaarsche markt)*. It is already critical of the trading practices in the Indies but carefully worded and apologetic in tone: "It is quite possible I looked too much on the dark side of things and pondered several negative aspects. Je ne sais quel diable me poussa, I don't know what possessed me, but a number of times I could not resist putting some wormwood and gall into my ink." Later on he would no longer excuse himself, not even for his involvement in shady trade practices, or for having been forced into "a real steeplechase of funny deals."

What kind of a man was Bas Veth, really, and where did he come from? He was born in 1860 and raised in Amsterdam but his favorite memories of his youth centered on the village of Alblasserdam, where he spent his vacations in "that ideal willow district . . . with its Waal River, streams, and willow-shaded ditches." There he loitered as a young troubadour, he wrote in 1912, like a Rip van Winkle reading Fénélon to the farm girls. The youth reveled in Heinrich Heine and Multatuli and there felt his first pangs of despair. Just a few years later he went to the Indies. No doubt he had a hard time of it there.

We have a letter Bas Veth wrote to his friend Henri Borel dated after his return to Holland in 1898, before he started writing his book. He was then thirty-eight. To Borel, still living in the Indies, Veth describes the interior of his room: Heine's bust and an ornament by Prikker grace his table; elsewhere, volumes of poetry by the aesthetics, Borel's book *The Lad (Het jongetje)*, Prikker's *Letters*, Heine's *Buch der Lieder*, Van Eeden's symbolic and autobiographical *Little Johannes (De Kleine Johannes)*, etc., and everywhere portraits of Byron, Schubert, and Wagner, as well as a large photograph of Van Deyssel and a picture of Ibsen. This was Bas Veth's world. One can well imagine how this man, who lived in the ivory tower of art, and who wished to continue living in it, must have felt among all those jolly, ill-mannered, noisy, and chatty compatriots of his. These, it goes without saying, must have been pretty annoyed by his arrogant and artistic personality. These people, which Daum, incidentally, renders much more believable than Veth, no doubt took their revenge by mocking and teasing him.

There is a sketch by one of Veth's fiercest opponents, Paul J. Koster, who in turn rants on about Holland for some 400 pages: "I remember that businessman very well. He was one of those pudgy, round-cheeked little fellows trying to look dapper while having himself introduced left and right with desperate urgency. Tirelessly he emitted his miserable sounding 'howdeedoo,' offering his flabby hand. On the surface, he seemed a vain, assertive little fellow, although he didn't look Jewish, and I've lately been told that he came of sound, Reformed stock. Apparently degeneracy runs in the best of circles." This brief quotation, complete with the ever latent anti-Semitism of those years occurs in *Excerpts from the Pages of an Indies Curmudgeon (Uit de nagelaten papieren van een Indische nurks, 1904)*. Koster, for that matter, was not the only one to attack Bas Veth. One L. C. van Vleuten, who introduced himself as an officer who had lived in the Indies for thirty years, had already attacked him earlier. Using his "meager literary talents," as he correctly assessed them, he wrote a pamphlet which he had printed in Batavia at his own expense called *The Truth about Life in the Netherlands Indies. A Protest against the*

Book by Bas Veth (De waarheid omtrent het leven in Nederlandsch-Indië. Protest tegen het boek van Bas Veth, 1900). Van Vleuten tells us that "Veth's book," from the moment it appeared, continued to be talked about by everybody but, he adds, "fortunately nearly always accompanied by a cry of indignation." Bas Veth's opponents were none of them lacking in indignation. Anyone checking the daily and weekly newspapers, even those well past the year 1900, will come across his name and the title of his book. Nearly everybody combatted him, sometimes under an assumed name, and called his accusations exaggerated, deceptive, or perfidious. They pointed to his numerous exaggerations and errors, as if indeed Bas Veth had been concerned with arguments. He had clearly stated that his book was written out of revenge, that it was his final reckoning, "settling the account and closing the books once and for all, just to make sure I would never return to the Indies."

When he was finally able to leave Padang, he kicked the dock, he tells us, "probably cursing as I did so." From the ship he happily watched "the Indies sink below the horizon at sundown." His first letters from Holland reveal how he felt on seeing Europe again: "Oh, these are incomparable moments of intense joy, of great happiness, believe me." Even so, the Indies nightmare was not quite over yet. Before too long, its ghosts returned and began to haunt him. That was the reason he began to write his book. Bas Veth epitomizes the uprooted and therefore embittered European in the Indies who could blame the banyan tree for not being more like his native willow, who considered tropical nature claustrophobic ("the Indies landscape is joyless"), who considered the food out there "a dirty mess," and who thought that all the girls in the Indies were calculating.

This judgment of young women in the Indies, of women there generally, aroused the ire of a certain Mrs. Koopman, who also wrote a book to counter Veth, called *Women's Paradise (Het paradijs der vrouwen, 1900).* Her book was counterproductive, however, in that her argument was altogether too naive. Bas Veth had described Indies receptions as the height of silly pretense. All Mrs. Koopman does is to alter their description. She describes these affairs as cosy places, where one makes a date for a picnic and a swim in the country. As to his assertion that women are pale, anemic, or dingy looking, she proposes they should be seen in the water: "What a marvelous sight to behold their youthful shapes cavorting in liquid crystal, their sarongs tied above their breasts. Most of them can swim, on their backs even, with just their heads out of the water, the clear water flowing over their firm breasts and slender arms." She goes on and on like this in her attempt to negate Veth, without the slightest idea she was playing directly into his hands. No doubt Bas Veth in his Amsterdam apartment had a good laugh at her.

As late as five years after the appearance of *Life in the Netherlands Indies*, a reaction appeared in the form of a hefty tome. Its author was J. B. Ruzius, who called his book *The Sacred Indies* (*Heilig Indië*, 1905). It became famous, more on account of its title than its content. For years, *The Sacred Indies* continued to be regarded as a sacred cow. Ruzius was the kind of Indies person who had lived too long in the Indies to be happy in Holland anymore. At times he thought he would suffocate within the walls of his living room in The Hague, and he had to take a deep breath whenever he thought of the Indies. He would then be overcome by visions of space and breadth, of faces and vistas. Bas Veth had offended him too in everything he held dear and sacred, and he too considered Veth unreasonable and rancorous. He simply did not understand Veth. However, his book prompted him to ask himself what "that fair country" had meant to him, the country that was never out of his thoughts. He tells us somewhere that what started him writing his book was "partly the urge to cleanse the Indies of all the blame which those writing out of spite and rancor have heaped upon it." Ruzius, however, is no polemicist.

What he does is to oppose Veth's view with his own "positive attitude." For that reason his protest is more dignified than that of all the others who attacked Veth so vehemently. Still, his reminiscences lose themselves too much in futilities and sentimentalities. In addition, they are simply not interesting enough. Ruzius shows himself to be the true retired official that he is. Even his style, probably copied from the Eighties Movement, shows us as much.

Among all those who wrote about Bas Veth's book there is one who refused to join the pack who were out to get him. This was Otto Knaap (1866–1917). In his booklet entitled *Bas Veth*, he introduces himself on the cover as "an Indies person," although to him the term meant something other than it meant to Veth. He was a Eurasian, born July 29, 1866, in Cheribon, Java. It is not known when he was sent to Holland to be educated, probably when still a child. Around 1895 or so he surfaced in Batavia as an employee of the K. P. M. Royal Shipping Lines there, following unfinished literary studies at Leiden University. From early on, he had been, like Bas Veth, an aesthete of a type associated with the Eighties Movement in Dutch literature. When he arrived in the Indies, he must have had an illusion of playing a part in the artistic life of the colony, for he wrote: "I wished to enhance the country dear to me by serving the cause of music through improving people's tastes. In my innermost being the firm plan had taken root to advance the arts in the Indies in some measure." He came into direct conflict with a society reveling in dilettantism, one where social position and not art held sway. It was a hopeless job in fact, his wanting to clean up the arts. Those "obstinate gentlemen and giggling ladies" cheerfully went about their business of playing games through every performance. Knaap should have started by first changing society. He realized that, of course, but he felt powerless. The only thing he could do was criticize, and Bas Veth gave him the opportunity to do just that. With everybody else attacking him, Otto Knaap sprang to his rescue with his booklet *Bas Veth*.

It was characteristic of him to do something of the kind, even though he had his objections to Veth's book. Nonetheless he wrote: "Bas Veth is basically right." All Otto Knaap had to do was to reproduce what he himself had published in the newspapers before Bas Veth's pieces had appeared. Veth had written: "The ability most esteemed here is that of making a fortune. Pay, promotion, making money, those are the things that preoccupy most people in the Netherlands Indies." This had made people mad as hornets. "But after all," Otto Knaap asked, "that's how it is. What other ambition do people here in the Indies really have?" Concerning morality in the Indies, Bas Veth may well have overdone it, but Otto Knaap asked his readers: "How many bounders out here are not respectfully referred to as clever fellows?" He also believed all those other things Veth had pointed out were true, to some degree at least, such as the prevailing pretentiousness, keeping up with the Joneses, and the fact that there were scores of nouveaux riches in the Indies. As Knaap wrote:

> People in Batavia like to put on a fancy show but it is mostly ludicrous. Indies society, after all, is largely composed of parvenus. I don't think it is anything to be ashamed of, on the contrary, it is only commendable if, for example, someone whose father sold groceries back in Holland has managed to work his way up to a position of power and authority. However, the moment a person like that starts putting on airs or pretending his descent is nobler than that of the other folks in town, then I think the whole business becomes extremely silly. Unfortunately there are plenty of people like that here. For that matter, social position here often means nothing other than that someone has just "arrived," and not necessarily by way of the straight and narrow, or by virtue of personal merit. Even so, there is hardly any place in the world where social position is so highly esteemed as it is here.

It was precisely this sort of social snobbery that stood in the way of any development of musical and artistic life in the colony. It was inevitable therefore that someone such as Otto Knaap who harbored all sorts of illusion of ameliorating the arts had run afoul of a society like that.

2   Creusesol

L. C. van Vleuten, in his previously mentioned attack on Bas Veth, while admitting to his own "meager literary talents," says that he had really hoped the author Creusesol would give Bas Veth the reply he deserved. Only because Creusesol had remained silent did Van Vleuten feel called upon, despite his literary handicap, to write and publish his booklet. His notion that Creusesol would have been just the man to put Bas Veth in his place is not so odd. Van Vleuten had good reason to suspect that he would be the one to defend the Indies, even though his supposition was based on just one small book.

In 1896, Creusesol had published a number of "sketches from a coffee plantation" in the Surabaja Courant (Soerabaia Courant), which were well received. Early in 1899, the collection appeared under the title Around and About Suka Sepi (Op en om Soeka Sepi; "suka sepi" meaning the desire to be alone). Again readers in the Indies took a liking to his sketches, and for good reason. Daum liked them very much, for example, and the reading audience recognized itself in them. They were written well enough, conversational and jesting in tone, somewhat self-satisfied perhaps but not nearly as chummy and banal as Justus van Maurik's Impressions of a Newcomer.

Creusesol, for that matter, was no outsider as Van Maurik was; he knew what he was talking about. He was a full-blood European, to be sure, but he had been born and bred in the Indies. Otherwise we know little more about him than what he tells us: "First I was a planter of coffee, which got some leaf disease; then I went into sugar, to finally end up in printer's ink." He was born in 1851 in Semarang. In 1897 he lived in Surabaja, then already working for a newspaper, to leave permanently for Holland in 1898 or 1899. In any case, he turns up living in The Hague in October 1899, like an outsider and a bit ill at ease. In fact, he feels exactly the way Ruzius did, and the way so many people who have lived in the Indies for a long time do after they have just returned to Holland. He misses the sun, he is cold, and he stares out of the window "some ten meters above The Hague's old sod," watching the snow come down, which he calls "udjan kapok," a shower of kapok puffs. It is at moments such as those that memories begin to overtake him:

> The features of friends and enemies, images of well-known places, the memory of sounds such as the wind sighing through the wa-

ringin tops, the sound of rice being pounded in the village; all this returns and becomes audible and visible in the most colorful mixture, . . . appearing on the wings of memory, which destroys distance and leaps across oceans in the oddest way, without rhyme or reason, and voilà, right next to your hearth in Holland you behold in your imagination, framed by the mists of time, a panorama of that country, of that rich, lovely, splendid island, our Java! . . . There is a story that says that the volcanoes of that island have powerful magnets inside of them. These magnets are at their strongest when people are surrounded by Dutch fogs and when the skies hang leaden above a dismal winterscape. . . . Those of you on Java now, would you want to change places with me?

The above is quoted from Creusesol's "Sketches of a Returnee" ("Schetsen van een terugkerende") and, like his first sketches, was published in an Indies daily, this time in the *Java Courier (Java Bode)*. They were later collected and called *Back to Holland (Naar Holland, 1900)*. One reviewer immediately recognized them as the very antidote to Bas Veth's venom, although these sketches do not mention Veth's name at all for the simple reason that they were written a few years before Veth's book appeared.

At times, while talking and quoting from French, German, and English poetry, Creusesol manages to convey a certain mood. That is when he is at his best, but he can also go on about trivialities (according to Veth, one of the characteristics of people from the Indies). Both his good and his bad points are present in all his writings, more so in some than in others. In his first collection, *Around and About Suka Sepi*, he knows how to evoke that dreadful feeling of desolation which can overcome the young Dutch planter as the sole European up in the hills somewhere. Creusesol also succeeds in making us feel something of the great excitement of living in the very midst of imposing surroundings. However, the moment he starts talking about his native houseboy, his stableboy, his cook, or his gardener, he begins to pall. He obviously wants to be informative and he wants us to know that those servants are not bad at all. Then he begins to debate others on that issue, without noticing that he is just exchanging one fashionable opinion for another. Sometimes he agrees with his opponents, and then again he does not. "Nonsense, all of it! As a people, the Javanese are no more honest or dishonest than any other. . . . It is wrong to either approve or disapprove of other people merely on the basis of our own opinions or point of view." All of this sounds intelligent enough but it is the kind of observation that does not go very far. Creusesol talks about natives, such as his cook, his houseboy, and so on, as if they were big children, much in the way a father would, one sure of his place in the patrimonial past of *tempo dulu*, the days gone by. He is unable to go deep enough and show what their lives are like, for despite his familiarity with the country and its people, he remains a European. For example, when he tries to convey what a tropical night up on his coffee estate is like, the sky dotted with a million stars (he calls them "les hiéroglyphes brillants"), with the music of the *gamelan* coming from afar, he still thinks of Europe: "If only one could have a little music on a fine night such as this. I don't mean the *gamelan*, of course, but something like a tune by Bilsen or Mannstädt." Once he is back in The Hague, however, with all its opportunities to go to concerts, operas, operettas, and vaudeville, he gradually begins to change his mind. Then the *gamelan* is not "a stupid *gamelan*" any longer, and the *suling* (Javanese flute) no longer "a damned squeaky, whining instrument." Now their sounds are dear to him because they tie Creusesol to unforgettable memories of an unforgettable country.

In 1908, his *The Kimono (De Khimono)* appeared, a new collection of stories "including two other East Indies stories." The first and longest one is about the life of a *nonna*, a young Indies woman. As subject matter, the likes of this story had, as far as we know, never appeared in Dutch literature before. Even so, Creusesol shows little understanding of this sort of Indies woman. As a *totok*, as the outsider he is, he is far too prejudiced about his subject. No wonder he sees fit to warn the boys from Holland, using a French proverb no less, against marrying this sort of girl. He himself is safely married to a "Dutch Eve," he confides.

The final story, "Don't Judge the Flour" ("Bij 't scheiden van de markt"), deriving its title from the proverb "Don't judge the flour before the bread is made," is unique in that Creusesol introduces a *njai* and has this native "housekeeper" or concubine tell the story of her life. No doubt it is based on fact but it still gives the impression of being warped by Creusesol's Dutch way of looking at things. Moreover, its literary overlay detracts from its authenticity.

As the economic situation in the Indies improved between 1905 and 1910, the need to "import" women increased, and this bettered the chances for young people to go the Indies. Many hesitated, of course, because there had been quite a number of ugly rumors about the Indies and Bas Veth had not been forgotten yet. There existed a need to be better informed, and as had been the case in the previous century, now too all kinds of old-timers came to the fore to supply that very need. They wrote scores of pamphlets, articles, and stories concerning the now acute problem of "going to the Indies." Quite a debate got started, in fact, involving a great many people. It was said that the colonies needed European workers but no longer the former variety of flunkies, adventurers, fortune hunters, or impoverished youths of bourgeois homes; what was needed instead were "people of education and polish," young people of "decent backgrounds," as Creusesol invariably called them. With people like that in mind, he wrote a number of discursive sketches entitled *To the East* (*Naar den Oost*, 1908). He mentions "the Great Obstacle" and "Indifference" and talks about the chances to succeed in the Indies. He discusses the necessary wardrobe, describes the departure, the boat trip, and the inevitable phenomenon of women married by proxy. He ends all this by saying "I have said it once, and I will say it again: Dutch Youngsters of Good Family, why are not more of you headed for the East?"

There were of course people who cautioned against optimism, including those, such as Bas Veth, who regarded going to the Indies as the first step to a failed life. One of these was Henri Borel. In 1913 he entered the arena against Creusesol with a pamphlet called *A Career in the Indies* (*Een werkkring in Indië*, 1913). As we could have guessed, Creusesol was in favor, and Borel against. Creusesol starts out by admitting that the fabulous careers are a thing of the past, but he maintains that there are plenty of opportunities left. He also repeats what all the veterans say, that life in the Indies offers a great deal more freedom and is much less tied to social convention and rules. In addition, and apparently to reassure parents, he states that Indies immorality is nothing to worry about. Borel is much less optimistic about the situation and mentions the dangers of "Indianization." He writes: "It is absolutely untrue what Bas Veth's infamous book crudely alleges, that the Indies are crowded with innumerable bounders, upstarts, fortune hunters, and so on. I would not wish to support that notion because I would not be telling the truth. However, the process of Indianization is less obvious, more subtle and insidious because it takes place unperceived. It amounts to an indistinct bastardization of taste and of one's clarity of perception, of conscience, of feeling itself, especially in matters sexual and ethical." Creusesol can only counter that with his denial, his nostalgia, and his inborn optimism. In summary, he is a sympathetic man from the Indies who can tell a good story once he gets going but who is not lacking in a certain degree of vanity, the vanity of the self-made man. He is proud of his position in Indies society, which he admits he owes to his white skin. He quotes a great deal from various literatures but it is hard to escape the impression that he consulted something like Bartlett's *Familiar Quotations*. He likes showing off his Indies experience and dropping pearls of wisdom, oblivious to the fact that he is spouting nothing but prejudices, and the typical prejudices of the (well-meaning) old-timer at that. We do have to grant Creusesol that he does not take himself too seriously: his discourse is light and he likes to make fun of things, including himself, and that is one thing that argues well for him.

It should be pointed out in conclusion that he derived his pseudonym from the French "creuse," which means "graaf" or "to dig" in Dutch, and the French "sol," which means "land" or "earth" in Dutch. I. P. C. Graafland died in The Hague in 1918.

3   The Other World

It is increasingly obvious that the Europeans in the Indies must have been living in some sort of enclave in the midst of millions. They lived in their own closed community, which was vastly different from society in the mother country, making every European quite different from his counterpart in Holland. His way of looking at things was determined by the new social relationships he encountered there. The subjects of Indies novels derive from this Indo-European society, and the "native" is described only insofar as he or she enters this society. He is approached from a world quite different from his own, often with good will and fondness, but still judged by norms derived from European society.

We have to distinguish between Europeans living in the cities and those living in the interior. In the interior, one lived much closer to the native Indies world. Social adjustment there meant something quite different from what it did in places such as Batavia, Semarang, or Surabaja. Deskbound officials who had always spent their time in the cities could correctly say they "personally had had little contact with the native population," as Daum has one of his characters explain. To the government official and the planter living far in the interior, the situation was quite different, of course. They were the ones who constantly dealt with the native population. Not surprisingly, they also understand the private world of the native Indonesians better. Among them were those who even became fully assimilated and anonymously disappeared into Indonesian society. Their number is impossible to estimate but probably larger than one suspects. Every once in a while, the Indies daily and weekly papers carried a story of such a European living among the native population, far from other Europeans, similar to Resident van Oudijck in *The Hidden Force*, who, at the end of the novel, withdraws deep into the interior of Java.

Several novels feature this curious kind of European as their major character, as does for example G. Gonggrijp's *The White Tiger* (*De blanke tijger*, 1935). G. P. Rouffaer, who in the 1880s undertook a trip through Java, met several such characters, Van der Tuuk among them. Another such, a former assistant resident, Rouffaer used as an informer for his study on village relationships. These people, some of them recluses, others not, lived their "plantation" lives away from the other Europeans, either as patriarchs or Western medicine men. They had, as it were, removed their white skins. They were accepted by the native population, and upon their death they were buried like one of them, in native fashion, as happened with "the white tiger," or the Belgian soldier, the pariah, in the harrowing account by M. B. van der Jagt in *Koloniaal Tijdschrift* I (1917): 62. "These people," Rouffaer tells us, "had so completely identified with Indonesian society through some quirk of mind that they became totally devoted to living solely for its benefit."

There were innumerable gradations between these so-called odd-balls and the Europeans from the cities living in their own cliques. There were also a number of people, quite a few in fact, who ended up living between two worlds. They were people who had not severed their ties with other Europeans but who had nonetheless changed in their thinking and habits. They were often planters or government officials. Some of them lived with a native wife, others had a European wife and children, but they lived in the midst of the native population, nearly always surrounded by the aura of European authority even if they had none to exercise. They were addressed either as *kandjeng* (lord) or *bapak* (father), as in the case of the well-known planter Karel Holle, who really lived like a friend and a father among the Sundanese. All these Europeans spoke the indigenous language, knew the customs, and were familiar with village life. They also knew the forest paths, were accustomed to the smell of the villages, and lived much closer to both the people and the country than the majority of their compatriots. These were the ones "who understood much," or, as the native people might have put it, "dia jang mengerti." They did understand much because they spent all their time with these people and saw much that eluded the other Europeans. They also knew how poor the people had been for years and the kind of whims they were subject to.

One of these was P. C. C. Hansen (1867–1930), who wrote under the pseudonym Boeka. He was a *totok*, a full-blooded European, born in Amsterdam, who for many years had run a coffee plantation up in the hill country of central Java. This meant that for days, or even weeks probably, the only people he could talk to were his Javanese housekeeper, his servants, overseers, some native chiefs, and, once in a while, a European or Eurasian. Because of leaf disease in the coffee plants (about which he wrote in the *Indies Mercury [Indische Mer-*

cuur] of 1898) and the decline of coffee cultivation generally, he was forced in 1897 to return to Europe. He could not forget Java, however, and neither could he forget the fate of its people. He published numerous articles in weeklies and monthlies such as *De Amsterdammer* and *The Indies Guide (De Indische Gids)*. In the September 15, 1902, issue of *De Amsterdammer* he published under his own name one of several articles concerning the perpetual impoverishment of the Javanese. Under his pseudonym Boeka he published an essay in *The Indies Guide* (2 [1903]: 1137) called "The Native Indonesian" ("De Inlander"). This essay, which he called "a study," is in fact more nearly a private act of piety. It certainly bespeaks his great fondness for the Javanese people, especially for those living in the countryside.

He defends them against the usual prejudices of most of his compatriots, which make the Javanese out to be apathetic, fatalistic, or subservient. According to Boeka, this judgment is superficial and only illustrates their inability to judge by anything other than Western standards. Javanese society is hardly idyllic and the Javanese does have his shortcomings, Boeka does not deny this; but these are not of his own making: "External influences are to blame, the tyranny of his own chiefs, an alien and remote government, in short, a lack of insight and sympathy on the part of his rulers which make his life into an oppressive burden" (p. 1183). Boeka made it his mission in life to draw attention to the situation, to point out ways of improving it, and to warn his fellow Dutchmen of the consequences of their colonial rule. He also says what his fellow countrymen either do not know or do not care to know, and that is that the Indonesian is filled with "a glowing hatred for his rulers, kindled and fueled by his hatred for all the injustice heaped on him" (p. 1169).

Boeka thought to further his aims even more by writing fiction, which he too must have regarded as a form of "pleasant relaxation." The preface to his best-known novel, *Pàh Troeno*, says as much: "To acquaint the reading public with all sorts of wrongs in Java's interior, in order that justice may prevail where injustice is done, and improvements made where people have been waiting for too long."

Boeka wrote four such "didactic novels," as he himself called them. His first book, *An Overseer (Een koffieopziener, 1901)*, concerns the life of a small Eurasian, the son of a full-blooded Dutchman and the "usual housekeeper." Upon his father's death, he has to find his own way as a Eurasian among Europeans and as a European among the natives on a narrow strip of no man's land. His position is a difficult and vulnerable one. Boeka did not write his life history of Karel Steenstra, the Eurasian pauper, as a polemic but it did have a didactic aim. It was meant as an indictment against a government that had never bothered to do a thing for the social position of the Eurasian. All Steenstra can do is to endure: "Yes, he was worn out, and those he had worked for and who had reaped the benefits of his work were now mercilessly putting him to pasture. It would do no good to get annoyed or angry because those fine gentlemen were all-powerful and could afford to be indifferent to his protest" (p. 284). He becomes a pauper and can only salvage his dignity by allowing himself to be totally absorbed by Javanese society, "because then at least he did not have to endure orders from those arrogant Hollanders" (p. 287). However, Javanese society, of which he becomes a part, is anything but ideal. Boeka deals with this world more extensively in his second novel, *Pàh Troeno,* the history of a simple villager helplessly caught in a world of "whim and oppression." Boeka lists a number of abuses such as the use of opium ("a cancer"), usury ("cause of poverty and famine"), the judicial system ("very dismal"), the tax on tenant housing ("people being bled white"), and, particularly, the general lack of safety everywhere, which "causes scandalous conditions." All of these abuses, Boeka concludes, "have long since caused the Javanese to lose all faith in the government."

Boeka criticizes the self-satisfied way people in the Netherlands regarded the colonial administration. He points out how both official reports and articles in the press disguise the real condition in the Javanese countryside. Boeka knew what he was talking about. Having lived among the Javanese for years, he knew a great deal about their world. He knew a lot more even than someone such as Douwes Dekker, for example, but even so Boeka is now an unknown and forgotten author. There is only one explanation for this. His slow and compact style lacks the sparkle and convincing rhetorical power which Multatuli has in such abundance. This, incidentally, illustrates once again the extent to which the effectiveness of one's social involvement depends on how well one can handle the chosen means of expression, in this case, writing.

Boeka's two-volume novel *Civilization (Beschaving,* 1903) repeats and expands his earlier writings. He does add one thing, however, and that is the decline of a formerly civilized and unspoiled population because of the presence of European enterprises which throws the village system out of kilter and demoralizes people. In and around the plantations and factories, crime, prostitution, and gambling thrive. This is also the major theme of *Pàhkasinum* (1904), Boeka's last and best novel. It is probably his best because here the moral had been integrated with the story and is no longer just scattered throughout in didactic statements. In 1903, Boeka published yet another two-volume work concerning the *Government in the East Indies (Bestuur van Oost-Indië)*. Its conclusion is that the Indies have little chance of amelioration without a change from their dependency on the mother country.

Boeka's publisher also issued a novel about the Indies called *Sakinum* (1899), under the name of G. Dompers, a didactic novel similar to those of Boeka's and written in a style almost identical to his.

Because he was a private planter, Boeka had the advantage of not being regarded as someone in a position of power. This enabled him to get to know better what went on in the mind of the Javanese, especially what they thought about the government. Because the typical government official represented government policy and held an "elevated" office, he was thereby cut off from a great deal of information. Even so, there were officials whose knowledge of the country and its wants and needs was impressive. For that reason they could be relied on to help their "younger brothers and children," i.e., their native subordinate officials and the population. Among these informed officials were people such as Jasper, Opheffer (whose real name was G. L. Gonggrijp), Westenek, and various others who, it so happens, did *not* write.

Of all of these, J. E. Jasper (1874–1945) must have considered himself the most literary. He wrote scores of articles in all sorts of magazines about government, industrial arts (quite a lot), about drama, police matters, superstition, self-hypnosis, and mysticism; about the life of a medicine woman, the history of the city of Tuban (on the north-east coast of Java), about legends in the Minahasa region of northern Celebes, and so on. Besides all that, he wrote "real literature" which dealt largely with Javanese life without the presence of a single European.

In an article published in the *Indies Weekly* (*[Weekblad voor Indië]* August 7, 1904), Jasper complained that junior government administrators were insufficiently informed about conditions in their districts: "They know nothing, see nothing, and they only get to know a little bit about their immediate surroundings. This is why they fail in the most essential aspects of their duty, which is to learn as much as possible about the life of the small villager." This sort of statement is characteristic of Jasper. He, of course, was in touch with the population and knew his district well. On his rounds, he left the main roads and penetrated the remotest villages, talking to the people in their own language. He knew how they lived, knew their customs and rituals, and would never tamper with their private customs and laws, their *adat*, in other words. Knowing the people through and through, he wrote about them. He was moved by the condition of the little man, although in a way that bespeaks the interest of a literary observer. He does not protest or accuse, as Boeka does. His political conservatism is partly owing to this "objectivity." Jasper's stories invariably deal with little people. All of them are touched by tragedy or pathos. They are defenseless, can not find their place in society, they are incapable of coping with the situation they are in, they commit sins, and they are weak. In Jasper's stories, however, they all retain an endearing quality because he understands their sins and shortcomings in terms of their situation. It is their situation that in his opinion remains a constant, one that is unlikely to change.

The long, separately published story called *The Life of Ardja and Lasmi* (*Het leven van Ardja en Lasmi*, 1908) is one such tale of human error and frailty, on the part of Ardja, and of touching loyalty on Lasmi's part. It is a simple, somewhat too precious village story which Jasper proceeds to tell us with, unfortunately, altogether too much embellishment. When Jasper started writing, he must have wanted his work to resemble the kind of writing he admired in a number of authors of the period. He badly wanted to be an artist but because he was not enough of one, he thought to avail himself of a formula. More clearly, Jasper was an imitator of the Eighties Movement who tried to prove his artistry in letters by making the sort of impressionistic observations that leave nothing to the imagination of the reader: "Amidst drooping leaves on stiff and upright bushes topped by pink blossoms did the gentle rays of sunshine descend on lumpy chunks of freshly tilled earth, and there the rays continued to vibrate for a while longer, an orange yellow over black" (*Of Java's Roads* [*Van Java's wegen*], 1904, p. 67).

Literary landscapes such as these crowd out his story and detract from what he has to say. Instead of suggesting something, his style merely irritates. As a writer, Jasper had fallen victim to something fairly common in his time, and that was the misunderstanding that created discrepancies between the writer's real aims and his literary pretensions. His entire oeuvre, although less so as time went on, bears the stigma of this misunderstanding. It is indeed a pity that because of this so many opportunities were lost. It is easy to see what good things he might have done with his stories in the collections *Of Virtues and Vices* (*Van deugden en dwalingen*, 1910) or *Quiet Influences* (*Stille invloeden*, 1906). The subject of nearly every story from the gallery of Indies lives he displays, about Javanese, Eurasians, and *totoks*, is fascinating. Every once in a while, whenever life triumphs over literature, as in the sketches "Granny" ("Oudje"), "Turnabout" ("Ommekeer"), or "The Music Master" ("De muziekmeester"), we are happily allowed to forget that we are in the sacred presence of literature. Then these stories leave an everlasting impression.

Also in 1910, a very productive year apparently, Jasper collected another batch of stories that had first run in all kinds of periodicals (*The
Guide* among them) and in dailies (especially in the *Java Messenger
[Java Bode]*). He called the collection *Deep Currents (De diepe stro-
mingen*, 1910). They dealt with those currents that to him were the
passions that ruled man's life and determined his fate, such as love,
hate, jealousy, desire, and the lack of it.

One thing stands out in Jasper's work, and that is his ability to identify himself best of all with the emotional world of the so-called Indiesman or half-caste. The Eurasian had always been forced to take
a back seat to the European, and the former was filled with rancor
against the outside *totok*, while at the same time feeling automatically superior to the native Indonesian. As his Eurasian character puts it:
"There is hatred smoldering everywhere." Jasper himself was an Indiesman, born in Surabaja. Although he became a high official and attained the rank of governor of Djokjakarta, he retained his feeling of
solidarity with his forgotten fellow Eurasians up to a point. Jasper,
however, also understood the Javanese, although not quite as intimately. He understood him and, without identifying wholly with his
fate, he knew as much about him as any non-Javanese could. He knew
exactly how the Javanese male headdress was folded and how the
Javanese woman wrapped her sarong. He was an expert on Javanese
batik and weaving and organized many exhibits. In his position as
controller he was appointed in 1906 to investigate the state of arts and
crafts. With the exception of two years' furlough in the Netherlands,
he continued at this task until its completion in 1915. Between 1912
and 1930, the magnificently produced standard work appeared which
Jasper wrote together with Mas Pirngadi, *Native Arts and Crafts in
the Netherlands Indies (De Inlandse kunstnijverheid in Nederlandsch-Indië)*, five heavy volumes containing numerous colored
plates and reproductions.

Upon his retirement, Jasper did not return to Holland as did most
people. He regarded the Indies as his mother country and chose
to stay on. In 1945 he died in the Japanese concentration camp at
Tjimahi.

Looking at Jasper's service record, it is clear he was a "Java man,"
an official who had spent virtually his entire career on the island of
Java. L. C. Westenek (1872–1930) was a man from the outlying districts. The outlying districts prescribed a different way of life, a more
primitive existence but also a different talent and personality. For
that matter, Westenek, like Jasper, was born on Java, where his father
ran a coffee plantation. His mother was an Indieswoman, of mixed
descent, coming from a large family. When he was seven years old his

father took him to Holland, where he came to stay with an aunt in the city of Deventer. Even so, he was to retain his Indies habits of speech and, like Jasper, remained an Indiesman in many respects. This is where their similarity ends. Jasper was a man of certain refinement, artistic, who headed an arts circle, and who was a sociable man as well, with something of the aesthete about him. In any case, he was quite a different type from Westenek. Damsté, who had been his friend for years, informs us about Westenek's years as a youth in Deventer. As early as that, he stood out. He could spit furthest, run fastest, and hit hardest. When he got older, he went in for rowing, swimming, skating, and walking for hours on end. He was clearly a lad destined for the outdoor life.

His father decided he should become a government official, and so he did. He could not stand his desk job in Bandung and got himself transferred to the island of Borneo somewhere on the banks of the Kapuas River. There he was the only white man in an area of some ninety square miles. Twenty-three at the time, he lived in a house on stilts above the river, with many plants and flowers, especially orchids, and a whole menagerie of pets. "This is the life," he wrote home, "for it makes it also possible to study the land and the people, and to collect ethnographica and so on."

And that is how his life was to continue. Sumatra's western coast was in time to become his particular territory. He liked to hunt and was fond of dogs and horses. Wherever he was stationed, he had a race track built and organized races. Westenek was not what one would call introspective but rather a practical man of action, less an administrator and more a leader. He made long tours of inspection deep into the jungle, accompanied only by a couple of guides and bearers. On the way, he talked with anyone he encountered. He was a born storyteller who was to make a deep impression on Louis Couperus. During those day-long journeys, living among and with his people, he got to know the population, their customs, ideas, and *adat*. That was how he came to understand a great deal and how he acquired his authority. He knew far more about his territory and its people than most administrators, and this impressed everyone, his colleagues as well as outsiders. His personality was marked by the fact that as a young official he had already learned to make decisions and to command. He did much for the population because he truly loved those people after his own fashion, although there were instances when he behaved like an authoritarian father who brooked no contradictions. This also got him into trouble with other officials, his superiors included. Not surprisingly therefore, Westenek's career was not without incidents but his excellent administrative record always saved him, especially his vast knowledge of the native population. Every page bears witness to this knowledge in his books *Where Man and Tiger Meet* (*Waar mens en tijger buren zijn*, 1927) and *The Realm of Bittertong (Het rijk van Bittertong)*, published posthumously in 1932.

Westenek was not "a man of letters," but he writes well, in a simple, straightforward style. It is not a grand style but it does lack artifice and wordiness. He did not write either stories or novels ("no make believe," as he said himself) but wrote about his own adventures. These included encounters with tigers and deal with tiger lore, with an old chief, with "superstition" and magic, with jungle people or the *orang pèndèk* (pygmies), with the mysteries of the jungle, with hunting for big game, with the *tjinta manis* (love of sweets), or with the poisonous snake that dreams, about Penjoe the tortoise, about Telegoe the skunk, about Joseph the hornbill, and so on. Whatever he talks about is rare, curious, fascinating, and interesting. To the question of whether it is the story itself or the way of telling that makes his books so compelling, the answer has to be that it hardly matters. Westenek succeeds in making us enter into an unknown and intriguing world, and he does so by the magic of writing.

IX
The World Beyond

1 The Ethical Movement

No matter how much each European living in the Indies was subject to a process of change, or however much he became a different person, he could never completely shake off his origins. To some extent, he always remained a bit bourgeois, this because the middle class, often the lower middle class, had invariably exported the greatest number of Hollanders. A middle-class person rose in social position the moment he set foot in the Indies. By virtue of his white skin alone he could immediately assume a privileged position. The Indies provided him with the incalculable advantage of giving him the sense of moving up several degrees. Having left behind a life involving a great deal of insecurity, humiliation, and narrowness, this new sense of self-esteem in the absence of old values did at times lead to boisterousness and excessive behavior. He became most aggressive where he was least opposed, which was among the native Indonesians. Hence the infamous bossy manner and exclamations such as "Ajo, lekas!" ("Come on, let's get a move on!") and "Godverdomme" ("Goddamn") were typical, as Bas Veth observed. For that matter, this bossiness is something taken completely for granted in every Indies novel.

The very traits that Veth so accurately observed at times were the result of the social structure. Indies society can not, however, be judged on the basis of Veth's work alone, but requires all sorts of correctives from other sources, also from those that lie outside literature.

Even Bas Veth, so clearly out to settle a score with the Dutch in the Indies, allowed for exceptions. Those exceptions, which he no longer called "Indiesmen," were to be found among officials, officers, doctors, planters, and merchants—nearly everywhere, in fact. They formed the top layer of European society, which was still extremely thin in the nineteenth century, so thin in fact, that it did not exert any influence on that society. Moreover, they were so few in number and spread out over such a vast area that they had little or no contact among themselves. An old-Indies hand wrote in 1897, in a book called *Our East (Onze Oost)*: "The Europeans living in the Indies are too few in number and live at such great distances from one another that they can not possibly form a community, let alone a society. For that reason, they are not sufficiently sympathetic toward one another to satisfy a mutual craving for intellectual pursuits." That same old-timer, however, also wrote that increasing numbers of "civilized men and women" were settling in the Indies. This meant, in his judgment at least, a qualitative as well as a numerical increase. The latter is a matter of record: between 1860 and 1900, the number of Europeans had doubled. Available statistics make it seem probable that the quality of life did indeed improve. The relatively large influx of European women was also to leave its mark on this society. In any event, a process of normalization began to set in. This, coupled with the increase in population, made possible improved communication among its elite, at least in the cities. This elite too regarded the native Indonesian the way newly arrived foreigners did, in contrast to the attitude of Boeka, Jasper, or Westenek, and they too mentioned the "inscrutable faces of the Javanese," and felt themselves unable to penetrate their private and spiritual world. Still, they no longer regarded them as "a servile people," as Creusesol had done, or as a people content with a simple life. They began to realize that such "views" only served to gloss over their own responsibilities and that the true economic condition of the population was simply deplorable.

The journalist Brooshooft from Semarang wrote as early as 1884: "I'm a Dutchman who profits every single day from the income of the Colonies. I should really favor the interests of the Netherlands over those of the Indies but I do not doubt for a single moment that the Netherlands have done a great injustice to the Indies, an injustice that must incense every just person." In 1887, shocked by what he had seen during a trip through Java, he took the initiative to write to twelve important Dutchmen. He asked them to please acquaint themselves with "the dreadful results of Dutch administration in the Netherlands Indies."

Brooshooft accompanied his request with his own *Memorandum concerning the Situation in the Indies (Memorie over den toestand in Indië)*, an excellent piece of writing the size of a book. Brooshooft did not get much of a response in the Netherlands. Not until the end of the nineteenth century did the government become aware of the seriousness of the situation and begin to face up to it. Maybe it took the government that long to realize that its past policies of colonial exploitation had resulted in a stagnation of welfare generally, ultimately afflicting its own "well-considered self-interest."

Economical and ethical considerations overlapped and this resulted in 1902 in the appointment of a commission whose task it was to investigate this "diminished welfare." This so-called Commission of Diminished Welfare produced a report of twelve volumes which was not completed until 1914. It is a gold mine for the social scientist. In addition, in 1904 the ethical Minister of the Colonies, A. W. F. Idenburg, appointed C. Th. van Deventer, member of the Chamber of Deputies and its Indies specialist, to write a report concerning *The Economical Condition of the Native Population of Java and Madura (De economische toestand der Inheemsche bevolking van Java en Madoera)*. This report, which appeared in the same year, went straight to the heart of the matter. Its conclusion was an official sounding and politely phrased denunciation of the government. The fact that Idenburg had asked Van Deventer to write the report was no accident, of course. It was really more an act of collaboration. Minister Idenburg was familiar with Van Deventer's ideas, which had appeared as early as 1899 in *The Guide* in a much discussed article entitled "A Debt of Honor" ("Een eereschuld"). That article had argued for a restitution of the monies that the Netherlands had extracted from the Indies in the course of time. Now that the population found itself "in an alarming condition," to use Van Deventer's words, the time had come to make such a restitution. In his opinion, there was no policy for the Indies better than one of "justice and honesty." Idenburg could not have agreed more.

"The Ethical Movement in Colonial Policies" ("De ethische koers in de koloniale politiek"), also the title of Brooshooft's article, became the title of a political movement that is traditionally thought to have dated from the Royal Address to Parliament of 1901, in which the government makes mention for the first time of "a moral obligation" toward the people of the Indies. This ethical course of action led to improvements in native education, modest enough at first, which were patterned after Western ideas, because the idea of development could of course only be interpreted in a Western sense. It also led to a cautious policy of general welfare (including irrigation works, improvement of native financial credit, establishment of small native industries and workshops). This "new sense of justice," as Brooshooft had called it, never quite became a modus operandi the government could adhere to, much less the European community in the Indies at large. It remained restricted to a small, albeit influential, group including governors-general such as Idenburg and Van Limburg Stirum, politicians such as Van Deventer, Van Kol, Kielstra, Abendanon, academics such as Snouck Hurgronje and Van Vollenhoven, writers such as Augusta de Wit, Marie C. van Zeggelen, and others, as well as Brooshooft himself. At a certain level, an exchange did take place between Dutchmen and Indonesians. The Indonesian began to penetrate European sensibilities, while the European too came out of his confines to seek out the Indonesian. The European discovered a different world which he tried to understand as well as enter. No longer did he remain locked up within his own sphere of interests. As his interests increased, he broadened his horizons.

The ethical movement or course of action, if one will, was a little presumptuous, to be sure, and at times too devout and precious, but it did represent the colonial government's conscience. There is no doubt that it was supported by a real sense of compassion with the plight of the Indonesian, which it tried to raise above the level of material poverty and social discrimination. For this to succeed at all, it was necessary that the Indonesian free himself from feudal traditions and seek development along Western lines, a process of emancipation and education aimed at independence. Then, it was hoped, Dutchmen and Indonesians would build the future Indies together. This goal was called "politics of association." Beyond that, adherents of the ethical approach did not look. The colonial structure of society was nowhere called into question and any advance the Indonesian was meant to make was to be made within this colonial system. As it happened, the ethical approach amounted to little more than a humanitarian corrective. To be sure, there were some Socialists among its adherents, such as Van Kol and, later, Stokvis and others. However, even those who condemned the colonial situation and recognized Indonesian nationalism as "a welcome and fortuitous revival of the native masses" could only envision change on a long-term basis and believed that European leadership would remain necessary for many years to come. For all his good intention, his genuine interest in and respect and admiration for various aspects of Indonesian culture and society, even the most well-intended Dutchman naturally assumed that Western ways were superior. For that matter, without such an assumption he could not have begun to undertake the task of elevating and educating others in the first place. This kind of mission put him in the often repugnant role of the well-meaning guardian who could not desist from watching over his wards, not even when the latter were quite ready to go it alone. The nature of this tendency to remain a perpetual guardian has been described by J. S. Furnivall in his *Netherlands India: A Study of Plural Economy* (1939, p. 389) as follows: "All these people want to help so much: 'Let me help you,' one can almost hear them say, 'let me show you how to do it, *let me do it for you.*' "

The life and work of Kartini (1879–1904) are inseparable from the ethical movement. Her place in history is really owing to the initiative of the then "ethical" director of education, J. H. Abendanon. In 1911, seven years after her death at age twenty-five, he had her correspondence published, although unfortunately not completely.

Kartini has since become a legend. She has been officially declared a national hero, in fact, but one wonders what would have happened if the Abendanons had not regarded her as their spiritual foster child, if Mr. Abendanon had *not* seen to the publication of her letters, if he had not happened to be director of education, and if, later on, no schools "under the protection of her name" had been founded. Maybe people would have continued to talk about her for a while, for the Kartini case was a cause célèbre indeed. People would have spoken of her as the emancipated daughter of the regent of Japara but in time she would have become little more than just a name. What we know about her, about what she felt, hoped for, and thought, all that is owing to Abendanon's edition of her letters. Despite all subsequent studies, this edition is still our principal source. It is incomplete, however, and leaves a number of questions unanswered. For that reason perhaps, Kartini gradually grew into a legendary figure, principally in the eyes of Dutch adherents to the ethical movement who wanted to see her as a symbol of cooperation between "white" and "brown" people. They also regarded Kartini as personifying their idea of what the modern Indonesian should become.

To the supporters of the ethical movement, Kartini then represented the Javanese woman who had freed herself from the severe constraints of Javanese tradition in order to develop according to Western ideas. The title *From Darkness to Light* (*Door duisternis tot licht*, 1911), which Abendanon gave to her collected letters, underscores this assumption. The Dutch legend surrounding Kartini was first adopted, and then expanded by the Indonesians. From a woman who fought for the rights of women against male selfishness, against polygamy and prostitution, she became "the symbol of the awakening of the Indonesian people," in order to finally evolve into a "national hero." By then, we have quite lost sight of the real Kartini.

From what we know from her letters and other sources, the real Kartini was a quick, extremely sensitive Javanese, very intelligent, courageous, and perceptive—far too perceptive to be happy in her time and situation. Something pathetic surrounds the figure of Kartini. Her life, the things she writes about, and her manner of writing all inspire a sense of sympathy, respect, and pity for her. We take pity on her for all the things that were denied her, and we respect and like her for her courage in fighting her "silent battle." For there is much within and beyond Kartini's letters that goes unmentioned.

She was born in 1879. Her father was one of the first enlightened regents to send his daughters to the Dutch school, then something unheard of. He was not modern enough, however, not to keep them "under lock and key" after they reached age twelve. In other words, they could not set a foot outside until they were properly married and then only to a husband their parents had selected. In all fairness, his appointment as regent had a limiting effect on his actions. Whereas the elder daughter had easily submitted to the severities of Javanese tradition following her years of schooling, Kartini, the younger daughter, proved exceedingly obstreperous and rebellious. "I don't know how I managed to live through that period," she wrote a Dutch friend, "all I know is that it was horrible." Her father had bowed to the demands of sacred tradition and had succumbed neither to European pressure nor to the copious tears and pleas from his twelve-year-old favorite, his "little Ni." He tried to ease her imprisonment as much as possible. He never denied her Dutch books or her correspondence with Dutch friends, and he did all he could to get her more reading material. "He spoiled me with presents of books," Kartini was to write. "Reading and writing meant everything to me and without them I probably would have died." But with all the books, the periodicals, and the letters, her desire for freedom and independence only increased. She could not tolerate the fact that her surroundings demanded complete obedience, dependence, and subjugation. She became rebellious, she demanded to be educated and to be trained in order that she too might educate others and help "raise up" her own people. Wherever she turned, she met with difficulties, antagonism, and slander. She found herself torn between love and duty, between progress and tradition. She ended up feeling a failure in her mission, although she tried to keep this from herself and from others. She did return to her old, familiar world. On November 8, 1903, she married the much older regent of Rembang, a widower. To this union she brought a few scraps of her former ideals. She died on September 17, 1904, a few days after being delivered of her child.

Kartini's letters, written in a well-nigh flawless Dutch, are an irreplaceable human document. Nowhere in the Dutch language can one hope to find such a specific process of acculturation traceable from within. Only if one were to argue that a compilation of letters such as *From Darkness to Light* lies beyond the pale of literature could we leave these letters undiscussed here. For the rest, whatever Kartini read and wrote was very much within the literary tradition of the

Netherlands. In one of her letters, she admits to having literary aspirations, as, in fact, did most of her correspondents.

What did she read? She herself writes that her reading educated and formed her. She read the newspaper, and that was in her time *The Locomotive (De Locomotief)* from Semarang, the paper edited by Brooshooft. Kartini must have regarded him as an ally. Her reading also included *The Guide*, as well as *The New Guide (De Nieuwe Gids)*, *Scientific Pages (Wetenschappelijke Bladen)* and *Contributions (Bijdragen)*. Her letters show that she read these with interest, quoting from several on occasion. They also indicate her interest in social problems, not just female emancipation. She was among the first to regard the women's movement for equal rights, for freedom and independence, as part of a much larger social movement. Her interests were wide-ranging and they broadened themselves in time. Multatuli was certainly among the authors she read before she turned twenty. She owned a copy of his *Max Havelaar*, and before the turn of the century she had read his *Amatory Letters (Minnebrieven)* twice. In November 1901, while she was desperate and despondent, she haphazardly took a book from its shelf which turned out to be the *Amatory Letters*. In it, with a shock, she came upon the very phrase that applied to her own situation: "Father says that *knowing, understanding* and *wanting* are sinful in a girl." She also read Couperus, whom she expected to write "a splendid book about my country."

By then, she had thrice read the then-popular feminist novel *Hilda van Suylenburg* by Goekoop-de Jong van Beek en Donk, and found it a "fine and beautiful book." She was also familiar with the poet De Genestet and had enjoyed Van Eeden's *Little Johannes (De kleine Johannes)*. All in all, an odd assortment perhaps. We are better informed about the things she read from May 1898 on, when her letters commence, up to the day of her death. They mention authors and titles such as Van Eeden, Augusta de Wit, Fritz Reuter, Vosmaer (his *Consecration [Inwijding]*), and others. She also read the Dutch translation of Bertha von Suttner's *Lay Down Your Weapons* and, indeed, Bas Veth's work, which naturally annoyed her a great deal. Kartini depended on luck as far as her reading was concerned, although she did once in a while order books directly from Holland. The book trade in the Indies had all sorts of shortcomings and she had a hard time finding her way around in contemporary literature. Nonetheless, she does reveal her predilections and we realize how thoroughly Javanese she really was: she shows a clear preference for tracts, moral tracts especially.

This is not surprising, of course, when we remember that she had not as yet entered into "the other world" and that her entire frame of reference was still none other than her own ancient Javanese culture. It stressed the unity of the beautiful with the philosophical, religious, and ethical. This also explains her lack of what we are in the habit of calling "literary discrimination." What she was looking for in literature was something quite different. To put it another way, her frame of reference involved different categories and values. She admired Couperus immensely and called his language "simply beautiful," but she considered his characters "what we tend to call sickly." Remarks such as these are typical. In addition, she called Multatuli "a genius" and she read him "with ecstasy," but still she considered Henri Borel "most exciting" as well. While she praised *Little Johannes* as "deeply sensitive," she also held the highest opinion of a mediocre writer such as Marie Metz-Koning. To anyone with a sensitive ear, Kartini's taste is clear enough: her preference is tuned to a particular tone, one that is all too frequently sharp and sounds off key. All of her favorite authors have this high tone in common, but the better ones among them produce it as an overtone only, whereas among the lesser writers it dominates everything else. Kartini had ambitions to become a writer herself. As a Javanese-speaking person, however, she felt unsure of herself, and that explains why she practiced writing in the manner of her older and younger female correspondents, all of them "dedicated to literature." They wrote, in fact, for a fancy sounding and genteel ladies' magazine called *The Holland Lily (De Hollandsche Lelie)*, to which Kartini subscribed and in which she published. As such letters go, moreover, Kartini's were better written than the books her Dutch friends held in such high esteem. Some of her letters have the power to captivate and hold us. At times, quite frequently in fact, her voice has a great immediacy, despite all her stylistic clichés.

Just as her name will be forever linked with that of Abendanon, so too will Kartini's name be forever associated with that of the Van Deventers. Upon Kartini's death, the Van Deventers, acting "in the spirit of her name," made possible the establishment of girls' schools in order to try and realize Kartini's ideas concerning the education of native girls.

Conrad Théodore van Deventer (1857–1915), a cousin of the critic Busken Huet, had gone to the Indies as a young legal official. On account of his legal practice and owing to the revival of the plantation system, as well as the new explorations of oil, he had managed to make his fortune within the span of slightly more than ten years. Although he mockingly called himself "a passionate moneyman," he was in fact a man with "social tendencies," as he confided in a letter to his parents, dated April 30, 1886. He was aware even then of the fact that a great deal more *needed* to be done for the Indonesians, "because otherwise the day will come when the dam bursts and the sea of revolution will drown all of us."

Having returned to the Netherlands as a financially independent man, he dedicated all his efforts to the "Indies cause." Van Deventer became and was to remain the spokesman for the ethical movement in the Netherlands by dint of his articles and as a member of the House and, later, of the Senate. In addition to his previously mentioned "A Debt of Honor," which appeared in *The Guide*, and his report for Idenburg, the Minister of Colonial Affairs, he wrote scores of articles, most of them appearing in *The Guide*. One of these was called "Indonesia's Future" ("Insulinde's toekomst"), which appeared in 1908 and deals with his expanded views on Indies development according to ethical guidelines.

The appearance in 1911 of Kartini's letters made a deep impression on Van Deventer, and he wrote a lengthy review in order to make her ideas more widely known. Her ideals, which Van Deventer learned from reading her letters as well as her famous "note from the heart," complemented his *own* ideals exactly, i.e., the spiritual and economic development and emancipation of the Indonesian people. He felt encouraged by what a Javanese person like Kartini had to say. It provided evidence that the same desires and longings also existed among the people living in "the other world." Kartini's writings stimulated him, and she became his sounding board. His review of her *From Darkness to Light* emphasizes her ideas, although he fails to see the tragedy of her personal situation. Here Van Deventer's shortcomings as a human being become evident. He was a man of high ideals, moved by social causes and needs, but without real understanding of the human heart. In fact, it is this shortcoming that makes him the typical supporter of the ethical movement, precisely because of this somewhat ethereal and abstract characteristic of his.

One wonders whether the Van Deventers did not actually know Kartini earlier. He had met her when she was a twelve-year-old in Japara, but by the time she was writing her first letters to her girl friends in Holland, he and his wife had already returned to the Netherlands. They seem to have been in touch with one another through Kartini's brother Kartono, who was living in Semarang, attending high school, while the Van Deventers lived there. This was insufficient cause, however, for either Mr. or Mrs. van Deventer ever to have paid a visit to Kartini in nearby Japara. This only goes to prove that Indonesia and the Indonesians did not begin to play an important role in the lives of the Van Deventers till quite late. Not until they had left the country and settled in The Hague did they become aware of their "late calling."

Even though they knew of Kartini, they did not discover her until after Abendanon published her letters. From that moment on, Mrs. van Deventer began to assume a prominent role. "In the spirit of her name," to use Van Deventer's expression, and "in keeping with the ideas as they are to be found in the letters and her famous 'note from the heart,' " they took the initiative to found schools for Indonesian girls. That is how, on June 27, 1913, the Kartini Foundation came into being. This foundation, with its headquarters back in the Netherlands, grew into a far-flung organization that included thousands of pupils. Mrs. van Deventer devoted all her time and energy to its administration. Her unflagging efforts accomplished a great deal. There were times, especially following her husband's death, when she ran herself ragged. Her life became one long series of meetings and conferences. She was the one to choose the teachers and arrange for their being sent abroad and this is how she gave the schools her personal stamp. As to the atmosphere and spirit of those schools, a former pupil summed them up by saying "no better life than that in the Van Deventer boarding schools."

Mrs. van Deventer died during the German occupation in 1942, when she was eighty-five years old. In her will, she left her capital to Indonesia and for the use of Indonesians, later facilitated by the establishment of the Van Deventer-Maas Foundation. In conclusion, one more detail which better than anything else characterizes the Van Deventers' relationship to the Indonesians: in the "Oud Eik en Duinen" cemetery in The Hague, two young Javanese men who had studied in the Netherlands lie buried, one having died in 1913, the other in 1923. Both of them are in the Van Deventer family plot.

2   John Company

Arthur van Schendel's *John Company* (1932) is a historical novel dealing, from a Dutch perspective, with the first Dutch settlement in the Indies. The novel shows a great deal of unity throughout. No doubt Van Schendel, while unfolding an important phase in Dutch colonial history, aimed at monumentality.

His novels, especially those written after 1930, have a broad perspective and a carefully worked-out plot. The critic Jan Greshoff, in his *Notes concerning "John Company" and "The Waterman"* (*Aanteekeningen over Jan Compagnie en De Waterman*, 1934), compared

Van Schendel's *John Company* to a mural. The comparison, when one thinks of it, makes a great deal of sense, especially because it illustrates so well how carefully Van Schendel went to work.

[John Company] is a detailed portrayal of the colorful first years in the history of the United East Indies Company. One mural, as it were, depicts the young city of Amsterdam and its growing port, its trade, and its rivalries. Placed in the foreground, and somewhat more clearly outlined than the other figures, we see a lively, overconfident young fellow who is anxious to escape the narrow confines of the town and who heads for the Indies.

The second mural reveals the Dutch establishing themselves in the Banten area on Java's West Coast. And again, among a multitude of natives, Chinamen, Englishmen, and Hollanders, we discern the more pronounced figure of De Brasser, soldier, corporal, and sergeant. The third tableau gives us a marvelous view of the Moluccas. It shows us the descendants of the Portuguese living their amiable, naive lives among the natives but it also shows all too well the servants of the Company destroying their idyll through fire and sword in order that they may send even more pepper and cloves back to Europe. The central figure here too is that of Jan de Brasser, now a free man, a landowner, a planter and merchant, who with care and hard work makes his fortune. He also makes it a point to remain as morally upright and just as circumstances allow.

In conclusion, the fourth mural shows the city of Amsterdam again, now much more crowded, greater, more colorful and richer, as the center of European commerce. Against this great national backdrop, old De Brasser stands out again as somebody not quite at home there, albeit for a different reason this time. As we look around us and examine one tableau after another in this manner, hundreds of details begin to stand out, far too many to describe here. Van Schendel shows us an amazing variety and number of things but he has managed to arrange them in such a way as to make them into a harmonious whole. All the parts contribute and are essential to this larger concept, and for that reason, whenever *John Company* comes to mind, I invariably think of it as one, inseparable whole.

Greshoff, aiming to praise Van Schendel, considers his prose devoid of "literary embellishments," but this does in no way mean that Van Schendel uses a lively and natural prose that follows the vagaries of the human heart, as does Multatuli's, for example. On the contrary, Van Schendel employs a stylized, classical, and somewhat archaic

Dutch, which certainly reveals a good deal of literary preoccupation on his part. His style is cool and most effective whenever it contrasts with a dramatic incident, which is the case in most of his novels. Even when the dramatic element is lacking, however, his prose retains this quality of always progressing slowly and steadily, but its effectiveness is then diminished or lost altogether. This is the case in *John Company*, where his sober style could not quite function to effect, because the story lacks real human and dramatic content. For that reason, *John Company* does not quite measure up to an earlier novel like *The Frigate "Johanna Maria" (Het Fregatschip Johanna Maria)*, and even less to his subsequent tragic novels. Greshoff has a different opinion and tries to forestall any criticism of this kind in the last few pages of his critique. He finds *John Company* just as successful a novel as Van Schendel's *The Waterman*, or his *A Dutch Drama (Een Hollands drama)*, or *Gray Birds (Grauwe vogels)*, or *The World is Dancing (De wereld een dansfeest)*.

The critic H. 's-Gravesande, in his 1949 monograph dealing with Arthur van Schendel, regrets the fact that there is relatively little biographical information available. Van Schendel was a man little inclined to reveal private details of his life, to be sure, but we do know quite a bit about him even so. For our purposes it is interesting to know that Van Schendel was born in Batavia in 1874. His father was an officer there and took his family back to the Netherlands when Arthur was just five years old. The formative years that any child spends in the Indies are quite decisive, however. 's-Gravesande informs us that Van Schendel's father died when the child was still quite young, which meant that he was largely brought up by his mother. Hers was a family with long-standing ties with the tropics, a colonial family, so to speak, which meant an Indies family with Indies traditions, Indies aunts and uncles, nephews, nieces, and so on. If not distinguishable from the Hollanders by their looks, they must surely have stood out on account of their different way of speaking, their way of life, in short, through their different habits. Van Schendel must have known these people, also in later life, after they had returned to the Netherlands, "repatriated," as they called it. His mother's family must have been quite close to him afterwards in Holland too. He was part of them, while he could at the same time stand back far enough to see how typically *Indies* and different they were, living in Holland but according to their own cultural pattern. Even so, Van Schendel wrote remarkably little about his family. For one thing, he did not emulate Couperus's habit of modeling his fictional characters after living family members.

Once, in *The World is Dancing*, he introduces an Indies lady whom he draws admirably, mostly by just allowing us to overhear her talk. Her authenticity leaves little doubt that she is modeled after one or several members of his Indies "clan." This remarkable portrait of a lady should be seen within its proper framework, or within the whole gallery of portraits called *The World is Dancing*. This novel deals with the tragic history of the dancing couple Marion and Daniël as told by nineteen different people who knew them at various stages in the past. One of these people is the Indies lady, Mrs. Hadee, "née Odilie Harings." ("How old am I? Oh, Sir, I've quite forgotten that.") She is the piano teacher of Marion, Mr. Ringelinck's little daughter. She talks about her relationship with Ringelinck in a self-satisfied and coquettish sort of way ("I'm not sure whether I could really accept such a present, people so quickly jump to the wrong conclusions. But then again, Ringelinck never did give me the idea that I ought to be careful, he is such a thoroughly respectable gentleman.") She is flattered by his attentions but she feels that his friends insult her: "My God, the number of insufferable men in this world, always after something." Her speech is a mixture of cunning and innocence, the somewhat romantic jargon of so many older Indies ladies ("What a dear, what a pretty!"), larded with French words and exclamations. What characterizes her most as an Indies lady is her particular tone of voice. Van Schendel conveys it admirably.

X
The Netherlands East Indies

1 The Young Dutch Wives

In 1905, 1906, or a little later perhaps, the Indies began to improve economically. The commission looking into "decreased well-being" had hardly commenced its exhaustive inquiry when the world economic climate began to have a salubrious effect on the Indies also. As early as 1890, but especially after 1905, European and particularly Dutch businessmen began to invest large sums in the Indies. It became a period of incorporated businesses. In 1909 alone, 175 new ones were established. As commerce, industry, and new crops developed, the need for more employees from Holland increased, in commerce as well as in government. These could only be accommodated if a great many things were changed. They needed greater comfort, greater safety, life needed to be normalized and made more like that in the home country. Gradually the notion was abandoned that young employees and officials should come to the Indies as unmarried men who could take a concubine for a start. The government had been more progressive on that score all along, and now the business world began to follow suit. The Deli Company, for example, did not rescind its demand that its employees be unmarried until 1919, but other businesses, particularly on Java, had dropped this requirement sooner, and more were to follow. Now more than ever in the previous decades, the employees and officials came to the Indies either with their wives, or they had them come over as soon as their economic circumstances allowed, usually through a proxy wedding back in Holland. All the statistics bear this out. The percentage of women leaving for the Indies rose between 1905 and 1915 from 18.7 percent to 40.6 percent.

The influx of a far greater number of European women caused gradual but definite changes in the Indies way of life, both in the hinterland and in the cities, but particularly in the latter. The first years of the twentieth century were transitional. From then on, certain shifts in the old Indies pattern of life began to take place, for a while leaving a number of characteristics of the old pattern intact everywhere, with the old and the new overlapping. However, European society, which had altered structurally very little in the previous decades, now began to show signs of accelerated change, and in a direction it had always tended toward, that of Europeanization. This was a process that, naturally enough, took place from the (white) top on down, and that was especially accelerated by the new influx of European women then entering the colonies, bringing their customs and habits with them. They also had different desires and new demands, which were to leave their mark on Indies society and had a wide and profound effect in setting new standards. All of Indies life began to become much more European, among the Eurasians as well and even among the Indonesians who had advanced themselves in colonial society. Even so, the good old life of the Indies plantation did continue to exist for quite some time afterwards. Especially deep in the interior or in the outlying districts, far from the European centers, people continued to live as if time had stood still, with the *njai,* or native concubine, as "mother of the children," kerosene lamps throughout the house, and white-caulked flower pots in the garden. And at night, they still sat endlessly on the veranda "shooting the breeze." They did not call in a doctor but sent for the native medicine man or obtained counsel from other wives or Indonesian women, or otherwise consulted Mrs. Kloppenburgh-Versteegh's herbals. But this way of life too was doomed to disappear.

The Indies were also made "more inhabitable" for European families. Tropical medicine developed and could begin to combat more effectively such virulent diseases as malaria, cholera, typhoid, and dysentery. The appearance of the six-volume *Kromoblanda* (1915–1923) by H. F. Tillema, a pharmacist from Semarang, is symptomatic of this. A number of books date from this period too, bearing such titles as *To the Indies and Back (Naar Indië en terug),* advertised as "a guide for the family and especially a vademecum for ladies." Another was *Our Home in the Indies (Ons huis in Indië),* "a manual on the selection, decoration, habitation, and care of the home according to the demands of modern hygiene." This included advice on the use of drinking water, on healthy clothing (advocating the homely, long housecoat), on ventilation, on the furnishing of a proper bedroom (no more chamber pots, dividing screens, or kerosene nightlights), and also dealt with the advantages of a modern kitchen (no more sooty kitchen with a charcoal grill but a "Perfection" kerosene oven, and especially a "good drain"!). And it contained something on the use of disinfectants. Also to become popular was an ever-increasing number of books on medicine written for the layman, designed to supplant *Tips and Suggestions (Wenken en raadgevingen)* by Mrs. J. Kloppenburgh-Versteegh, which, nonetheless, continued to remain the classic of many an Indies housewife.

Those young Dutch wives who annually left Holland during the first decade of the twentieth century had a difficult enough time of it, especially if they came from the Dutch upper-middle class and were somewhat intellectual or artistic, painted or played an instrument, read or recited poetry, or if they were accustomed to going to concerts or plays. In the Indies life was monotonous and they had to make do without all that. One day was exactly the same as the next, the same sun, the same foliage, and the same endless boredom. In a letter dated April 20, 1916, which is somehow preserved, an unknown young Dutch woman writes to a girl friend in Utrecht, Holland: "Every day is the same here. Breakfast is over at seven in the morning. The bread is sour here. That leaves that enormous stretch from seven until noon to get through! Toward eleven o'clock, moreover, it's already terribly hot and you feel so tired and miserable, you just want to collapse. After lunch is over around twelve-thirty, most people take a nap, and the streets are desolate and deserted. I find it impossible to sleep in the afternoon, however. How, you may well ask, do I spend my time? At times like these, I think again of going shopping in Amsterdam, and drinking coffee someplace nice, with a small orchestra playing in the background somewhere." The same letter continues: "For days on end, I'd lie in a lounge chair on the front veranda, arms under my head, just staring into space, dreaming about that distant world so incredibly far away, and I'd fight back the feeling of homesickness that just comes over me, and against which I am so powerless. . . . Do you know the feeling, Nell? It's so miserable." Even one year later, she writes in a letter dated August 7, 1917: "Oh, I can't stand it anymore! Nell, tell me, is there still no change, is there still no end to this?" The letter this young woman wrote could have been written on behalf of hundreds of other young wives. They nearly all had to give up their illusions, their values, background, and sense of security. It is no small wonder they felt themselves cast out and lonely, and in that alien condition they cursed "that miserable country" where they were aliens. Very often they ended up in a society with totally different values, many of them coming from the confines of a Dutch province. They found themselves confronted with a free, crude, and often unbridled life of bachelors. They introduced a sense of home and comfort, and they were the ones who effected changes and stability, but there was a great deal they had to endure. In many instances, they were the ones to replace the native concubine, with all the ensuing tensions and complications. Many Dutch women simply could not stand it, just as the writer of the letter quoted could not. They would either fall ill or become too homesick, and then they would have to go back. Others managed to adjust much better and even had a few good things to say about the country, but most often not until they were safely back in Holland. Seen from that distance, the Indies were "not so bad after all."

2   M. H. Székely-Lulofs

Madelon Hermine Lulofs (1899–1958) came to Deli, Sumatra in 1918, following her marriage to a planter. Her father was a government official, which meant that, like an army brat, she had lived in a lot of different places. "I was born in Surabaja," she writes, "during a lunar eclipse, in a hotel room, and similar circumstances were to govern my life throughout." She grew up in cities as well as way out in the interior, "where we were the sole representatives of the entire white race." Her work certainly bears the traces of these experiences.

She married when still very young, "just a silly girl," she writes. She lived an unexamined life and simply put up with Deli, which was a new town to her. She remained there till 1930. Her first three novels are situated in Deli: *Rubber* (1931), *Coolie* (*Koelie*, 1932), and *The Other World* (*De andere wereld*, 1934). She knew nothing about literature when she first arrived in Deli. Her family was anything but literary, and her first husband, she tells us, lived a life "totally beyond the realm of literature." Of course she had been writing all along, even when a child. She made her debut in 1925 in a local paper for plantation people, getting several stories placed in it. Not until her second marriage to L. Székely, a Hungarian, also a planter at Deli, and particularly following her return to Europe, did she take up writing seriously. She wrote first of all about Deli. Then it occurred to her to write about her own experiences, and this resulted in her novel called *Rubber*. Its success came unexpectedly and was something unheard of. *Rubber* enjoyed numerous translations, it was made into a play that was performed over a hundred times, and was finally made into a movie. Székely-Lulofs was famous practically overnight. At the time she was pleased with the general acclaim, but later on, she confessed that even thinking about her novels *Rubber* and *Coolie* made her blush: "Afterwards, I was embarrassed, but by then the damage had already been done. The books were simply devoured by everyone and translated everywhere." It is to her credit that she was not fooled by her initial success and could own up to her feelings in this way. She may just possibly have heeded Menno ter Braak's negative assessment of her first books, the critic for whom, she tells us, she retained "a masochistic admiration."

However, it was precisely this success and the fact that her novels were so generally known that troubled the Dutch colony, ever mindful of losing its prestige. The *Deli Courant,* to its credit, had no part in this but merely limited itself to a literary opinion. It was totally wrong, to be sure. "There are numerous pages in this book," the paper wrote, "which possess great tragic force without being in the least written for effect." Another segment of the Indies press, probably less informed about conditions in Deli but also much less guileless, got very excited about the "infamous manner" in which plantation life in Deli had been depicted. If the author thought for one minute that she could impudently "drag European society through the mud," people in Batavia would give her to understand that her portrayal "was no representation of real life." Something else was at issue, however. With an attitude of "I told you so," papers such as *The Locomotive* and the *Java Courier* featured the opinion of a certain Mr. A. Hoogesteeger ("from Hilversum, Holland"). He "had heard from a good friend" or "read somewhere" that translations of *Rubber* in Sweden and in Germany had occasioned adverse political commentary. This made him exclaim: "And then there still are people who dare to claim that this book is not injurious to the reputation of the Indies?" Reactions such as these are typical of the times. The *Java Courier* wrote in undiluted bureaucratic style: "The intent and purpose of the novels written by this married couple can only be judged with disapprobation." Of course, Székely-Lulofs's method of writing did not in the least involve a premeditated slant on things. She said in an interview with Jeanne van Schaik-Willing that she had written her first novels "just for the fun of it." This seems indeed typical of her approach. What she meant by it was that she wrote without any abstraction whatever, and in so doing attained a level of "tempered realism." Herman Robbers, associated with *Elseviers Illustrated Monthly (Elseviers geïllustreerd Maandschrift),* recognized and admired her from the very first. She corresponded with him from 1932, one year after the appearance of *Rubber,* until his death in 1937.

In assessing her work, one has to keep in mind that her realism aims at representing reality and nothing else, without any preconceived notions. In this respect, Székely-Lulofs has admirably acquitted herself in trying to depict the life of plantation people in Deli without any reservation. Her dialogue is as lifelike as possible, interspersed with all manner of punctuation marks, so many in fact, that Du Perron likened them to "swirling confetti." Within the confines of her settings and the inherent limits of the novel (and there are limits, after all), she has tried to compress numerous typical details, which—as in her novel *Rubber*—are meant to evoke the essence of Deli as much as possible. Indeed, her details have a great deal of veracity but the novel as a whole seems unreal, because, after all, a novel about Deli is something other than a sociographical study of Deli society. However, Székely-Lulofs's novels show us that she saw Deli differently from the way Europeans *wished* to see it. Her "different way" of looking at things, she said, had not begun till after her second marriage, and particularly after Deli had become just a memory and a thing of the past. Only then had she begun to understand Deli. From a mere participant she had turned into an observant participant. Her husband's influence may well have helped this process along. He too wrote a book about Deli (two, really), which she translated from the Hungarian, entitled *From Jungle to Plantation* (*Van oerwoud tot plantage*, 1935).

It contains a great many observations that could well keep a couple of sociologists busy for some time. For example: "Here a man conforms, he just conforms and joins the ranks. He wants to become a planter, after all, and a Deli planter at that, nothing less will do. Deli men are a race apart. In Deli everyone gives up his personal traits and simply forgets what he has learned or how he was brought up. All that dissolves and merges here and helps to bring into being a new type of man." We have to allow that the Székely-Lulofs were not a couple that would ever adjust anywhere, and that they both retained something of their personal traits. One can read between the lines and see to what extent they were indeed true members of Deli society, while still remaining outsiders. It was this trait that the well-adjusted members of the Deli world could not forgive them.

In 1936, a former planter by the name of Kleian brought out a book called *Deli Planter*, which was intended as an answer to *Rubber*. Kleian clearly wished to show the other side of the picture. His book introduces a *singkeh*, a newcomer to Deli, who, unlike Székely-Lulofs's character, adapts at once to his new environment. He undergoes his initiation as a rejuvenation, even though a pioneer's life is terribly hard and the bosses curse (forgivable, that, because they all really have a heart of gold). No scandals in his book, but the inevitable native concubine and sneaky half-caste provide the necessary dissonants. Once in a while, a government assistant is treated unfairly. The story trundles along through endless dialogue, and, unintentionally, this boring book turned into a meaningful protest.

If, besides Kleian's, one reads still other books dealing with the Deli region, such as those by Ton Vonk, H. P. van den Bergh, Jo Manders, or H. Gorter, it becomes apparent that Székely-Lulofs is a relatively good author. Among these, Manders (born 1900) was the most controversial. She too wrote things about Deli that were considered "detrimental" to the Indies and that could also undermine colonial prestige at home and abroad. Her *The Lawless* (*De bandeloozen*, 1929) contains a moral portrait of "perverse abnormalities," as some scared colonial critics put it. Her *Stag Club* (*De boedjangclub*, 1933) relates rather a few excessive things about planters, while *Half Caste* (*Indo*, 1935) deals with all kinds of misery befalling two Eurasian girls forced to suffer society's racial prejudices in Deli. The author seems most impressed by her own sense of being above it all.

To return to Székely-Lulofs, however. Two years after *The Other World*, her *Journey of Famine* (*De hongertocht*, 1936) appeared, which may well be her best book. *Journey of Famine* is no longer situated in Deli but in northern Sumatra's Achin region, called Atjeh by the Dutch. She knew Achin very well. She spent the very first years of her life behind the barbed wire and palisades of a military outpost there. Words such as "bivouac," "ration," and "patrol" she knew firsthand. The world "patrol" to her evoked an armed reconnaissance party going out into the jungle, carbine in one hand, the short machetelike *klewang* sword in the other, all the men wearing their wide-brimmed hats. She was also well acquainted with Achin's jungles and its wild interior with its many mountain ranges and deep ravines through which sometimes a *kroëng* (river) flowed, and she had sensed the oppressiveness of the jungle. Her natural descriptions are among the best sections of the book, even though she again betrays her penchant for the all-inclusive listing of things. Nonetheless, *Journey of Famine* is clearly better than her earlier works. Its story is based on actual events.

In 1911, one Second Lieutenant Nutters (called Nyhoff in her novel) was ordered to take two detachments of infantry armed with forty jungle carbines on a patrol from their bivouac at Meureuduë (on Achin's northern coast) to Pameuë, situated in the mountainous jungle of northern Sumatra. This group was accompanied by an Achinese guide and numerous bearers consisting of forced laborers and free coolies. Such journeys were extremely difficult. To their commanding officer, their successful completion was a question of honor and also a test, as it were, to see if he would be allowed to continue to serve in Achin's elite corps. Nutters left on July 11. After about a week, he lost his way. More than a month later, the remaining members of his patrol were found by a rescue party commanded by one

Lieutenant Van Arkel (Van Brakel in the book). The latter found them by following their track of skeletons and emaciated human wrecks. The commander survived the journey. He was called to account and found guilty. He was not discharged, however. They even sent him out on other patrols but his position had become untenable both at the post and in the surrounding villages. During his fateful journey, he had allowed his group to make camp on the shores of a mountain lake inhabited by spirits without asking their "permission." The local population ascribed the fate of the patrol to the might and anger of the lake spirits. No doubt Nutters had made a tactical and psychological blunder in choosing this camp site, an error that lowered his men's morale, especially when things began to go wrong. Following a talk between one of the Achinese village heads and his bivouac commander, Nutters was transferred to a different post. A year later, he left the service and was pensioned off. The question of guilt and responsibility continued to trouble him, however. Twenty-five years later, no less, he wrote an essay about the affair and forwarded it, together with all the facts pertaining to the incident, to Székely-Lulofs.

Nutter's essay and relevant information were "essential in shaping" the tale of the journey, she writes. Nutters had supplied her with the material for a book. "All I did," Székely-Lulofs wrote, "was to add the circumstances as I understood them." Intentionally or unintentionally, her book turned into a plea for Nutters.

Journey of Famine features him as the victim of an 'incomprehensible error." This is debatable. The question remains why Nutters did not turn back when he knew himself to be lost. Székely-Lulofs allows Nutters himself the answer that "that was against orders." She makes his commanding officer say "An order is an order, and turning back only means one thing, incompetence." Somehow this does not sound convincing. Still, it is possible that Nutters allowed his military ambitions to sway his better judgment, unlike Lieutenant Dieleman from the same post who, in the previous year, had turned back from a similar assignment. Yet, in all fairness to Nutters's deliberations, we ought to be mindful of his military position, i.e., the psychology of a second lieutenant and military discipline generally. The latter was, particularly in Achin, extreme if not overstrained.

During an interview with the editors of *Morks Magazijn*, Székely-Lulofs said that as an author she found it easiest to identify with her main character if he or she were heroic. But, she added, the heroic to her did not necessarily mean the hero's success so much as the tragic and human condition surrounding him or her in every action. That explains why Lieutenant Nutters strikes her as heroic, even though he fails in the fulfillment of his assignment.

In her later novel *Tjut Nja Din (Tjoet Nja Din)*, her leading character is an Achinese princess, the widow of Teuku Umar, the resistance hero killed by the Dutch. She too is heroic, and she too goes down to defeat. It is precisely her defeat, however, that constitutes her humanity and tragedy. Thus far her concept of the heroic is consistent. For the rest, the differences are vast. The author's feeling for Lieutenant Nutters is of an entirely different nature than her feeling for Tjut Nja Din. Her attitude toward Nutters lacks the very element that forms the basis of *Tjut Nja Din*, and that is her identification with the heroine. Whereas *Journey of Famine* is still largely a series of events and a taking of sides from a safe distance, *Tjut Nja Din* is characterized by her tendency of total identification. There is, in addition, a clear difference in tone between *Journey of Famine* and *Tjut Nja Din*. The restrained narrative of the former, partly necessitated by the listing of events, has drawn frequent praise. In the latter, the author's tone of voice in uneven, at times uncontrolled and fierce, even rhetorical, then again too matter-of-fact, but in any case indicative of the strong emotional element that went into the writing of it.

As was said before, Székely-Lulofs spent her childhood in Achin, "where I learned to walk." She remembered its natural grandeur, peaks, and plateaus; she had heard of ambushes, seen the dead buried, she had heard of "the brave Achinese enemy," and of course she knew about the "traitor" Teuku Umar. It was through him that she traced the woman in the background who continued the war against the Hollanders after his death. Tjut Nja Din was a ferocious woman dressed "in long, black Achinese trousers and jacket." She was possessed by an implacable hatred of "the Company," i.e., the Netherlands Indies government and the Dutch generally. That is how she appeared to Székely-Lulofs from Dokarim's Achinese chronicle, the *Hikajat Perang Kompeunie (History of the War against the Company)*, which H. T. Damsté, an authority on Achin, had read to her in translation.

Tjut Nja Din was first a name, then an outline, but gradually began to take on a human form to her, and she began to compare her circumstances to her own, somewhat similar ones. She transferred her own hankering after freedom and her own protest against and hatred for the Germans in occupied Holland to Tjut Nja Din and made her into a heroine resisting the Dutch.

Dokarim's *Hikajat* informs us that Tjut Nja Din was captured only after strong resistance. Even then she did not give in. She is said to have yelled and cursed, and only after Captain Veltman asked her if she were indeed the one and only regal Tjut Nja Din did she desist. General van Daalen had her banished to Java, and there she spent the rest of her life. Székely-Lulofs draws her final portrait this way: "She sat motionless except for her hands lying loosely in her lap, which she would raise and clasp together and drop back into her lap, still clasped." Székely-Lulofs also refuses to accept the myth that she was resigned when she died: "Why should we not at least allow her that ultimate hatred toward us, through whom she lost all she had and loved?"

The Literary Museum in The Hague has one loose, anonymous, and undated newspaper clipping on file that claims that Székely-Lulofs had failed in her purpose and ended up somewhere between history and epic. She, however, emphatically tells us that she did not write either an epic or a history, but a biography, which, in turn, amounted to an identification of sorts.

One does not need to regard *Tjut Nja Din* as a masterpiece nor even as her best book, to realize that the author herself was most deeply attached to it among all her works. Her *Journey of Famine* may well be her more successful story but *Tjut Nja Din* was a far more exacting book, so exacting in fact that it may well have strained her powers. Even then it still remains a pity that *Rubber* has gone through numerous reprints, and that *Tjut Nja Din* was never reprinted.

XI
The Idea of Federation

The Indonesian professor and poet G. J. Resink wrote a number of brilliant essays, collected in 1968, which once and for all destroyed the myth that the Dutch colonial empire in the East had been in existence for three uninterrupted centuries. Instead, he shows that the Netherlands East Indies did not actually come into being until about 1910. Before that, there were really only native states within the Indonesian archipelago which were to some extent dependent on the Netherlands and to some extent independent. Outwardly, they formed a state called the Netherlands Indies. The assumption that there was such a thing as a Pax Neerlandica that applied to the entire realm before 1910 is also erroneous.

Assuming that every myth has a pragmatic character and is designed to serve some purpose or other, the logical question to ask ourselves is where this myth came from and what purpose it was supposed to serve. The answer is that the myth of a 300-year-old empire dates from the 1920s or earlier, and that it served the purposes of a particular administrative and political view. This view held that unity between the various parts of the empire did exist and that Dutchmen and Indonesians were equally interdependent. This concept is extensively worked out in the three-volume work by De Kat Angelino. The ideas of De Kat created a broad, firm base that was meant to give substance to the myth. The appearance of his work generally made a big impression, and also influenced government policy.

It served as a compelling justification of the colonial regime that was clearly viable, economically speaking. It also gave shape and direction to numerous attempts to come to some form of cultural synthesis. "Political unity" and "cultural synthesis" are terms that we encounter time and again in the literature of that era. They were interpreted in various ways but they always assumed close collaboration between the people of Indonesia and the Netherlands, politically as well as culturally. Some, or, rather, quite a few people, added something else, either spoken or unspoken, and that was that in order to make this synthesis possible, European leadership should be secured for the duration. This is also the conclusion that H. Kraemer reaches, following his incisive and extensive analysis of De Kat's work. The idea to hold on and to conserve, in more ways than one, was widespread in the European community. "Wij willen Holland houen" ("we want to hold on to Holland") they sang in the Harmonie Club in Batavia, "en Indië daarbij" ("and the Indies too").

Insofar as the facts and events of history do indeed always relate to one another, we may safely assume that the idea of political ties and cultural synthesis would have been unthinkable without the ethical movement preceding this idea. We could even see it as an extension of the ethical movement, although we would then be guilty of obfuscation and find our terminology clouded. It is perhaps better no longer to speak of the ethical movement from the twenties onward if we are indeed to preserve the criterion of the "ethical impulse." For it was precisely this ethical impulse that found itself gradually replaced by the "impulse to preserve." The idea of federation obscured the fact that this ethical impulse was gradually being replaced by the impulse to hang on to the Indies. The facts are more complicated, more nuanced, and less antagonistic, of course. Even so, this juxtaposition is enough of a political reality and has enough tangents to fit the thesis of E. J. Stokvis. Between January and February of 1915, he published a series of articles in *The Locomotive* arguing that the ethical movement had been short-lived indeed and that by 1915 it had already passed its zenith. It is possible, of course, that Stokvis makes a premature claim concerning the movement's demise. More likely, the ethical movement continued as a viable force at least through the administration of Governor-General Van Limburg Stirum, himself a proponent of the movement. Shortly thereafter, the government clearly changed its policy by appointing D. Fock to the governor-generalship in 1921.

To be sure, De Graeff took over from Fock in 1926, and he again was a man of strong ethical persuasions. Still, he was unable to make much headway against the strong currents of patriotism. His improvised policies generally foundered and he has since become a shadowy figure. During his administration, the magazine *The Dam (De Stuw)* was founded, mostly advocating progressive programs. Among its founders was Van Mook, who was to play an important part in Indonesia's postwar period. Its views were followed with interest during De Graeff's time, or in any case condoned and not judged negatively. *The Dam* also carried authority and was respected because it counted a number of colonial professors and higher officials among its contributors. After 1931, however, following the appointment of De Jonge to the governor-generalship, government permanently abandoned ethical directives. De Jonge eschewed the progressive ideas of *The Dam*, which in retrospect are only very moderate, and called them "hyper-ethical." His administration broke completely with the Indonesian Nationalist movement. Instead, he advocated a Dutch-Indonesian federation, which notion he elevated to a vision of still many more centuries of Dutch rule to come.

In his disappointment over the relatively negligible results of the ethical movement for the population, Stokvis blamed the colonial bureaucracy. Whereas business initially cooperated with progressive ideas and tendencies, government, according to Stokvis, felt itself threatened from the start. Former Resident and Governor M. B. van der Jagt's *Memoirs* (*Memoires*, 1955) is symptomatic of the general uneasiness among civil-service bureaucrats and Europeans generally about the ethically inspired administrations of Governors-General J. P. van Limburg Stirum and A. C. D. de Graeff. Van der Jagt's book is one long critique of ethically inspired government. He protests against all modernization, against all government reforms, in short, against everything that could, in his opinion, diminish the powers of the colonial civil service. He thought that only the civil service itself, because it was constantly in touch with the native population, was in a position to gauge the wants and needs of the people. Only the civil service could judge not only how to administer but how to *govern*. While Van Limburg Stirum was governor-general, Van der Jagt did not have a chance. Upon the arrival of Fock, he was made resident by his own choice. Later on he became a member of the Volksraad, the colonial council. There he twice delivered himself of a "fire and brimstone speech," as he called it, against Indonesian nationalism. His *Memoirs* contains one of these speeches in extenso. He may not have been politically far-seeing, but he was nonetheless an excellent administrator who knew his territory through and through, and who got on very well with native government. But these memoirs also show that a sound administrator is not necessarily a man of distinction. They prove him to be a man of limitless vanity (he devotes a separate section of his book to "Honors" he received). Not knowing his own limitations, he also hazards to write "literature," employing the most horrible clichés. Just a few examples: "The pale orb had already risen in the pristine firmament"; or "Before me, the full moon rose, fast coming away from the horizon, soon floating in the sky, pouring out her magic light"; or, concerning the postwar government, "It depends on the Netherlands government, returning from its stray and errant ways, whether or not our tricolor over there will unfold to new fame and glory. . . ."

Van der Jagt is forever talking about justice and duty, about loyalty and incorruptibility, and invariably within the context of "law and order." Prosperity and law and order were regarded as one and inseparable. Those same words were also engraved on the monument dedicated to the conqueror of Achin, General van Heutsz, in Batavia. The monument has long since been demolished. To be sure, prosperity did in fact exist. Law and order were considered essential conditions for maintaining it. There did not appear the slightest plausible reason for disturbing this order. After a brief decline, economic life was flourishing. In the twenties, the relationship between the Indies and the mother country seemed particularly rosy. The term "mother country" was used emphatically to stress the nature of their relationship. Economic expansion was indeed so exuberant that there seemed no reason to doubt the desirability of their symbiotic relationship. These were times of great expectations and mighty optimism. One need only scan the magazines of those days to note the overall tone of satisfaction, confirming that Holland and Indonesia were indeed "tightly joined, for better or for worse."

The Indonesian nationalist movement operated on entirely different principles and assumptions: it wished freedom and independence. It held that the entire communication process between motherland and colonies passed it by, that it was purely a Dutch business affair that only involved the population obliquely and passively. The colonial government took Dutch leadership for granted; the Indonesian leaders did not. Collaboration on the basis of political unity did not appeal to the nationalists. On an individual and institutional level there did exist some areas of contact between Dutchmen and Indonesians but an ideological and political basis for any real collaboration was lacking.

What the colonial ambiance would not allow or made barely possible did however take place back in the Netherlands. There, collaboration was possible thanks to the ethical movement, even though it had lately fallen into disuse. It was based on a sense of solidarity mindful of 300 years of common history that had forged an inseparable destiny between two peoples. On the part of the Dutch, collaboration was especially sought with the Indonesian *prijaji* group, consisting of the Javanese ruling class, regents, and princes, and constituted primarily cultural ties. Yet another manifestation of Dutchmen and Indonesians working together existed among university students. As early as 1918, a number of Dutch and Indonesian students got together to form an alliance that listed political *independence* for Indonesia among its aims. This was only a very small alliance, however, but the fact that it existed at all, and at such an early date, is remarkable in itself. Then too, the Indonesian Student Group in the Netherlands, to which Mohammed Hatta belonged, and which was known as the "Hatta Club," had many personal contacts in leftist and radical circles. This group was to have great political influence on the future of Indonesia.

The idea of political unity, then, found greater response among the Dutch. It was a very popular idea in the twenties and helped determine the overall mood and attitude toward the Indies, while making the Dutch much more aware of their existence. An important number of Dutchmen became more noticeably involved in the colonies, and Indies' prosperity became visible in the Netherlands too. The notion that they needed one another was indeed widespread. All manner of clubs were started, exhibitions organized, and meetings planned; the queen officially received important Indonesian guests.

The idea of federation and unity with Indonesia found its monumental expression in the Colonial Institute in Amsterdam, now the Royal Institute for the Tropics. The business community had planned it, as was to be expected in those days of private enterprise, and the government added little in the way of support, at least not much by contemporary standards. Construction started in 1913, stagnated during World War I, and was resumed in 1919. In 1924 and 1925, the building was partially occupied, and in 1926 it was completed. By then, it had become a symbol of colonial wealth, both material and spiritual. Eastern designs embellished the exterior as well as the interior. The murals were meant to bear witness to prosperity, idealism, and cooperation.

In the Indies too, the strong economic resurgence created the need to erect representative banks and corporate headquarters. The increasing influx of Europeans also necessitated all sorts of urban expansion in the big cities, such as the Gondangdia area in Batavia, the hilly Nieuw Tjandi area in Semarang, the Gubeng and Darmo areas in Surabaja. Medan, Sumatra, was in fact transformed into a new city. "Modern European architecture" got its chance. The architectural firm of Cuijpers and Hulswit even began publishing a richly illustrated magazine, *The Indies Home, Past and Present (Het Indisch huis, oud en nieuw)*. Its first issue of January 1913 explains its purpose: the development of European architecture "through a serious study of the aesthetics of ancient native culture." It contains contributions on the houses of the Dayak and the Buginese, on native crafts, on Javanese architecture, as well as richly illustrated articles dealing with new edifices such as the Java Bank, the Netherlands Trading Company, the Hotel des Indes, the Hong Kong and Shanghai Banking Corporation, and so on.

A similar development took place in the arts. The new, white urban elite began to develop tastes and demands different from those of old-fashioned Indies society, which ranked the cosy atmosphere of any get-together as the utmost. Otto Knaap's fierce personal fight against dilettantism and dabbling around the turn of the century had been the first sign of future changes. We know also that he failed, by his own admission "that whosoever tries to do away with routine and convention will be done in himself."

Meanwhile, in 1902 a group of prominent citizens in Batavia, officials and such, had founded an arts council which was first of all to concern itself with the much neglected plastic arts. After a somewhat disappointing start (the daily paper apologetically called them "idealists"), the group proved to have sufficient vitality in following years to grow into the kind of cultural center the likes of which had never been seen in the Indies before. It was no small feat of the council to salvage the arts from the philistine sphere of amusements and to give them their rightful attention among the "new elite." And even though something such as the arts council could for the time being only hope to succeed in a city the size of Batavia, still its success was symptomatic of the changes taking place within European society. Gradually, the "stray bourgeois" that Bas Veth had inveighed against was being flushed out of the higher social stratum by the educated European with cultural needs.

The arts council was not wanting in interest, not even official interest. Financially, however, it was dependent on the business community and private individuals. These made significant donations, and finances were not primarily what limited its activities. Rather, the question repeatedly was what needed to be done. As soon as it considered importing Western art into the Indies, all manner of insoluble problems presented themselves. There was a lack of sufficient gallery space, first of all, and people back in Holland were not willing to bear the risks involved in shipping collections of any size or importance. The council had to fall back on its own resources and either avail itself of material available in the Indies or help itself in some other way. To its credit, it pursued a progressive policy. In 1906, it commemorated the tricentennial of Rembrandt's birth by purchasing reproductions in Europe and showing them, with explanations, in a number of cities. In 1907, the same was done with copies of Roman bronzes. Exhibitions featuring Western art from private collections proved not to be of high enough quality. Exhibitions of Eastern art offered greater artistic possibilities. Its first great success was an exhibition of Chinese art in 1904, complete with a catalogue prepared by Henri Borel.

It was followed by an exhibit of Indonesian brassware in 1912, of Balinese art in 1916, and of Japara woodcarving in 1921. Exhibitions such as these, moreover, fitted in very well with the idea of federation and the dream of synthesis between East and West, as the arts council management was fully aware.

Thanks to grants from banks, corporations, and the government, the arts council was able in 1914 to move into its own premises in the new European suburb of Gondangdia. Its president was the then well-known architect and painter P. A. J. Moojen, who had himself designed the building in a somewhat heavy "modern style." At its dedication, the poet Jan Prins declaimed one of his own poems in the presence of the governor-general and all sorts of higher officials imaginable. His poem gave expression to the fairly lofty ideas of the times:

> Whoever looked on Beauty, fair, inviolate,
> Will revel in her pleasure everlasting.

In the meantime, in Bandung and other cities, arts councils had been established which collaborated with the one in Batavia. In 1916, the Society of Netherlands-Indies Arts Councils was founded. Following the establishment of the society, cultural activities were widely extended, especially by sending foreign artists, musicians particularly, out on tour. Owing to the improved means of communication, Western art was increasingly emphasized. The general tendency of Europeanization of society was also reflected in the arts council's development. Its activities took place entirely within European society. A few prominent Indonesians were members, most of them high officials, but Indonesians generally did not belong. The young, Western-oriented intelligentsia among the nationalists purposely kept to itself. The arts council was an entirely European affair and interested the nationalists just about as much as the notion of federation. Typically, the long list of names of administrative and honorary members, extending up to 1928, does not have a single Indonesian or Chinese name on it, and in this exclusiveness, the arts council reflected the social relationships in the colony.

Similar events were taking place back in the Netherlands. On May 3, 1899, two years prior to the well-known Royal Address of 1901, the East West Society was founded in The Hague. Its immediate cause was a national exhibit of feminine crafts where Indonesian art was amply represented. It drew a great deal of interest but it would be wrong to conclude that this was caused entirely by an intellectual and political change of attitude toward the Indies. It was rather more related to the development of "modern art" in Western Europe with its preference for arts and crafts, handicrafts, and applied ornamentation and embellishment. Symbol, ornament, and expressive power were recurrent words in any discussion of the plastic arts in those days. Not surprisingly, therefore, Indonesian weaving, batik, crafts, and woodcarvings proved a veritable treasure trove of the very geometrical, leaf and vine designs favored by art nouveau. During the first two decades of the twentieth century, Indonesian art invaded the Dutch living room. The Japanese vases already there were now flanked by brass bowls, sometimes with even a gong hanging from its frame; divans covered in Sumba cloth were placed in front of a screen showing two herons and a twig with blossoms; a batik cloth was invariably draped over the mantelpiece.

The East West Society, whose scope was much wider, gave birth to the Buatan Society, which specialized in arousing interest in Indonesian art through organizing permanent as well as temporary exhibits. Meanwhile, a host of artists were making their grand tour of the tropics, such as Berlage, Van Lelyveld, Poortenaar, Isaäc Israels, Nieuwenkamp, and—last but not least—Louis Couperus.

In 1916, the magazine *Netherlands-Indies, Past and Present* *(Nederlandsch-Indië, oud en nieuw)* began to appear in Amsterdam. It could well be regarded as a Dutch sequel to *The Indies Home* except for the fact that its scope was much wider. Among its editors were the architects Cuijpers and Hulswit, as well as Noto Suroto, and there were others. This magazine was expensively printed on heavy stock and embellished with numerous illustrations and photographs. At times, it even featured excellent color reproductions of, for example, *ikat* cloth from the Batak and Dayak areas and from Bali. Clearly, there was sufficient money and interest to support such a publication. In 1917, others commenced publishing the weekly *The Indies* *(Indië)*, which, in a slightly more popular format, was similarly inspired by *The Indies Home.*

Noto Suroto

In a great many of these new publications, the name Noto Suroto (1888–1951) crops up. His earliest known article decries the frequently negative opinion Dutchmen had of the Javanese, expressed even in official reports. He was twenty-two years old at the time. He was to write a great deal more, poems and also essays dealing with Javanese music, Javanese culture, East-West relationships, Javanese legends, cockfights, *wajang*, "the noble Aim," the painter Van Lelyveld, the poet Tagore, and so on. His contributions appeared everywhere, in weeklies and monthlies that even remotely dealt with Indonesia, but he really came into his own when he himself started a magazine. It was called *Oedaja*, which means sunrise, and its first number appeared in May 1923. (It would now be spelled Udaya, for the same reason Suroto is no longer spelled Soeroto.) Its editorial stated that it was "not influenced by any political party whatever, nor by any private interest." The editor, who was Noto Suroto himself, would "allow himself to be guided only by a positive attitude toward the Dutch-Indonesian relationship." "Tranquil order, gradual progression and naturalness, symbolized by the sunrise itself" were to be the guidelines for the magazine's intended support for the ascent of Indonesia. Here was something that appealed to many Dutchmen, i.e., a positive attitude toward a Dutch-Indonesian relationship, and an orderly, gradual, and natural development of Indonesia. That sounded reassuring enough. It provided a medial position between the colonial diehards and the Indonesian nationalists. Even so, Noto Suroto found himself caught in the middle at times, and needed to do a lot of explaining in order to clarify his position and his actions. His explanations were not always successful. Politically speaking, he remained ambiguous, altogether too vulnerable to external influences and forces.

For a while, he was listed as one of the permanent staff members of *The Federation (De Rijkseenheid)*, a very reactionary weekly. Only with some difficulty did his friends persuade him to give up this membership. Politically speaking, he gave the impression of being somewhat naive. Still, it would be hard to maintain that his political opinions were vapid, just because his entire ideology was of an ethereal nature. On the contrary, he was a thinker, a pensive man, a philosopher almost, and certainly a cultural idealist, but one who escaped into the clouds whenever he was pressed for his precise point of view. This did not, however, stand in the way of his friendships. His elusive and inconceivable behavior were altogether fitting the development of Western art after 1900, characterized as it was by aestheticism, exoticism, humanism, mysticism, symbolism, and so on. Noto Suroto was an amiable man of integrity who had many friends, particularly in the artistic circles of The Hague. For a while, he was a central figure in the city's cultural life, admired and loved for his wise and conciliatory behavior. He was in great demand as a speaker by all sorts of idealistically oriented societies. For example, in 1930 he addressed the then well-known artists' society "The Wigwam," and was clearly in his element: "Artists, if you really consider yourselves among the blessed of mankind," he began. He talked about the idea of federation and the colonial relationship, which he presented as "a meeting between two cultures on a spiritual plane." "Our generation can only hope to acquit itself of the demands of these times if we mutually join our physical and organizational faculties. The latter, our ability to control, should be ever guided by the spirit, for only it can hope to fathom the beauty in the most obscure design." In the course of his lengthy lecture, he dropped words such as "world harmony," "the harmony of humanity," and "universal purpose." On this basis he argued for cooperation between the Netherlands and Indonesia as two equal partners within the framework of a federation. His position was shared by the Netherlandic-Indonesian Union, of which he happened to be president. The Dutch diehards ridiculed him and the Indonesian nationalists avoided him, calling him a "traitor," as one of the letters from Mohammed Hatta reveals. Meanwhile, he continued in good faith to bear witness to his belief in a "spiritual osmosis."

This "osmosis" was something that he only sought for himself, however. What he wanted was to reach a synthesis between his Javanese self and his acquired Western culture. He availed himself of the Dutch language, the tongue, he wrote, in which he could best express himself, also as a poet, but his soul remained Javanese. An article from *Oedaja* (3 [June 1926]: 150), concerning "Dutch poems and Javanese thoughts," gives us an insight into his difficult, divided position. His views, written from a defensive position and in a—for him—unusually emotional style, are particularly remarkable for the insecurity they show: "There is not a single star for us to follow, and we do not know whither we shall go. Such is our cultural plight as well."

He shared this insecurity with numerous Indonesians who were forced to live between two worlds. His predicament was aggravated by the fact that he was a descendant of the ruling house of the Paku Alam, one of the four independent ruling houses on Java which was loyal to authority, and respected and revered by the Dutch. His father, a prince of the blood, saw to it that his son got a Javanese as well as a Western education. He sent him to the Netherlands to study law at Leiden University. There Noto Suroto met the future ruler Mangku Negoro, who became his friend and whose secretary he later became. Upon the outbreak of World War I, Noto Suroto followed his family's tradition by joining the Blue Huzars as an officer. During these years, while the Netherlands remained in a state of armed neutrality, he began to publish. 1915 saw the appearance of his first prose poems, *The Budding Melati (Melatiknoppen)*. Shortly before, he had gotten to know Rabindranath Tagore through Frederik van Eeden's anthology. So impressed was Noto Suroto by Tagore that he became lost in emulation of the Indian poet. One year after *The Budding Melati, Moth-*

er's Fragrant Hair (De geur van moeder's haarwrong, 1916) appeared,
followed by other collections, Whisperings of the Evening Breeze
(Fluisteringen van den avondwind, 1917), Garlands (Bloemeketen-
en, 1918), Lotus and Morning Dew (Lotus en morgendauw, 1920),
New Whisperings (Nieuwe fluisteringen van den avondwind, 1925),
and Wajang Songs (Wayang-Liederen, 1931). Noto Suroto wrote impeccable Dutch but his tone and style belong to classical Javanese. He
unfortunately did not succeed in bringing about a synthesis of form
and content. Instead of a synthesis, the two different worlds slide past
one another. His use of the (Western) sonnet form, for example, does
not go well with the Javanese form of expression. Still, there were
people in the Netherlands as well as abroad who were sufficiently
convinced of the wisdom of the East to regard his poems as a precious
gift.

Not until the collection Wajang Songs did he sound a personal
note. Noto Suroto rediscovered his human condition as it was expressed in the mythology of the wajang. He felt consoled and fulfilled
the moment he entered the sacred realm of the holy tales: "My tem-
poral life is filled with difficulty and strife, and my enemies, who are
many, laugh at me. Their mockery hits home more quickly than
feathered arrows, their words cut deeper than the kris. My battle is
not over yet. . . . Lord, make me a wajang puppet in Your hands. Then
Your hand can make me move again a hundred or a thousand years
from now. Then, after my time will have become a part of Your eternity, You will take me up again, and I shall speak again and do battle.
And there will come a time when mine enemies will be silenced and I
will have slain the demons. Lord, make me a wajang in Your hands."
The Wajang Songs were translated into French as well as German.
The pompous tone of their introductions gives one an idea of what
people expected to find in them.

Earlier, Noto Suroto had introduced Tagore through a "biographical sketch" (1916), then through an essay dealing with Tagore's peda-
gogical precepts (1921), and through an adaptation of Tagore's The
Parrot's Apprenticeship and Speeches in Shanti Niketan (1922).
Early in 1931, he personally met Mahatma Gandhi. In The Fatherland (Het Vaderland) of December 1931, he published three articles,
typically entitled "An Hour of Devotion with Mahatma Gandhi." He
was deeply impressed with Gandhi's ideas, including his political
ones, but he rejected for the time being his ideas of passive resistance
and noncooperation.

Noto Suroto returned to Indonesia in 1932. Following the Japanese
invasion, he was interned by the Kempetai (the Japanese equivalent
of the German Gestapo) and maltreated. Populist postwar national-

ism was repugnant to this aristocrat and he became totally isolated. He continued to write a great deal nevertheless, and he even revived his *Oedaja* as *Udaya*. He died in Surakarta at the age of sixty-four. His legacy contained an unfinished manuscript of animal stories. This was finally published in 1956, together with *Wajang Songs*, by his Dutch friend Ben van Eysselsteijn under the title *Gods, People and Animals (Goden, mensen en dieren)*.

These animal stories, fables rather, contain many of his ideas and memories. Some are not devoid of bitterness. In his "Wolf Country" ("De staat der wolven"), werewolves control accomplices who in turn control the fighting wolves, and these threaten the wolf masses, hungry, scurvy-ridden, and disgusting to see. His reference to the Indonesian revolution is unmistakable.

In another story, the large old white monkey called Hanuman is shown, among the other apes in the cage, thinking: "I have to get away from all this busyness around me. I'm an old fellow who would much prefer to sit in some small, quiet spot and meditate about the purpose of life, of my own in particular, which is rapidly coming to an end." Writing this, Noto Suroto sensed that his own end could not be far off either. As Hanuman had wished, he himself died in a quiet spot, totally forgotten.

XII
Between the Thirties and Forties

1 Country of Origin

There was a time in the thirties when people seriously asked themselves whether "Indies belles-lettres" had any future at all. The general consensus was that they did not. Professor Gonggrijp argued that
the physical nature of the Indies was simply too overwhelming, and
its society "lacking in elevated pursuits." Brom too got himself involved in the question, and put forth a fairly gloomy prediction at the
end of his book. The only hopeful signs he could perceive were missionary tracts and parliamentary speeches! The senselessness of all
this crystal-ball gazing was revealed a few years later when E. du Perron's *Country of Origin (Het land van herkomst)* came out, and by
the general stirrings of positive literary activity which would not
reach its stride until after the Second World War. The Dutch literary
world was to become thoroughly aware of the striking vitality of Indies belles-lettres, and its postwar continuation would be lacking
neither in interest nor in possibilities.

All this still lay very much in the future when *Country of Origin*
came out in 1935. The book was met by a kind of resistance, prejudice, and misconception almost impossible to imagine today. It was
said, for instance, that Du Perron had written an autobiography and
not a novel. It would have been a moot point if people had not then attached a value judgment to the distinction, which they did. It so happens that many Dutch critics in the thirties were still operating within the confines of known genres only, such as the novel, poetry, and
the novella. These were regarded as the specific forms of literature,
against a larger backdrop of a romantic classification of art and literature as belonging to a "higher plane" and as "superior expressions of
life." It was based on a philosophy that regarded life as raw matter and

regarded a work of art as cooled-down crystal brought into being through the "creative powers" of the artist. A literary magazine of the times was in fact named *Crystal (Kristal)*. They believed too that only the imagination could transmute life into art. *Country of Origin* was obviously autobiographical, not at all a product of the imagination, and as a life history it ranked on a lower plane. Du Perron, for that matter, had written "a novel" on its title page because he had imposed all sorts of changes on reality. Altering the facts did not, however, constitute an act of creative imagination, and it was sooner regarded as the author's hiding behind the facts "so as not to reveal all." "In order to pass this work off as a real autobiography," Du Perron wrote, "I would, in all honesty, have to enclose a list of all the changes which as a novelist I had the good right to make." Later on, Du Perron did exactly that but only for his friends, not for his readers. The Literary Museum in The Hague has that faded copy of *Country of Origin* in which Du Perron (for the benefit of Jan Greshoff) has reduced all fiction to fact, while still leaving unsaid what had been left unsaid before.

This same copy also allows us a closer look at Du Perron's method as a novelist. It shows clearly that he composed this book, whether novel or autobiography, and that he definitely arranged his materials. The result is not a formless novel in the least but a precise and detailed whole. Vestdijk's article "Du Perron's Great Anti-Novel" ("Du Perrons grote anti-roman") in *Lyre and Lancet (Lier en Lancet)* points out that a work such as *Country of Origin* was not unprecedented in foreign literatures. Vestdijk's particular point is that Du Perron had come to be disgusted with the "real novel" or what passed for it in the Netherlands. His book was an antinovel in the sense that it reacted against the standard recipe for the novel of "order and progression," consisting of the initial exposition, gradual development, a timely anticlimax, then the denouement and a tidy ending.

Discussing the "real" and the "artificial" novel, Du Perron once quoted Valéry's memorable statement: "I simply can not get myself to write down: Madame la Comtesse est rentrée à six heures." To this Du Perron adds: "But that's exactly what it's all about. A born novelist knows that he *has* to write down facts like that; and whether he has to or not, he does time and again, and with relish" (*Collected Works [Verzameld werk]*, 6:302).

In Du Perron's own book, none of these novelistic tricks of the trade are employed though and its intentionally open ending is somewhat of a taunt. Du Perron's *Country of Origin* is exemplary in that his antinovel became an example in reverse of the kind of "real novel" enjoyed by a wide audience. To be sure, he never for a moment intended to attack the "solid, dependable novel format of the nineteenth century." Its importance he fully recognized, especially in his admiration of Couperus. What he meant was that its rules and values did not apply to him personally, and he repudiated them especially because they were still used as criteria of the novel generally.

Du Perron invariably defended his *Country of Origin* by invoking *Max Havelaar* (which he regarded as the supreme work of Dutch literature) along with *La Vie de Henri Brulard* by Stendhal.

The method used in *Max Havelaar* of working on two separate chronological planes (the Drystubble chapters and the chapters situated in Lebak) Du Perron applied even more rigorously in his own book by alternating the chapters situated in Europe with those taking place in the Indies. Even the final convergence of these two chronological planes reminds one of Multatuli. *Max Havelaar*'s Dutch chapters finally fuse with those in the Indies when, following chapter ten, Amsterdam and Drystubble cease to be heard from in the book. *Country of Origin*'s chapters situated in the Indies similarly fuse with those dealing with Paris. Following chapter twenty-five, only Europe remains as a locale in the novel. There are naturally also several formal and informal differences between the novels, with Du Perron keeping his own options. For example, his relationship to his alter ego Ducroo is quite different from Multatuli's relationship to his major character Max Havelaar. In this respect, *Country of Origin* is nowhere near the "auto-hagiography" Douwes Dekker's *Max Havelaar* is. (The term "auto-hagiography," a self-sanctification of sorts, is used by Sötemann in his dissertation on *Max Havelaar*.) More so than Multatuli, Du Perron was simply too self-critical to allow that to happen. Multatuli's mocking and ironical treatment of his character Drystubble is *never* applied to his character Max Havelaar, for example, whereas Du Perron subjects his character Ducroo to the same irony he applies throughout, just as Henri Brulard can not escape the self-mockery of Henri Beyle (Stendhal). Ducroo resembles Du Perron the same way Henri Brulard resembles Stendhal (or Henri Beyle, if one prefers).

Their egos and alter ego can not be identified with one another because they continuously pursue and keep an eye on one another, while commenting on and correcting their actions and thoughts. In addition, the unconscious memory of Valéry Larbaud's *Barnabooth* can have influenced him, for Du Perron repeatedly mentions this book, which is yet another autobiography in novel form. The critic Ter Braak is correct, however, when he asks rhetorically why it is so important to start fishing for Du Perron's spiritual ancestors when Du Perron's own presence, in voice and gesture, is already so imposing? His presence is recognizable despite attempts to avoid the straight confessional. He tried in all sorts of extra ways to create distance, using irony, for example, and by following a special procedure that is related to the arrangement of the entire book. On reading the Indies chapters, one notices that the first person, the speaker, is always present. In the Paris chapter, however, Du Perron frequently uses dialogue. He must have done so to avoid the autobiographical dilemma. The narrator from an earlier phase naturally could be dealt with as a character later on. Du Perron tells us therefore that he *sees* the child Ducroo walking, talking, and acting. He is related to it while at the same time it is moving through the book as an independent character. Whereas the problems relating the "I" with the speaker were easily solved as long as they concerned the past, the real problems began in the present. Because the distance created by time and the past had ceased, Du Perron now came face to face with his alter ego and he could no longer write about his contemporary Ducroo in the same fashion he wrote about him as a child. In other words, Du Perron realized that he had to treat the present differently from the way he had treated the past. He decided to use a different method, one that would utilize his phenomenal memory. Following a sober sketch of a particular situation, he would often continue with authentic dialogue and thereby exclude himself as the biographer, transferring that role to the reader who had to act as an additional character. These different ways of describing one and then another narrator explain the obvious ambivalence in *Country of Origin,* which must have bothered the reader accustomed to "real novels." Those who indeed object that *Country of Origin* consists of two different parts would do well to remember, however, that neither part will function without the other.

The Parisian dialogues show us various aspects of Du Perron's state of mind at the time he started writing. Similarly, the chapters situated in the Indies, the country of his origins, try to explain his mental state during his childhood there. Some people prefer the Indies chapters over the Paris ones, and with good reason. As Vestdijk already observed, Du Perron's dialogues are totally lacking in dramatic tension, and they are effective only in terms of the action. This becomes all the more objectionable as the book progresses, leaving the past behind. The dialogues are also burdened by excessive detail, as a consequence of the author's sound memory, and the Indies chapters too are burdened by it. Even so, they are an indispensable and integral part of the book.

"Novel for Jane" is what Ter Braak wrote above his discussion of *Country of Origin* (see *Collected Works [Verzameld Werk]*, 5:518), and what he meant by this was that *Country of Origin* did not address itself to the anonymous reader but to just one person, the character Jane. The book is dedicated to her, its first sentence deals with her, and the book's final words are addressed to her. Her presence in the novel is continuous even though she remains in the background. She is the ever-listening figure, just as she is seen listening and smiling in the only portrait Du Perron drew of her in chapter nine, at home with the Héverlés. *Country of Origin* becomes fully understandable only when we read it as a "novel for Jane." The return to this country is undertaken for Jane's sake, in order to fully explain to her who he is and why. This also explains the need for the device of alternating chapters between Paris and Indonesia. It also explains the presence of the one constantly audible voice, one of the book's best points. The Dutch poet Nijhoff said somewhere that writing was difficult but that it was hardest of all to write in such a way that the reader can hear a voice actually speaking. This kind of voice is continuously present, talking, telling stories, and arguing (about the past and the present). The novel owes its voice to the book's concept as a "novel for Jane," as the history of a life told to her.

2 In Search of the Country of Origin

Jane's presence gave *Country of Origin* a basis of actual fact. While writing the book (Du Perron tells us it took him two years and three months), reality encroached even more with his mother's death. This signaled new changes, because he was cut off from the last remaining ties with his youth, as well as the family income. As the book progressed, there is no doubt that the Indies increasingly began to insinuate themselves into his everyday reality, and that their memory became more intense and poignant with the increasing insecurity of the present, exacerbated by the worsening political situation. We are talking about Europe in 1934–35. Du Perron had always lived with a longing for the Indies and a nostalgia for his own childhood even before meeting Jane and before starting *Country of Origin*. Just as Europe had always remained close to the horizon in the Indies, now the Indies were always remotely present in Europe. There, they would be crowded out occasionally by day-to-day affairs, only to reassert themselves in dream and daydream: scents and images "from the remotest past," from "the domain of memory," pushed their way back up from a "submerged life."

The house of his birth was a recurring image, "a house that remains loyal for the same reasons animals are, but vaster and more intimate." These are quotations lifted from Du Perron's poems, but nothing so well captures this mixed feeling of sadness, melancholy, and happiness as that one passage in *Country of Origin* that should really be quoted in full (it occurs in *Collected Works*, 3:26–27), although a synopsis and quotation will have to suffice here. Du Perron tells us he is lying in bed in a mean room in Brussels, "my back turned to the woman who was not of my choosing," when all of a sudden the clear, sharp image of his parental home in Tjitjurug appears.

> Everything was there before me, even when I opened my eyes in bed. And what's more, my body had shrunk to where it was a boy's body again, although I knew myself to be thirty years old, that Suzanne lay behind me and that I was living in a miserable apartment over a haberdashery in Brussels, still I felt like a four- or five-year-old lying on the leather sofa in the oval gallery of Tjitjurug in the exact same position I was now lying in, and that I was looking at Mount Salak. I felt the short, brown leather bolster, wrinkled, lying under my head and pressing hard against my neck, my hands touching its flat little buttons in the leather. And down in the fields where the small train rode by, I had just seen my mother go past, stout as she was then, wearing a gray dress, one with those puffed sleeves which were then in fashion, waving from the train window. . . . I must have held my breath to . . . hold on to this metamorphosis for as long as possible; and all at once, while I was still my old, small self, I sensed how completely it had all been lost, and before I knew it, I lay there and cried with such intensity of emotion as people call uncontrollable.

Later on, as things clearly begin to get worse, after the fight with the lawyers has been lost, and as World War II slowly announces itself in a number of ominous ways, a return to the Indies begins to look increasingly more like a refuge of sorts. Then the idea of going back there begins to take on more substance. When all his friends disappear one after the other to volunteer for the Spanish Civil War, and the atmosphere in Paris becomes poisoned by "political madness," he makes the decision. Du Perron's decision to return was influenced by some considerations, and then again *not* influenced by others, partly because he was unaware of them but also because they simply did not apply to him. Moreover, this sort of decision is not made all that rationally anyway. Given a certain situation, longing and homesickness can have powerful effects: "I keep wanting to go back to the Indies." Also, something as simple as his hope for a financially secure position may have had its effect: "does wanting an inexpensive house during this depression seem sufficient reason to you . . . and in my present circumstances?" We know now more clearly than ever before what Du Perron's going home resulted in, thanks to the study by J. H. W. Veenstra entitled *D'Artagnan against the Mob; E. du Perron as Indies Polemicist (D'Artagnan tegen Jan Fuselier; E. du Perron als Indisch polemist,* 1962). In order to get any idea at all of the "misunderstanding" between Du Perron and the Indies, we have first got to know what kind of a man he was and later became. We ought to know also what the Indies were like when he left, and what they had turned into by the time he returned fifteen years later.

Charles Edgar du Perron was born November 2, 1899, in Meester Cornelis, present-day Djatinegara, a suburb of Djakarta, in the then well-known country house of Gedong Menu (called Gedong Lami in *Country of Origin*). It was a big Indies house, a "besaran" as it was then called. There were a number of such huge places between Batavia and Bogor (formerly Buitenzorg, meaning the same as Sans Soucie). They were mostly pompous edifices with thick walls, a high roof, large rooms and galleries all around. Du Perron's birthplace was one of these, and he remembers it in his book with scarcely concealed emotion. In that house he saw, most important, his mother, larger than life, dressed in native sarong and kabaja, his father clad in a white linen suit, his personal maid Alimah, and then the little boy Ducroo, himself, wearing a thin union suit or a sailor's outfit. "Only the house remains loyal," Du Perron had written in *Country of Origin*, before he saw it again. But what indeed was left of it by 1936? It appeared to have been altered and modernized, "irretrievably restored," as Walraven would have put it. It had lost its original purpose too. The immense yard, one exactly as Du Perron had described, now looked abandoned and desiccated, and only the old pavilion was the same. The house was occupied by a military uniform shop. It is some measure of Du Perron's dogged attempt to retrieve *his* Indies and his childhood that he showed the need to return there. During his stay in the Indies, he lived in the garden pavilion for several weeks or months. Had the house indeed remained loyal to him? Who is to say? Walraven wrote that later on in Bandung Du Perron frequently mentioned the house to him "as if only there he had found back what had driven him to return to the Indies."

Country houses such as Gedong Menu had meant something, they had embodied the way of life of the colonial patriciate of the nineteenth century. They may not have had much in the way of style but they did have a certain air, the same air as their inhabitants, in fact. They created the particular sense of spaciousness and openness that Du Perron remembered whenever he spoke of the Indies. These manors were truly baronial. The colonial patriciate of landowners was essentially a nineteenth-century phenomenon that extended here and there into the twentieth. Their number was limited to just several scores of families, such as the Hoflands, Aments, Boutmys, Motmans, Arnolds, and Du Perrons, families with extensive branches and, what is more, all deeply rooted in the Indies. They lived in baronial splendor in a particularly Indies style, incomparably grander than that of the Dutch "sugar lords" and "tea squires," and even more so than the "big bosses" of Deli did. All of these were mere latecomers and strangers to the Indies landowners. They were owners and proprietors, while those Deli rubber planters and those superintendents of sugar plantations and factories were mere "wage slaves," as they put it. With the influx of European capital, however, these Indies landowners who could not keep up with industrial development were overtaken by the companies with their well-trained, imported employees. Large parcels of land had to be sold and divided, and the family property was swallowed up by the new corporations. For a while yet, they continued to live spacious and well-to-do lives, but in the course of the twentieth century these houses were nearly all abandoned and dilapidated. What was lost particularly was the way of life that Du Perron had been just old enough to have known.

In order to fully understand Du Perron, we have to see him in this Indies milieu. He was descended from a powerful family, so powerful in fact as to taunt the civil service. Even shortly before and after the war, their dilapidated mansions, statues, and elaborate gravestones still bore witness to their former presence. The family plot of the Du Perrons in the cemetery of Tjilatjap (on Java's south coast) was a striking example.

When Walraven met Du Perron for the first time, he was struck by his "Indies-looking face," with its *kulit langsep*, (light brown color). "Du Perron is an Indies fellow," he wrote elsewhere as something that was a matter of course. In chapter one of *Country of Origin*, the character called Goeraëff asks: "Isn't there some Indies blood coursing through your veins, Ducroo?" There the answer is negative. In chapter five, entitled "Family Album," Du Perron's family history is correct. It is certainly not complete, however. Not that racial admixture is important, of course. What matters is one's social and cultural milieu, and one's way of life. Du Perron was indeed in many respects an Indies fellow, in his gestures, in the way he sat, and the way he spoke, with a slight but unmistakable accent of an *anak Betawi*, a child of Batavia. Nobody doubted that he was, really, and neither did he himself. Early in July 1936, Du Perron wrote to Greshoff: "I think I'm still an Indies fellow in many respects." And in his well-known open letter to Sjahrir, on the occasion of Du Perron's departure from

Indonesia in 1939, he wrote: "Just put me in the company of a bunch of real Indies fellows, and they'll know me as one of their own within ten minutes."

The Du Perron family lived according to Indies traditions very much determined by Mrs. du Perron. In *Country of Origin*, Du Perron draws an unforgettable portrait of his mother, which, although it may not be complete, can still serve as the prototype of the Indies lady, the typical *njonja besar* (literally "great lady"). The fact that hers is both a portrait and a description of a general type goes to show what a good likeness it must have been.

Whichever way one looks at it, the Du Perrons were extremely Indies, and had become so as the result of a historically evolved cultural pattern that included a lot of native sense and sensibility. They really lived almost entirely in *tempo dulu* still, in the grand "good old days." Not surprisingly, they had absorbed almost nothing of the new Dutch way of life. The family had been in the Indies for several generations. Of Du Perron's four grandparents, three had been born on Java and one in Singapore; of his eight great-grandparents, one had been born in Colombo (Ceylon), three in the Netherlands, two on the island of Réunion, and two in France. All of them, however, had established themselves on Java within the first decade of the nineteenth century. They had died there too, except for two who died in Singapore on account of accidental circumstances. The other family members also stayed on and mixed with other well-known Indies families. Only in the twenties and thirties of this century did a number of them begin to move away to Europe.

Everybody who knew Du Perron first through his work and reputation and only later met him personally was struck by his Indies appearance. Walraven, who looked him up in Bandung, wrote in his newspaper about their first personal meeting: "I was standing there near the entrance when I saw the face which I already knew so well from all those illustrated literary histories. It was clearly an intellectual face, but an Indies face nonetheless." And he kept harping on that Indies exterior as something that had particularly struck him, probably because he too had first gotten to know Du Perron through his work as a European intellectual. This Du Perron undoubtedly was, but at the same time he had continued to behave according to the social pattern of his youth.

Indo-European, hence truly "Indies" culture—insofar as one can generalize about such vast social distinctions—the culture in which Du Perron was raised, was a typical culture of grand seigneurs, a ruling class with a pronounced romantic and heroic tinge. Du Perron was aware of this romantic-heroic characteristic in himself and called it his "espagnolisme," after Stendhal. This trait characterized his behavior and really his subsequent literary and polemical activities as well. Two excellent articles by Gomperts in *Hunting for Survival (Jagen om te leven)* also stress this aspect. But although he quotes Du Perron ascribing this "espagnolisme" to his Indies upbringing, Gomperts treats it rather as a typical aspect of Du Perron's personality than as something typical of his background. This "espagnolisme" is, of course, closely related to a particular phase in Indies adolescence. When applied to an Indies milieu, however, the term is unworkable. A different one is required, and "d'artagnanism" presents itself as a much more appropriate description. This "d'artagnanism," which could easily border on bravura and posturing, apparently fulfilled a need of Indies youngsters. Indeed, as Du Perron tells us himself, discussing his boyhood reading: "Dumas' *Three Musketeers* outshone all else, d'Artagnan's rapier cleared away everything that had come before. . . . D'Artagnan, Athos, Porthos, and Aramis ultimately became to me what the heroes of the *Iliad* must have meant to the Greeks, in that they became both example and poetry at the same time, myth, in short" (*Collected Works*, 5:259).

This "d'artagnanism" at once explains, to a degree at least, Du Perron's unmistakable admiration for a man such as the Achin officer Arthur Hille. In *Country of Origin*, Du Perron's alter ego, the "European intellectual" tells us that a man such as Hille "would have made a great Nazi S. A. leader." There existed in the Indies a whole D'Artagnan cult which was not even over after the twenties. The cult began with the showing of the serialized movie *Les Trois Mousquetaires*, which ran for months on end in the numerous cinemas. All the kids in the Indies were crazy about it. The well-known theatrical group Komedie Stamboel also played *The Three Musketeers* as part of its regular repertory. The result of all this was a true D'Artagnan cult that made its demands on daily life and that for a while at least determined the schoolboy's way of life. It is typical of the spirit of those times that the name D'Artagnan should also occur as a first name in its abbreviated form of "Dart," as "Uncle Dart" in the family of the author Tjalie Robinson.

Gomperts also pointed out in his study that Du Perron's friendships had something of a conspiratorial character and that Du Perron regarded his circle of friends as some kind of secret society with its own laws and its own secret oaths of admission. Gomperts calls it a clan spirit and explains it as having its source in the nature of colonial society. This was a small society, after all, which could not hope to maintain itself without a sense of solidarity. This clan spirit or coterie spirit did indeed exist, but maybe it was really more akin to d'artagnanism. For that matter, this so-called clan spirit ought sooner to be called a "gang" spirit. Du Perron's relationship to his friends clearly shows the Indies gang spirit with its small and large groups of friends sticking together, emulating one another's example in order to become the chivalrous, noble, and strong characters of their literary and movie heroes. It was difficult to become a member of these gangs. The initial fight necessary to gain admission reminds one of the "entrance examinations" Du Perron writes about in his letters to Marsman in a half-serious, half-mocking way. This again shows Du Perron's participation in an Indies tradition.

Much later, definitely not at the beginning of his career but especially after his death, people praised Du Perron's independent and detached way of looking at things. But much of what Gomperts calls his "autonomous spirit" can be traced to those elements in his Indies past that were different from the Dutch norms. Let us not forget that he grew up in a society that Dutch idealists condemned as utterly materialistic, and perhaps rightly so. In any case, the literary world in the Indies was not exactly something people looked up to. Rather, it was regarded as part of social activity and as a form of (superior) amusement. There was no such thing as a separate literary tradition; literary groups were nonexistent, and there were no literary authorities either. Hence it was completely natural when Du Perron did not appear impressed by the literary luminaries in the Netherlands. Imagine his situation. He arrived in Europe as a twenty-two-year-old, and when he entered literary life two years later he must have looked about him in a surprised and uneasy way. Surprised, surely, that something like this could and did indeed exist. And right away, he became involved in all manner of literary skirmishes. He fought in the manner of D'Artagnan, often fighting for fighting's sake but always mindful of a code of honor dating back to the days of his youth. He observed rules that hardly conformed to the Dutch norms of "responsibility and basic good manners," in Anthonie Donker's phrase. Du Perron must have seemed some sort of spoilsport who blew down the whole house of cards of value judgments and who wanted to stack them in a new hierarchical order of his own. Not long after Greshoff had introduced him to the world of Dutch letters in 1927, he got to know his first Dutch friends. First of all there was Ter Braak, with whom he founded the literary magazine *Forum*. This allowed Du Perron to continue meddling in Dutch letters ("meddling" is the word Gomperts uses), a characteristic that is directly related to the typical need of the Indies ruling class to organize the lives and the affairs of others. There is, in fact, a uniquely Indies expression for this kind of meddling, to "urus"; old Mrs. Du Perron too was one who wanted to "urus" each and everyone and would issue commands either from her chair or from her bed.

His literary tastes too were characteristic in that the authors he liked were of a heroic nature. He realized this in himself: "I spent my youth among heroes . . . and some of them had taken such possession of my imagination that I would walk around for days as in a dream, not knowing whether I had assumed their shape or was merely the page attending on these knights and heroes." And after all, he wondered, did not Balzac and Stendhal, Stevenson and Conrad, Sawinkow and Malraux become the psychological and subtle replacements of the heroes from his youth? And Valéry Larbaud and Paul Léautaud, were they not really a corrective and refinement of the early heroes in their attitude toward women, on "a higher level but with the same aims"? And Du Perron ends these notes (in *Collected Works*, 5:257 ff.) with a meaningful remark which can only be regarded as an understatement: "A person does not really change all that much, after all. . . ." All this adds up to just one thing, that he had remained true to type.

Something had changed, however, and that was the pattern of Indies society to which Du Perron returned in 1936. In an interview for *The Fatherland* shortly before his departure, someone asked him if he expected to find back the Indies he had described in *Country of Origin*. His answer was: "That would be asking rather too much." He did not discount the possibility either, he said, that too much in the way of poetry might perhaps have crept into the memoirs of his youth, and that this might have made the Indies less real to him. He did not yet take into account that society itself might have changed. He does not seem to have anticipated either social or political changes, at least he never said anything about them. The only thing that concerned him was literature. This is typical enough, and not just of Du Perron but of many of the intellectuals of those days as well. However much they may have been politically or socially committed, still they could only accept an individual approach to problems. A friend from his youth who had himself just returned wrote him: "Don't come back, the Indies are different and no longer what they once were, you'd only be disappointed." "And what of it," Du Perron added to this, clearly intending to throw this counsel to the wind, and ascribing its sentiments to "a traditional European turn of phrase." Time and circumstance would prove this traditional writer correct of course, painfully so, for Du Perron did indeed end up in a country different from that which he had known in his youth.

He had left Java, with his parents, in August of 1921. He returned to his native soil in November 1936, together this time with his wife and child. In the interim fifteen years, the Indies happened to have undergone a phase of Europeanization and normalization that profoundly changed European society there. Changes that had begun to take place back in 1905 had gained increased momentum following World War I to the extent that they were truly revolutionary. The old Indies had been swept away for good.

In order to get a clearer picture of all these important changes, one should know that the number of Europeans in the colony was a mere 100,000 in 1905. This number had increased threefold by 1940, mostly on account of new "immigrants." Moreover, the improved working methods used on the large estates, combined with the higher demands business began to make for the education and training of its employees, had attracted a different kind of European to the Indies. The planter who used to tramp around his estate gardens with bare feet, wearing a bamboo *tjaping* hat, found himself replaced by an employee trained in the colleges of Deventer or Wageningen. Similarly, the "business employee" had replaced the merchant of the kind Bas Veth had still known and described as the "bourgeois without a leash," and a university-trained official now replaced the self-made man who had gotten to the top quite rapidly.

Even more remarkable, compared to the increase in the number of Europeans, was the relatively greater increase in the number of women. In 1880, there were only 471.6 women to every 1,000 men but the 1930 census showed that the ratio had radically changed. By then, there were 884.5 women to every 1,000 men and the number of women was sure to have been even higher by 1940. This did not mean that the *njai* or native housekeeper had disappeared, certainly not in the interior, but the life of the *budjang*, or bachelor, living with a concubine as a matter of course, had become a definite thing of the past. An important indicator of normalization and Europeanization is the increase in racially mixed marriages from about 15 percent in 1900 to about 25 percent in 1930, as well as the important increase in women not born in the colony, which meant they were mostly European born. Whereas the number of nonnative women was about 4,000 in 1905, it was six times that by 1930, having risen to 25,600. And insofar as it is true that women are the civilizing force in society it becomes clear that people began to live increasingly in a more European fashion. Life in the Indies became more comfortable, especially in the cities, where the greater part of the Europeans lived. They got good schools, first-rate hotels, asphalt roads, water mains, and electric light, refrigerators, and air conditioning, while up-to-date hospitals and good medical care now protected everybody against the dangers of yesteryear. In large as well as small towns European suburbs came into being, the so-called *kampung belanda,* where the Hollander or *belanda* lived among his own kind in his own village, so to speak. Even the style of architecture adapted itself to the new way of life. Those large cool Indies houses with their marble floors, surrounded by immense yards, were replaced by small bungalows with a tiny garden in front and in back. Some of these new suburbs even looked like the Dutch towns of Laren or Bussum, during a heat wave, to be sure.

In addition, and this was very important, the European way of life became the norm. If we draw the borderline between *tempo dulu* and the more recent period as lying somewhere between 1914 and 1918, then it is fair to say that the European arriving before World War I was forced to adapt himself to the colonial way of life, especially since he often lived with a native concubine, and that he either made a mixed marriage or got married to a Eurasian woman, but after World War I, Indies families began to adapt to European ways, often for social reasons, and thereby started the process of adaptation in reverse.

Indies society had evolved, relatively speaking, from an easygoing, hospitable, and congenial world to a more dynamic, tougher, and more impersonal one. During *tempo dulu,* European contact with the "natives" invariably took place by way of the *njai* and the servants. This relationship bore a patriarchal character, as indeed it did among the indigenous social groups. Their relationship was often extremely intimate, as any older Indies novel will prove. By means of the housekeeper—in her role as caretaker and bedmate—the European learned to know the language and the people, and his contacts with the other, native world ran through her. As the *njai* gradually came to disappear, a vital link between the two races was lost too. The relationship to the servants also changed. Formerly they had made up a community within the family, often on a personal basis, as was the case with Du Perron's family, for example. Now, the relationship became one based exclusively on a wage contract. This new arrangement also meant a loss of intimacy. "The old family servant," often a personal maid such as Alimah in *Country of Origin,* became a curiosity and an anachronism.

The Indies were indeed no longer what they once were, and certainly no longer *his* Indies. Even so, Du Perron tried to retrace and recapture his youth, looking up old people and things in a country that he had either outgrown or really never known at all. In doing so, he often encountered things strange and unfamiliar to him. Walraven, who had come to the Indies in 1918 and who had witnessed the entire process, knew the explanations readily enough, but Du Perron found them surprising, "even things that seemed perfectly natural and ordinary to me," Walraven wrote. Once in a while, he rediscovered something of his past and was touched by it. In the first place, he rediscovered the unchanging natural world of the Indies: "When I'm riding in the train and see that red soil again, I realize, without having to think about it even, that this is where I belong." As to his old friends and familiar places, he wanted to see them all again, the Odingas, Junius and Rudi van Geen, but halfway through he stopped. Somewhere, somehow, the old sense of belonging and loyalty was still there but it did have its limits. All of his friends, one a planter, another an officer, a third a government official, and another an important member of the Indo-European Society, turned out to have adapted to the colonial situation and had conformed to it, without seeing its arbitrary nature. Du Perron, however, had made it precisely his business to doubt the soundness of the colonial arrangement.

"This country repels me morally and intellectually," he said, "it's a pedestrian and hypocritical colonial society." As a "European intellectual" he came into direct conflict with colonial mentality incarnate in the person of Mr. Zentgraaff, Nazi sympathizer and editor-in-chief of the *Java Courier (Java Bode)*, the Indies daily with the widest circulation. Veenstra's *D'Artagnan against the Mob* makes the conflict with Zentgraaff central to his study of Du Perron's Indies period. To Du Perron, Zentgraaff represented everything repugnant about the colonial Dutch. Veenstra's book provides us with an excellent array of annotated letters and documents showing how totally these men disagreed. Du Perron's letters sound a note of desperation, also about his social position. There did not appear to be a niche for him anywhere, although hindsight explains readily enough why this was so. European society out in the Indies was a relatively simple affair. It consisted of three groups: officials, people in the private sector (in business and on the plantations), and the military. To be sure, there were the free professions such as law, medicine, and several others, but these were few. Someone like Du Perron who had fallen outside of his profession, as it were, one whose strong point was writing, ended up in some sort of vacuum. Society had no way of absorbing him because its structure was not differentiated enough. All this is a rational post-mortem. His disappointment was painful and it made him desperate and rebellious at times, and these feelings were compounded by the fact that neither he nor his wife was in good health. Veenstra gives us a blow-by-blow account of the fiasco.

Reduced to his own work—and Du Perron wrote and read a great deal while in the Indies—he increasingly began to regard Multatuli as an ally. He pictured himself to be in the same kind of social situation Multatuli had had to endure while in the Netherlands. In the Indies, Du Perron came to understand more than ever before Multatuli's clashes with the elusive powers of the law, morality, and officialdom, the very forces in retrospect that were of course designed to hold the heterogeneous Indies together. And more than ever perhaps he discovered that Multatuli's temperament was similar to his own. In describing him, Du Perron characterized himself and his own hopes: "His oversensitivity, impressionableness, his hankering after action combined at the same time with an ability to dream, his constant need to assert himself, his sense of injustice and his unflagging fight against it, all these traits, every single one of them mark him as a man of youthful spirit" (*Collected Works*, 4:443).

Multatuli became his spiritual friend and model, and Du Perron became almost obsessed by him. In a very short time, using new documents, he wrote *The Man from Lebak* (*De man van Lebak*, 1937), then added *Multatuli, Second Plea* (*Multatuli, tweede pleidooi*, 1938). Back in Holland, he continued his studies in the Multatuli Museum. All his writings about Multatuli are to be found in the fourth volume of his *Collected Works*. His pleas for Multatuli are indeed pleas *pro domo*, as Veenstra calls them, and it is best to read them as Du Perron's personal testimony.

In addition to his two books about Multatuli, while still in the Indies Du Perron completed *Fairy Tales of Crime; Discussions of the Detective Story* (*Het sprookje van de misdaad; dialogen over het detektiveverhaal*, 1938), two extensive anthologies with biographical notes of Indies literature, *John Company's Muse* (*De muze van Jan Companjie*, 1939) and *From Kraspukol to Saïdjah* (*Van Kraspoekol tot Saïdjah*, 1939), which was never published, and finally the novel *Scandal in Holland* (*Schandaal in Holland*, 1939), concerning the family scandal in which Onno Zwier van Haren got involved in all kinds of intrigue. This is still a most readable novel which has received too little attention (see vol. 3 of *Collected Works*).

Back in the Netherlands, Du Perron started a book about Dirk van Hogendorp which was to have had the title *To Give Account (Zich doen gelden)* but remained unfinished. Dirk van Hogendorp too can with some justification be considered an anticolonial figure who became equally embroiled with his surroundings. His is another example of Du Perron's identification with his chosen subject, albeit from a greater distance in time.

3   Critique and Reconstruction

Du Perron found himself a haven in two places; one was on the staff of the magazine *Critique and Reconstruction*, and another with the *Ba-*

tavian News (Bataviaasch Nieuwsblad, edited at the time by J. H. Ritman). He felt most at home and least constrained (where his writing was concerned) with *Critique and Reconstruction; General Independent and Progressive Indies Magazine (Kritiek en Opbouw; Algemeen onafhankelijk en vooruitstrevend Indisch tijdschrift,* 1938–1940).

From *Critique* he launched his attacks on Zentgraaff. Appearing every fortnight, it was a sort of safety valve for people from the Netherlands and from Indonesia who held opposing views and felt constrained and lacking in freedom under an authoritarian system of government. They were essentially democrats, some of them social democrats, and belonged to a political minority (very much a minority, in fact), but they were much more politically aware than most Dutchmen. What was happening in Europe frightened them as much as did developments in the Indies. In a society deeply shaken by the Depression, the fascist National Socialist Party (Nationaal Socialistische Bond or NSB) won wide support, especially among those hardest hit by the world recession. And it was not really so much a question of how many active members the NSB had but of how many open and secret sympathizers there were who tolerated at least "the good qualities in the party's principles." Between what we may fairly call the "colonial mentality" and national socialism there existed a definite affinity, especially where their support of a strong central government was concerned.

To counterbalance the advance of national socialism, the Unity Through Democracy party was founded. Its original plan had been to establish a sister organization in the Indies but its statutes did not provide for Indonesian membership. Therefore several people in the town of Bandung decided to found a separate General Democratic Group, which even managed to secure one seat in the municipal council. During its initial and subsequent meetings, many Indonesians and Chinese showed a great deal of interest in this group, thereby bring about a political alliance which was something entirely new in the colony. One year later, *Critique and Reconstruction* was founded, which had its roots in the General Democratic Group but operated independently from it. The magazine was the brainchild of D. M. G. Koch, a staunch Social Democrat. Koch became its chief editor and performed with unbelievable dedication. The staff consisted of Dutchmen and Indonesians, among them ardent nationalists who under any other circumstance would have been against all form of cooperation. The decisive factor for their attitude was very likely that *Critique* emphatically supported the Indonesians' right to independence.

Du Perron got the job through Koch and joined the staff sometime during 1938. From then on, the magazine became livelier and took on a slightly more literary tone, although it continued to retain its character as a magazine of the political opposition. Personally Du Perron had imagined something else, something different from *Critique,* although he saw nothing wrong with its spirit. He did not want something like *Colonial Studies (Koloniale Studiën)* either, or anything on the order of the publication issued by the Batavian Society, but rather a more topical and lively magazine that would not be primarily politically oriented. Between December 1939 and June-July 1940, there were meetings to plan a magazine of the sort he had in mind. Those attending these discussions included Du Perron, J. van Leur, H. Samkalden, P. J. Koets, and Sujitno Mangunkusumo (whom Du Perron had meanwhile befriended). Achmad Subardjo joined them at a later stage. What tied them together was, remarkably enough, once again a political point of view. They shared a dislike of all forms of dictatorship, a strong feeling against fascism, and a recognition of the right to freedom for Indonesians. They were not outspoken Socialists such as Koch but generally leftist-oriented intellectuals. The magazine they contemplated was to focus on Indonesia, in other words, was to assume an Indonesian-centered point of view. They adopted Sujitno's proposal to name the magazine *Nusantara,* meaning "archipelago" and also the oldest known name for Indonesia. They got as far as talking with a printer. Yet nothing ever came of the magazine for financial and other reasons, and Du Perron stayed with *Critique,* where he published regularly and started a dialogue going with Indonesians about culture and politics. This was quite exceptional, if only for the fact that he managed to get Indonesians to publish in a Dutch magazine at all because, politically speaking, the situation was a poor one in those years and the color bar, which exists in any racially mixed society, had become more pronounced than ever. There was a lot of mistrust on both sides and contact between Netherlanders and Indonesians was at best limited to voluntary meetings and dinners of Dutch and Indonesian colleagues. Spontaneous and unprejudiced exchanges hardly ever took place between them, certainly not if the subject were politics, and that was precisely what had become the prime Indonesian concern and on which everything depended—their dignity, their independence, their self-respect, and the future of their children.

They were disappointed in the Netherlands government and felt cheated. As Sukarno put it: "but time and again our expectations are not fulfilled and therefore a feeling of regret has stolen into our hearts." When Du Perron arrived in the Indies in 1936, the erstwhile noisy propaganda of the nationalists had fallen silent. Their leaders had been banished, Tjipto Mangunkusumo, the father of the nationalist movement, as early as 1927; Sukarno was banished in 1934, following his arrest on August 31, 1933; one week after Sukarno was transported to the island of Flores in February 1934, Hatta and Sjahrir were arrested. A year later, they were banished to Upper Digul, deep in the interior of New Guinea. Hundreds of nationalists, arrested under the infamous article 153 *bis* were incarcerated in the concentration camps of Upper Digul, and a similar fate awaited hundreds more. It was a form of repression that sought to decapitate the movement, break the organization, create uncertainty, and instill disunity and doubt. Meanwhile, a political and police apparatus was keeping a sharp eye on the movement. On the surface, these repressive measures seemed to have their desired effect but psychologically they backfired and created feelings of bitterness, distrust, and rancor even among very moderate and reasonable people such as Sjahrir (see his *Indonesian Thoughts [Indonesische Overpeinzingen]*, 4th ed., March 7, 1938, p. 181). Contrary to their sentiments, many regarded *every* Dutchman as a potential enemy, and considered a showing of personal sympathy a form of betrayal. Du Perron entered into this atmosphere of repression, fear, and suspicion, seeking contact with Indonesian intellectuals. Initially, he also complained about mistrust and how difficult it was to meet anybody, but he persevered and overcame it simply by presenting himself for what he was. He did not skirt the issues and also made very clear what his own position was: that if matters got worse he would be on their side. He broke through barriers and obstacles.

There exists a small article by the author Suwarsih Djojopuspito that appeared in *Free Netherlands (Vrij Nederland)* of December 14, 1946, describing Du Perron's manner of getting through to the Indonesians, and the impression he made on them in doing so. To Suwarsih Djojopuspito and her husband, meeting Du Perron and his wife seemed like some kind of miracle. She wrote: "Anyone who is at all acquainted with the colonial relationship will understand what it meant for us to have felt at home in European surroundings."

Indonesians were struck most of all by his naturalness. "He lacked precisely what we detested in the attitude of colonial Dutchmen, their ethically inspired pity for us," wrote another Indonesian lady, Mrs. Pringgodigdo, a militant nationalist and feminist in the Indonesian magazine *Attitude (Sikap)* in 1951. Du Perron never fully realized how much he meant to his Indonesian friends. After all, such things are not easily discussed. This only happened after the news of his death (on May 14, 1940, in Holland) reached Indonesia, and *Cri-*

tique and Reconstruction devoted a special commemorative issue to him. All of his Dutch and Indonesian friends were represented in it, except for Sjahrir, who could not be reached in time in his remote prison camp. One of these, of whom Du Perron had been especially fond, Sujitno Mangunkusumo, concluded his "In Memoriam" saying: "Do I really have to write and speak of this man, to whom I owe so much, in the past tense from now on? The words fail me to convey the emotion that overwhelmed me when I realized I had to. And I could kick myself for the fact that despite (or should I say because of) the great friendship I bear him, I can only find these banal words to honor him who meant so much in my life." Another Indonesian, Sugondo Djojopuspito, wrote: "What he meant to his friends makes up for three centuries of colonial injustice." And Sjahrir, with whom Du Perron corresponded, was to say after the war: "He did not approach the Indonesians from without, as if they were an interesting subject for study, as did so many 'ethically minded' people, but rather he approached them as equals and as people in whom he recognized a common human bond. Friends such as he was are the best ambassadors that the Netherlands could send us."

What exactly did Du Perron mean to his friends? Different things. To his Dutch friends something other than to his Indonesian friends, but all agreed that he was devoted, and open and stimulating to be around. Koets said: "Eddy du Perron made it possible through his own personality for his Indonesian and Dutch friends to also become each other's friends." Beb Vuyk was even more cryptic when she wrote in the *Batavian Courant:* "He left us his friends."

Suwarsih Djojopuspito explained (in *Free Netherlands*) that without Du Perron she would never have written her novel *Beyond Constraint (Buiten het gareel)*. Nor for that matter would this *Mirror of the Indies* have been written more than thirty years after the fact, without the "written instructions" which Du Perron sent this author in 1939. Of course Du Perron was influential but influences are hard to trace and harder to evaluate, because it is always a matter of how one applies them. Du Perron's presence certainly set something in motion and engendered cultural activities such as never existed before his arrival. These activities continued in the prison camps during the war and especially after the war with much less constraint, resulting in mutual contacts. Without these contacts, the publication of a monthly magazine such as *Orientation (Oriëntatie)*, which began to appear toward the end of 1947, would never have been possible.

It would be a myth to assert that Du Perron's influence on Indonesian intellectuals generally was great. It remained limited. The Indonesian postwar generation, the Angkatan '45 (the generation of 1945) never knew him. To them, he was little more than a positive-sounding name. Only a few among them, such as Chairil Anwar, Sitor Situmorang, and Ida Nasution knew his work in part. To the older generation, to which belonged Suwarsih Djojopuspito (1912–1977) and her husband, to Sujitno, and to many others who had known Du Perron personally, he meant a great deal, however. He meant less to Sjahrir (1909–1966), who had never met Du Perron because of his internment on the island of Banda. Sjahrir was also more of an intellectual, more mature in his opinions, partly due to his studies in Amsterdam, and more policitically oriented than Du Perron. Du Perron held Sjahrir in high esteem and expected great things from him. His farewell letter to Indonesia was addressed to Sjahrir (see *Collected Works*, 7:124) in fact, because he expected Sjahrir to understand his situation and his choosing to return to Holland. He felt that only the politically and ideologically educated Sjahrir would understand this choice, which was also politically motivated.

In his *Indonesian Thoughts* (of March 20, 1937), before he began to correspond with Du Perron, Sjahrir wrote that he had read Du Perron's *Notebook, Small Format (Blocnote, klein formaat)*, had liked it a great deal, and then he added: "I only wish the lads on Java who are now busy practicing so-called literature would feast their eyes on young writers of *this* kind in the Netherlands, instead of reading those old fossils writing for *The New Guide [De Nieuwe Gids]*." He was clearly referring to the group associated with *Pudjangga Baru* (literally, *The New Poet*). Without knowing Du Perron, he read Malraux's *Les Conquérants*, and without Ter Braak, he read Nietzsche. He also read the Bible, Marx and Engels, as well as the English positivists who were gradually replacing the German speculative philosophers. We can follow his literary and political development easily enough, and when he writes about his apprehension of approaching fascism, his mental grasp of the situation is all the more astute and admirable considering that he wrote this from an isolated, Dutch-imposed exile. He read Dutch literature as well and very perceptively criticized authors such as Maurits Dekker and Van Gogh-Kaulbach for their "petit bourgeois sentiments." He did not like Vestdijk. He read Jef Last, called him "pathetic," and found him lacking in "human perception," someone who indulged in "word play." He then also attacked the kind of Dutch stylistics that Ter Braak and Du Perron were always scoffing at. Ter Braak and Du Perron in fact shared his every opinion—except when it came to Vestdijk—and often even worded their objections in the same way.

Independent of those two who headed *Forum*, Sjahrir wrote in December 1936 (he was twenty-seven at the time): "Gradually I have managed to free myself from the slavery imposed by the official arts and sciences; inwardly, authority does not affect me much anymore." In May 1938, Sjahrir contributed to the commemorative issue of *Pudjangga Baru* an article dealing with the relationship between people and culture. Du Perron saw it early in 1939 and included it (in translation) in the May 1st and 16th issues of *Critique and Reconstruction.* Du Perron then added his own comments to this article (*Collected Works,* 7:96). Apparently Sjahrir and Du Perron began to correspond with one another from this time on. Du Perron must have considered Sjahrir a like-minded person, up to a point, and certainly a political ally. In the *Critique* dialogue they talk a bit past one another, with Du Perron only contradicting him on certain details. Judged from a distance of so many years, one is now inclined to find Sjahrir more in the right, especially where he knew more about the Indonesian situation and its needs than Du Perron could. In any event, Du Perron was never Sjahrir's "guru" (also the Indonesian word for teacher) although he was, by their own admission, such a figure to Suwarsih and her husband and, to a lesser degree, to Sujitno ("he taught me to be myself").

Du Perron left us his friends, as Beb Vuyk said. True enough. During the ensuing Japanese occupation, Sjahrir and Sujitno found one another in their mutually negative stance against the Japanese conqueror on the basis of principles that Du Perron would undoubtedly have understood.

4   Beyond Constraint

Before Du Perron joined the editorial staff of *Critique and Reconstruction,* Suwarsih Djojopuspito (1912–1977) had submitted several contributions. As a result of an article of hers demanding the release of nationalist leaders from exile, *Critique* was for the first time threatened by a government-imposed press curb. She was a teacher at a so-called wild school. An important component of the nationalist movement was educating people in the national spirit. There were a number of such wild schools, private and unsubsidized schools, which, especially after 1923, were placed under increased surveillance, because the authorities feared that the educational system would be abused by political propaganda. Life for the teachers was hard, and their idealism sorely tested. Suwarsih's book *Beyond Constraint (Buiten het gareel,* 1940), written in Dutch, testifies to this hard life. However, a rumor had already preceded the book, a partial account of which is in the book itself. It appears that she had originally written it in her native Sundanese language and forwarded the manuscript to Balai Pustaka, the official bureau for native culture. It was found unsuitable, however, and very likely the story's character Sudarmo could have told that the editors did not like the book because they found it useless, nonpedagogic, nontraditional, not simple enough, and too political. Disappointed and unsure of herself but still not willing to abide by the editorial rejection, Suwarsih turned to Du Perron. He advised her to write the book directly in Dutch, the language she thought in. She promised to start afresh but had several talks with Du Perron beforehand.

We can almost guess what they talked about, the problems of the novel format, of the autobiographer, of the rendering of reality, of literary honesty, and so on. Du Perron's advice is to be found on page thirteen of her book, where her husband "Sudarmo" says: "Do what your heart dictates because there are times when one's intuition is stronger than the keenest intellect." Du Perron took the first manuscript chapters with him on vacation and returned them fully annotated. They met again, and as the book gradually began to take shape, she rediscovered her self-reliance.

Although the book's plot is too transparent, her story too slow and too wordy in places, the novel has a unique charm. Its charm lies in its uncertainty or rather in the absence of certainty. Her book is really an account of her search for identity. It is fascinating to follow her spiritual conquest, her recognition of feelings, and her juxtaposing sentiment and intellect as the book progresses. The fact that the reader is so closely involved enforces the book's impression of incompleteness, but this same lack of perfection protects it against anything remotely smacking of self-satisfaction. What is most striking in Suwarsih is the way she comes to grips with certain situations, how she analyses her own feelings and balances them with humor and irony. It is true, however, that her ironic self-criticism is a bit forced because she in unsure of herself and runs the risk of being overcome at any moment by an ever-lurking sentimentality: "Why always this terrible sentimentality," Sulastri berates herself as she is once again on the verge of tears.

The book creates the impression that its author, both as an Indonesian and as a woman, has in a nearly superhuman way tried to keep her feelings at bay without losing her sensitivity. Suwarsih has the capacity to focus on everything that goes on between people. She has an eye and an ear for relationships and can especially convey the mood of a conversation and the "electricity" that can permeate it. Her omissions are often the most important part of a statement. A single sentence or a single remark can reveal the slightest tension between people, such as suspicions, suppositions, uncertainties, clues, no more and no less. Feelings are barely touched upon, never clearly defined.

A good example of this is a fragment from the book that one can not easily forget: the description of Sulastri's trip to Djokja.

Traveling alone with her baby, she meets a soldier. She has all kinds of defensive feelings toward him but it is only her fear that she is conscious of, a fear transmitted from parent to child. After all, to her a soldier is also the symbol of authority, repression, and rape. Yet gradually, and to her own amazement, they arrive at a human understanding. Even a feeling of tenderness comes over her when the soldier holds her baby in his arms, and for a moment the situation, in Suwarsih's phrase, is precarious where she herself is concerned. Nothing happens, she gets off at Djokja and is picked up by her family, and yet she has the feeling of just having lived through a special episode in her life. This kind of thing happens time and again in Suwarsih's work, this hint of an underground current that gives her dialogue a distinctive character.

For an Indonesian woman with an inherited sense of reserve, it represents a great personal triumph to have reached the frankness that surprises us on every page. She must have had a great urge for honesty and intellectual purity, for her work represents a radical attempt to come to a different awareness of life.

This is likely where Du Perron's influence shows, as well as in the book's strong autobiographical strain, which in turn has influenced the way her characters are portrayed. The latter she does after the fashion of Du Perron, using her "creative memory" sooner than her "creative imagination." This method results in fashioning her characters according to recognizable models, although ultimately, as the book illustrates, the process makes little difference to the reader. At times we have the sensation of actually knowing some of her characters, especially the main characters, but others are so vaguely sketched that they leave no lasting impression. This is the case, for example, with the sketchy outline of the person of Sukarno, whom one would have liked to have gotten to know much better. Possibly her vagueness here has something to do with the author's attitude toward this historical figure. Although Suwarsih invariably keeps her distance from the characters while still maintaining contact with them, where Sukarno is concerned her distance became so great that he eludes her critical grasp. She does make an attempt to see his shortcomings but only mentions some minor faults without really pointing out the man's weak points. Nor is she aware of his real value, and nowhere does she approximate an explanation of the legend that grew up around Sukarno.

Her method of reproducing characters from memory does not escape falsification any better than any other method. Suwarsih gives the impression of thoroughly understanding the figure of Sutrisno, for example, while his true value escapes her. Sutrisno was modeled after Sujitno, one of Du Perron's most intelligent Indonesian friends, who possessed a finely tuned mind.

What is curious about this novel is that so much of the social and political background remains obscure. To be sure, there is mention of a Partai Kebangsaän and a Partai Marhaen, of the struggle for national education, of difficulties with the secret police, of searches and meetings, and from the titles of books and subjects we can reconstruct the ideology of the nationalist movement, but we still do not get a clear picture or presentation of the political situation. Time and again Suwarsih emphasizes human relationships and whether or not the movement had an effect on people. Suwarsih does not keep silent about the demeaning compromise she gradually had to make, and its effect on human relationships. She can not have made these confessions without feelings of guilt, especially because her novel was written in the Dutch language, but she had reached a point where prestige was not nearly as important as self-criticism and reclaiming her own identity.

5   Willem Walraven: A Colonial Tragedy

The great *literary* discovery Du Perron made during his stay in the Indies was Willem Walraven (1887–1943). Yet, Walraven was no "literary figure" in the strict sense of the word, because he was neither a poet nor a novelist. Ever since 1926, Walraven had been a free-lance journalist with *The Indies Courant (De Indische Courant)*, a newspaper that appeared in the city of Surabaja. He did write some four or five short stories just a few years before he died, but these were spin-offs from his journalistic work and were in fact adaptations of it. Walraven himself, for that matter, made no distinction between literature and journalism because either would have served his need to express himself through writing: "No matter what I do, I'll always be a journalist and a writer. That's just something you can't help doing because you are born with it, and because it's really your true destiny to express yourself, no matter how, in whatever form you can."

Whether journalist or literary figure, Walraven was a born writer, and especially a writer of letters. He must have written hundreds, maybe even thousands of letters, although only a relatively small number have survived. He was obsessed by writing, and writing letters was to him the most direct form of communication or, more exactly perhaps, of bearing witness. Nearly everything Walraven ever wrote in fact is his bearing witness, and this goes for the greater part of his journalistic output as well. Whether writing about books, people, Indies conditions, or Indies cities, he always came back to himself and what really mattered to him: his experiences, his memories, his own life. The little announcement of a book dealing with needlework, for example, somehow gets related to a childhood memory of his. In another instance, a new edition of Brusse's *Little Scoundrel (Boefje)* provided the occasion for him to write about the city of Rotterdam as he had known it before World War I, during the brief period in his life when, as he tells us, he felt free and happy. Everything Walraven wrote is crammed full of memories. Time and again, he retrieves something from the past, with the help of his powerful memory. This burden he had to carry with him throughout his life. He perpetually reactivated his memory, and intensified it more profoundly than reality itself. It was filled with the most contradictory feelings of hatred and love, but intense hatred and abundant love only. As Walraven confided: "I am a man of extremes: I can only love or hate, very intensely, there is nothing in between."

Writing to him was a way of turning inward, into a world where he could be himself ("If they were to lock me up in a cell, I would still not be alone for I have my thoughts and my memory") and only then did he feel unconstrained. "Only when I'm writing am I happy."

The image that Walraven's eldest son later conjured up of his father is unforgettable:

> I remember my father as an older man, dressed in pajama trousers and a shirt, seated behind a table with a typewriter on it. . . . I can still hear that typewriter banging away for hours, sometimes days on end. I remember waking up at times and hearing the machine going. That meant that he had found "a start" and from then on the typewriter would bang continuously. I call it banging, because my father would put his typewriter on a stack of old newspapers, probably to muffle the sound. For that reason the characteristic ticking noise was lacking, just the banging instead, especially because my father's touch on the keys was rather powerful. . . . My father would also say about his work: just go and sit down behind the typewriter and start. Make a start, and the rest will come by itself. And as soon as he had a start, the letters would fill the page, one sheet after another.

In his newspaper articles as well as in his letters, Walraven wrote with both speed and precision in a style clearly attuned to a conversational tone in order to establish close contact with his reader. In his style, he remained truly himself, clear, open, expansive, with a dislike for shading and obscurity, and he always aimed for reality. Writing to him was a solace, never a flight from reality: "I don't really have to write pure fantasy, my own life's experience is quite enough, meetings, memories, ups and downs, but it often hurts to dig deep down because so much of it I buried so long ago." In his letters Walraven frequently mentions what writing means to him, and that whatever he wrote he put down spontaneously, that it had to be done without preconceived notions and that reworking anything is wrong: "Whatever is written with verve is best." And this is precisely what is so marvelous in Walraven, that whatever he wrote does give the impression of having been done with verve and élan. Everything he wrote, he wrote straight at you, with his entire, big body behind it, often with a shocking honesty, baring his life for all to see. That is the way it strikes us at any rate, but there must also have been a great many things he kept silent about, all the things that would have called forth emotions too strong and too unmanageable.

Occasionally, Walraven hints at this in his letters. Be that as it may, it is impossible to separate his work from his life, because the latter is its only subject. This is why a biographical approach is really the only way to write about Walraven. Yet someone who wrote as he did and who was as obsessed by it must have had a reason for that obsession. The reason was his isolation, a lifelong isolation which to him seemed to take on the characteristics of exile. He often used the word in his letters: "I, the exile."

Willem Walraven was born in 1887 in the village of Dirksland near Middelharnis on the island of Goeree-Overflakkee, and he died in 1943 in a Japanese concentration camp in east Java. He was the son of a vendor who traveled from one fair to another and who made enough money later on to buy himself a store and sell groceries. On his mother's side, he descended from a family of skippers, who owned a sizable house in the village. More on Walraven's youth can be found in his "Life Lines" (Levenslijnen), a series of articles included in his journalistic work Ephemera (Eendagsvliegen, 1971).

Walraven wrote somewhere that he grew up in a purely Protestant place, even symbolically, with a landscape just as flat and angular as the thinking, a barren place forever surrounded by sea and wind. And even though he had liberal parents, they were still real islanders and that meant a great deal. To Walraven, Dirksland was the embodiment of conservatism ("my father admired the status quo"), narrowness, dullness, and, particularly, lovelessness. To a young man who wanted to be free, who was bursting at the seams, and who hankered especially after understanding and relationships, Dirksland was an impossible place. The quarrels at home were fierce and endless. He sought his own way in Delft and Rotterdam and lived among what were then called bohemians. In those days, he was also much taken by the new Socialist movement, a persuasion he never abandoned. Till the very end he called himself a Marxist. Later on he was to write: "I think that I only long for those days." He returned home to study for a bookkeeping certificate. Shortly thereafter he emigrated to Canada. Those must have been five terrible years while he lived in a number of different places. Walraven kept mostly silent about this period. Upon the outbreak of the First World War he returned to Holland, but within half a year the situation at home was as tense as ever. In August 1915, Walraven signed up for the colonial army.

In his letters from the Indies to his brother, who had stayed in Dirksland, he repeatedly says that he never wants to return to Dirksland but also inquires after people and things and writes about them as if they were still around him. "I would most prefer to be totally free of Dirksland but that is impossible of course; on the contrary, it has such a hold on me that not a day passes when I don't think of Dirksland." Dirksland was a barbed hook deeply embedded in his flesh. Even as late as 1941, just two years before his death, he still wrote that just thinking about Dirksland made him feverish, and gave him "a hot forehead, I mean, so that I can't get to sleep at night, not with all those memories rushing in on me and all those feelings aroused again." His letters contain bitter remarks about his relationship to his parents: "Give my regards to father and mother. I don't want to write them because I'd just say too much and I'd be too sharp and hurt their feelings. Then again, they're already so old it makes me want to cry that it has come to this. But I can not very well change myself and too much has happened that I can not forget, much of it my own fault, but also a great deal that should not have been necessary if they had only supported me a little when I needed it. But enough, I had best keep still because I do not want to start that all over again" (letter from March 23, 1925). Repeatedly he touches upon the same thing in his letters, that his parents left him in the lurch, that they were unloving. "I can only think of those people with hatred, with an intense hatred, even after all those years, and don't you forget it" (letter dated April 20, 1930).

Walraven became a telegraphist with the army's communication branch and was stationed in Tjimahi. He had a desk job there and sometimes he also went out on maneuvers. For the rest he kept aloof from military life. However, he was and remained a low-ranking soldier, and in colonial society anybody who was not an officer but belonged to the so-called lesser ranks lived an isolated existence. Such people had no contact with the European civilian population, they were unwanted in the European cafes, restaurants, and clubs. They were cast out, certainly in Walraven's time, and forced to live on the edge. The same thing happened to Walraven.

During the time he was a soldier, he met Itih, the woman who was to assume such a dominant role in his life. His story called "The Clan," which is among the best things he ever wrote, is about Itih. Walraven wrote about her with a barely contained tenderness, "Itih, with her small name and her big heart."

His army contract ran out in 1918, and he left for Banjuwangi on Java's extreme eastern coast facing Bali, where he got a job as a bookkeeper for a factory. He felt lonely out there, asked after Itih in a letter to an acquaintance and heard that Itih had been asking after him as well. After a brief exchange, Walraven made a decision and sent twenty-five guilders for travel expenses ("with the shrug and the smile of a gambler putting money on a card expecting to lose"). Two days later, he stood face to face with her. Under cover of dark, they had abducted her from her aunt and uncle's house and put her on board the train. After having spent the night in a Chinese hotel in Surabaja, she arrived the next afternoon. "She could never afterwards bring herself to tell me what went on in her heart through it all. And I was never to know how she, the impeccable woman, managed to make up her mind to undertake that vast trip into the unknown." Later on, Itih filled in some of the gaps in Walraven's story. Her coming to him had been a flight, a calculated escape from a situation of near slavery. Arriving at Walraven's house in Banjuwangi, she right away walked over to the annex where the servants' quarters were, thinking to find her cot there. Only when she did not find it and finally saw the double bed in Walraven's room did she realize that he had asked her to become his housekeeper. After thinking this over for one night, she decided to stay, and after their first child was born they got married. Walraven had insisted on getting married, not Itih. She knew what it meant to become irrevocably European, never being able to return to her own society, which would never have taken her back. Where he was concerned, many Europeans would not accept him with his "native wife." This was a very sensitive issue with Walraven. He demanded that they accept Itih, and he thereby isolated himself from a European world on which he depended for his "spiritual sustenance" and human contact. His eldest son wrote in his memoirs that his father, while drunk, once cried out: "Get me a European!"

Whichever way one chooses to interpret this, the fact remains that such a cri de coeur signals the desperation and loneliness of a man who does not socially or culturally belong anywhere, with the pertinent symptoms of frustration, psychic conflict, and neurosis. Walraven was "paranoid," in much the same way people also called Multatuli "paranoid." In 1930 he wrote to his brother: "I am often tense and excitable, I rave and rant from time to time, I'm terribly hot and" —and this is the point—"I don't fit here." It was his tragedy to be an outsider of the European community he abhorred, while the world his wife and children belonged to remained closed to him. That way he ended up in some sort of vacuum, on the borderline between two worlds, partly inside and partly outside. *His* world lay far away, if not in Dirksland, then maybe somewhere in Holland, but in Western Europe in any case, or so he thought. "There is really only one place to live, and that is in Western Europe." This was the world he tried to conjure up by reading and through writing about it. There is a letter to his brother that, in the simplicity of its request, makes us keenly aware of the degree of his longing. In it, he asks to be sent some herbs such as chervil, savory, garden cress, and he adds: "through the herbs I smell Holland, the meadows, the shoulder of the road and the dikes. I am often moved even when I add thyme to some food and then savor the smell. I'm not sure you'll understand this but it's a fact. You can *smell* countries in much the same way as you can smell people!"

The realization that on account of Itih and the children he would never again reach that world made him desperate at times. There were financial worries besides, as well as conflict and tension with the children, especially when they began to grow up. His children were to repeat the experience he had had with his own parents. He fumed over "Asiatics," scoffed at Europeans, and hated the heat, the bill collectors who were after him, his children's schooling, Indies food, Indies houses, and Indies yards. His son had memories of his father different from Walraven the author:

> When he had been drinking he would unleash everything he had pent up, and his hatred for this country, this life, and the people here would go unchecked. He would then also give free rein to his loneliness and misery. Like an old, caged lion he would restlessly pace to and fro, lift his hands up to heaven and look grotesque with his complaining and cursing. . . . He felt captive; he was not able to spread his wings, neither materially nor spiritually. His complaints were those of an old, tired man who lived alone and abandoned in

this country which, despite everything, had remained alien and hostile. . . . We avoided him, slinking through the living room like ghosts. Most of us suffered under all this, which did not help either. It made us hate my father and widen the rift between him and most of us, especially as we got older.

After a couple of days like that, the clouds would lift and the children would hear his typewriter banging away again. His newspaper needed copy. It is doubtful whether Walraven was always happy having to write for his paper. He had to interest his readers, he had to be humorous and witty because his readers expected this of him, for there were those who only read *The Indies Courant* for the sake of his pieces.

There were times indeed when his jokes would fall flat and his humor would turn into jollification, such as in one of his most popular columns, "Chronicle of Sins" ("Kroniek der zonden"), covering all sorts of court cases. Even so, Walraven was one of the best journalists writing in the Indies. Nobody could write the way he did, not about politics or economics but about books and people, to which he would add all sorts of views concerning marriage, concubinage, life in the Indies ("a mess"), labor unions, Marxism, smoking sausage and preparing pea soup, Indonesian nationalism and European arrogance in the Indies. He scoffed at the colonial system and the European colonizer and yet he had all the prejudices of a European in the Indies. At times he was fed up with the whole thing, with all the scribbling, everlasting worry, and his own incessant restlessness, and he would sigh: "Oh, if only I could get some rest and not have to look at these Asiatics anymore, if only I could be rid of literary quacks, children, wives, Eurasians, simple Javanese, household bills, doctor's bills, newspaper editors, cars on the street, lousy tobacco, etc., etc."

He claimed to hate the Indies, the westernized Indies in which he lived, but after more than twenty years he appeared to be quite attached to them, "despite everything," as his son said. He understood all sorts of Indies conditions and social relationships, and could often place them into some sort of historical framework, giving them a definite perspective. This was especially true about his descriptions of small Indies towns and places in the interior. Walraven made several trips through Java, reporting to his paper about the towns and cities he visited. These were places with either a Dutch or a Javanese past, such as Batavia, Rembang, Kediri, or places with no past at all but which were merely shrouded in silence, timelessness, dust, and heat. Like his admired predecessor, the Indies writer Daum, Walraven too had an acute awareness of Indies decay and decline, of everything that had either disappeared or had been cleared away or just left standing without sense or purpose. His articles are unforgettable and incomparable, and anyone capable of turning out work such as that is no longer a real outsider.

Nineteen thirty-eight was an important year for Walraven. In that year, an unexpected sort of emissary from his country of origin appeared in the person of an eighteen-year-old apprentice ship's mate, his sister's only son. The account of their first meeting, which he writes to his sister as early as the next day, reveals the happy impression this nephew made on him. From then on his letters kept coming, their tone uncommonly mild, breaking down his own barriers. It seemed as if his isolation had finally ceased. All his letters are about Frans, little Frans, or "my dear boy." It is as if he wants to care for the boy forever and keep him for himself, because he finally had found the son he had always wanted, white, blond, open-hearted, and free. His correspondence with this newly acquired son and his parents, Walraven's sister and his brother-in-law, which commences on August 28, 1938, and ends April 25, 1940, comprises nearly 400 printed pages!

When war broke out, Walraven was once more isolated from Holland but he had gotten to know Du Perron beforehand, first through letters, later personally. Du Perron had initiated their meeting. He had read articles in *The Indies Courant* signed M.C., written the editors, and gotten hold of Walraven's name and address. He told him that he could write, that he was a born writer. Walraven was extremely grateful for this, especially because it came from Du Perron. His feelings for him were a mixture of respect, admiration, and a sense of responsibility for his younger friend. This time also, he wanted to keep him for himself. He was apprehensive about him and told Du Perron when visiting him in Bandung: "Something is going to happen to you and I won't be around to help you." (Du Perron died in Holland on May 14, 1940, four days after the German invasion.) Du Perron tried to get him to write things other than journalism but the Indies offered no opportunity for getting literary work published. However, Du Perron gave Walraven access to *Critique and Reconstruction*, where he could at least express himself more freely than in his newspaper. He also introduced him to D. M. G. Koch and referred him to his friends before he left for Holland.

Through Du Perron, Walraven finally got the contacts in the Indies that he had always felt lacking, contacts with "real people," as he called them. Only during this period did Walraven experience complete recognition as a writer. In 1941, after *The Torch* (*De Fakkel*, a cultural monthly) was founded, he finally began to write fiction. Altogether, he completed four stories, two of which were published before the outbreak of the war in the Pacific in December 1941: "Borderline" ("Op de grens") and "The Clan" ("De clan"). Both of these stories are about Itih, and they would be the high points of any anthology of Dutch short stories. Even so, all this came too late, for as Walraven wrote to the editor of *The Torch* on March 15, 1941, his nerves were altogether too "frayed" by that time. The war and the ensuing Japanese occupation deprived him even of the last opportunity to write. The few friends he had disappeared; they were called up for military duty and were then imprisoned by the Japanese. As a civilian, he retained his freedom for a few weeks longer, but soon he and his sons were rounded up too and transported to a prison camp in east Java. There Walraven died on February 13, 1943, in a state of complete apathy. His son's account of those final weeks with his father are not easily forgotten: about his illness, Itih's visit, and then the end.

6   Distant Thunder

The war in the Pacific began on December 8, 1941, and was also the start of the great process of decolonization in Asia. It did not come unheralded though. Still, literature had been curiously silent on the subject. It was as if other people had felt none of the forebodings Walraven had never been without, and as if none of the rumblings around and about had ever penetrated their world.

Perhaps we can make an exception for several books. In the first place *The Book of Siman, the Javanese (Het boek van Siman den Javaan)*, which appeared as early as 1908, written by Multatuli's descendant, E. F. E. Douwes Dekker. Like his great-uncle, he too was considered a "jumble of contradictions," as well as a romantic revolutionary, a fervent nationalist, very anti-Dutch, and full of hatred for the white rulers. He was an Indiesman, born in Pasuruan of a Javanese mother. He was proud of the Javanese blood in his veins, he said, and never lost an opportunity for reminding people of it. Unlike most Indo-Europeans, he did not opt for social and cultural assimilation with the Europeans but desired assimilation with the Indonesians instead. He became one of the first leaders of the nationalist movement. He wrote a great deal, books, pamphlets, articles, all of them equally strident. At times he plagiarized from his great-uncle but lacked his talent, alas. His only novel, *The Book of Siman, the Javanese*, is written with a lot of bombast, accusation, and lamentation, an ineffectual method of writing because it perpetually drowns out the author's voice. His book is in fact a typical pulp novel, which only for this reason belongs to the Indies novelistic tradition of daggers and lots of moaning.

At the age of seventy his autobiography came out, which is a monument to his boundless vanity. One thing is certain, however: his life was very interesting and his political choice definitely merits the book's title, *Seventy Years of Action (70 Jaren konsekwent)*. Banishment, imprisonment, persecution, press offenses, nothing ever shook his conviction, he kept right on going. To some extent he was a fanatic, even a mystic (as he called himself), to whom doubt, including any doubt about his own importance, did not exist. Was he a hero or a martyr? An actor perhaps, who continued to play his own part with a great deal of sacrifice? Opinions about Ernest Douwes Dekker are certainly very divided but his importance to the Indonesian struggle for freedom is beyond any doubt.

Adolf ter Haghe's book *Mother Indonesia (Ibu Indonesia,* 1939) confronts the reader directly with the nationalist movement and the figure of Sukarno. Its very subject was an immediate source of concern to the European community, to its press, and to the authorities. Even though Ter Haghe (pseudonym for J. A. Koch) portrayed Sukarno as a "utopian" and did not regard the nationalists as altogether blameless or lily white, the authorities at once smelled a rat. Their objections were the same as those to Székely-Lulofs's *Rubber.* According to the *Java Courier,* typically enough, the book contained all sorts of "deceptive matter" about the Indies, it was presumed bad for colonial prestige (which always tipped the scale in such cases), and it was pronounced a "seditious book" for that reason. To anyone reading *Mother Indonesia* today, after more than thirty years since its first appearance, all of this sounds unreal. The book's only mildly sympathetic attitude toward the nationalist movement renders totally incomprehensible why the public prosecutor prohibited it and why the author, a schoolteacher, was temporarily dismissed.

Just as striking and curious, in retrospect, as the colonial uproar about a perfectly naive and innocent book as *Mother Indonesia* was the lack of appreciation in the Netherlands for H. van Galen Last's novel. *President Dramakutra* appeared at a time (1957) when the Dutch were busy trying to forget the colonial period as fast as possible. They appeared incapable of exchanging their role of ruler and partner for the role of outsider and foreigner on such short notice. The only option seemed therefore not to think about the colonies anymore and not to assume any role whatever. Van Galen Last did choose to play a part, however, and decided to face up to the new situation in as consequential a manner as possible. This he was able to do by virtue of a youth spent in the Indies and his long-standing interest in the

"Indonesian question." From the very first, his talent had predestined him to become an interested observer of the conflict, a position enhanced, moreover, by his stay in Europe.

Although Van Galen Last placed his story in an imaginary country called Somalesia, it shows a close resemblance to Indonesia if only because like Indonesia, it had recently been decolonized. It is clear that Van Galen Last had no intention of writing a roman à clef, and he says as much in his introduction. Somalesia only resembles Indonesia to the extent that as an Asiatic country it too finds itself in a position similar to that of Indonesia, especially in its confrontation with the West. Van Galen Last must have envisioned the treatment of this problem of acculturation in the novel format. It goes almost without saying that he based much of his material on the actual situation in Indonesia in 1957.

The character of President Dramakutra, for that matter, is not a portrait of Indonesia's President Sukarno but modeled after an intimate Dutch friend of Van Galen Last's who, although he was totally apolitical, resembled Sukarno in several ways. Various other Somalesians were also modeled after Europeans and were certainly not typecast as Indonesians. President Dramakutra is a charming and, if need be, jovial dictator, a genial tactician and born orator who is capable of playing upon an audience, as the phrase goes. He is also the kind of man who can change a demonstration around and turn it into a personal victory. All of this suggests Sukarno clearly enough. President Dramakutra is a juggler with power whom Van Galen Last observes ironically and not without admiration.

Actually the book concerns not so much the portrayal of Dramakutra as the question of how the colonial transplants have taken to Eastern soil. It asks to what extent Somalesia is a politically, economically, and technically underdeveloped country, judging by Western standards. Particularly, the book wants to know what the human situation in the country has become. The answer is provided by Dramakutra's wife during a conversation with the Hightowers, a Western couple staying with the president and his wife at their country estate called Sans Soucie. On page seventy-six of the novel, Mrs. Dramakutra observes that she is sorry to have to point out that Westerners view Somalesia exclusively as a technical or political problem. This spokeswoman, more sympathetic and intelligent than her husband, is principally interested in what has become of the Somalesian intellectual as a human being. The foreigner is bold enough to talk openly about technical and economical *under*development but never mentions the human side of the situation. He either does not talk about it or he tries to keep his judgment to himself, but Mrs. Dramakutra, as a

Somalesian, formulates it as follows: "We are especially, you understand, underdeveloped as human beings, much more so than in some technical, economical, or social way. This may well sound odd, considering the civilization behind us, and no doubt any Somalesian will deny it, but even so I am convinced that a Somalesian has absolutely nothing to say to a Westerner." Right away, of course, someone speaks up to deny this. It is Hightower who does, and he puts the blame on the West.

President Dramakutra is a satire because Van Galen Last's talent lends itself to the genre, but it is also an ironical analysis of a very important problem facing all decolonized countries, which Van Galen Last himself takes no less seriously, and that is their relationship to the cultural complex of the West.

In conclusion, we should mention three different memoirs written by Indonesians. They help us understand how even those who served in an official capacity and who availed themselves of the Dutch language perceived and experienced the colonial relationship and the ensuing revolution. It appears that there always existed a world to which their Dutch friends had no access. These memoirs could well act as eye openers to those Dutchmen who have always lived in and believed in a segregated colonial society as a matter of course.

In the first place, there are the *Memoirs of Pangéran Achmad Djajadiningrat (Herinneringen van P. A. D.,* 1936), who was descended from a well-known ruling family from Banten. These are unique and extremely interesting. They contain passages we will never forget, such as the childhood memories of the Tjilegon uprising from 1888, and particularly the public execution of a number of rebels. Much more recent are the equally very readable *Memoirs from Three Eras (Herinneringen uit drie tijdperken)* by Margono Djojohadikusumo. These were written in Dutch but first appeared in serialized form in the daily newspaper *Indonesia Raya (Great Indonesia)* run by Mochtar Lubis. They have since been collected and brought out in two different editions, one appearing in Indonesia in 1969, and the other in the Netherlands in 1970. Finally, there is that charming volume written by the widow of the TNI General (Tentara Nasional Indonesia, the National Indonesian Army), *Urip Sumohardjo,* which was brought out by Tong Tong Publishers. It is very informative reading for Dutchmen who still think that the colonial relationship had so much to recommend it.

XIII
Best Forgotten

1 "Asia Raya": The Japanese Occupation

"Best Forgotten" ("Niet meer aan denken") is the title of a story about a prison camp somewhere in Thailand written by L. A. Koelewijn. It is a tale told in exact and revealing detail, as if to document and relive everything for the very last time ever and to exorcise a nightmare best forgotten.

A number of events had preceded the nightmare: the attack on Pearl Harbor on December 7, 1941, the outbreak of war and everything that came after, the war itself. On December 11, the armed forces of the Netherlands East Indies were mobilized. Part of the Dutch civilian population joined the military, another part took up civil-defense positions or was asked "to stay at its post," as the phrase went. The mood was one of tense waiting. Radio and newspaper reports and the wailing of sirens brought war closer every day. There was a general need to work off tensions and every opportunity was seized to translate them into deeds. Meanwhile, no matter how cautiously worded, all manner of disastrous news began to trickle in. It made the peaceful, quiet mornings seem unreal. With the landing of Japanese troops, major and minor armed clashes followed, with the Dutch East Indies army ever retreating. The armed forces, with the exception of the navy, surrendered in March. In some places, the resulting power vacuum made things unsafe for many Europeans, there was some looting, and people were in danger of their lives. The Japanese were now expected to keep order. According to their prearranged plan, all allied military personnel was interned, and at a later stage the greater part of the European civilian population as well.

Throughout the entire Netherlands Indies, the Japanese set up camps: military camps, civilian camps, and separate camps for women and children. In this fashion, the entire Dutch population was practically eliminated and forced to lead an artificial existence behind bamboo and barbed wire. The life in which they had played such a prominent role now went on without them.

Once inside these camps, in totally different relation to one another, they again had to wait. This time they waited for the end of the war, which would not come for three and a half years and which a quarter of all prisoners would never live to experience. Anyone expecting that a mood of apathy or listless despondency prevailed in the camps would be mistaken. The will to live, the faith in an Allied victory, and maybe a latent feeling of self-esteem and even superiority, despite all humiliation, kept people going, especially in the beginning. Only later, when pressure and privation became too heavy to bear, did moral and physical decay set in. This began after the start of transports to Thailand, Burma, Sumatra, Flores, and the Moluccas for tasks such as laying the "railway of the dead" and building air strips. By then, thousands of prisoners could think of nothing more than simply staying alive. Yet, no matter how deplorable the situation in most camps became, there always remained a small opportunity for recreation. This was still the case in 1942–43 in the large camp at Tjimahi on Java, which boasted theatrical groups (such as the "Eternal Theater"), and courses and lectures (in the "Studio") which were a new experience to many. Moreover, in many camps, with an ever-changing population, people were thrown together who would never have met one another in peace time. This concentration of Dutch people not only resulted in a feeling of solidarity (put to the test frequently enough), but also created an opportunity for intellectual and cultural contact with often stimulating effect. Camp life did not always mean impoverishment, it also meant development, which could lead to spiritual reorganization. Not only did people talk and read a lot in all of these camps, but they also wrote a great deal. Paper and writing material were precious things and only the occasional distribution of Japanese toilet paper saved the situation. What some people had never dared dream now happened: they began to feel the need to give expression to their moods, feelings, and thoughts. They often did so in well-intended rhymes, but some of it was poetry.

Leo Vroman, who had barely published anything at the time, wrote a number of stories and his *Poems* (*Gedichten*, 1946) in a variety of different camps. Judging by their dates, it appears that Albert Besnard also wrote several of his poems appearing in *Doom and Thirst* (*Doem en dorst*, 1952) in an internment camp in east Sumatra. Willem Brandt also wrote poems, collected as *Inside Japanese Barbed Wire* (*Binnen Japans prikkeldraad*). These came out in 1946. While in camp he probably wrote other poems which found their way into sev-

eral later collections. During his incarceration, the government official H. J. Friedericy wrote his first stories and the novel *Bontorio*
which was published in 1947. Breton de Nijs (pseudonym for Rob
Nieuwenhuys) was working on his family saga *Faded Portraits (Vergeelde Portretten)*, although he did not complete the novel till 1954.
Others were busy preparing lectures, writing articles, or making
notes with plans to expand them into writing later on. Many drew
and painted (on walls or on the cardboard of their Red Cross pack-
ages), designed stage sets and costumes; and there were a great many
who developed detailed governmental and political plans for postwar
activities.

Even so, there were few who wrote about the war itself. To most
people the war had been a matter of only a few days, without too
much combat or privation. Not to all, however. Jan Eggink wrote an
account in 1942 to expunge from his memory a dreadful journey
made by troops who had lost their way. He did so without much ado
and without an excess of detail. Perhaps for that reason this brief account, published in 1948 under the title *Stray Journey (De zwerf-
tocht)* makes for such excellent reading.

Many people kept diaries or wrote down events and experiences.
Most of this stuff is hardly readable, dull, in a mediocre style, with an
altogether too frequent and annoying undertone of self-pity and self-
inflation. Rare indeed was the individual who managed to keep an
emotional distance between himself and the ongoing events. Such a
man was C. Binnerts, who on the island of Flores in 1943 kept a diary
using a good measure of irony mixed with a careful sense of the ludicrous as well as macabre aspects. He seemed to have hit upon an effi-
cient way of shielding himself mentally. It came out in 1947 as *Everything All Right, Gentlemen! (Alles in orde, Heeren)*, a title already
containing its own understatement. Unfortunately, this small book
got a bit lost in the subsequent and growing stack of poorly written
prison-camp literature, and few people seem to have heard of it. Years
later, one will still remember the account of a nocturnal cremation of
six dead prisoners, the huge flames shooting up, and the return by
torchlight of eight stark-naked men after a job well done. If ever a diary is to be reprinted, let it be this one. It is one of the best, and in an
indirect way one learns a great deal more about the situation in the
camps than from most of those later, wordy camp stories written
with such a fuss.

One of these is *Women behind Barbed Wire (Vrouwen achter prikkeldraad, n.d. [Batavia, June 1–Sept. 1, 1947])* by Jo Manders, born in
1900. Admittedly, Manders suffered much personal grief, much that
was horrible. But she did not succeed in making a reasonably good

book of her experiences. On the contrary, she fell into all the pitfalls related to writing about this kind of subject. As an author, she lost complete control of herself and her book shows no signs of either understanding or restraint. It just goes on and on in alternatingly quarrelsome or weepy tones, clenched fists, or a voice choked with emotion. In both senses of the word, a dismal book.

Willem Brandt (born 1905) wrote at about the same time as Jo Manders a book about the men's camp Si Ringo Ringo in east Sumatra. It bears the ominous title *The Yellow Terror (De gele terreur)*, is "dedicated to my dead comrades," and is preceded by a poem called "Cemetery at Si Ringo Ringo" ("Kerkhof Si Ringo Ringo"). It appeared in 1946. His book is considerably better written than that of Manders but still suffers from a tendency toward the theatrical and melodramatic, especially whenever his emotions become too powerful.

Brandt also produced a number of camp stories that were written within the span of the last ten or twenty years. A number of those were collected around a Christmas theme toward the end of 1977 and bear the fitting title derived from Dickens: "God bless us everyone!" These stories suffer from the same shortcoming and they ring hollow.

"The Candle" ("De kaars"), which first appeared in 1964, opens this collection of eight stories and "a Christmas suite for angels and shepherds." The story is representative of Brandt's method. It is apparently quite well known and was once read over the radio.

The story takes us to a prison barracks, in all likelihood at Si Ringo Ringo. The men are dreadfully hungry and their hunger is all they can think about, day and night. Only one of the prisoners has something edible left, a candle. Instead of eating it, he keeps it for Christmas Day. Then he lights it, and all those emaciated men crowd around it, the minister and the priest too, and Brandt writes that they saw things within that flame "which are not of this world." A number of those who had sat around the candle survived, others did not. "But when they died," Brandt writes, "their eyes were less dull than before." He ends with: "That was on account of that strange candle. The Light that darkness could not quench."

Brandt wrote another prison camp story which is not included in this collection because it has nothing to do with Christmas, but it too has become quite well known. It was also read over the radio, on May 5, the Day of Liberation for the people in Holland. This is odd, considering that the Japanese did not surrender in Asia until August 15, 1945. In any event, the story bears the title "The Secret" ("Het geheim," 1960) and is linked to the ninth chapter of *The Yellow Terror*, which describes the liberation of one Dutch prison camp in Indonesia. The story's basic plot is the authentic situation of a prisoner's managing to hide the Dutch national flag inside his little pillow for three and a half years and then hoisting it over one of the barracks the day of liberation. Indeed, an impressive and memorable event after so many years of hunger, misery, and humiliation, but even so Brandt once again strains too hard to be "literary" about it.

It so happens that these same events are described in another book about the camps: *Rationed Lives* (*Leven op rantsoen*, 1959) by H. L. Leffelaar who, as a fifteen- or sixteen-year-old, was in the same camp Brandt was. He experienced the same liberation therefore and experienced comparable feelings. He too gives an account of the overwhelming moment when the national anthem was sung for the first time and then taken up, from barrack to barrack. He also tells about the hidden flag and how moved they all were, and so on, but he does not make it into a pat little story. His choice of words is quite different from Brandt's, when he says "I was all choked up, couldn't utter a damned squeak and tears were running down my face." His use of "damned squeak" is typical of his attitude toward sentiment and literature. Leffelaar realizes the dangers of pathos which might get the better of him, as he says himself, and ruin his story. He is alert to these possible pitfalls and he keeps up his guard. This is one good reason why Leffelaar has managed to steer clear of "literature" of Brandt's sort.

H. L. Leffelaar (born 1929), whose father ran a printing business in Medan, Sumatra, was thirteen years old when he and his mother were put in a concentration camp for women. Only later did the Japanese transfer him to a camp for men, camp Si Ringo Ringo in this case. He kept a diary in the camps. *Rationed Lives* is not, incidentally, the diary of a fifteen-year-old but the story of a mature author who much later wrote down his memories of the camp. The excerpts from his diary only serve as a kind of measuring device and vantage point for the subsequent story. In his introduction, Leffelaar tells us that as he retraced his steps to his camp experiences, he stopped short at the edge of his memory and then looked back. Chronological time appeared to have lost all meaning for him and the events themselves had given way to his perception of them. The composition of Leffelaar's book, originally a prize-winning essay in 1945, gives his story a great deal of variety. Memories, anecdotes, comments, and speculations follow one another or merge. Leffelaar particularly reveals a talent for telling good anecdotes of the kind that illuminate. His so-called general considerations are not his strongest point. After he left prison camp, his memory of the events of the revolutionary war between the

Dutch and the Indonesians after 1945—comparable to those between the French and the Indochinese—never left him and marked him permanently.

Leffelaar also wrote *Through a Harsh Dawn* (1963), in English, a more complete retrospect of the war years. In it, he also quotes from his father's diary, written while he worked as a Japanese POW on the infamous Burma railroad. *Through a Harsh Dawn* ends with a chapter called "In Search of Myself." Here, Leffelaar tries to explain that what motivated him to write was the desire to free himself from his war experiences, not by forgetting or hiding them but by reviving them instead. His ultimate goal was the completion of a process of identification.

The April 1975 and December 1977 issues of *Tirade* contain short pieces that Leffelaar called "By Bits and Pieces," and which one hopes and suspects will lead to a larger whole. To any observant and interested reader with the ability to put himself in other people's shoes, these pieces are often moving. They are effective, again, because they maintain the balance between keeping and surrendering one's emotional distance. To this very day there are all sorts of strands and ties that lead him back to his earlier experiences. They are the ones, after all, which shaped the present and determined one's relationship to the ongoing events in the world with all their related feelings of insecurity, abandonment, desperation, loss, violence, leave taking, protest, in short, to everything. What is gained is our increased ability to imagine and share the feelings of others, of all those hundreds of thousands who are still caught up in the very situations Leffelaar recognizes. This explains his attitude to what took place in Vietnam, and his fierce and unreasonable protest against the American ambassador in Bucharest with his "war is war" argument.

Memories can be suppressed for years but are never forgotten. The slightest incident can unleash everything again. Something of the sort happened to C. van Heekeren (born 1912) when he talked to an old fellow prisoner. So many memories came rushing back and with such force that "it occurred to him," as he modestly puts it, to write about them. Van Heekeren became quickly enough aware of the dangers inherent in writing down personal memories, especially after so many years. He drastically changed course and took a different tack by turning his book into a kind of documentary involving other narrators as well. He called it *Olieman's Mess Kit (Het pannetje van Oliemans*, 1966), which had earlier been privately issued as *The Achin Party (De Atjeh-party).*

On March 8, 1944, a work party was sent out of Glugur prison camp near Medan consisting of 300 Dutchmen and 200 Englishmen to the interior of southern Achin. This was the so-called Achin party that turned into a nightmare. Eight months later it was disbanded and what was left of the men distributed over several base camps in Pakan Baru.

Twenty years later it became evident that the process of mental repression renders human memory unreliable: "When I finally tried to get a few things down on paper it became clear that the machinations of memory are treacherous." Little remained other than to call in the help of others. As it turned out, he was lucky. A former fellow prisoner came up with an aluminum mess kit of the Dutch East Indies army that had belonged to a certain Oliemans. While bedridden, the latter had engraved onto his small round pan the names of all the Dutchmen who had been involved in the disastrous Achin party. Using this curious list, Van Heekeren commenced his long search for the surviving members. He managed to collect over 200 names and addresses and what followed was a correspondence of nearly 900 letters. What had begun as a last ditch effort now proved to be an excellent method. Van Heekeren's book consists largely of quotations from this correspondence, but even so, *Olieman's Mess Kit* indirectly turned into a personal account. We still get to know the author intimately, fortunately not as "a man of letters," but as an author with no other ambition than to be a good reporter. And happily enough, his book is more convincing, better, and more spellbinding than many a work of fiction would have been. Van Heekeren knows when to smile and how to tell an anecdote, and knows when to keep his distance, as well. For these reasons he is also capable of regarding his enemies as human, such as Miura, the Japanese camp commander, whose actions he tries to explain in terms of his particular situation, without altogether excusing him. Van Heekeren is a man without bitterness, with a dislike for excitement and literary embellishment, and this graces him.

Following *Olieman's Mess Kit*, he wrote several other books according to the same method with lots of quotations and snatches of conversation. His second book is called *Batavia Signals: "Berlin"* (*Batavia seint: Berlijn*, 1967), "Berlin" being the codeword used to signal to Dutch authorities that all German nationals in the Indies were to be rounded up and interned. It is an excellent book, better even than *Olieman's Mess Kit*. The second book is a logical enough extension of the first. After Van Heekeren had completed his first book, he honestly asked himself: "How did we Dutchmen treat *our* prisoners?" In this instance, those were the Germans who shortly after the German invasion of the Netherlands were imprisoned in the Netherlands East Indies. As before, Van Heekeren started with extensive research, going through the available material, correspond-ing with and interviewing witnesses. Their names are all included in his "Sources." The resulting information was more than surprising, it was "perplexing," in the author's own words. As his research pro-gressed, he found himself thinking time and again "I never knew that," while realizing at the same time that he was uttering his own equivalent of the German postwar disclaimer on the subject of war atrocities—"Wir haben es nicht gewusst" ("We didn't know"). Typi-cally, Van Heekeren tries to explain the harsh and often brutal treat-ment of the German prisoners in terms of the psychology of the times and relates it to German behavior in Europe, especially toward the Jews, but he does not try to exonerate Dutch behavior. On the con-trary. He found witnesses and came up with all kinds of incontrovert-ible facts and proof which greatly diminish the right of the Dutch to accuse the Germans and the Japanese of war crimes. This book by Van Heekeren will anger all those who would like nothing better than to continue to believe in the comfortable and self-serving myth of the specific humanity of the Dutch. What we find most striking in Van Heekeren's book, by the way, is not so much the lack of human-ity as the blindness and stupidity of "the authorities." This often re-sulted in ludicrous situations although always against a background that "perplexed" Van Heekeren. His book is truly written in the name of humanity.

Van Heekeren's documentary reads like a novel not only because of his sense for vital and telling detail and his ability to make a balanced composition, but also because he included the testimony of several German internees who, it turns out, often wrote a fine, indeed excel-lent, Dutch. The account of the shipwreck of German prisoners on the island of Nias, west of Sumatra, after one of three transports tak-ing them to British India has been torpedoed, reads like a well-written tragicomedy more exciting than many an adventure story: "reality surpassing fiction."

In 1958 and 1959, two collections of short stories by L. A. Koele-wijn (pseudonym of Nic Beets, born 1915) appeared, one called *A Day at a Time (De ene dag, en de andere)* and the other *Best Forgotten (Niet meer aan denken)*. Each collection contains a story set in a Japa-nese prison camp. Neither of them is a documentary like Van Heeke-ren's books, nor are they direct reports such as Binnerts's or anything like Leffelaar's reconstructed memoirs. But their similarity lies in the fact that they too are the result of their author's possibly even greater need to exorcise the prison camp experience by coming to terms with it through a written confrontation. The title of the second and longest story, "Best Forgotten," is significant in this respect. For the rest, these stories differ from all others in their genre by virtue of the author's perspective. He uses historical and personal experiences as a backdrop only, while concentrating on the development of an inner process under duress. He purposely avoids any use of direct expression. It is odd that Koelewijn's work is still so little known.

This obscurity is understandable, on the other hand, when we realize that the intricacy of his work becomes apparent only after a careful, slow, and concentrated reading. Koelewijn writes a kind of diminutive prose built up out of minute internal and external observations. His small brush strokes gradually bring out his total concept, and only after completing his stories do we realize the conscious purpose of each brush stroke and its relationship to others. We then become aware of his fine distribution of detail, the purpose of repeated motifs, and the subtlety of transition. What is most striking is Koelewijn's craftsmanship, especially when we consider that he made his debut with these stories. No doubt he realized the importance of language as a means of communication, since it obviously means more to him than mere reproduction. He also realized that writing meant intervening in a psychological process. These stories give the clear impression of having aided an act of self-liberation. The interaction between language and experience is effective only at a high level of intensity. This explains why the stories not dealing with the war are not nearly as good as those two prison camp stories; the former lack the urge to free oneself that motivated the latter.

In the first place, there is the portrait of the Japanese interpreter Tamagashi in *A Day at a Time* which seems to have been written as an act of reconciliation. Tamagashi does not represent the stereotype "Jap" but is portrayed as an individual Japanese with human features. The portrait seems wholly authentic and is clearly modeled after someone the author saw as a human being deserving of sympathy. Koelewijn may well have known someone like Tamagashi in the small transit station for allied prisoners he describes. It lies in a village deep within the interior of Thailand, with a camp for the English, a camp for the Dutch, and a small compound for Japanese guards. Among the railroad cars, the trucks, the Japanese soldiers, and Allied prisoners, somewhat hesitant and unsure, Tamagashi moves about. He does not seem to be a member of his group and is unable to gain access to the prisoners. The latter deny him access by keeping their distance and by their correct and polite behavior toward him. As far as his relationship with his compatriots is concerned, Koelewijn informs us on several occasions that he did not seem to belong with them even though he was inescapably a member: "Among them, he was totally alone." Because he is an interpreter he has an officer's rank but no position or power. Even the Japanese sergeant and corporal wield more authority than he does. His background is sketched quickly, without interrupting the story. His father was a merchant with interests in America and now holds an important job in supplying food. He is a modern man, tolerant of Western ideas which have also penetrated his world. Tamagashi has studied English for a couple of years and read English literature, especially English poets, and he borrows paperbacks from the prisoners. He wants to study at Oxford and become a teacher of English. He is not a merchant like his father and brother but an intellectual who is attracted by the West. Unsure on account of his marginal position, isolated by his group, his sole consolation is the memory of his sister, two years older than he, who gave his life meaning and who is now a nurse somewhere terribly far off.

The story begins with everybody waiting for a transport of prisoners that is either not coming or delayed, nobody knows exactly, because communications are poor. There is really nothing to do for Tamagashi. He lies on his bunk and reads (English books, of course). Every once in a while he gets up and wanders about in a kind of no man's land. He is thinking of walking over to his compatriots but knows there will be nobody there to talk to and that they distrust him because of his good relationship with the opposition. Halfway there, he turns around, walks past his own quarters and then, naturally almost, he goes over to the English camp in vague hopes of contact. He asks to talk to the doctor, who has to be fetched first and then right away confronts him with a problem. He needs help moving a very sick man out of the Dutch camp. In his desire to please the Allied doctor, he gets himself into a confused and difficult situation which through some ensuing incident nearly endangers his life but ultimately turns out all right. When it is all over, nothing much has really happened. Even so, the events have excited him greatly because they have once again pinpointed his ambiguous position. His mental instability leads to an inward panic attended by fever and dizzy spells. The doctor diagnoses "malaria." During his hallucinations, he reveals his feelings of guilt and betrayal. These complete our image of an enemy with a human face.

The longer story, "Best Forgotten," seems almost certainly based on a personal war experience but the story is not written in the kind of shorthand dictated by immediate experience. Koelewijn has kept himself totally out of the story and in so doing creates a distance between himself and the events described. Although they remain his private experiences, they are assumed and recorded by a Dutch sergeant of the Indies army, Johan van Rees. Van Rees goes through everything Koelewijn himself experienced but he is of course still his own character with an entirely different past. Curiously enough, this Dutch sergeant turns out to have something in common with the Japanese translator Tamagashi because, despite their vast differences, they are both loners who have difficulty establishing contact with others. Van Rees, together with a small group of Dutchmen and several hundred Englishmen and Australians, is picked to make a trek up into the Thai highlands in order to make a new railroad bed close to the Three Pagodas Pass on the Thai-Burmese border. First they go by train and later on foot. After a while, Van Rees loses contact with his group, falls behind, and ends up among strangers, Englishmen, with whom he can barely exchange a few meaningless phrases.

This is hardly a coincidence. But during their journey through the dusky forests and open plains, past camps with the remains of human life strewn about and bleached out skeletons along the trail, past camps with well-fed work parties, in drenching rain or under a scorching sun, during this journey something happens to Van Rees. Exactly what does happen to him is something Koelewijn allows him to say in his own words. They add up to the long monologue which is the essence of the story. The narrator does not provide any clues or directions but transfers the story's interpretation to the reader, who gradually becomes aware of something happening to Van Rees, of something shifting inside him and of spaces opening up. Van Rees experiences the hitherto unknown feeling of human solidarity and transcends his own boundaries. It all starts on the railway bridge, with the swollen river below and the English captain's grasp that keeps him from falling in. The same captain sits down beside him at night in the forest while it is raining, and begins to talk to him. He wakes up with his head resting against another's body and hears the heartbeat inside. Later on, when they are passing through a cholera-infested area, Van Rees sees one of his fellow prisoners lying on the ground, vomiting up a wave of water. He knows what that means. The sick man turns out to be the captain. Like the others, his first impulse is to march on, but he stops. He is one of four men who stay behind and later bury the captain. Then their journey continues as they carry a sick man with them. Their exhaustion is almost complete, their bodies moving without volition. They have entered a dreamlike state and hallucinate, and Van Rees sees himself as a small boy whom he tries to entice to come closer. He is certain now that this means the long-awaited end. But when they have finally reached their destination and Van Rees rests, stretched out upon the ground, it appears that the end again has been postponed. In its place, an entirely new physical experience occurs, not as previously "something contemptible and not worth mentioning," but a feeling of fluidity, of spaciousness and deep contentment. "It would be all right if it came tonight. He had already been expecting it for so long. Everything was reconciled now, things from very long ago and other things that had just happened. It had all been reconciled. Nothing could happen anymore. He was satisfied. . . ."

This does not exhaust prison camp literature by a long shot. The authors' names do not matter but maybe their titles do, if only to indicate the general level of their output: *The Yellow Terror, The Yellow Peril,* and *The Yellow Hell,* the last subtitled *Slaves in the Jap Mines.* These books are on the whole very discouraging. One wonders why so few found an adequate way of expressing experiences for something that must have cut deeply. Most of these writers lose themselves in endless detail or drown in their own tears. This is the danger inherent in writing about the war because anyone disturbing old war memories comes upon an adder's nest, with no way of knowing what the consequences will be. It is like disrupting a seeming calm and being overwhelmed by the onrush of wave upon wave of memory. Each wave will first seem to merge with another, then clash, and so the tide of memory will flow on infinitely, it would seem. Each detail becomes meaningful in terms of the next and can not seem to function without it. The only solution that suggests itself is to write everything down but this is pointless, of course, because all distinction will be lost and the end result will be a sheer monotone. This kind of account only increases the distance between an author and his audience, and the only way to solve this clashing of interests is a rigorous change in arranging one's presentation. Most prison camp literature has had to do without any such surgery because all the pent-up facts and emotions proved too powerful, even as late as thirty years after the fact.

A case in point is the book *Taku'ang's Ring (De ring van Takoe'-ang,* 1974) by Ies van Bel. It is not known whether this is the author's real name or whether he is hiding behind one of his main characters, quartermaster Van Dalen. His introduction has a few indistinct things to say about truth and fiction but that is not the point here. The point is whether or not Ies van Bel has succeeded in living up to the claim on the book's dust jacket of an "exciting adventure story." Unfortunately, he has not turned his experience among the Dayaks of Borneo during the Japanese occupation into anything either exciting or adventurous. This is one of those books where a wealth of material is lost in the kind of expansiveness characteristic of people such as Mr. van Bel. They do not really have any idea what writing is about, and what it takes in terms of concentration, limitation, self-discipline, and so on, and more's the pity.

Two recent books which also concern the Japanese occupation ought to be mentioned here because they belong to the better kind in this genre, even though they display the same shortcomings. The first one is *The Crying's Got to Stop* (*Je kunt niet altijd huilen*, 1975) and the second *Mommy, I'm Dying* (*Mammie ik ga dood*, 1976) by Annemie MacGillavry and Margaretha Ferguson, respectively. They are not bad, despite their lachrymose titles. Neither author indulges in lamentation or great self-pity, although MacGilavry comes dangerously close at times.

Annemie MacGillavry (born 1908) was a *njonja besar*, a "great lady" before the war. She was Dutch and married into a well-known Indies family of planters and manufacturers. It is obvious that life was good to her and that it had style, an old-Indies style in fact, which she thoroughly liked and enjoyed. The first thirty pages of her book deal with life before the war. It strikes us as almost idyllic, and it may very well have been, certainly compared to the gruesome period that was to follow. Her account covers her experiences with her two children in prison and the immediate postwar or *bersiap* ("get ready!") period, the latter a revolutionary war cry usually resulting in bloodshed. Her story sounds incredible but the events she describes are authentic enough. Her book has page upon page, sentence upon sentence of minute descriptions of their suffering and unspeakable misery, their hunger, desperation, apathy, and fear of dying. The narrator's voice is distinctive, in itself a sign of quality, but the voice goes on far too long, indiscriminately describing one detail after another. We understand well enough that the author aims to re-create everything as completely as possible but it wears the reader down after a while.

It is obvious that writing about those years was meant to cure MacGillavry of an obsession. She tells us herself that she suffers from a post-concentration-camp syndrome, complete with an ego fixation as an attendant symptom. And although she does not say this, she must have written her book in the way of self-prescribed therapy. As a work of prose, however, the book is simply overwritten. It would be foolish to say that it is not effective as a human document; on the contrary, it is very impressive as such. It is not her shocking story that fails to impress but simply her talent as a writer. Especially when she most strains to be literary her sentences seem to come straight out of a ladies' magazine. Fortunately those sentences are few.

After all that has been said about prison camp literature generally, Margaretha Ferguson's book requires few comments. Hers is not a retrospective account, such as MacGillavry's and that of most other prison camp books, but an authentic diary, at the most edited by her. It records her war experiences on the inside and outside of prison camps haunted by the fear that she and her newborn child will not survive the war. Because it is a diary we ought to read it as one, that is to say, as a direct record of daily events, feelings, and thoughts. Ferguson's most striking characteristic is her honesty. She certainly dares express herself without reservation but even so, the distance between her and her reader is too great. It is all too long, too much, and too compact. Time and again the reader is distracted by her commentary. Whether prompted by her notes or not, her comments do lend her journal a certain variety but on the other hand they tend to impede her "story." Whatever we may think of her views and comments and their place in the diary, we should not forget that the author was barely twenty years old at the time she wrote them. The fact is that her observations functioned as a defense mechanism while helping her to escape from her daily, sordid routine, and that they were a means to keep her going.

In 1974, Paula Gomes (born Djakarta, 1932) made a trip through Indonesia after almost thirty years' absence. She had been born and raised there. Her father was a Hollander, her mother an Indo-European, her grandmother an Indonesian. She regarded Indonesia as her home, her country, whence the Indonesians had driven her out as a child. That is how she looked at it, even though she had come to understand events better when she was back in Holland. Now she had come back wondering what her own feelings would be. It proved to be her country still, with the same friendly people from before the war. The old enmity had vanished completely. That was perhaps the most difficult thing of all to understand. The hateful *bersiap* period was gone forever, it seemed, and so was her fear. In reality of course, her fear had always been part of her memory. It had always been there, if dormant most of the time. The moment she was back in Indonesia, however, all these suppressed fears were aroused again. She remembered the days spent with the Kempetai (the Japanese equivalent of the German Gestapo), the prison camp, and her mother's death. Worst of all, she recalled the madness of the revolution, an outburst of hatred and cruelty, and the unbearable feeling of enmity.

With a certain feeling of resignation Paula Gomes named her book *Sudah, Let It Be* (*Sudah, laat maar*, 1975). She thought she had left Indonesia for good when she managed to flee the country as a fourteen-year-old girl. She was taken to Holland alone, without her parents. Almost thirty years later, she took her leave from Indonesia again.

At the end of her trip, she says farewell to an old hotel servant, who to her is the personification of Indonesia: "I picked up my traveling bag. Still out on the veranda, I looked back. Through the window, I saw his brown, deeply furrowed face. Yes, *sudah*, let it be. This was the way the gods had destined it to be, I was to leave once again. Indonesia had become an independent country and Holland was my home." There is something tragic and insoluble about her situation which is shared by thousands of Indo-European people in the Netherlands. The title of her story reflects an attitude said to be typical of many of these Indies people, that things will just have to be accepted as they are. People with such a view will arm themselves and do not stand for tears or whining. Gomes lowers her horizons too, but strengthens herself as she writes, and she requires only enough words to fill a hundred pages.

2   "Indonesia Merdeka": A Free Indonesia

The Japanese surrendered on August 15, 1945, and the formation of the Indonesian Republic was announced on August 17. At the time, hundreds of thousands of Dutch people found themselves without adequate protection. The Allies, in this case the English, who were assigned to occupy the Netherlands Indies, did not arrive until weeks later. It was to take several months, in fact, before they could fully take over from the Japanese. The resulting power vacuum led to a wave of aggression, seemingly throwing the entire country into chaos. The revolutionaries exploited this situation. It started with the so-called *bersiap* period, attended by numerous killings of Europeans, Chinese, and Japanese, as well as collaborating Indonesians. To many Europeans, the "liberation" often meant either new imprisonment or death, giving the word a bitter taste.

During the first half year, British troops were almost in sole charge of the military situation but proved too few in number. The battle of Surabaja, involving air power, shore bombardment, and infantry units, pitted limited English forces against 100,000 Indonesians. Surabaja was taken but only with relatively heavy losses of 600 killed and nearly 1,000 wounded. Gradually, Dutch forces arrived on the scene. The former Dutch East Indies army fielded two battalions, while seventeen volunteer battalions from the Netherlands were put ashore, together with several thousand marines. Later followed an expeditionary force of military draftees which the regular troops nicknamed the *tentara susu*, which freely translates as baby-face army.

The Dutch attempt to regain power was opposed by an army of the young republic with its own improvised style. As the weaker army, it chose by necessity the guerrilla method. This meant the tactic of small units that would pull back, return and ambush, and only engage their enemy at times and places of their own choosing. The journalist Alfred van Sprang has one of his characters at headquarters say: "It's no use . . . we now have a measure of order and safety in our area but the moment you turn your back it's a mess again. We're patrolling night and day . . . we try and hunt them down, only to have them show up somewhere else. We never have the feeling of ever settling anything. They just keep coming back. The whole thing is so hopeless."

The situation was not the same everywhere and there was also a difference between conditions on Java itself and on the other islands. On Java anyway, two armies confronted one another, one an army of established authority, the other a growing revolutionary force. Typically, both armies appealed for support and favor to the local population. Dutch troops did so by liberating them from "hunger and terrorism," by creating "order and safety," while the Indonesian army appealed to national sentiment and the promise of *kemerdekaän* or liberty. Both sides had an entirely different point of view. To the Indonesians, the Dutch belligerents were the enemies of a newly gained political freedom, whereas to the Dutch the Indonesians represented rebels who hardly cared for the interests of the population at all. They considered themselves the protectors of "order and safety," words that occurred with great frequency then to justify their military actions. In his *Line of Demarcation*, a war story embellished with literary flourishes, Willem Brandt plainly and honestly says: "We know our job, and we know what we have to do: to protect and to guard these people."

The Indonesians saw things quite differently. Next to their regular army, the TNI, there were on the Indonesian side also a number of smaller fighting units that refused to join the regulars. These small units made up the "gangs" one heard so much about then, the real "pelopors," or "peloppers," as the Dutch called them, who went about their business in very destructive and radical ways. (The word "pelopor" seems to derive from the Dutch word "voorloper" or scout.) On several occasions, these small bands got in the way of the regular army. In any event, gradually a total war developed. As the Indonesian army got a better hold of the situation (and a better hold on the population), both sides became more radical. In the middle of 1947, after a period of infiltrations coming from the republican side, sabotage, ambushes, and seemingly endless talks, the Dutch government decided to launch its first "policing action." A year later, it was followed by another. The use of the word "policing" was not intended as a euphemism for a real and complete war but rather as a logical term stemming from the Dutch view of the conflict. These policing actions never had their intended result, certainly not politically. Militarily too they were to prove Pyrrhic victories. Gradually the Dutch potential to govern the archipelago declined. On December 27, 1949, the Netherlands recognized Indonesia's sovereignty.

As we said, the *bersiap* period just after the Japanese surrender was a power vacuum during which hundreds of Europeans, women and children included, were murdered. Until recently, little had been written about that time. To be sure, Jo Manders had written about it as a sequel of sorts to her camp experiences. So had A. Paul Cortenbach written *Mickey Behind Barbed Wire* (*Mickey achter prikkeldraad*, 1955), a rather weepy story. It was not until 1974, however, that someone would again write about it. The first to do so was Lin Scholte; a year later, in 1975, Annemie MacGillavry and Paula Gomes did. Gomes's writing is impressive for two reasons. First, because of her subject, which can only be called horrible, and second, on account of her controlled attitude and style. We mentioned her in the previous chapter.

Shortly after the end of the war, when Djakarta was in chaos, when nothing could be done and anything could happen, Johan Fabricius arrived from London as one among a score of foreign correspondents. He had arrived in a city with thousands of other people coming in and as many trying to get out, a city chock-full of military personnel, black marketeers, beggars, and prostitutes. Like his fellow journalists, Fabricius hung around a bit, talked, and made inquiries without getting much the wiser. Later on, he brought out a small book about his visit, *How I Found the Indies Again* (*Hoe ik Indië terugvond*, 1947). He really had not found anything at all. If we compare his account with, say that of W. H. J. Elias, *The Indies under Japan's Yoke* (*Indië onder Japans hiel*, 1946), then Fabricius's prose clearly wins out. Still, Fabricius had been too much on the sidelines, lacked firsthand knowledge of the camps, and knew nothing about the frustrations of thousands of civilians and former POWs who had found themselves suddenly in a vacuum. Fabricius has little to say about the desolate mood, the heat, dust, aimlessness, or anger of those times, nor do we find in his book anything of the feeling of alienation and emptiness that prevailed. These things are certainly touched upon in a story by E. R. Duncan Elias (born 1919) although it really does not pretend to be a war story at all. Its setting is Djakarta of 1946 and 1947, not its center or its streets but merely a house full of people, or rather, just one room in that house.

The story deals with a young Dutch official who has been sent over to "rebuild the Indies." We encounter him within the four walls of his room. He happens to be sick with malaria and he has nobody but himself to look after him. In his feverish state of mind, all sorts of memories crowd in on him, together with the sounds and voices coming from the adjacent rooms and beyond.

The narrator of the story is in a strange, somewhat keyed-up and feverish mood; he has headaches, he talks with people, gets irritated, and becomes angry with them. Meanwhile, he reluctantly plays the gallant gentleman, but every so often he slips off into faraway memories and images. His mind wanders to his school days, to the Tyrolean Alps, to a girl somewhere in Australia who waves a line of poetry at him and then disappears again. Elias called his story "Voyage autour de ma chambre," after a French book that happened to be lying around in his room. His trip around his room is an unreal voyage indeed. All that is really left amounts to lost chances, frustration, self-accusation, and doubt, perhaps best summed up by his exclamation: "What in heaven's name am I doing here, and how did I end up here?"

Meanwhile, at the time of Elias's story, outside his room's walls, there was fighting everywhere. It involved thousands of young men from the Netherlands, volunteers as well as draftees. The majority of them went without enthusiasm but also without any real dislike. They had come expecting an adventure that was not really there. What they found was a life consisting largely of guard duty, patrolling through the mud in the heat of day, not to mention the violence of reprisal, fear, and death. And all the while, beyond the horizon, their native Holland would beckon like a distant shore and leave them restless. A great many books inform us about the Dutch soldier's life, his motivations, and his thoughts. Their authors, such as war correspondents, clergy, and the men themselves, are often as cheerful as possible and stress qualities such as comradeship, morale, and bravery, with an occasional obligatory reference to their assignment. No doubt all these authors of war literature have together written a great deal of history. What they have not written is literature. The sheer monotony of their stories in which yet so many shocking events take place is astounding. Their numerous clichés are as many signs of their inability to write. Whether we read the books by J. W. Hofwijk (*The Heat of Day*, 1974; *Blubber*, 1948) or by A. C. de Gooyer (*Guarding the Dessa*, 1949; *Honorable Discharge*, 1952), or by Henk van Maurik, *Djokja Beyond the Horizon* (1949), or the quasiliterary *Diary of a Half Man* (1951) by G. J. Vermeulen, or whatever other book, they are all pretty much alike.

It is not easy to remain interested in all these books when nearly identical events are discussed in nearly identical phrases. One begins to realize after a while that perhaps the veterans themselves, the people involved, feel differently about these stories. These books were written for them, after all, and because of their great number, the publishers must have sensed a good market. Particularly popular became the books by Job Sytzen, the Jan de Hartog of our military crusades, *Not All Soldiers Die* (*Niet iedere soldaat sneuvelt*, 1953), *God's Ravine* (*God's Ravijn*, 1954), and *Compatriots* (*Landgenoten*, 1955). These enjoyed many reprints and even appeared in a collected edition.

The books by Albert van der Hoogte (1909–1970) are of a different caliber and of better quality, especially his *The Final Hour* (*Het laatste uur*, 1953) and, second, *The House in the Night* (*Het huis in de nacht*, 1956). Van den Hoogte got a temporary assignment as public prosecutor in the Indies just after the war. He ended up in "a problem area" and there he had to make decisions about the life and death of other people. In a sense, his was a privileged position in that, as an interested spectator, he could witness the revolution at close range. He saw the whole gamut of cruelty, ranging from looting and ambush to reprisal and execution. In between, he witnessed the "ordinary life" of the Europeans. Van der Hoogte was one of those younger Dutchmen one frequently encountered in those days, an erudite fellow, sensitive and intelligent. He was the kind of person who, despite all the mess around him, or maybe because of it, became inextricably involved with the times and the country. His books clearly reveal the need to get something out of his system. He must have come to the Indies, however, with the typical Dutch penchant for the profound and the spiritual, as well as with the ambition to translate these inclinations into literature. The shocking events he encountered in Indonesia must have gradually dampened his hankering to render life into fine prose, but never entirely. His style shows the attempt to outgrow the need to write preciously. Because of this he soon learned to write a swift and captivating prose. Nevertheless, he never quite managed to suppress his inclination to recite because the rhetorical quality of his writing continues to stand out. Van der Hoogte is one of those people who, as his emotions increase, feels the need to gesture a lot and to raise his voice.

His stories are exaggerated in places, and he consistently overdramatizes the cruelty of the events, the social and personal disarray, the moral reactions, everything. To his credit, Van der Hoogte tries to see himself from a critical angle in his book. As a public prosecutor, he confesses to having used far too much "hollow bombast," but although he realizes these shortcomings, nature passes nurture every time. He can not seem to keep his characters from talking for pages on end while they recite all sorts of dreadful platitudes, especially where religion or women are concerned. For example: "Women are chaotic. They are at best half-chaste, half-lascivious, or half-lewd and half-chaste. They have no sense of responsibility the way men do because their nature is altogether different. Their purpose in life is to worship at their own shrine" (*The Final Hour*, p. 5). And what are we to think of the following gems: "Desire swept through me like a reckless flame" (p. 126), or: "There had been a time when those tight, purple lips were soft, moist, and red, like an open fruit" (p. 175). One could go on quoting this way. However, the book also contains unforgettable descriptions such as the one of the barren, chalky island of Madura with a few poor huts scattered here and there. Equally powerful is his account of the execution of the seven murderers, especially his oppressive and concise description of the beach at Gresik in the early morning. That is the kind of description that remains vivid years later, but elsewhere Van der Hoogte's prose has an unpleasant background noise which culminates in the final sentence of his first book: "On such days it is as if the breath of eternity brushes past us." This is the kind of sentence, alas, that has all the sonority of literary sermonizing.

His second book also leaves one with mixed feelings. There is no doubt Van der Hoogte can write, and write well at that. In his *The House in the Night*, the house in question is the only one left standing amidst the ruins of others, and it makes for a memorable scene. However, its inhabitants are so woodenly portrayed that they seem like actors mounting a stage. They are three young men, carefully selected to represent three different social classes, and one woman, whose job it is to be the object of confrontation. She suddenly appears one night and leaves just as suddenly. They converse about a great many things such as the existence of a Supreme Being, and about love and passion, with a degree of cynicism not unusual for precocious lads. This is unfortunate, especially where his descriptions are otherwise excellent.

After a training in England "to fight the Japs," Jan Eijkelboom (born 1926) was sent to Indonesia in the middle of 1947 to fight the republican army instead. It was not that he disliked going but he was not overly enthusiastic either. The tropics held him under their spell, however, the moment he smelled rain-drenched Sabang Island aboard his troop transport. He was to stay in Indonesia for a total of two and a half years, one half of which was a pastoral idyll, the other half a harrowing experience. He took part in the first as well as the second military "policing" action, the latter in east Java. Neither of them got him into trouble, however. The worst part of his tour of duty did not start till afterwards, when he was assigned to convoy duty with a detachment of Bren gun-equipped half-ton trucks mostly patrolling the road beween Blitar and Kediri. "The only thing you could do was to wait till you either hit a mine or an incendiary bomb blew you up. It happened to me three times, but every time I walked away from it with only a scratch. Every time it was the guy next to me who got killed, which gave me a lugubrious sort of reputation. Shortly before the final cease-fire, I transferred out to Communications. My first assignment there was to establish contact with the TNI, the republican army. That was the first time I ever got a look at the enemy."

His story, "The Retreat," takes place during the second policing action. He prefixed it with a meaningful epigram from *Trader Horn:* "Aye, there's something in writing's like armour to the feelings." Writing was therapeutic to him, and it was to Koelewijn, a way of putting one's business in order after the war. "The Retreat" centers around a soldier's relationship with a Javanese girl called Sumiati. He first meets her in a brothel, then keeps her to live with him amidst the indescribably squalid atmosphere that is part of war, that of stinking uniforms, iron, oil, trucks, and land mines. Sumiati not only represents eroticism to him but also loyalty and affection, a human relationship, in short. Because of their relationship, he puts her and she puts herself in an impossible situation. She becomes a traitor to her own people and then an abandoned woman after the forced evacuation of Dutch troops to their homeland. After an attempt at suicide, Sumiati is taken to the military hospital in Surabaja. There he says goodbye to her. The seemingly innocuous title "The Retreat" purposely takes one's attention away from the story's drama. Its title also befits the restrained tone of the story, the only way Eijkelboom has of controlling the complexity of contradictory emotions. The feelings of happiness, relief, and revulsion, of pity, guilt, and betrayal are all resolved by it.

The story "The Cannons" ("De kanonnen") by A. J. Schneiders (born 1925) is not about soldiering, there are no artillery exchanges and certainly no personal drama. What little war there is is shown only as a rather boring excursion that includes a senseless barrage at an invisible enemy at the foot of a mountain somewhere in Banten, west Java. Schneiders lived through the policing actions quite differently from Eijkelboom, having been more detached and much more of an outsider. He wrote that he had felt more like a tourist with a gun instead of a camera, than a soldier. Either way, the things he describes must have bothered him, for besides showing us the routine firing of cannon amidst a majestic and otherwise peaceful landscape, he also shows us the dread and fear of a dismayed little man. He is only a porter who must stand by while grenades blast his son's only possessions, a village hut, and several water buffalos to bits. "The Cannons" was Schneiders's first story. He wrote it somewhere on the island of Riau, "where both the surroundings and the established Dutch colony were so indescribably dull that I simply had to find a way out via the nib of a pen. I thank God, or whomever, that for the first time in my life, my pen did not leave me in the lurch."

As was to be expected, little was written in the Dutch language about the Indonesian experience of the revolution and the war. Still, there were some publications.

Fairly recent are the *Memoirs of a Freedom Fighter (Herinneringen van een vrijheidstrijder)*, published in 1972 and 1974 by Roswitha Djajadiningrat. She is a niece of the well-known former Regent Achmad Djajadiningrat about whom the author, because of her republican convictions, has quite a few nasty things to say. Better still than these well-written memoirs are the writings of Joke Muljono (born in Bandung, 1925). He was educated in the Dutch language, studied medicine in Djakarta, and completed his studies in Amsterdam. He came from a Catholic family made up of Indonesians as well as Dutch people. When the revolution broke out and he had to make a choice, he naturally chose the Indonesian side but he did not deny the Dutchman in him altogether. His position was different from that of most Indonesian patriots who could hate the Dutch without reservation, since his feelings were much more ambivalent. It appeared that he had too many personal and cultural ties with "the enemy." Joke Muljono's work expresses this sense of ambivalence most clearly perhaps in his poems "Pemoeda," (a *pemuda* is a young freedom fighter). During his stay in The Netherlands, he had come in contact with a Dutch literary group writing for the magazines *Criterium* and *Libertinage*. His pieces appeared in these magazines also, especially in *Criterium*. It published several of his poems and stories, such as his brief but amusing "Queen's Birthday" ("Koninginnedag"), the story "No Man's Land" ("Niemandsland"), which takes place during the revolution, and "The Flight," a part of a novel, again showing the same ambivalence. These are remarkably well-written stories.

Meanwhile, he published a number of "letters" containing reminiscences of his youth addressed to a real or imaginary aunt in Holland. These appeared in *Orientation (Oriëntatie, 36 [September 1950])*, an East-West magazine published in Bandung. His letters deal with observations, events, and family affairs, typical of a youth spent between two cultures. These letters are clearly written to explain his later involvement with the revolution. Joke Muljono, who is a bacteriologist, has been living in Indonesia for many years now.

Gradually the interest in war stories subsided. The military policing actions were over, and so too were the Netherlands Indies a thing of the past. Only the hangover remained, the national trauma, as one could call it. The outside world learned little enough about it, however. Nearly all war veterans had developed an almost natural immunity toward the outside world, a feeling that their past was "nobody else's business." Everyone of them knew what dreadful things had taken place but most of them had kept their hands clean. The really dirty work had been done by only a very few. The others had been against it or had looked the other way, shrugging their shoulders and keeping quiet about it all. There were some who felt accessory to the fact and suffered psychological breakdowns, but no blame or criticism from outsiders was tolerated.

It was impossible to explain to outsiders that in particular war situations, violence and aggressions were forces that ethics could barely hope to keep in check. There were times, however, when someone would talk, often many years later and always with some reluctance. One such case involved statements made by the psychologist Hueting in 1969. This affair made the newspapers and television in the Netherlands. Possibly triggered by the American My-Lai war-crimes scandal in Vietnam, Hueting leveled comparable accusations of Dutch military misconduct in Indonesia. The public outcry against his indictment, and especially the reaction of war veterans, once again showed this characteristic defense mechanism at work. People reacted by categorically denying any involvement, "denials," as Jan Varenne said, "often coming from people who had definitely known what went on."

Even so, the Hueting incident had started something. The whole stream of war books which had all but dried up now began to flow again. Several books that had either remained unpublished or had never been completed now found a market. These included *Playing Soldier in the Emerald Isles (Soldaatje spelen onder de smaragden gordel)* by Jan Schilt; *Soldier in the Indies: History of a Platoon (Soldaat in Indië: de geschiedenis van een peleton)* by J. Zwaan; and *Ere the Cock Crows . . . : A Young Soldier among the Rebels on Java (Eer de haan kraait . . . ; een serdadoe soesoe tussen de peloppers op Java)* by Jan Varenne. All three books appeared in 1969, the year of the Hueting affair. The most striking thing about these books is their detachment, or rather the extent to which they demystify the war. Schilt, Zwaan, and Varenne are miles apart from their predecessor Job Sytzen and his ilk. Whichever way one looks at *Playing Soldier*, for example, it is a sordid thing. Only a good measure of indifference, irony, or vulgarity could arm one against it, but what the book did was to change the emphasis of the genre once and for all. Far and away the best of the three is Jan Varenne's book. It was originally a much larger work written back in 1951 and 1952. *Ere the Cock Crows* is an abbreviated and updated version of the original manuscript with a clear reference to the present. Jan Varenne can obviously write, there is no doubt about that. He would have done a better job, in fact, if he had not allowed himself to be influenced by his own prejudice against literature. His composition is not sufficiently natural and therefore too transparent. Also, the division between the author Varenne and his fictional character Jenver (an anagram) strikes us as artificial. This split either does not work or it must have been forced at times in his attempt to put things cleverly. Varenne's potential as a writer, however, appears clearly enough from a great number of well-written passages. These indicate that he knows how to capture the right tone while maintaining his distance and his faculty for self-criticism. On the whole, *Ere the Cock Crows* is one of the best books dealing with the policing actions.

Happily too, the passing rumor of the Hueting affair stimulated a different kind of literature about the policing actions, as critical of the period as the novels dealing with soldiering had been. One result, among others, was that after twenty years' preparation, the voluminous *Diary of Schermerhorn (Het dagboek van Schermerhorn)* could finally be published. It is the impressive monument to a great but tragic figure who played an important role during the transfer of power to Indonesia. The Hueting affair also stimulated the sociologist J. A. A. Doorn, in collaboration with W. J. Hendrix, to complete a manuscript that had remained unfinished for quite some time. Both of them had been soldiers in Indonesia for three and a half years. They were not outsiders therefore but had been directly involved. Their recollections resulted in a study about the nature and the effect of violence. They called it *Violence Unleashed (Ontsporing van geweld,* 1970). It is a moving, well-written work that does not raise the question of guilt but takes the responsibility for military and violent excess away from the individual and places it squarely with the system that sought to reestablish control over Indonesia. "Anyone assuming responsibility ought to know that any form of violence shows a tendency to get out of hand once it has been unleashed." Their work turned into a happy combination of scientific detachment and personal involvement.

3   "Irian Barat"

When Indonesia became independent in 1949, not all the territory that had made up the Netherlands East Indies was transferred. For a variety of political and other reasons now difficult to understand, the Netherlands had held on to West New Guinea. It should have been obvious from the start that the incomplete transfer would lead to a continuation of the colonial war, if only on a limited scale. During the period prior to the United Nations plebiscite that gave the territory to Indonesia, Dutch officials still governed the area. One of these was C. J. Schneider (born 1932). For four years he was a controller, and during his final two years he was stationed in the recently discovered Balim Valley with its Stone Age culture. He returned to the Netherlands in 1962. There he was told that he was no longer needed, simply because western New Guinea was henceforth called Irian Barat. So he stayed home with his nostalgia for a country where he had worked for four years. In the end, he found a form of release in writing about it and he adopted the pseudonym F. Springer. Later still, after Schneider entered the foreign service, his experiences were no longer limited to his stint in New Guinea but even so his interest in Indonesia remained and it shows up directly or indirectly in his subsequent books.

He started in 1962 with a very modest, small volume entitled *Message from Hollandia (Nieuws uit Hollandia)*. People realized right away that Springer could write and liked his sober, rather broad and straightforward approach. Of the three stories in *Message from Hollandia* "Toetie's Death" is probably the best. It shows us that something definitely happens to a Westerner once he has entered that other world of magic and voodoo, enough to change his view of things generally. His second book, *Ghosts around the Parula (Schimmen rond de Parula, 1966)* contains just one story. It is situated in the Balim Valley, called Zakar Valley here. It is essentially a gruesome tale but Springer tells it in a sufficiently ironical way to keep it from being a mere horror story. Irony was apparently the only defense the author himself had against the superabundance of missionary zeal and so much gruesome barbarity. His third book, *The Slippery Pole of Power (De gladde paal van de macht, 1969)*, is a novel of slightly over one hundred pages dealing with the power struggle in a developing country. The story is a perfect satire which Springer prefixed with an epigram by Chamfort, one of France's best moralists: "Amitié de Cour, foi de renards et société de loups," or political friendships having the trustworthiness of foxes in the company of wolves. It is a genre that apparently suits Springer. New Guinea is immediately recognizable from the descriptions he made earlier of Hollandia (now the city of Jayapura), of the islands, bays, and beaches. The names of his characters too are revealing, although they belong to white people here and not to the Papuans. His satirical world knows neither racial discrimination nor a colonial complex because the state of D'Unia possesses "the only white-skinned autochthonous people in this exotic part of the world." Apparently its inhabitants are descendants of the explorer Abel Tasman's mutineers who were put ashore with their wives, although they might also be descendants of Vasco da Gama. Otherwise the country of D'Unia does have the social structure of a former colony. The country has a very small upper class and, lower down the scale, no middle class, but a large, uneducated mass. High up in its central mountain ranges, white tribes still roam that adhere to all kinds of rituals, such as the killing of people to placate the gods. Inasmuch as whites and not Papuans practice these rites, they suddenly attain something of an Old Testament quality. Laurie, the American wife of one of the main characters, writes to her stockbroker father in the United States: "The savages here are white people, or rather, the whites are the savages. Here you can see, Daddy, what we used to be like, or would still be like if we had had just as little in the way of opportunity as the D'Unians did."

The tale is primarily about climbing "the slippery pole of power." The chief contenders for reaching its top are Premier Wister Hazeltor, appointed by the governor, and his declared opponent, Brigadier Ohme, chief of police. The story starts out with a coup and ends with a countercoup that backfires and finishes in a minor bloodbath: "Twenty meters before Wister was to have turned the last corner, someone flung his arms around him. A hand moved past his elbow and turned the ignition off, while other hands took over the wheel. He did not even have time to be surprised. They cut his throat very quickly, very painlessly, and very neatly. His head sagged to one side but they carefully held it up straight till the jeep came to a stop with a slight jolt before the last corner had been reached. Only then did they let go of Wister." A gruesome ending, to be sure.

So Long, New York (*Tabee, New York*, 1974) heralds a new phase for Springer. Its style is more personal and its basic tone is one of effective self-mockery of the kind one finds in Willem Elsschot's stories. The emphasis of its main character has not increased but has been reduced instead, while he still continues to act as the author's alter ego. This character, called Rudy, ends up in situations that the author may well have experienced himself, although probably not to the same degree. Rudy is expected to be an energetic fellow, which he really is not and which also shows in his inability to get himself out of some pretty tight spots. Instead, he usually runs away, and this is exactly what he does when faced with the consequences of his romantic feelings for a former girl friend. She too is originally from the city of Bandung, and he meets her at a party for Indies-Dutch immigrants somewhere in upstate New York. It turns out that she is married to his former school rival, the loud-mouthed Flash Gordon fan then known as "Menno Cool with his Tool." In America, this fellow has only grown in years, not in wisdom, and he is still in fact his same old noisy and boastful self. Dollie has now changed her name to the more American sounding Dola, but now Rudy changes it back again to Dollie. This Dollie is determined to give their former high school flirtation a little more physical substance, hoping also to get rid of her husband ("Oh, Rudy, I'm so unhappy," and "I'm all yours now, your very own"). But then, like a deus ex machina, his transfer to the consulate in Lagos, Nigeria, comes through ("Apparently they were in great need of a busy bee out there"). That same weekend, Dollie comes to stay with him, and after having happily consummated her stay, she sings "Turks do it, Germans do it, Eskimos do it, . . ." adlibbing Cole Porter's "Let's Do It." By this time, Rudy is hopelessly in love with her but his impending transfer makes everything pointless. Time and again he wants to tell her, but something always interferes. Finally, he allows Dollie to depart in a joyful mood, off to arrange her affairs and scotch her marriage. After she has left, he goes to attend a farewell party given by his colleagues. He feels lousy, but everyone at the party thinks it is because he is upset. Only after his plane is off the ground does he ask himself in a panic: "What in heaven's name have I done?" A delightful book this is.

Springer's latest is called *Overseas Business* (*Zaken overzee*, 1977). It contains four stories, in the way of a central panel with a few smaller panels to the side, something like a lopsided triptych. These are jolly stories about some pretty gruesome things. Quite a lot transpires in them, a couple of murders and suicides, as well as several accidents and other bloody business. However, Springer describes these events in the style of a picaresque novel, without a show of scruples or moralizing but with a great deal of irony and self-mockery. In any case, his stories are anything but depressing; on the contrary, they make us laugh every time. Life gets us into funny situations, after all, and people never stop trying to make it to the top, not even at the expense of their soul or their happiness if necessary. Often they bite off more than they can chew and then get their comeuppance. Fate deals harshly with such as these. And what of their expectations and hopes? Nothing at all: either they are murdered, like Robbie Frederiks in "Pink Eldorado," or they do themselves in, or they disappear without leaving a trace, the way Max Flier does in "Happy Days," or else they simply die like army captain Visser, or, finally, they stay alive but only after leaving their possessions behind. There is also a final reckoning with the memory of the Netherlands East Indies: it takes place in a bar in The Hague with a bunch of New Guinea old-timers seated around a table. No dramatics are involved here, just a bit of a queasy feeling.

Springer bases his work on real situations and events, but it is obvious that he manipulates these in order to create his own freedom and breathing space. Reality by itself is simply too clumsy and its limitations would pin him down too much. Springer's method is the reverse of that of the typical novelist who does not intrude on the action. Springer purposely uses the first person in order to involve himself in the novel's action so as to create an illusion of authenticity. He is then at liberty to move about within the pale of reality. Once on the scene, he can solve problems, bring about meetings, create relationships and dissolve them again. This method of operation shows most clearly in the first story where the scene he introduces is recognizably based on an actual situation. Although he can not possibly have been on that particular scene himself, he engineers things in such a way that he becomes a witness to the occasion without participating in it.

He tinkers more with reality in one story than in another, and probably least in the lead story called "Overseas Business." This deals with Springers's own experiences as a government official in western New Guinea. New Guinea became an adventure to him in more than one sense, a marvelous, at time frightening, and, ultimately, ridiculous adventure.

In the evening of colonialism, people were still putting on a performance of sorts. Even after the first Indonesian infiltrations, after the first families had already been evacuated, and the whole denouement was already clearly visible, people continued to speak about their "cultural mission" and about "rebuilding the country," while still more troops were being brought in. "What a lot of nonsense," a sober corporal was overheard to say, "to fight against people you're going to invite over for coffee later on." But in the Netherlands, they were apparently of a different opinion. Toward the very end of the war, they sent out an antiaircraft contingent, complete with its own administrator. This was the job assigned to sociologist, writer, and poet Aad Nuis (born 1933). Having been drafted and then sent overseas was bad enough to begin with where Nuis was concerned, but there was something else. It so happened that he was one of many people in the Netherlands who opposed his government's policies. Not only did he consider the transfer of power to Indonesia inevitable, he believed it was far and away the best thing to do for all parties concerned. This made his position difficult and made him extremely loath to go. Nevertheless, Ensign Nuis was shipped out in April 1962 from Den Helder naval station to be deposited in Sorong, New Guinea, "right smack on the beak of the Bird's Head Peninsula."

The title of his book *The Barf Bird* (*De balenkraai*, 1967) requires some explanation. As the author himself tells us on page thirty-two:

> There was an amazing bird there which for months on end lived in a tree right outside of my little office, next to an abandoned tennis court. I never got a good look at it but I think it was black and tiny. Anyway, every fifteen minutes this bird would make a sound like that of somebody who is dreadfully sick and tries very hard to vomit but can't. I called it a puking bird but the men came up with a better name and called it the barf bird. "Barfing" was a very popular expression among soldiers at the time. They applied the word to everything, especially to that mixture of boredom, rage, frustration, and apathy military life produces in people. I got very fond of this little bird. It was the one creature in Sorong I totally agreed with.

The mood of the barf bird sets the tone for this book. Aad Nuis's chronicle is happily lacking in the kind of heavy-handed protest a troubled conscience is likely to produce. One of the book's positive traits is that Nuis warded off "boredom, rage, frustration, and apathy" by reminding himself as much as possible that he was at least in a unique position to observe a particular community, a military one in this instance, at close range. He became, in other words, a participating sociologist without, fortunately, using the abstruse jargon of his curious profession. *The Barf Bird* became a personal chronicle of events, variegated by observations and speculations, but especially enlivened by scores of effective anecdotes that characterize people and conditions. His opinions are never vague but always based on fact and that explains their liveliness. Sometimes Nuis employs the essay format, sometimes that of the eye-witness report, then again a straight narrative, but they all blend and merge naturally. What remains is his natural tone of voice with a slightly mocking undertone. This binds and holds his story together.

The Barf Bird is a book that one reads with a great deal of quiet glee, although it can not have been all that much fun for the author out there. This too becomes apparent as one goes along. This book does not depict Holland's last colonial war in Asia as a tragedy of great magnitude but as a tragicomedy. Its many and varied characters reveal themselves in all their strengths and weaknesses, especially in the latter category, not least the author himself. Aad Nuis knows all about self-criticism and self-ridicule. These are good qualities to have when one's temperament and profession both call for judging others.

The Barf Bird ends with the evacuation of Dutch troops, the author among them ("Turning in one's gear, enduring the colonel's final speech, going home"). For him this was the end of a boring military excursion. The story's conclusion has something of a death knell. It brings to an end a period that now only exists in retrospect, to be regarded with either mixed or unmixed feelings.

XIV
Not to be Forgotten

1 Maria Dermoût

Maria Dermoût made her debut as a writer with a book of barely 200 pages, which she called *Only Yesterday (Nog pas gisteren)*. It was about memories of a childhood spent on Java, that was obvious. The title too pointed in that direction. The memories were so alive and clear it seemed indeed as if they had all occurred "only yesterday." One could really go one step further and say that Dermoût's memories constitute a world that also makes up the present, for she is part of both worlds. Her memory is furnished with a large house, a real *besaran* with annexes, stables, coach houses, and guest pavilions. It is an ample, cool house surrounded by tall trees, by plants and animals, and with a view of Mount Lawu. And inside of that house and that garden, there lives a little girl of about ten or eleven called Riek. It is inhabited also by her parents and, most important, by the servants who are always there. These are Urip, her personal *babu*, or maid, then Mangun, the "inside boy," Roos, the seamstress, the cook with her two little nieces Assi and Nèng who help her in the kitchen, the coachmen, the water bearers, the guards, a whole host of servants as was customary in those days in a house belonging to a sugar refinery's chief administrator.

Maria Dermoût was born in 1888 on a plantation in the northern coastal area of central Java near the town of Pekalongan. Following the death of her mother when she was still a baby, she was sent to Holland. She returned and was sent to Holland once again. "Before my sixth birthday I had already traveled to and from Holland twice," as she put it herself (*Singel 262*, 1954, p. 22). From her sixth until her eleventh birthday, she lived with her parents, her father and her stepmother, on the sugar estate Redjosari near Madiun, with indeed a view of Mount Lawu.

On her father's side, Dermoût was descended from a family that had been in Indonesia for several generations. Her great-grandfather had sailed for the Dutch East India Company. He returned to Holland but his son went to Java to stay. His son, in turn, who was Dermoût's father, was born there too, as she was. At age eleven, she returned to Holland a third time and came back to Java when she was eighteen. She was married in Semarang. All but one of her children and grandchildren were also born in Indonesia. Hence hers was a family with definite roots there. For many years, she and her husband lived "here and there and everywhere," on Java, but particularly for many years on the Moluccas, "the islands I loved so dearly." She died on June 26, 1962, in a hospital in The Hague. In keeping with her express wishes, she was quietly buried, a last wish which fitted her restrained character.

She was sixty-three years old when she made her debut although she had been writing for years, of course, and had experimented with a style which was to resemble the spoken language. Several small stories had appeared in a newspaper, others she had kept in her portfolio. Still, her greatest productivity came after her work appeared in book form. She was not to have much time. Moreover, she was physically frail and often sick. In addition, she was wont to think about her stories a great deal and she worked slowly. During the ten years allotted to her, she wrote two novels, *Only Yesterday* and *The Ten Thousand Things* (*De tienduizend dingen*, 1955) and five collections of short stories, of which the last two appeared after her death. The titles of these collections are: *The Playing of Tifa Gongs* (*Spel van tifa gongs*, 1954); *The Jeweled Comb* (*De juwelen haarkam*, 1956); *The Chest and Other Stories* (*De kist en enige verhalen*, 1958); *The Sirens* (*De sirenen*, 1963); and *Dark in Appearance* (*Donker van uiterlijk*, 1964). It was possible to publish her *Collected Works* (*Verzameld werk*, 1970) in just one volume of 645 pages. She had been working on several of her stories until the very last, even while in the hospital. She was in the habit of working on several stories simultaneously, and she must have had the feeling that she still had all "the ten thousand things" to write about. Dermoût was not sure that her books would mean much to later generations. She herself knew that her style of writing was quite different and bore an entirely different relationship to reality. That reality was different in itself. She realized that her position in Dutch literature was singular and outside its mainstream. Until the very last she lived in Indonesia with and through her books. They are very closely tied to the country, especially to the Moluccas and its people, both the living and the dead. Dermoût's world is neither sober nor clear but somewhat diffuse. It consists of past and present, of reality and tradition, and it is populated by the living and the dead, real people as well as mythological figures, human and animal at the same time. She is not a real Dutch author. In the first place, her stories lack a Dutch view. They lack Dutch streets and houses, there are no meadows, and there is no rain. Their setting, instead, includes the sunny Moluccan sea, the islands, gardens, streams, mountains, waterfalls, old Indies mansions, the shells, corals, jewels, gongs, cannons, and numerous other things. Part of those "other things" and certainly not least among them are also the traditions, consisting of hearsay, superstition, belief, and so on. The people in her books are different as well, even when they are Westerners, in that they experience things differently. They are not characters with psychological problems or clearly outlined flesh-and-blood people but sooner shapes that move through the story. And there is always something going on between them, be it love, friendship, hatred, sadness, departure, or death, just as there always is a relationship with the supernatural that determines the life and fate of human beings. Although she rarely provides a complete description of what she sees, the curious fact is that the living world is always present. Animate nature surrounds everything and holds people, animals, and things in a cosmic embrace.

Even assuming that *Only Yesterday* contains a considerable amount of autobiography, we still do not have sufficient reason to think that Dermoût identifies wholly with the character of Riek. After all, a backward glance at our own childhood always involves a certain amount of distortion. We do notice, however, that the young girl Riek, whose point of view is identical to that of the story, has a fairly distant relationship with her parents: "Riek loved them well enough, but really not too much." The parents are always seen together. They take walks in the garden together, with Jimmy, the monkey; they pay visits together; they receive people together; and their child is never present on those occasions. Often she has to eat alone and *babu* Urip has to take her to bed. Urip is really the one who brings her up but, then "upbringing" is a word that is altogether too Western. What she receives is not an upbringing because she actually lives alone in the world of Urip and the other servants. "Say something," Riek says, and *babu* Urip begins, telling long stories about wondrous things that are taken for reality. She is told stories endlessly and it is precisely this that is so important because being told stories is her entrance into another world. This is not a starkly dualistic world like our own with a heaven and an earth, but a world where the visible and invisible merge, a world in which the soul of a human being can dwell in an animal or in a tree. The stories contain any number of references to the supernatural, to something that can either bring happiness or misfortune, such as the call of a bird. Objects such as krisses, rings, and cannons are animate, and a house too can be *sial*, that is to say, bring about bad luck. There are propitious and unpropitious days, and there even exist rules and tables by which to determine them. There is one scene where Riek and her mother go over to stay with "the old gentleman." He is a wise old man who has written a book about *The Javanese Spirit World (De Javaanse geestenwereld)*. That book contains the additions or numbers or "petangans," the Javanese mysticism of numbers. "The old gentleman" referred to was modeled after H. A. van Hien, the actual author of *The Javanese Spirit World*. As a character in the story, he also helps introduce a sense of the occult into the life of the little girl.

"My little heart," Urip calls her, a direct translation of the Indonesian term of endearment *hatiku*. Together with Urip and the cook, Riek goes bathing in paradisaical surroundings near the waterfall with the big boulders. Its description is unforgettable. But apart from everyday life, there is also a hidden life, "one of goodness and evil both, of light and darkness. Of life and of death." This frightens her. The houseboy Mangun takes her by the hand along a dark road. "Best not be afraid," he says.

Evil does intrude nonetheless, maleficence is born, and death comes. Roos the seamstress is murdered, and there is the tragedy with Uncle Fred and Aunt Nancy, and Uncle Fred's suicide. As disaster steals its way in, all sorts of things happen to the grownups around her who talk in a language the child does not fully comprehend. She sees things happen but can not very well relate to other events. The technique of looking at events through the eyes of a child is particularly effective here. It is Riek who sees dear Aunt Nancy in such a way that she thinks she loves her better than her own mother; she sees Uncle Fred, Papa's younger brother, and loves him too, very much in fact. She wants to be Aunt Nancy's child because then she will be called Riquette, not Riek, because Riquette is what Aunt Nancy calls her. And Aunt Nancy loves Uncle Fred and Uncle Fred loves Aunt Nancy, but Aunt Nancy goes back to her own husband and Uncle Fred leaves for Australia. When the telegram announcing his death arrives, the catastrophe is complete. Urip also goes away, taking little Assi and Nèng with her. The others have either died or disappeared. Then Riek leaves too, for Holland, all by herself. Papa tells her: "All that hanging around with the servants has got to stop, you understand?" But he probably never realized the degree to which this "hanging around" had already had its effect, and that the seeds had already been sown that were to influence Maria Dermoût's later outlook on life.

It would be wrong to assume that *Only Yesterday* is an autobiography. It is not even an autobiographical novel like Du Perron's *Country of Origin*, with its slightly altered arrangement of reality. Dermoût's method was quite different from his, and much more imaginative. Memory and fantasy merge in her writing, just as nature and people either change places or alter their appearance, and only the experiences themselves are authentic. These experiences connect childhood with later life and permeate it.

We could, if we wanted to, and only considered length, divide Dermoût's work into so many novels and so many short stories, but all she actually ever wrote were stories, some just longer or shorter than others. She never wrote novels in the ordinary sense of the word, the kind fitting in with Western tradition. She was a storyteller more than anything else. Stories and tales derive from an oral tradition, of course, and they are told, not written. Some of them are written down, such as those of Dermoût, but continue to show the characteristics of the spoken word. The source of Dermoût's stories is often overheard recitation, as for example the first snake story in *The Sirens*. This is not always the case, however, for sometimes she would get her story from a book and retell it in her own fashion.

One such is the story about the elephants. It is the story of a young woman who, as she is walking through the forest, comes upon a small group of elephants. They surround her and nuzzle and smell her all over, for she has just bathed and anointed herself. Slowly and gradually they remove all her clothes. That done, they run back in to the forest, loudly trumpeting. The original text of this story is in C. J. Leendertz's *From the Shores of Achin* (*Van Atjeh's stranden*, 1890, pp. 280–82). If we compare it with Dermoût's reworking of it in *Dark in Appearance*, it becomes at once clear what a lively tale she has constructed out of the otherwise identical but stiffly worded original. What she has actually done is to restore it to the realm of oral tradition, but to a tradition of her own making.

Dermoût was very fond of tales and telling stories. Some stories that she had heard at a particular time and place were just as important, possibly more so, than the actual events and incidents of the same period. "Among the things from the past that survive and remain very much alive, to my mind, are the stories that were told then."

The literature of the Netherlands Indies generally evolved from an oral tradition but Dermoût's way of telling a story is different. Her style comes closest to "charming monotony," it has been pointed out, and is closely related to the Javanese *dongèng*, which has an incantatory and infinite quality, one seemingly without either beginning or end. No doubt Dermoût was greatly influenced by the Indonesian way of storytelling. She affirmed this herself: "I have been privileged," she wrote, "that throughout my life I have always been around men and women who were storytellers." In this context, she singles out her housekeeper Louisa from the island of Ambon in the Moluccas ("which I still love so much").

In the short story "The Good Snake" ("De goede slang") from the collection called *The Sirens*, Dermoût introduced Louisa and tried to capture her exact manner of storytelling, "using short words only, constantly breaking off sentences, using sentences hardly at all," imitating the sounds of animals as they appear, making the appropriate gestures with her hands and especially her fingers, all the while keeping her eyes fixed on one point. Naturally Dermoût does more than retell other people's stories and imitate a certain manner of presentation, but it would be hard to imagine her style without the Indonesian tradition of storytelling. It greatly influenced her technique as shown by her use of pauses, truncated sentences, suggestion rather than description, using a single word at times, and short dialogues.

This manner of writing is not always effective. The moment the relationship to her own personal experience is either weak or lacking, the structure of her stories is weakened, as in the case of those in *The Playing of Tifa Gongs* and several later ones. In those cases, only her technique stands out. Curiously enough, none of this applies to the final tale in *The Playing of Tifa Gongs*, "The Cannon" ("Het kanon"). This happens to be an excellent example of meshing reality and tradition.

The Playing of Tifa Gongs can be regarded as an interlude of sorts and as a transition to her novel *The Ten Thousand Things*, which is a much larger and more ambitious work. In a way too it is her own test of herself, which became the masterpiece that ended her apprenticeship. One may regard it either as a novel or as a cycle of stories. Dermoût used the work to express a philosophy in which man coexists on a subordinate plane with "the ten thousand things" that together make up all creation. She has not done so in philosophical language but expressed her relationship to the world in the life story of an older woman.

She is called Felicia and lives alone on one of the abandoned estates on an island in the Moluccas. That the island is immediately recognizable as Ambon is irrelevant. Felicia's story is more than a vehicle for Dermoût's philosophy in that it also expresses her own attitude toward violence and death. Here too she has assimilated her private experience, although in a most guarded way.

The title is explained by the epigram that quotes a Taoist poet from the eighth century who alludes to "the ten thousand things." The ten thousand things are all emanations of creation, and man is only one of them, "a part of the immense multitude we call Creation, good and cruel, beautiful and ugly, ever moving and ever at rest. Man is neither more, nor less, than the tree or flower beside him, than a bird or a jellyfish, fair as a jewel. Indeed, he is neither better nor worse than what we have come to regard as inanimate or nonliving things, such as an empty shell without its inhabitant, or a tiny crystal, or even a small pebble" (Maria Dermoût in *The Hague Post [De Haagse Post]*, Nov. 26, 1955).

Maria Dermoût consistently turns this concept into literature. Her description of the island in the first chapter already includes the trees, the sea (the "inner bay" and the "outer bay"), the river, the casuarina trees, the sea snails, the shells, the garden in the sea, everything. There are still a number of overgrown spice plantations on the island, and Felicia, "the lady from Kleyntjes," lives on one of them in an old guest house. Everyone knows her. She is always dressed in sarong and kabaja, she is small and has a thick-set posture, "freckles and liver spots, never wears a hat, with springy graying hair." She lives all by herself. But she is not quite alone because she has servants living with her, and then there are all the people of the island, and nature. She lives there with her memories, with the past and the traditions of the island: "Still something seemed to have remained of the old things that passed, of all that was so long ago." In one of the gardens, "the three little girls," who have been dead for years, are playing. Felicia has never seen them play but she has heard about it and wonders "was it necessary to see them? For as long as she could remember, she had heard people talk about them. They belonged, and they had their own special place in her garden, on the island in the Moluccas, and in her own life as well." There is a man walking on the beach who was murdered not too long ago. In the bay in front of her house live a large and a smaller shark who used to be people, a father and his son. And "the mother of Pokjes" lives there too, the one who is forever looking for children, and "the man with blue hair," and "the coral woman" (who also appears in Rumphius). The strains of old melodies can still be heard also, such as dirges for the dead; so are the shells there, and eau de Cologne, the jewels, the incense, and the wind coming out of the sea. "All these things, and still others, the heavens included, were the island."

The second chapter gives us the life history of Felicia, of her parents, of her grandmother, and of herself. She was born on the island but her parents left it to go to Europe and took Felicia with them. Felicia gets married, but her husband leaves her. She bears him a son and returns to the island. For many years she lives alone with her grandmother, from whom she has "learned such a great deal." Felicia once asks her whether she believes in the "other" and "invisible" world, and her grandmother answers her in almost the same words Dermoût would have used. She says: "I don't really know; don't forget that I have been living here these many years alone with the servants." This is precisely the influence of the "Eastern world" which should never be underestimated and which also determines the outlook of so many Indies people, Dermoût included. Not to keep this in mind and recognize it for a fact means to risk missing the point of most of her books.

Later on, Felicia's son also goes to Europe. She waits for him. He too returns to the island, as an officer. He is called "Himpies" because the servants can not pronounce his nickname "Wimpie." Felicia is a historical figure, insofar as she is modeled after a woman everyone in Ambon knew who answers fairly closely to Dermoût's description of her. She used to receive many visitors because she was a special, bossy, and, at the same time, helpful and friendly woman. That is probably how Dermoût met her also, when she arrived on Ambon newly married. Up to a point and from a great distance, Dermoût identified with this woman, that is to say, she used Felicia's life to express some of her views concerning loss, death, and sadness. During an expedition on the island of Ceram, a native of the mountains hits Felicia's son "Himpies" in the neck with an arrow and kills him. After that, she is the only survivor, the last in a line of Dutch spice growers who had run the estates for five generations.

After the first two chapters, which introduce us to the garden, to the grandmother, and Felicia, and the ten thousand things, a number of fairly independent stories follow. Even so, these stories all take place in or near the garden of Kleyntjes. All of them are tales of murder. "Himpies" is murdered, even though the officers say that he has "fallen in action." As far as she is concerned, he has been murdered and that is different from dying. The government deputy is murdered also. He has drowned, they say, but he has still been murdered. Constance, the maid who always danced during the rattan pulling games, is murdered by a sailor, and the Scotch professor who came to the island to study its flora and fauna is also murdered. And what about the three girls, were they not murdered too? Murder arouses fear, revulsion, and anger, while death alone does not. Dermoût's work shows a repugnance of violence but not of death, while it most cer-

tainly lacks any obsession with death. Her world is too still, too remote, and too resigned for that, all bitter experience notwithstanding. There is only sadness, "more bitter than the bitter water out of
the bitter earthen jar," as Dermoût puts it. Even so, one is to keep
one's pride (just as grandmother tells the child Felicia that she must
be "proud" and should not cry). Man must remain conscious of his
worth, not by fighting against fate but by accepting it *without being
broken by it.* This is how Dermoût puts it almost literally and with
the same emphasis. Death means sadness and parting (*The Ten Thousand Things* contains several fine passages about sadness), but the
dead are never fully departed. Once a year, at All Hallows', Mother of
Kleyntjes sits down in her rattan chair at night on the small beach in
front of the house underneath the plane trees, and there she com-
memorates the dead. Then too the annual reunion with the murdered
ones takes place. On that day of reconciliation she also thinks of the
murderers. She no longer feels any anger or revulsion, only pity, "as
if they were not the murderers but had been murdered also." And
when she sits like that in the moonlight, with the quiet water before her, the dead come and visit her. Felicia talks to them as if they
were ordinary people. She even quarrels with them. She is annoyed
by the deputy and gets cross with "Himpies" when he again answers
with "yes and no," the way he used to, instead of with a clear "yes *or*
no." She also talks briefly with Constance and with the professor.
Then she gets the feeling that they have left, one after another. "Stay
with me," she whispers, but a fishing boat enters the bay. The end is
unforgettable.

> She sat quietly in her chair. There were not just a hundred things
> but many more than a hundred things, and not just hers, but a hun-
> dred times a "hundred things," next to one another, apart from one
> another, touching, sometimes merging with one another, but with-
> out any ties anywhere, and at the same time forever united. A unity
> she did not quite understand: there was no need, it could not be un-
> derstood, but given to her for a moment to behold above the moon-
> lit water. . . . Then the lady of Kleyntjes, called Felicia, got up out of
> her chair, and without looking back again at the inner bay in the
> moonlight—it would certainly stay there, always—she walked un-
> derneath the trees and went indoors to drink a cup of coffee and get
> on with the business of life.

The Ten Thousand Things is an exquisite story (the term "novel"
hardly seems to fit anymore) which yields new and meaningful details at every reading.

After *The Ten Thousand Things,* four more collections of stories appeared, two of them after her death. Dermoût has a way of telling a story that never reveals everything at once but that suggests more than it says, suggests more than it conjures up, and yet she is a very precise author. In her stories, however, especially in the shorter ones, this precision can turn precious at times and become too stylish. Whenever that happens, we sense the lack of something characteristic of her as a writer, we miss the cadence of her voice. "The Buddha Ring," for example, is really a well-told tale but nothing more. Another example is "The Brass Dancer." The story never gets off the ground because too much time is spent on the description of the statue. In addition, the transition between the interpretation of the statue and the human situation in the story gives the impression of being forced. Not so, however, the conclusion, which describes the parting of the man and woman, because here the story recaptures the mood it established at the outset. The slight shock we feel makes us realize what the "stakes" involved in the story really were. The same holds true for "The Bracelet" ("De armband," in *The Jeweled Comb*) and "The South Sea" ("De Zuidzee," in *The Sirens*) and in "Toetie" (in *Dark in Appearance*). Then we become aware, despite a lot of restraint on her part, of the great measure of intimacy we are allowed to share.

In conclusion, we can say that Dermoût's stories vary somewhat in quality, either internally or when compared to each other. What is immediately noticeable, as others too have observed, is that she sounds off key as soon as she situates her story outside of Indonesia. Apparently her experience required the sustenance of its original soil.

Of course there were things about Holland she liked. The final years of her life were spent in the town of Noordwijk, alternated by a sometimes extended stay in Ascona on the Swiss-Italian border. She lived in the dunes, with a wide view overlooking the North Sea. Much space is devoted in her diary to that wide prospect in the early morning or at dusk, with rainstorms slanting down and clouds towering by. In the village of Noordwijk-Binnen, further inland, stood the knotted lime trees she has Nancy and her father dream about.

When Maria Dermoût died in 1962, it appeared that she had been working on several things at once. This explains why so much has remained fragmentary. Her estate contained a number of finished and unfinished stories, and even different versions of the same story. It also contained a large number of loose notes often jotted down on odd scraps of paper with lots of sentences stricken out or corrected, some of them restored to their original version. This tells us something about her method of working. She worked extremely slowly and conscientiously. Consciously or unconsciously, she was forever occupied with writing. She would take a long time hunting up the right word, the right sentence, or the right turn of phrase. As a writer, she was forever involved with words and language, while aiming for the greatest possible naturalness. She herself called it experimenting with "prattle."

Her literary estate was sorted out by her daughter, in collaboration with the author Johan van der Woude, who had the honor of having discovered her. They were able to put together for publication two collections of short stories, *The Sirens* (1963) and *Dark in Appearance* (1964). For the time being, the rest had to wait. It included some completed stories (which were not set in Indonesia), incomplete work, and numerous notes and letters.

The Sirens contains several fascinating stories. In the first place, there is the title story about the young woman. She too is from the Island and goes in search of the Continent. She buys herself a proa with the All-Seeing Eye painted on its bows, and takes along a ship's mate who becomes her lover, as well as an orange cat for the mice. Dermoût's story is inspired by W. W. Skeat's *Malay Magic* (1900). She added different elements to it, however, which she had heard from others, elements such as the sirens, who are really sea cows. The rare manatees or dugongs live close to the Malaccan coast, and indeed graze on sea meadows, feeding on kelp, and they sometimes make sounds. In Dermoût's story, they have been made into legendary creatures that can sing and so they become an integral part of the tale's magical atmosphere. Despite the story's fantastic elements, its human elements have been greatly increased as well, particularly through the relationship between the woman and the young man. The unmistakable erotic undercurrent in the story is enforced by the presence of the manatees resembling bare-breasted women that call out and sing.

"Old Men Forget" is a moving story that also hides an intimate element. It is about an old man commemorating his very first love, while his children are worried about his "increasing forgetfulness." Among its nine stories there is one written as early as 1910 that already shows Dermoût's manner of telling a story. The editor's note informs us further about dates of composition and the publishing history of these stories, information sadly lacking in her *Collected Works*.

One year later, in 1964, *Dark in Appearance* came out. It was originally to contain three stories but only two could be published. These were "The Island Princess" ("De prinses van het eiland"), which was ready for publication, and "Toetie," which was put together from various fragments. The third story, "The Table" ("De tafel"), about an old Indies woman telling a young man her life history, could not possibly be reconstructed. Dermoût derived her title *Dark in Appearance* from the Mahābhārata, the Hindu epic where Draupadi, wife of the five Pandawas, is said to be "the first among women, her eyes shaped like the petals of the lotus blossom, dark in appearance." Like the five Pandawa princes, princess Draupadi too "faces East" as she goes on her way to depart from this world.

In all three stories, which are real Indies family tales, the female characters stand out not only because of their dark appearance but also because they distinguish themselves through their own intellectual and emotional lives. Judging only by the two published stories, the world of these women is invaded by evil and bitterness, as is often the case with Dermoût. This intrusion temporarily upsets the balance of things but does not create havoc. Women and men prove themselves capable of finding their destiny "without ceasing to be themselves." All these women possess the same "pride" Felicia's grandmother spoke about, not an arrogant pride but self-awareness and self-possession, despite everything, and despite their lesser development in the Western sense.

Another recurrent theme in Dermoût is that of two worlds that have contracted a relationship of sorts. They are close together and even touch one another ("without saying anything, he took her hand in his and continued to hold it"), but they still remain apart, maybe because each world is sufficient unto itself. This theme is also present in both of these stories. They end rather abruptly and it is hard to escape the impression that they really require the more elaborate format of the novel. This is especially true in the first story, "The Island Princess," where both beginning and end are too brief, while its central part, located in Holland, is overextended. The format of the chronicle in the first twenty pages or so changes over into a style of writing that does not fit. The story does not work somehow. Although Dermoût herself completed "The Island Princess," and "Toetie" had to be put together from various sections, with gaps clearly showing, this second story is more successful. Its theme is also worked out more consistently and convincingly. More is the pity therefore that it was never completed, for it would probably have been among the best Dermoût had ever written. Like the first, "Toetie" is a family history, this time about a Dutch government official, his Indies wife, and their children. The wife is the central character of the story. She is "very Indies" and knows little Dutch. She is not an educated woman but she possesses an intuitive intelligence and she is, moreover, tactful and wise. She lives for her children. He too is very concerned about the children's welfare, although he has different ideas about their upbringing. As a character he is of secondary importance. They find each other through their children but live past each other for the rest, without drama, without divorce, but still separated by the borderline that divides two worlds. Dermoût suggests their mutual impenetrability in a single conversation and in a few words. In between, the children's story is told and here the story becomes incomplete. Several children are mentioned but we never hear anything further about them. Some succeed in life and "go far," while others fail. The portrait of Tjrot, a vagabond and "good-for-nothing," is particularly well done, and so is that of "little Tsjalie" who ends up in a London prison. For his sake, Toetie goes to Europe, accompanied by her personal *babu* Mah Itih, while the man stays behind. After six years they return. The man has aged and she too has visibly gotten older. Their attitude toward one another is touching. Sometimes he strokes her face with his hand, "just that, no more; they did not now desire any more."

The ending is rather abrupt, and one wonders if there is not a large gap here. Only Mah Itih is left. Toetie and her husband have died, and Itih now visits the cemetery where both lie buried. She places five different kinds of flowers on their graves, and burns incense and candles. Nor does she forget to pay hommage to the grave of "Captain Jacket," the legendary patron saint of the graveyard, in order to beg him "to be good" to her dead. "And Captain Jacket was Death," Itih muses, "crazy, those white people, an old soldier in an old greatcoat. To her, Death was the young archangel Gabriel with his long wings."

Maria Dermoût continued to work on this story till the very last. When she wrote the conclusion, she could almost see the end of her own life before her, like a vision.

2   Beb Vuyk

One of Beb Vuyk's best books is *The Last House in the World* (*Het laatste huis van de wereld*, 1939). At first glance, it is little more than an account of her life on the island of Buru in the Moluccas. It is a very personal account, to be sure, because the delights and fears of a pioneering existence far from the civilized world determine its tone. The book's emphasis is on delight, the delight in the great adventure of primitive existence. Fear is present too, if only as a lurking threat. The fear also exists in Beb Vuyk herself. What comes to mind, curiously enough, is the memory of a painting that has nothing to do with Indonesia at all. It is a painting by Mondriaan from 1907, from his expressionist period, painted with broad, rough brush strokes, showing a clear blue sky with a red cloud in it like the beginning of a threat. This is also the atmosphere in Vuyk's book, although it has an entirely different decor. In *The Last House in the World*, Vuyk, a woman scarcely thirty at the time, tells us about the daily life of herself, her husband, and their very small children. It was a hard life but not one she would have traded for the kind "channeled between promotion, a bonus, and a pay raise," as she puts it.

Her oldest child, called Hans Christiaan after the Danish writer Hans Christian Andersen, was born on Ambon, where there had been a doctor present at least. Her second is to be born in Namlea on the island of Buru, where there is no doctor at all. Fear invades her life from without and from within. She expresses open fear about the future but harbors a "hidden fear" about death as well. "Anybody getting a child pays for it, either with money or with death. I am paying for mine, without discount, with all the horrors of a limitless fear." At the start of her first contractions, she begins to read poetry, just as she read Rilke when she began nursing Hans Christiaan, an important moment to her. This time she is not reading Rilke, however, but Marsman. She reads "Marsman's splendid poem, 'In Memoriam P. M.-S.' " aloud. She does not quote it, as she had quoted Rilke. This particular poem of Marsman deals with fear, pain, and death:

> [she was] wounded by pain but deeper still by guessing
> felt life as something so immensely dark
> that sought in vain a desperate escape.
>
> but failed; and there, unseen and hiding
> something sobbed with widely opened eyes
> and bled to death mysteriously and slow.

This must have been a question of immediate recognition in the most direct sense.

Marsman had been Vuyk's favorite poet of her youth, more so than Slauerhoff, for example, with whom she seems to have much more in common at first glance. The curious thing is also that up to a point she remained loyal to Marsman, even though he strikes one as too rhetorical for her tastes. Still, he can always provide consolation, especially in hard times. There must have been something else as well that kept her loyal to the poet of her younger years, because throughout his work, Marsman's main themes have been life and death. Marsman's work, which is described in every school anthology as "vitalistic," is indeed marked by its desire for a strong existence, which ought to be "grand and rousing." Vuyk had a similar desire for a strong, primitive existence and an intensive life, with a need to break out and to gain a view of the horizon. But mention life, and one mentions death. Later on, Marsman realized what his vitalism was worth, and that his call for life was actually not much more than a loud cry to drown out his fear of death. Marsman's work features death as an invisible shape which attacks one from behind when least expected: "Oh pinion in my back, oh blade!" Death is always present as a companion of sorts, a figure that strikes all at once and wreaks havoc. Death is a horror-inspiring figure. Death in Marsman's work has something macabre because he is portrayed as realistically as in a medieval woodcut, or as in some poems, the "danses macabres." He is not depicted as a skeleton but as a body with the flesh removed. In her notes about her childhood, "My grandparents" ("Mijn grootouders") in *The Wild Green Fragrance* (*De wilde groene geur*, 1962), Vuyk tells us about a gruesome experience. While a young girl, she was playing immediately below a dyke near an old, overgrown cemetery: "While we were playing hide and seek, I had hidden myself in some bushes while two men were busy cleaning up old graves. The skulls and bones they collected had not been cleaned, bleached, and polished as the skeletons in the doctor's waiting room are, but they were brown, with the remains of rotten flesh and matted hair still clinging to them." This shows the same "medieval" sensibility one finds in Marsman.

During a newspaper interview in 1969, Vuyk readily admitted to these feelings. When the interviewer pointed out her fondness for the "friendly" fairy tales of Hans Christian Andersen, she answered that Andersen had "certain gruesome elements" too, and that in his story of the little mermaid, for example, the witch scours the pot with a bunch of toads. Vuyk noticed this kind of detail that would have escaped others. The same repugnance for death and decomposition is found in a different section of the same book. When she is up in the attic playing with her brother, they find their long-dead grandfather's false teeth among some moldy clothes. "They didn't bury him!" she screams, "This is all that's left of him!" And later on she adds: "I was especially afraid because I imagined . . . that I would not find him like the man with the sideburns from the portrait, nor as a white ghost but much, much worse, that I'd find him back as chunks of bone and filthy flesh."

There is another element accompanying life and death, and that is violence. Not surprisingly therefore, one of her later and best collections of stories is called *Sound and Fury* (*Gerucht en geweld*, 1959). It deals with the rumor of the impending Indonesian revolution and the subsequent upheaval in senseless violence—killing and murder, fear and nightmare. Beb Vuyk had herself faced violence while imprisoned by the Japanese Kempetai, the equivalent of the German Gestapo, when the cries of people being tortured entered her cell every night and when she too was tortured. Then her experiences during the revolution followed. Her account of the execution of a traitor is harrowing, particularly because of her dispassionate description.

The intensity of this horror, which is part of her fear of violence and pain, can once again be traced to the story of her childhood. As she tells us: "From the rear, the house looked out over pastures. There was not really all that much to see, except when my father was shooting rats. . . . You could clearly see their heads, then the shot would follow, and then you saw the water colored red with blood." An even stronger trauma of her youth was caused by a copy of Foxe's *Book of Martyrs*, which she found in the attic upon another occasion. It contained horrible pictures which clearly showed the details of every gruesome torture. As a little girl, trying to dispel her fears, she began to tell stories, and her tales served as so many charms to ward off evil. In winter, she told them in the nursery behind the overhanging table cloth: "I was afraid of the dark and in order to keep my fear at bay, I told the most horrible stories." Herein lies the source of her stories concerning life and death, apprehension and horror. Life and death are recurring themes in her work, as in the final story of *The Wild Green Fragrance* called "The Ultimate Dignity" ("De laatste waardigheid"). It is a story that takes place during the Indonesian revolution. Although it is told by one of the characters, the author herself is deeply involved in the story. With great verve the story relates how Bennie Nambela, a Batak officer and tribal chief, takes the town in an open truck without cover. Then follows the history of his father, Dr. Nambela, whom the author knew personally, and who crossed over to the Dutch. The story takes place during the Dutch period still, at the time of the insurrection.

The writer, or the narrator in any case, meets old Dr. Nambela at a reception somewhere on the island of Sumatra in what appears to be the city of Medan. The city is full of damage and decay after war and revolution, and Vuyk evokes its desolate atmosphere in a few telling details. Dr. Nambela carries a photograph around with him which he shows to everybody. It is a ghastly photo showing a huge stack of corpses of women and children all piled up. "I found my wife and daughter in a pile like that," he says. He keeps the photograph inside a small Bible which he carries on him always as if to accuse God himself. Then the author remembers that a friend of hers in Djakarta had told her his story. Later on, she has a chance to talk some more with Nambela when they have both been accidentally left behind and everyone else has gone on an excursion tour. Then he tells her the same story about the murder of his wife and daughter by the Indonesian republican army. They had kicked him and tried to drown him in a burlap bag, but his son managed to save him. He is now a member of the Dutch-installed Negara Council for East Sumatra. Even so, he openly confesses to being a nationalist. He has been a nationalist since his student days but still he wants to avenge what his own compatriots have done to him. His wife and daughter were murdered by a Batak army detail intent on settling an old tribal feud, which could go undetected during the revolutionary turmoil. He is driven by vengeance but because of it he has maneuvered himself into an impossible situation, for he also hates the Dutch who humiliated him in the past. Now he lives with a double hatred, but his greatest contempt is for himself. At a later point in time, he visits the story's narrator in Djakarta. The story's ending, whether authentic or not, is a great find. Other Indonesians, all republicans, are gathered in his house for a visit. Then a car stops and Dr. Nambela is asked to go over to the governor's palace to see Van Mook, the leading Dutch official. Dr. Nambela gets up from his chair with great dignity and tells his compatriots as he is ready to leave: "My grandfather was a king and a cannibal. I am a Christian and a physician, but he was worth more than I am," and continuing after a brief pause, "He was a free man, and all I am is independent." He then turns and slowly walks away to the car. This is his "ultimate dignity." Truly a grand story, excellently wrought, with every scene just right and placed in such a way that this complicated story remains clear from beginning to end.

The most characteristic of Beb Vuyk's attitude toward violence is the first story in *Sound and Fury* bearing the title "Full of Sound and Fury," which, like William Faulkner, she took from Shakespeare's *Macbeth* (act 5, scene 5). It too has assimilated some of her experiences with the Japanese secret police, the Kempetai. Again it is a mixture of storytelling and personal experience molded into a new story. It is an account of the author's trip taken with a number of Indonesian journalists from Pontianak (in West Borneo, now Kalimantan Barat) into the interior via the Kapuas River. It contains evocative descriptions of Dajak tribes and feasts and of interiors decorated with human heads, but the story's emphasis lies elsewhere.

On board their small ship, she meets Tjondro, a veteran of the revolutionary war. Although he is still young, he too is forced to live with his experiences and fears and he can only vent these by telling about them. ("He told his stories so graphically, I was right there with him.") Tjondro's story is so full of gruesomeness and violence that only someone filled with terrible pain and fear could tell it. He is a journalist but unable to write about any of it. Later on, we learn why he cannot. All he can do is talk about it, just talk and talk. He tells about his being tortured by the Dutch intelligence service. His scars are clearly visible. It appears he was part of a plot that was betrayed for reasons of personal vengeance. He tells about a Dutch nurse who helped him escape and about the execution of the traitor they had meanwhile tracked down. Later on, the author hears the identical story told by another person who was also involved in the plot. But his story is slightly different and it now appears that Tjondro himself was the traitor. "Full of Sound and Fury," together with "The Ultimate Dignity," is among the very best stories Vuyk ever wrote.

The Wild Green Fragrance contains plenty of biographical data about Vuyk, lots of facts that are very much interwoven with her work. She always writes autobiographically or semiautobiographically, and she tells us as much in the previously mentioned interview.

Beb Vuyk, or Elizabeth de Willigen-Vuyk in full, was born in 1905 in Delftshaven, a suburb of Rotterdam, where her father was a shipbuilder and where, for example, her story "The Loser" ("De verliezer") is situated. In *The Wild Green Fragrance* she mentions how she wrote her very first stories when she was still under the influence of the expressionist method of writing in brief sentences. This also involved the rigorously applied use of the present tense, which so annoyed Du Perron. These first stories are: "The Friend" ("De vriend"), which first appeared in *Free Pages* (*De Vrije Bladen,* 1930); "The Loser" ("De verliezer"), which appeared in *Twenty Dutch Stories from North and South* (*Twintig Noord- en Zuid-Nederlandsche Verhalen,* 1930), edited by Constant van Wessem; and *Many Names* (*Vele namen*), separately published in 1932 in the same magazine that was then coming out in copybook format. Part of it had already appeared in *Free Pages* of 1943. All of these first stories share a theme that was to develop in her later work. It is the theme of longing for a freer life, the desire for "a life out of the ordinary," with the attendant fear of alienation and loneliness. The fear of being different is also a theme in *Many Names,* where the character Hank stands out because of his disfigurement. This character owes much to her father, who had a Madurese mother but who was sent to Holland at an early age and who married a real Dutchwoman with a Calvinist background. Like Hank, he too was a bit shy and withdrawn, and in a way also a bit "disfigured."

Of the three children, two girls and a boy, Beb Vuyk was the only one, she tells us, who stood out on account of the dark color of her skin. They called her names in the street such as "blackamoor," "dirty nigger," "biglips," "darky," and suchlike. "That's when I began to fight back and went to school with a ruler in my hand." This

singled her out, despite her Dutch speech and her Dutch, even bibli-
cal, upbringing. It also subjected her to all kinds of emotional confusion. This made her, even as a child, into an individual who was both
aggressive and defenseless, ruthless and hesitant, sure of herself but
shy at the same time. It determined her fate and it helped her ultimately decide to become an Indonesian. It made her choose the society of colored people. During this period also, in *Many Names* for example, her writing refers to the Madurese grandmother she never saw
and to whom, for that matter, her father never once referred.

Through her literary contributions to *Free Pages*, Beb Vuyk met the
editor Constant van Wessem. He recognized her as one of the younger
authors who had answered his frequent calls to write a modern short
story. He promised her a splendid literary career if she chose to stay in
Holland. She left Holland all the same when she was twenty-five, and
went to Indonesia, then still the Netherlands Indies, and she never regretted it. On board ship she met her future husband, who had an Amboinese mother and who was therefore "an Indies fellow."

From that moment on, all her work is set in Indonesia. In 1937 her
first novel appeared, then still more or less under the auspices of *Free
Pages*. It came out in its "Pathfinder" ("Voortrekker") series, then
edited by Anthonie Donker. He provided the book with a kind of introduction on the inside of its dust jacket. There he mentioned her
earlier novellas and counted them among "the best that younger
writers have brought forth in the way of narrative prose." The book itself he called "first-rate." This praise irritated the critic Ter Braak,
who was not about to consider *A Thousand Islands (Duizend eiland-
en)* first-rate but who still thought the book "unmistakably pure" in
tone. Ter Braak's criticism is milder, for that matter, than Du Perron's, which mocked the book's method and its use of the present
tense but did not overlook its qualities of describing landscape without clichés. Ter Braak wrote that the landscape in it could be "seen,
smelled, and touched." For the rest he objected to the novel's charac-
terizations, which are indeed unsatisfactory to a point of nonexist-
ence. It certainly must have been her intention to reconcile and make
into friends the Indo-European Carl van Waarlaerden and the Dutch
newcomer Ab Daalders, but their relationship remains too brief. In
addition, its attempt to camouflage reality is far too transparent. The
book's opening has been praised at times and indeed deserves to be
but as the novel proceeds, we completely lose sight of the relationship between Ab Daalders and the girl. The result is that the whole
thing is left dangling. Obviously Vuyk had a harder time constructing
her stories in those days than she did later on. What we are ultimately
left with are its descriptions of nature: the mountain slopes, tea plan-

tations, the quiet native people squatting down, and everywhere the rain, the all-drenching rain that leaves everything wet and sticky. It reminds us of her description of the sound of rain coming down among the citrus trees in *Many Names*, which Vuyk wrote when she did not know the country yet, something quite remarkable, really. *A Thousand Islands* already shows her attempt to simplify but it often appears as if she is trying to overcome a deeply rooted habit. In this book she has not discovered her own style yet, or rather, she only does so in the final chapter, when Carl and Ab leave for the Moluccas together, to the place of "a thousand islands," among them Ceram, Haruku, Buru, Manipa, across "a sea smooth and glistening as steel." In real life, the history ended with her husband losing his job during the Depression. Both of them left for the island of Buru, where her husband had inherited a run-down cajaput oil plantation. On this island, in a wooden house facing a white beach and the sea beyond, she begins to lead the kind of life she had dreamt of in Holland. She gives a straightforward account of this primitive but adventurous life, without changing names or making up clumsy anagrams. In 1937, she wrote a number of serialized articles for the *Haarlem Daily (Haarlems Dagblad)*. After drastic changes, she used these to write her second book, *The Last House in the World (Het laatste huis in de wereld*, 1939), its title derived from a poem by Rilke. Her short story "Journal of a Prahu Voyage" ("Journaal van een prauwreis"), which appears in *The Wild Green Fragrance*, complements and in a way supplements this book. It is simply a splendid reportage.

The Moluccan islands also feature in another short story, as well as in her new novel, if we may call it that, *Bara's Wood (Het hout van Bara*, 1947). Vuyk started it before the outbreak of the war in the Pacific and continued working on it in prison camp. The story is not entirely autobiographical. The names have been changed, it starts out with a story about someone else but, not surprisingly, Vuyk gradually relates it to her own predicament. The remainder of the book is definitely autobiographical if we ignore some name changes and some nonessential modifications. This is one of Vuyk's least known books and unjustly so. At first, the book seems to be about one of those classical quarrels with the Indies government. As it progresses, we realize that it is much more than that, and that its real subject is the use and abuse of power and especially the insufferable injustice at the hands of authority. The book ends with: "They sold their house and the property around it and left for Java. One month later the war broke out."

Both Beb Vuyk and her husband ended up in Japanese prison camps. She stayed on Java and he was taken to Thailand, where, as an Indies fellow who knew his plants and herbs, he stood a better chance of surviving than most of his fellow prisoners did. Her "A Spectator's Story" ("Verhaal van een toeschouwer"), which first appeared in *Orientation* (*Oriëntatie*, April 1950), is partly situated in Thailand. Later on, it was included in *Sound and Fury*. This story too deals with violence in all its fury as her husband, not she, experienced it. Even so, the story is told in such an intensive way that it almost seems a personal experience. It also addresses a number of problems for the first time. The story introduces a new kind of storytelling in her development as a writer and it is an attempt to point a new way to the solution of personal difficulties. The predicament in "A Spectator's Story" is that of the Indies fellow Hermans, an Indo-European who shares some of the characteristics of Hajo in *Bara's Wood*. The spectator's story concerns Hermans. This spectator is no outsider, however. Both men are tied by their common fate of having spent the war years working as prisoners of the Japanese on the so-called railway of death somewhere in Thailand. There, the spectator got to know, admire, and envy Hermans. He admired him for the quiet and unassuming authority with which he could lead and earn respect from his fellow prisoners without the least inclination on his part to be authoritative. He was able to do so simply because, as an Indies man, he was used to the jungle and he was their superior. His campmates relied on him, on his knowledge of edible plants and herbs, and on his ability to bear hardship. To the spectator, he was an example, and an enviable one at that, because he was able to put up with prison life as if it were a slight imposition, whereas it threatened to get the better of most other men, himself included.

After the war, chance brings them together again in a small hospital somewhere in west Java where Hermans is in charge of a small plantation. There the spectator realizes that not his but Hermans's life has been devastated by the calamities of war. Hermans has lost his country. He is no longer allowed to return to the island in the Moluccas he talked about in prison camp and his farm there has been destroyed. His wife has been killed by a revolutionary gang and his son has left for America. Hermans is totally alone. Even so, his wife's murder has not changed his attitude or impaired his judgment. He still understands and recognizes the Indonesian aspirations toward freedom, and he harbors no feelings of hatred or vengeance because those feelings are alien to him. But the soil where his roots were has become inaccessible and unattainable, and with it his aim in life as well. This is irreparable. There are several different strains and subplots running through the story, again dealing with cruelty and force, which are not always integrated with the main story. Still, they all ultimately come back to one central point, the character of Hermans, who even in the end manages to find a formula for living on: "In any case, it makes sense to be planting food in a hungry world." This story is told by the spectator with an undertone of compassion for his former prison mate. His overall attitude is one of admiration and love for this man who cannot be praised enough. The spectator's story has become the author's homage to her husband.

Vuyk is not a prolific writer. Over the years, she has produced several, mostly short, stories and a longer one once in a while. Only in 1969, a new collection containing two stories appeared, "Villa Sonja" ("Huize Sonja") and "Ngawang," under the title *One's Own World and the Other (De eigen wereld en die andere)*.

"Villa Sonja" starts out with a sentence that is almost identical to the closing sentence in *Bara's Wood*. Where one ends, the other begins. But for the fact that Hajo and Eli are henceforth called Harry and Etta, they are the same people who are now living in "Villa Sonja" in the town of Sukabumi. They are waiting for the gradually approaching war to start, although nobody can imagine what it will be like. It is connected with *Bara's Wood* in yet another way. The latter book starts out with the story of Hajo's return to his Amboinese clan, this time accompanied by a foreign element, his Dutch wife. His mother accepts this woman "in much the same way she accepted life's disasters." Eli, the Dutch wife, is forced to live in the family dwelling, and it is clear from the start that the mother wants to bring the son back into the old pattern of the clan. The Dutch wife, however, has her "own world." For several months the tensions remain dormant but then an angry outburst occurs over the way of feeding the first-born baby. Out of sheer self-preservation, she forces her husband to choose either her world or his mother's, which is a choice he has actually already made. This forces Hajo into a position between his mother, with the Amboinese family behind her, and his wife on the other side. In the end, he definitely chooses for his wife and thereby for her world. This theme is the same as that of "Villa Sonja," except that the game of move and countermove between mother and daughter-in-law behind Harry's back is worked out more clearly. Their ensuing departure for Java means her liberation and her victory. There, she practically swallows him up in her world. But something happens to her in Sukabumi because of the war. As the Japanese occupy the country, an odd feeling of dispossession and alienation overcomes her. This feeling is made complete by a remark from one of her children. As the Japanese troops move closer, the rumor spreads that all Europeans will be murdered. Simon, their confidant and servant, who has come along with them from the island of Banda, flees the house.

She goes looking for him with her children. During this search especially, she gets the all-encompassing feeling of being a stranger, an all-
engulfing feeling that extends to her relationship with her children.
She does not find Simon but it turns out that he has already returned
to their house. "Mommy does not have to worry anymore . . . I have
told him that he has no reason to be afraid *because we are Ban-
danese.*" And all of a sudden Etta realizes that despite everything, the
children consider themselves part of "the other world." The story's
conclusion is clever but maybe too much so: she recognizes the birth-
mark on her own foot as a sign of her own identity. Because Vuyk
keeps coming back to the same theme, we realize how much rancor
she must have felt, potentially at least. It also explains how her potential fear, or, better still, how her latent fear may have contributed to
her general sense of alienation.

Vuyk's ability shows to best advantage in the kind of story that
combines human problems and reality. Her mastery means a great
deal more than just technical ability. Her second story, "Ngawang,"
is no exception. It is about a young Indo-European woman, the Indies
girl Ernie. She is married to a Hollander. During the war, she flees to
her Indonesian mother where she finds her own world again. Here we
have a reversal in the move from one world to another, from the European to the Indonesian, but both cases deal with the attempt to preserve one's identity and one's world. In "Ngawang," Vuyk has also
added another pair of opposites through the character of the youngest
sister. She is married to an Indo-European who desperately chooses
for the European world and so loses her identity in occupied Djakarta.
Once again we are presented with a perfectly closed intrigue with all
kinds of autobiographical experiences interwoven. The interview
with Beb Vuyk in the *New Rotterdam Courant* (*Nieuwe Rotter-
damse Courant,* November 29, 1969) has more to say on this score.

Critics have generally praised Vuyk's ability to structure and com-
pose. Even so, the clever construction of this story is perhaps too
striking. For that reason, although this is not her fault, her latest
stories have fallen prey to petty critics. It is true, however, that both
stories are lacking something. They lack the "charged" quality of
"The Ultimate Dignity," for example, which was also very well constructed. This time, the interest and care expended on the composition seem to have taken away from the intensity of the experience,
i.e., her identification with her subjects. It is possible that the power
of her personal experience will find greater opportunity for expression in a more loosely constructed format. Given her degree of craftsmanship, it would seem to be a rewarding experiment, especially in
view of the fact that the impulse of innovation has always been one of

Beb Vuyk's potential strong points even where she is no longer among the younger authors.

3   Johan Fabricius

Johan Fabricius has produced several times more books than Maria Dermoût and Beb Vuyk put together. The author of more than sixty books was born in 1899 in Bandung of *totok,* or full-blooded Dutch parents. He was the son of the well-known journalist and playwright Jan Fabricius. Johan loved and greatly admired his father and has devoted several moving pages to his memory. From his father he inherited restlessness and the need to wander, to acquire new impressions, and to see a great deal of the world. Fabricius has traveled far and wide and lived a particularly varied life that has been anything but ordinary. He lived abroad for the longest time but returned to the Netherlands after the war as a cosmopolitan Hollander.

Not until the country of his birth was occupied by the Japanese did Fabricius realize what his Indies childhood and the country where he had lived the first fourteen years of his life had meant to him. He was living in London when the news of the war in the Pacific and the defeat of the Netherlands East Indies reached him. From that moment on, the Indies began to furnish material for his books. The background of his stories, their plot, characters, and things, all of them became inseparable from the country he had begun to feel closer to as the war pushed it increasingly further from his reach. During his stay in London, he wrote *Night over Java* (*Nacht over Java,* not dated, but written in 1942–43), a story about the resistance movement during the Japanese occupation, as well as the novel *Halfbreed* (*Halfbloed,* 1946). In order to write the first, he was forced to rely almost exclusively on his own resourcefulness and imagination. For the second book, he could fall back on his youth and impressions he had gathered during a round-the-world trip in 1935. In neither case, however, did he succeed in putting across anything essential about his "special ties" with his native country.

Fabricius is a prolific writer who gives the impression of never wanting to stop. This is in itself nothing to hold against him; on the contrary, it takes a great deal of inventiveness to come up with new subjects all the time and render them into stories. But the truth of it is that only great writers can permit themselves to write so much. Even an accomplished novelist such as Couperus could not always realize his great potential.

There exist a great many conflicting opinions about Fabricius as a writer. He has his admirers, such as the critic writing for the *Hague Courant (Haagse Courant)*, Rico Bulthuis, who talks in awed terms about Fabricius's books. To admire Fabricius the way Rico Bulthuis and several others (such as Ben van Eysselstein and Anne Wadman) do is to willfully ignore his limitations and shortcomings. To revile him as Jan Greshoff did ("a born chatterbox with nothing to recommend him") is to ignore Fabricius's qualities that make him the novelist he is. In several interviews, Fabricius has rightly objected to people regarding him as exclusively a storyteller. "I think I am a perfect example of a novelist," he said in an interview in *Free Netherlands* (*Vrij Nederland*, Nov. 19, 1968), "in a country that has not had many novelists since the death of Anton Coolen." He considered Jan de Hartog more the storytelling type, "but I'm no storyteller, I don't base my work on external events but on people." Whether this is altogether true or not, the fact is that Fabricius is not simply a teller of tales and that he is indeed also interested in people. He features them in his novels according to the classical method of the "real" *romancier* by setting up a plot, which he seems to do effortlessly, and then by developing his characters from then on. How they develop is a different question. Sometimes they turn out as people, most of the time as mere figures, and once in a while as cardboard cutouts.

Fabricius may well be a "real" novelist and not just another storyteller but he lacks sufficient psychological intuition to be able to do what, for example, Couperus can do so well, and that is not only to typify people but to penetrate their characters as well. This explains why he has never been able to write a "great novel" and only several good ones, as well as a number of competent books, some of them very competent indeed. Unfortunately, he has also written several bad books, such as *Halfbreed* or *Easy Chair* (*Luie stoel*, 1957), or worse, the novella *The Dark Blood* (*Het duistere bloed*, 1954). All three books take place in a racially mixed society, the first two in an Indonesian-Dutch world. What is striking is that Fabricius, who likes to create the impression of knowing the world of the Indo, or half-caste, actually cheapens this world in his desire for dramatic writing. Discussing his own novel *Halfbreed*, Fabricius claimed that "anyone familiar with Java" would easily recognize the characters in his novels. In reality, however, they are about as recognizable as walk-on characters in a contrived melodrama replete with torrid scenes, murder, and mayhem. His style is equally rife with clichés which Fabricius uses indiscriminately, especially when it comes to love scenes: " 'Non, Nonnie my dear . . . I think I'm falling a bit in love with you,' he whispered. She found it hard not to cry out, not to faint in his arms or burst out in tears on his chest. . . . 'Oh, Frits,' she moaned, 'oh darling Frits. . . .' " These are the kind of sentences that no self-respecting person should ever write down, least of all the man who uttered the exalted opinion that Dutch literature was little more than the product of a "literary cottage industry." In *Easy Chair*, the main character is an indolent "white Indies fellow," who, as the story progresses, turns into a caricature. Its descriptions of the various milieus are overdone and tiresome because of that. Its dialogues are so desperately calculated to suggest "typical Indies" idiom that the entire story, whatever its possible authentic source, creates an unbelievable impression in a literary sense. An intelligent critic such as Kees Fens, who does *not* know the Indies firsthand but who is always a good reader, could tell from its style and the book's entire intent that it presented a false image. He called *Easy Chair* "a piece of romanticism with cheap pretensions" (*The Times [De Tijd]*, August 30, 1957). It is a pity indeed that Fabricius's qualities as a storyteller and novelist are hidden by his shortcomings, with the inevitable result that any evaluation becomes lopsided.

Among the better Indies novels Fabricius wrote are *Setuwo, the Tiger* (*Setoewo, de tijger*, 1956), *The Sacred Horses* (*De heilige paarden*, 1959), and especially *Shadow Play* (*Schimmenspel*, 1958). *The Sacred Horses* is set on the island of Sumba in eastern Indonesia. The subject for this book, the history of the rebel Pombu, the landscape descriptions, facts about customs, habits, land, and people, all this Fabricius garnered from a number of books written by D. K. Wielenga, a missionary. Fabricius got much of his material particularly from *Umbu Dongga (Oemboe Dongga)*, which he mistakenly calls an autobiography. It provided him with his plot outline, several scenes, and most of his characters. He gave them different names and some got to play a part different from that in *Umbu Dongga*, which contains the *real* story.

If the island of Sumba, as Fabricius describes it and where *The Sacred Horses* takes places, should by any chance fail to please someone who knows Sumba, then this would still not detract from the book's literary value. The only thing that matters is whether or not Fabricius has managed to create an impression of the island's authenticity, and he has indeed succeeded in doing this.

The account of the rebellious village chief "Umbu Dongga" (whom Fabricius calls by his real name, Pombu) ends with his surrender and his subjugation by the Dutch. If we compare *Umbu Dongga* with *The Sacred Horses*, it becomes clear that Fabricius has made several changes, one essential change in particular. His Pombu of *The Sacred Horses* does not surrender but continues to fight the Dutch until he is killed. He is the implacable foe of the white invaders who desecrate his *adat*, his traditions. This is the way Fabricius sees Pombu, alias Umbu Dongga, and this is his good right as an author. But its integrity is damaged as soon as Fabricius, for reasons unknown, introduces a love story that is absent in Wielenga's account, and that, moreover, has no function whatever in *The Sacred Horses*. Fabricius pushes aside the character of Anakami, a friend of Umbu Dongga and his counselor and intellectual equal who accompanies him on his exhausting flight. In his place, he introduces the young female slave Maja. During a raid, Pombu finds Maja naked inside the house of his enemy: "he saw her naked body rise up to him, soft and with a lovely sheen. She smiled at him . . . and lo . . . she opened her arms." With such romantic hodgepodge, including the oratorical "lo," Fabricius does indeed harm the literary integrity of his book. Maja's presence offers Fabricius a few additional dramatic possibilities in that she arouses the jealousy and hatred of Pombu's wife, Dahi Waha, the mother of his favorite son Pati. Unbeknownst to Pati, Pombu and his wife have a quarrel which ends in veiled patricide resulting from the son's "betrayal." As a result, Pombu is unintentionally ambushed and killed by the informed Dutch military.

Despite everything, *The Sacred Horses* is a well-written novel but it remains doubtful if we can agree with the critic Anne Wadman, who praised its "grand epic style." Its style of writing is strong and clear but still lacks sufficient resilience to be able to carry the numerous events and descriptions to their conclusion.

When we compare Fabricius's novel with *Umbu Dongga*, we notice at once that Fabricius is a more gifted writer than Wielenga. On the other hand, *Umbu Dongga* contains rhythmic pieces, speeches, prayers, and dirges which are most impressive for their metaphor and feeling. They were translated by Wielenga from the Sumbanese, leaving their truly "grand epic style" intact, which is an accomplishment in itself.

Shadow Play, which is perhaps Fabricius's best book, is not a novel. It is his biography of a Javanese man of high nobility. The young man studies in Leiden, marries a Dutch woman but ultimately leaves her in order to return to Java and its princely courts. The first part of the book is especially good. We are made aware of a quiet narration which is neither humdrum nor routine, and then we realize what a good storyteller Fabricius really is. Although he disclaims any intention of having written a roman à clef and makes his chief character a dancer (possibly modeled after Jojana), it is clear that he must have had Noto Suroto in mind. This book shows what Fabricius is capable of as long as he is personally involved in the story he is telling. Then he no longer addresses a public but a small circle of friends whom he hopes to acquaint with the tragic life history of his Javanese friend and his European wife. He divides his sympathies between the two of them. He has been a witness to their tragedy, from very close up at times, sometimes from a distance but ever involved in both their lives.

4 H. J. Friedericy

H. J. Friedericy (1900–1962) was at least forty years old when he began to write, that is to say, write something other than reports, memos, articles, and a dissertation entitled *Class Differences among the Buginese and Macassarese (De standen bij de Boegineezen en Makassaren, 1933)*. His notes and memos are no longer traceable but his articles, especially those that appeared in the *Colonial Times (Koloniaal Tijdschrift)*, and his dissertation are. These give us no hint of the remarkable writing talent he was to display. The letters he wrote home during the first six years of his administrative career are written with a mixture of decorum and ease, of traditionalism and originality, of perception and detachment.

Publication of *The First Stage (De eerste etappe, 1962)* came without introduction or explanation, which led to much guesswork about its nature and origin. Some people thought the book consisted of fictitious or rewritten letters, others thought it was a combination of letters and a diary, but it was generally assumed that the letters had been reworked. It turns out that they were only slightly changed or corrected in order to clarify a few things, and to protect the anonymity of some people, and that they are otherwise authentic. The author also left out those parts directly addressed to his parents and those dealing with family matters. The letters had functioned as both journal and letter at the same time. The personal element was removed as much as possible, but the general account was left intact. Friedericy's intention had been to publish something about an administrative career in the Indies as seen by an insider. It is not a political statement but a private one.

The letters are marked by the careless charm of youth. He says that he is "proud" to be serving in the colonial administration, and he speaks respectfully of his superiors, always adding "Mr.," and never referring to them only by their last names. Also, he does not mind letting on how well he is doing on the job and how much they appreciate him; in short, he is not without vanity. The letters show him as he was then, with all his weaknesses and positive qualities, a charming young man and a typical social creature who always needed other people around him and was willing to adjust himself for that reason.

It is amazing to see just how quickly he did adjust to everything. Right away he was in his element, and his letters abound with expressions such as "I am happy," "it is wonderful," and "I'm really fortunate." As an administrator too he felt right at home, in the midst of well-intentioned people, splendid natural surroundings, and a population that interested him from the very start. In an interview he was asked why he had opted for a career in the colonial civil service (always abbreviated as "B.B." for Binnenlands Bestuur). Friedericy clearly had difficulty answering the question. Had he come to the Indies for idealistic reasons perhaps? Yes, there had been those, no doubt about that. Had he come for the adventure of it, a desire to see the mysterious East? Yes, he most certainly had. Perhaps the longing for adventure and that desire had indeed been the major incentives but "a desire to rule . . . to lord it over other people . . . no, not that." He believed that in his administrative capacity he had a useful task to perform, a Task with a capital T, in fact. Not a political task but an assignment to govern to the best of his ability in the interest of the population. In short, he was a good student of the ethical ideas then propounded at Leiden University. The Leiden school of thought was essentially apolitical. It is interesting to read, for example, in a letter dated October 22, 1924, what Friedericy wrote to his parents from Celebes. The island had just gotten a new governor and this governor saw his task as chiefly political in nature. This very much surprised Friedericy: "I could see the roads and bridges opening up the countryside; I envisioned a multitude of irrigation works so that fields measuring ten thousands of *bahus* would provide an assured harvest; I could see public and personal safety increase year by year, but what I did *not* see was the need and the possibility to develop the people and their chiefs. Now here is this new governor, and he considers it to be his principal task to build up this internal political structure. So that's where I am right now, caught in the middle, in an atmosphere like that." He believes in the necessity of government and in his own branch of it, but apart from that Friedericy shows a natural capacity for objectivity which enables him to make a place for himself within a given pattern of organization. He has a sense of the ridiculous inherent in the hierarchy of the higher and lower authorities to which he himself belongs. "Everyone here is a boss," he writes, and his capricious mockery of the authoritarian and hierarchical structure of the Indies world is a delight.

Even so, many critics regarded *The First Stage* as a disappointment compared to his other work. One reason for this is that these letters from 1922, 1923, and so on, were for a long time not regarded as authentic. In disregarding their proper chronology, people did not know that they were actually juvenilia. Because his letters had been published in 1962, people erroneously considered them as sequels to Friedericy's other work, such as his novel *Bontorio* (1947), his collection of stories *Princes, Fishermen and Peasants* (*Vorsten, vissers en boeren,* 1957) and *The Councilor* (*De raadsman,* 1958). To say that Friedericy's letters are impersonal is to miss their humor, which is very much a part of his personality.

Humorists are always relativists who keep their distance and express themselves indirectly. They will invariably show the other side of their personality in the hope that people will also bother to discover the negative side. On March 3, 1923, Friedericy wrote his parents, not without self-satisfaction, that at his new post in Macassar everyone already knew who he was: "in short, they knew nearly everything there is to know about me, except of course the things I myself value most. But those things are nobody's business, after all." This characterizes Friedericy entirely, because the impersonal and detached element is very much a part of his personality.

Friedericy was a curious man in a way that should not be misinterpreted. He was forever curious about people and situations and this disinterested inquisitiveness provided him with the material for his stories. He was really in his element when he was writing and there was no limit to the stories he could tell. He was a great raconteur because he had developed his natural inclination into a special skill rarely found among the Dutch. Friedericy told his stories, also when writing, with the greatest possible intensity. In an interview he said: "It is as if I am physically present in the place I am writing about. I see the moon, I smell the fragrance, I hear the drums, and I take part in the conversations." This intensiveness not only gave all his writing a plastic and tangible quality but gave it, more than anything else, a lasting tension, even when Friedericy told a simple tale or simple event. This complete absorption also made him vulnerable because it made him overly sensitive. He knew enough to protect himself against this or else he would have failed as a storyteller and writer. His tendency toward detachment and toward viewing things in a relative way, as well as his ridicule and self-mockery, were his natural defenses against a perennial threat of sentiment. Friedericy wrote in a manner calculated to hide himself and to insure maximum privacy. Only when he knew himself to be in the presence of a good listener with whom he could converse in understatement did he give himself away. Stories and literature were his means of getting through to people, but he himself meant to determine how close he should get to them, all the while ready with a wink for anyone who understood. Friedericy deserves no less than to be read with this in mind.

Friedericy did not begin writing till late, did not consciously practice literature as an art form, that is, until the Japanese locked him up,
together with many others, in Struiswijk prison. When the London
correspondent of the *Business Daily (Handelsblad)* asked him why
he had never thought of writing sooner, he answered more or less to
his own surprise: "The idea simply never occurred to me." How then
to explain the fact that it did occur in a Japanese prison camp? "My incomprehensible change of heart in subjecting myself to perform hard
literary labor in Struiswijk prison I can only explain as an attempted
flight from reality." The flight in question led him back to a stylized
memory, to experiencing a world consisting of an earlier reality but
one that was itself no longer real. And without noticing it, Friedericy
had slipped into the world of literature where the only thing that was
real was reality *transformed.*

In prison camp, Friedericy started with the story "The Dance of the
Heron" ("De reigerdans"), based on an experience which he tried to
transform to imaginary reality. The story betrays its author's literary
background. Asked about this in the aforementioned interview, Friedericy confessed to having admired the typical wordsmiths Ary Prins
and Adriaan van Oordt in his "formative years," and even to having
admired Querido, but that at a later stage Van Schendel made a great
impression on him. Suddenly we realize that by the time he began to
write, Ary Prins and Van Oordt had already vanished, and that only
Van Schendel remained. His first stories, "The Dance of the Heron"
and especially the novel *Bontorio,* particularly the opening pages of
the latter, have the smooth style, the same poetic sobriety, the same
slightly archaic word choice as Arthur van Schendel's work. But they
are also different and develop very differently until they gradually
reach a more natural and more direct prose. Throughout, they are also
more narrative and less evocative than Van Schendel's prose. Van
Schendel's influence was not to last long. Friedericy worked a long
time on "Dance of the Heron," his literary debut, let us not forget,
and wrote it out in very clear, slow longhand, filling half a notebook.

His second story, "Blood" ("Bloed"), took much less time because
he had a far clearer idea of what he was aiming for. It turned into a particularly well-presented story, the best Friedericy ever wrote. It is
much less "poetic" than "The Dance of the Heron," if we must use
this word at all, and its language is much more direct and sparse, more
even, with a half smile and barely concealed admiration for the mur-
derer, Daëng Sisila. ["Daëng" is a title used to address persons of nobility.] The story's Daëng Sisila is the one who avenges himself on his
opponent Hadji Mustapa, because Mustapa, who is a bastard, has
dared to meddle in regal affairs: "He overlooked the fact that it is dan-

gerous to get mixed up in the affairs of a prince of the purest blood."
After "Blood," several more stories followed, also situated in the
same society in southern Celebes. These are "The Double Spike"
("De dubbele aar") and "Vassal" ("Vazal"), stories in which Friedericy himself makes an appearance as the Tuan Petoro, the title referring to a European government official. Together with the postwar
story "The Gangleader" ("De bendeleider"), they were published in
one small volume called *Princes, Fishermen and Peasants*, which
was not issued until 1957. Its title indicates exactly the feudal world
in which all the stories take place.

In yet another prison camp, in Suka Miskin near Bandung, one or
two years later, Friedericy wrote another story, which he called "Bontorio," and which he gave his colleague Alberts to read. Alberts, who
was himself to write several splendid stories later on, said something
rather unexpected and curious which took Friedericy aback some. He
said that "Bontorio" had all the potential of a novel and that some
sentences even contained the germ of entire paragraphs and chapters.
Thereupon Friedericy, obedient to his literary mentor, began to make
notes in the margin in order to work them out some other time. This
is how the novel *Bontorio* came into being. It was published in 1947
but barely found an audience at the time. Friedericy just left it at that
until many years later when, pressured by a friend, he took his stories
over to the publishing house of Querido in Amsterdam, which did
more than publish his stories, it turned out. Querido reissued *Bontorio* under the new title of *The Last General* (*De laatste generaal*,
1958), containing only two of the original three stories.

Bontorio is a unique novel, not only because it is one of the few to
take place entirely within an Indonesian setting (this is also the case
with *The Sacred Horses* by Fabricius), but because of Friedericy's
ability to penetrate a society with entirely different cultural patterns.
In this case, he has entered into the noble classes of Bone in southern
Celebes. Friedericy knew what he was writing about because he had
been an administrator in those areas for years and had enjoyed daily
contact with the *arus*, *karaëngs*, and *daëngs* there.

In previous letters to his parents he had written that he considered
his daily contact with the princes and rulers "uncommonly fascinating." It appeared that he had been able to think himself into their part
to such a degree that they thought they recognized themselves in his
book later on. In an interview in *The Fatherland* (*Het Vaderland*,
April 9, 1959), Friedericy told that he was once addressed by a man
who introduced himself as the son of Bonterihu. Even though Bonterihu was in fact a historical figure, Friedericy had indeed fashioned
him vaguely after a village head he knew. His dissertation about the

social classes among the Buginese and Macassarese had already dealt with these princes and their offspring. Here too he had crawled under the skin of their lives to such an extent that subsequent researchers thought he had viewed south Celebes society too much from the perspective of the nobility. What might have been considered a shortcoming in his thesis, however, proved to be a virtue in his novel.

Friedericy must have considered *Bontorio* as a test of strength. He was already writing about a subject that dictated its own distance in terms of space and culture, and now he was to increase that distance even more by writing a historical novel. Moreover, it was to encompass no fewer than three generations. The book is divided accordingly into three parts, "The Mother" (1870–1890), "The General" (1890–1906), and "The Son" (1906–1930). The book is named after the mother, the female Aru Bonterihu, "Aru" being the title of a princess or prince, the chief of a people. She is not the main character, however, her son Mappa is. He is "the last general," the great hunter, drinker, and fighter. An even less important character is Mendapi, the general's son in part three.

Bontorio appeared in 1947 under the pseudonym H. J. Merlijn, when Friedericy was already well into his forties. Friedericy's late debut as a writer about the Indies is curious, as is his apparent need to separate his identity as an official from that as a writer, and to disguise his identity as a writer, for the time being at least. The exact meaning of the pseudonym that covers him like a magical cloak of sorts is anybody's guess. We do know, of course, that Merlin, spelled "Merlijn" in Dutch, was a medieval sorcerer.

The novel, or maybe we should simply call it a story, begins when I Base, a female vassal, is declared Aru or chief of the small mountain state of Bontorio. She is brought to life on the very first page, a hard woman with a broad, flat face who talks in a loud voice. She is cruel and unpredictable. Hatred and contempt are the emotions that govern her attitude toward her subjects. She arrives in Bonterihu on horseback, seated on seven pillows as befits her station. She is followed by her husband and her first-born child, a boy seven months old, carried in the arms of a nurse, also on horseback. It starts to rain and four men with umbrellas go out to meet her in the ever-increasing downpour. When she sees them approaching, she slowly turns her head to her husband, and in a sharp, loud voice speaks the words that all the country of Bonterihu "knew in less than one day and would not forget for the next hundred years: 'I see that I am fated to rule over a bunch of monkeys.' " The new female Aru of Bonterihu, already pregnant when elected to Aru, begets two sons. Tappa, the eldest, resembles his father. Mappa, the younger son, is broad shouldered, coarse, and dark like his mother, with a peasant's face. He grows into a great warrior, deer hunter, gambler, and womanizer. Both brothers are invited to the court of the Arumpone, the King of Bone, to whom the Aru of Bonterihu is subject. The eldest, Tappa, develops into a half woman who paints and powders himself. At court, he joins the so-called *bissus*, priests who are in charge of the crown jewels and regalia, and who also have an important role in interceding between people, gods, and spirits. We are to assume that these priests are homosexuals, especially because they sometimes go about dressed as women, and behave accordingly. Tappa is murdered following a love intrigue. The younger Mappa flees from court but returns later, and is installed as one of the most loyal vassals of the Arumpone. His heroic life commences then. Far and wide he becomes a feared and admired man. "His heavy cheekbones were covered by a deep brown and healthy looking skin. The small Mongolian eyes looked respectful. There was a half-shy, half-sly smile about the large mouth that had a thin long moustache growing over it. The bright red sarong wrapped high above his waist revealed his heavy calves. The king of Bone nodded. Mappa made a deep bow, his right hand touching his head-cloth, flung himself onto his nervous, pale yellow stallion and galloped away, holding in his right hand the deer lance with its bow tied to the top." The fine description of the deer hunt follows and is one of the longer passages in the book. A reader will remember this scene for a long time after.

Mappa's fame as a warrior grows. He remains undefeated in the many civil wars and even saves the Arumpone's life. In the ensuing wars against their foreign enemy (the Dutch), Mappa succeeds in dealing their invading forces a heavy blow by defeating them on the beaches. However, after the capital city of Watampone falls, and the aging king of Bone is taken prisoner, he too surrenders. " 'I am Aru Bonterihu,' he said, 'I have come to put myself into your hands.' " But he surrenders only after he has amused himself by leading the Dutch troops down the garden path for several weeks.

The book's third part, which takes place in the present, is the weak-est. There have been critics who have fiercely attacked Friedericy, alias Merlijn, concerning scarcely more than twenty pages or so of part three. In this section, Friedericy, in his function as government official, speaks about a great task lying ahead and about a just govern-ment, by which he ultimately implies that of the Netherlands. Mappa's son, called Mendapi, develops into precisely such a just gov-ernment official after the democratic Dutch model. At the end, he re-pudiates and denies his father Mappa, when the latter tries to get his son to steal money from government funds. Fate enters like a deus ex machina: Mappa is killed in a car crash. This is really a pretty far-fetched and rather abrupt end to both the book and Mappa. It is as if Friedericy is trying to say that the old potentates are gone and that the era of justice has arrived. The reader, however, is more likely to sympathize with Mappa, no matter how big a freebooter and a drinker he is, than with his boring, well-educated, and obedient son Mendapi. When the book came out in paperback as *The Last General*, its previous subtitle, Friedericy left the final chapter out. Even though the story now no longer reaches to the present, as had been, no doubt, the original intent, it does contain, intentionally or not, a somewhat too programmatic justification of Dutch rule. This caused it to fail as literature, and that was the reason Friedericy decided against the final section.

The Councilor (De raadsman), written more than ten years later, was Friedericy's ample revenge on the failure of this third part. Instead of rewriting it, which would have been impossible to do, he cast it in a different form and used a different style. He based the book on his earlier experiences as a government official. At the beginning of his career, he was stationed as a very young Tuan Petoro, a Dutch administrator, in the subdepartment of Gowa, with Sunguminasa for its capital. All the literary background noise still audible in *Bontorio* has vanished in *The Councilor*. Its sentences are shorter and more compact and the phrasing is much more sober. The tone too has changed, and it is as if we can hear Friedericy talking, not in elevated or ponderous tones but with gentle irony and self-ridicule. It is a reserved kind of prose, fitting his personality. The central character is the councilor, an older government assistant Tuan Anwar (who is a composite of two former characters). The account concerns several incidents that took place during Friedericy's posting in south Celebes and is a mixture of reality and fiction, with reality its principal component. The book opens splendidly with the description of the quiet townships, their inevitable *alun-alun* or village squares, and the portrait of "the councilor" himself, Tuan Anwar. He becomes a friend and a father to the Tuan Petoro. There and then, in sublime fashion and with restrained humor, a series of stories are told. They are stories about people running amuck, about a fraudulent clerk, about a dying dog (a particularly fine story), about village chiefs and royal offspring. And every story touches upon the councilor, who features in every chapter. These sober, restrained tales move along almost imperceptibly. Quite different from the third part in *Bontorio*, here the mutual feeling of love and attachment between the young Tuan Petoro and the older Tuan Anwar becomes indeed a justification of the ethical kind of government that Friedericy espoused and practiced. The last part is especially moving, and not merely the one page describing the scene where the now no-longer-young Tuan Petoro and the old and shrunken councilor meet again. Most moving is the end when the Tuan Petoro (who by now has not been a Tuan Petoro for a long time) is taking three young Indonesians to their plane at the San Francisco airport. It is well after the war, and Indonesia has been an independent country for some time. At the airport, somehow the name of Tuan Anwar is mentioned, whereupon, in the midst of the hubbub of public announcements and people, one of the young Indonesians whispers: "Please excuse me, Sir . . . but in our opinion he was one of the collaborators who have done our country irreparable harm." Then the former Tuan Petoro falls silent, and the book too falls silent about the ensuing feeling, the painful feeling of an irrevocable "misunderstanding," of an insoluble difference between politics and humanity.

5   A. Alberts

A. Alberts (born 1911) was also well over forty when his first stories appeared in *Libertinage*. Shortly thereafter, these and some others came out under the collective title *The Islands (De eilanden,* 1952). This marked Alberts's debut as a writer. It was not a debut in the ordinary sense of holding out a promise, for the simple reason that the author had shown himself to be a "perfect" writer from the very start, having set precisely the right tone for his tales. In other words, Alberts already possessed his own style when he started writing. It is not known what apprenticeship, if any, preceded it. In an interview with Bernlef and Schippers in *The Guide (De Gids),* he said he had never written anything before. He had never even considered writing, he said, not even when he was in the same prison camp with Friedericy in Bandung, where the latter followed Alberts's advice to make *Bontorio* into a novel. Only when Alberts returned from the Indies did he begin to replace Dutch reality with a tropical decor by writing down very restrained, very short little sentences. This created a peculiar effect, a kind of transformed reality, one in which structure has been altered, just as in very lucid daydreams. In Alberts's work, the attributes of reality are always present and recognizable in people (who do not use many words), in islands, coasts, forests, sometimes mountains, the sea, and yet reality is prevented from entering completely into any of these. Alberts keeps it at bay by purposely being incomplete and by withholding the opportunity to recognize. Everything that could lead to either recognition or identification, such as place names or comments on certain situations, is lacking. Only a few Indonesian names give us some hint. Because he has cut down all signposts and indicators, we are presented with an almost lifeless and surreal background. His stories take place in a landscape without either milestones or warning signals. They have nothing but a road, a village, trees and bushes, and at the most, an outpost or a fortress somewhere.

We know when we are on an island only because the sea is all around or because of an opposite shore. Against this ever-present tropical decor, the action takes place and the story moves, and moves very slowly sometimes. But his sentences always have a tension that forces one to go on reading and, as one realizes afterwards, this tension is brought about by something other than the course of events in the story. It is the tone that propels, a somewhat casual, mildly ironic tone with a great deal of self-mockery. It expresses itself in a few words, in brief, almost lapidary sentences with much repetition. This is Alberts's "writing technique" which, he tells us, he first used unconsciously, then consciously when he realized that "it worked for him." It worked well enough to allow him to do what every writer wants, and in his case it meant expressing his own alienation from reality. Alberts is really a bit of a stranger who meets people and talks with them but always in a roundabout way, without giving them a direct answer or any assurances. He always has an absent air about him, partly because he wants to, but also, as he says himself, "in order not to bother anybody," by which he means allowing other people their freedom too. An essential aspect of Alberts is that he hides his own basic makeup. This is of course the protective device par excellence for all those somewhat uneasy and basically melancholy people like Alberts who are in constant danger of being overwhelmed by their own emotions.

Alberts's work abounds with situations where people are trying to outdo one another in courtesies, as for example in the funny story "The Car and the Nuns" ("De auto en de zusters"). It is about three nuns who have to be evacuated from the island as the war draws nearer. He himself, as an assistant comptroller, the patih and the regent (the highest Indonesian official), the missionary and the wealthy merchant Taronggi III are all engaged in acting out some sort of contest in manners. Each vies with the other to be allowed to convey the nuns to safety, a trip of three hundred kilometers down, and three hundred kilometers back. During an interview, Alberts tried to trace this motif of a contest in courtesy back to the formality and courtesy inherent in Indonesian social intercourse, which "really struck" him. But he forgets to tell us, consciously or unconsciously, that these courtesies are part of his own personality in the first place, and that they function as ritual gestures of sorts, in order to create at least some sort of endurable climate between people who do not really have much of anything to say to each other.

The same is true about the conversations in Alberts's stories. They ebb away to a point where they can hardly be called dialogues anymore, just talk with a few words, long silences, pointless questions, and answers that do not answer the question at all. Conversation is more a question of putting out one's feelers and then retracting them, complete with misunderstandings, near misunderstandings, and fear of misunderstandings. One such conversation, for example, is that with Mr. Naman (a palindrome that suggests Noman or nobody). Naman is an odd European who has more or less gone into seclusion by living beyond the swamp. The name of the story is "The Swamp" ("Het moeras"). Mr. Naman, another well-mannered gentleman, can hardly be reached by anyone and then only by the one path that does not get submerged. When the narrator asks him the "dumb question" why he went to live all the way beyond the swamp, Mr. Naman answers him twice: "Because there isn't anybody to talk to in the village." This may strike us as a strange answer but to the narrator (one is tempted to say Alberts) this answer is indeed comprehensible enough: "Maybe that was not such a bad idea after all. Maybe it was less awful to be alone than to live in a village where there was nobody at all to talk to." One repeatedly comes across such question-and-answer games, complete with the usual misunderstandings, in Alberts's work. They are interspersed by conversations in which people do not understand each other at all. This motif occurs in almost every story. Human communication is a problematical thing. In the story "The Uncharted Island" ("Het onbekende eiland"), such a situation ends up being nearly catastrophic. A plane is forced to make an emergency landing on one of the islands. They have a wounded man on board. Only after several days is the crew able to communicate that they want to be taken across to another island where there is at least a telephone. They are close to despair and half crazed with fear when someone finally drops the obvious and recognizable word "tilpun" (telephone). Only then do deliverance and rescue follow! Another story like this is called "The Last Island ("Het laatste eiland"). It is about a man who sails from island to island in search of swimmers who can retrieve sunken fishnets. He is convinced that there are swimmers to be found on at least one of the islands. On every island he asks the same question and every time he gets almost the same reply. Maybe such an island does exist and has swimmers and divers on it, they have heard about it but do not know exactly which island it is. On the last island it appears that an old man has heard of such divers for nets. For a moment it seems as if their goal has been reached but instead of delivering him a swimmer who can dive, he tells a legend about a fisherman who once caught a beautiful woman in his nets. Again all communication has broken down.

In one of the best stories in *The Islands*, "The King Is Dead" ("De koning is dood"), any form of communication whatever is impossible. In this story, the speaker, clearly a person of authority, asks all sorts of questions of "old Mr. Solomon" ("the ex sergeant-major bandleader"), who is so old that the wrinkles on his yellow bald head already "began to sag away." But none of his questions gets an answer. Old Mr. Solomon, also known as the "King," just laughs and nods. The office clerk replies in Mr. Solomon's stead. The "King" expires in regal fashion in the end but before anything resembling communication has transpired.

People do not understand each other and they are nearly always strangers to one another, but with things it is different. Between man and mute nature an intimate relationship is possible. Such a relationship exists in a strongly autobiographical book called *The Trees* (*De bomen*, 1953), which came out one year after *The Islands*. Alberts himself has said that his story can be located in the royal forest near the town of Apeldoorn, where he spent his childhood. There exists a friendship between the little boy Aart, who is partly Alberts himself, partly a friend of his youth, and the trees of the extensive forests. He talks with the trees, and the trees enter his room and talk with him. Their understanding is complete. There exists a firm bond between them which only his teacher Barre can guess at. Much more so than in *The Islands*, *The Trees* shows the application of the technique of simplification to a point of invisibility and inaudibility.

Alberts had here reached a point where it seemed he was playing with fire. When he reread his book after eight years, he was disappointed. He thought he had overdone it out of a fear of identifying too closely with his subject: "I might have been a little more explicit." Nevertheless, *The Trees* is a fine little book. In an article in *The Green One (De Groene)* of October 13, 1956, entitled "The Autumn of Longing ("De herfst van het heimwee"), Alberts clearly mapped out the place and the time of the woods where he spent his childhood by giving names and indicating places. He did so with the ostensible intention of writing a straight, informative article. Still, the vibration of his emotion is felt in nearly every sentence, especially toward the almost lyrical ending: "A woods in autumn is autumn itself. It is rest, resignation, sadness. There is nothing deathly or final about a forest in the fall. The forest is only getting ready for the night. It creaks and rustles and goes on living. There is nothing mysterious about a forest.

Abandoned houses can inspire dread but a forest never does. Only at times does it remind us of our own autumn and of our own longing."

The woods where he spent his youth also appear in the longer story called "Chase" ("Jacht") in *The Islands*. Here they are interwoven as memories with an ulterior function. At first, "Chase" strikes one as a rather bleak and barren story, the kind one expects from Alberts. It tells about the pursuit of a rebel, one Captain Florines. Alberts gave him the characteristics of an existing captain in the so-called *barisan*, an army corps on the island of Madura, who was a "terrible drinker and a great skirt chaser." The local man in charge is forced to go along with the armed party that is trying to hunt him down, although he would much prefer to stay home. The story ends with Florines being shot and killed, and his body cremated. The killing, historically perpetrated by a chief constable, is done in the story by the narrator. He does not particularly relish his own role in the chase. On the contrary, his sympathy goes out to Florines, the "game" they are pursuing, just as his sympathy had gone out to the boar they were chasing when he was a child, which he helped escape in the forests around his home. Alberts ingeniously intersperses other, similar memories, and he succeeds in making his solidarity with the pursued even more convincing by having him recall how, on a different occasion, he too was once pursued himself, after he had strayed into forbidden territory. As a child, he had been pursued, just as he had chased the boar. Now Florines is the boar; he is now Florines being pursued; he himself is really the one that is being hunted down.

Although he would not quite put it this way himself, Alberts does call forth some such sequence of associations in the reader just by telling the story. For this is also an aspect of Alberts's technique as a writer, that he relies more on reference and allusion than on clear-cut statements. It is a most effective technique. Every single one of Alberts's stories bears his personal stamp, no matter how impersonal the style of his writing may seem. Alberts always figures in one of his own stories too but only after the fashion of a visual puzzle. He is there somewhere but he is not always easy to spot.

Especially memorable is the conclusion of "Chase," the cremation of Florines's body. Here, as in every good ending, we get a brief restatement of the essence of the story, Alberts's own relationship to the hunted man.

Right away they started gathering wood and soon they had built an enormous pyre. Put him on it, face down, I said. This they did. Set fire to it, I said. Moments later the flames appeared from all sides. The constables were laughing, they thought it was a good joke on my part to fix Florines like this for one last time. But I was not really thinking about Florines anymore. I just looked at the flames, my last farewell to the boar, to my friend. Whenever the fire threatened to go out, the men tossed more wood onto it. It had gotten dark and the flames lit up the house and our faces. The wood snapped and the constables were yelling and laughing. Finally though everything became quiet. The fire went out and it became dark. Dark and terribly cold. It got so terribly, so terribly bitter cold after burning Captain Florines.

Alberts's first story in *The Islands* is called "Green" ("Groen"). This time it is not the green of the woods where he spent his youth but the green of the much more extensive forests of a tropical island. They are an almost impenetrable mass of tall trees, with here and there a cut clearing. Thinking about the woods in his youth gives Alberts a sense of peace and tranquillity but the forests on the island are his enemy. They slowly attack the human mind. The theme of the European going mad amidst the desolation of the primordial jungle is not a new one. In fact, it occurs quite frequently in Western literature, but it has never yet been used the way Alberts uses it.

For that matter, it was no mean task he set for himself. It must have been something like this: put a European on a tropical island and watch him go crazy. And then use some kind of diary to record the process. From then on, everything depends on the description.

A government official is carried ashore in a palanquin. There he is greeted by his colleague who has come to meet him. Just to meet him he has had to walk through the forest for two days. The colleague, called Peereboom, appears to be nothing but "a bundle of nerves," and he drinks an inordinate amount. Alberts shows us that the green jungle already has him in its clutches. During a later visit, Peereboom suddenly screams: "Chop down the whole damned forest, beat the whole mess into a pulp!"

The island appears to be totally covered by trees. There is a thin coastline but the forest starts immediately behind it and extends all the way inland. There are trees everywhere, and everywhere things are a light green color. Two days' march away is the western forest where Peereboom (literally "pear-tree") lives. There is also an eastern forest but it dead-ends on the beach because the coastline curves there, and then there is a northern forest. The western forest is still penetrable and it is possible to find one's way in it but nobody really knows much about the northern forest, not even the village chief. There is said to be an abandoned settlement in it somewhere but for the rest it is just primeval forest. This northern forest is different from the one in the west in that it is more impenetrable and much less hospitable, while at the same time completely uniform till the very edge, some hundred kilometers further on. The plain is reputed to begin there. The desire to reach this plain becomes an obsession. At first, the narrator makes brief reconnaissance trips. The forest turns out to be dreadful. When he returns to his house, actually nothing more than a wooden lean-to in the woods, he notices something peculiar: the oil lamp is swaying from side to side without casting any shadows. Something has happened to him. Still, he decides to make the great trek through the forest. When he finally reaches its outer limit, he sees the open plain beyond, which to him signifies light, rescue, freedom, truth, the end. It is wide, barren country with lots of boulders and a hazy blue mountain range on the horizon. The light is bright but, oddly enough, there does not appear to be a sun. The sky is "mildew gray," and "below that sky, right up against it, the forest lay, a venomous green in the harsh light of the gray sky, a layer of undulating, crawling snakes. I stood on the outside of it and I was terribly afraid. I had to go back, and with my eyes wide open I had to walk toward this fearful creature and enter it. . . ." When he returns to his station, he discovers that Peereboom has stopped by and hanged himself from the lamp post. The next morning, in a state of hallucination, he buries Peereboom: "I'm standing by a freshly dug grave. Our Father, I hear myself saying, who art in Heaven. When I move to turn away, I realize that my legs are still drunk. I leave the burning lantern hanging on its post as usual. Because I'm still alive."

"Green" is the kind of story that should be read line by line, especially because its writing is so compressed and because each word counts. This way it proves to be an obsessive story which might easily enough have turned into a piece of melodrama but which, owing to Alberts's "technique of simplification," is transmitted as a moving process of spiritual disintegration.

Ten years after *The Islands*, in 1962, there appeared *Putting Names to Things: Just a Few Unusual and Frank Memories of Life in Paradise Lost, Formerly Known as the Netherlands Indies* (*Namen noemen; zo maar wat ongewone en openhartige herinneringen aan het leven in het verloren paradijs dat Nederlands Indië heete*). Alberts's own comment on it was: "If I had to describe it briefly, I would say that it's really *The Islands*, except that this time around I'm putting names to things." This not only meant that he mentions the names of people, places, and islands, but also that he ties his stories to reality. To the extent that we had not already been able to guess from the text, we now know the names of those islands. They are the large island of Madura and the smaller islands to the east and to the south of it, among them "the fairest island in the world," Kangean. Alberts informs us about the people who lived on these islands just before the war, and about the events that took place. He does so, to use his own words, "just as it happened." In *Putting Names to Things*, we find the same islands and recognize the same people as those in *The Islands*. We encounter "Mr. Zeinal," for example, whose real name was Zainal, and the three Taronggis, who were really called Dirk I, Dirk II, and Dirk III, merchants with the dignity and power of princes. We also recognize all kinds of events that happened a little differently from the way they did in *The Islands*. It is tempting in fact to want to note where and how they differ, in order to get to know the method Alberts used in *The Islands*, until we realize that the difference between fiction and reality is actually not essential, least of all to Alberts. The difference between the two lies elsewhere.

Alberts is anything but a facile and happy writer, who writes purely for the joy of it, in an easy and routine manner. On the contrary, he is a man who has to overcome a disinclination or something else each time before he can get himself to sit down and write letters, words, and sentences. This "something else" must often appear insurmountable, enough to frighten him away. This explains why he said that he really liked writing on assignment. However, even then it was only with the understanding that people could refuse his stuff if they did not like it, just as they should feel free to spurn "just a few unusual and frank memories" in *Putting Names to Things*, for example.

During the same, previously mentioned interview, Alberts also said that he saw no difference between his early and his later work, not as far as method was concerned anyway. At first glance, this assessment seems somewhat doubtful. There is a distinct difference, for example, between the manner of writing in *The Islands* and that in *Putting Names to Things*. We can only hope to understand his assertion if we take it on his own terms. By having committed himself to reality in *Putting Names to Things*, he could no longer avail himself of simplification and omission, of combination and compression, the method so effective for him. On the other hand, this also meant that he had become less dependent on what we might call "the wayward course of the imagination." This independence meant that in a certain way he could now feel freer and write a little more easily. For the rest, Alberts has of course remained Alberts as far as he is concerned. He is a writer with a pronounced sense of the curious, the macabre, and the absurd. All these are interrelated, of course. His frequently amusing situations, his often humorous style, and his generally light-hearted tone serve to disguise a much darker undertone in his work. For that reason we have to make it our business to read *Put-*

ting Names to Things with a great deal of attention, which goes for all of Alberts's work, needless to say, all the while keeping our ears attuned to what W. F. Hermans once called the "ultra sound." The book appears to contain something other than mere light-hearted memories.

6 Two Authors: Hella Haasse and Aya Zikken

Anyone writing nowadays about Dutch literature of the Indies is in a position far different from that of past writers. For us, the literature is complete as far as Indonesia is concerned. One is no longer forced to look into the distant future as Brom had to in the early 1930s. That distant future no longer exists, there is no longer a road forward, only the road back. For this reason it would seem that all the conditions for a nostalgic literature are available. People often say, as if it were something self-evident, that Indies literature is a "literature of longing and homesickness," without realizing what they really mean. Just as frequently, people relate this nostalgia to the "loss of the Indies" and the "severing of ties." The relationship exists, of course, but the question is how one looks at it. The massive repatriation of people from Indonesia to the Netherlands, timely or not, forced a lot of those people to regard their past in the Indies as nothing but a memory. But memory is not quite the same thing as nostalgia or "a longing for that which has been lost." This nostalgia exists, naturally, among broad segments of the Indies community in the Netherlands, part of which—particularly its older members—considers itself to be in some kind of exile. This feeling of being cut off creates the nostalgia, which in turn colors people's memories. These memories can extend so far and so deep that they cause pain, even a great deal of pain.

These feelings can indeed be directed at what many people have come to regard as the best years of their lives, but they are invariably directed at one's childhood. Remembering "the child that we were" (Du Perron's phrase) has been the greatest need for many people, for writers particularly, even if this remembrance meant a significant coming to terms with things, and a settling of accounts. The desire to return to one's youth is common to all mankind, however. Not specifically related to Indonesia, it is a familiar theme in, especially, romantic literature.

The further back the domain of one's childhood lies, the less one's active memory will be able to exercise control over it and the greater the freedom will be for the writer to write. These unlimited memories that cannot be warded off have always provided the most in the way of creative impulses for a writer. The Indies authors we are here concerned with are certainly not to blame if they happen to have been born in Indonesia. Nor are they to blame if their childhood happens to be tied to a personal native nurse, one's "own" *babu*, such as Alimah was to Du Perron, for example, or Nènèh Tidjah was to Breton de Nijs. And can they help it if their childhood involved Indies scents and Indies sounds, the tropical rains, the mountains, jungles and terraced rice fields, charms and exorcisms, *selamatans* and ghosts, such as the *gendruwos, wéwés,* and *kuntianaks?*

It is hardly possible to speak of a typical Indies childhood, in fact. It made a big difference whether one was brought up in the cities, in the small towns, or in the outlying districts, and whether on Java, in the Moluccas, or in the Javanese principalities. Another thing to keep in mind is that society in the smaller cities and in upcountry towns was more mixed and that life there was much more Indies—in any event much less Dutch—than in, for example, Medan, Batavia, Bandung, or Surabaja. In these cities, the *totok* or Dutch-born community always constituted the upper layer and was sizable enough "to keep to itself."

In one such closed European community lived Hella S. Haasse as well as Rini Carpentier Alting, the author of a charming book of memoirs about her youth. In a community not quite as closed lived Margaretha Ferguson and Aya Zikken (who spent her childhood in a small town in the outlying districts). Lin Scholte was brought up in a community that was even less European. She made her debut with a fine book of memoirs of her childhood called *Army Brat (Anak Compenie,* literally "child of the Company" or soldier's child) which is situated in a typical mixed community, even more Indonesian than European.

Hella S. Haasse was born in Batavia in 1918. She is the author of what is a sizable oeuvre by now, but we cannot say that Indonesia takes up an important place in her work. It is present in her small novel *Urug (Oeroeg,* 1948) and in *Scratches on a Rock (Krassen op een rots,* 1969), which is her account of a trip through Java after a thirty years' absence. Indonesia also features in several shorter and longer fragments in the autobiographical works *Self Portrait as Puzzle (Zelfportret als legkaart,* 1954) and *Identity Card (Persoonsbewijs,* 1967), and maybe elsewhere, but it does not altogether amount to much. It is amazing that there is so little about Indonesia in her work because Haasse spent the greater part of her youth there. There is an explanation for this—really little more than a hint—in her *Identity Card.* From this it appears that the war years spent in the Netherlands rather than her years spent in the Indies were responsible for the important change in her life: "Without exaggeration, I can say that around 1940 I was born for the second time." Even more telling for her attitude toward Indonesia is that this change in her life also meant a break with her childhood: "In the first place, I knew that I could not go on living as an extension of my parents' mentality." She discusses her parents in both *Self Portrait as Puzzle* and *Identity Card*, and describes their way of life as well as her own. As she tells us herself: "We did not live in Indies fashion." Their home life was Dutch, as was common in so many *totok* families during the twenties and thirties. They were sufficient unto themselves, lived outside of the Indonesian world, even beyond that of the Indo-Europeans. "I was born in the Indies but even so I was perhaps never anything more than a stranger there" (*Self Portrait as Puzzle* [7th ed.], p. 99). She regards this fact as a severe limitation of her overall experience. Even with this limitation she must have been receptive as a young girl to all sorts of impressions which inevitably must have become part of her memory and imagination. That explains why she never lost Indonesia.

In the first place, there is her novella *Urug*. If we exclude a small volume of poetry and two volumes of translations and adaptations of folk poetry, *Urug* was her prose debut in 1948 that right away received recognition of sorts. A panel of nineteen anonymous judges had selected it to be the promotional copy in a national book advertising campaign. This made Haasse's first work widely known, and *Urug* has enjoyed numerous reprintings since. Its initial success was probably owing to its topicality, the fact that the Netherlands and Indonesia were at the time engaged in a colonial war on Java and elsewhere in the so-called policing actions.

The story deals with the friendship of a Dutch boy, the narrator, with an Indonesian boy called Urug. Urug is the eldest son of a *mandur*, a supervisor on a plantation of which the Dutch boy's father is the manager. And although the white boy lives in the manager's house and Urug in the simple dwelling of the supervisor, they are sworn friends of the same age who depend on each other. They are always going off together, without their social or racial differences making the least bit of a gap. Only when they get older do they gradually begin to pull apart. Urug becomes aware of his inferior social position as an Indonesian and starts looking for different friends, Indonesian friends who change his political perspective about conditions in the colony. The narrator goes to the Netherlands to study, while Urug remains. After the war, the narrator returns at a time that coincides with the first policing action. Naturally he starts looking for Urug but he can not find him. Not until the end, anyway. The narrator returns to the place where he and Urug spent their youth together, to a lake, Telaga Hideung. Right there and then, fate has Urug coming out of the bushes. He is a *pelopor* now, an insurrectionist, and, therefore, an enemy. "Go away," is Urug's reaction, "you have no business here." As Urug stands there with his threatening revolver silhouetted against the dark treeline, the narrator slowly removes himself. "I'll never see Urug again," he thinks, and at the same time he realizes that he never understood Urug, because Urug is "like the mirrored surface of the lake whose depths I never fathomed."

It is not so easy to fathom the meaning of this little book either. If one had not read her remarks about it in *Identity Card* (pp. 66–67), one would have thought the author had intended to express personal tragedy in revolutionary times or the conflict between politics and humanity. According to Haasse, however, *Urug* has a far more personal and much more symbolical meaning: "The character Urug is really her other half, the dark side of herself living in the shadows she does not know."

It is obvious that Haasse indeed does not know this side. How could she have, after all, a white girl brought up in Dutch surroundings? Tjalie Robinson, an initiate to her world of shadows, sharply critized her work in *Orientation* (*Oriëntatie*, no. 9 [1948], p. 56). He objected particularly to the incorrect assumptions inherent in her story, and her errors resulting from them, as well as to the generalities she resorted to. He objected to everything not experienced and to things untrue. These objections he substantiates with numerous examples but they can all be traced to Haasse's impossible initial point of departure, her attempt to fathom "the dark side of herself living in the shadows." She ought to have done so first, and really gotten to know Urug before even starting to write. No amount of explanation after the fact can make up for her erroneous approach. Such an approach, moreover, always shows up in the style as well, which is sometimes conventional, then again literary and metaphorical. But we should also bear in mind that *Urug* constituted her literary debut.

Just how closely "nostalgie tropique" and longing for one's childhood can be related is shown by *The Atlas Butterfly* (*De atlasvlinder*, 1958) by Aya Zikken (born 1919). Her first impulse must have been to relive her childhood again and to conjure up a memory that in her case could only be related to Indonesia. After all, nobody can write about one's memories and not write about the physical surroundings of these memories too, and this naturally includes Aya Zikken. One critic, however, complained of being unable to recognize Indonesia in her book. An outsider and stranger to the country, Jan Greshoff said he missed "the all-pervading splendor and danger of that country." He blamed Zikken for not having applied enough local color. For that matter, he was not the only one who missed "the scent and atmosphere of the Indies" in her story. Many people who had lived in the Indies had a similar objection. Of course, it is one thing to note the absence of something and another to consider an omission a shortcoming. For that matter, these complaints that the novel is lacking in an Indies atmosphere are not entirely true. It is really impossible to separate the story from its Indonesian background, and all one needs to do to confirm this is to read her description of the rain, for instance. All we can say is that Zikken, possibly in her endeavor not to overburden her story, may have left out too much to satisfy all those looking for the "typical Indies" elements in it. This was never her aim, of course. What she was after was to write about the people and their relationships that made up her childhood world.

Her book concerns people such as Ferdie and Per and Manna and Scotch and Sibert, but most of all the emotional and fantasy life of the girl Gembyr Egelie, who impersonates the author herself. To do it this way was Zikken's prerogative as an author and also something befitting her nature and her talent. After all, she determines what eyes shall see and ears shall hear, leaving out "all the other things that may very well have been there too," as she puts it somewhere in her own book.

Anyone returning to his childhood has to rely on memory, but memory is an unreliable thing and alters or misrepresents what really happened. In other words, remembrance distorts the reality that was. One's *active memory* is something different from *remembrance*. The better one's ability to actively recall is, the more the distortion created by remembrance can be corrected and the past be restored to reality. Again, the stronger one's ability to recall things, the more likely remembrance will be to abandon its peculiar diffuseness and chaotic character. In other words, only factual memory can force remembrance to regain its recognizable form again. Remembrance and memory cannot work without one another and although they seem to be at opposite ends of the spectrum, they need one another's corrective influence in order to bring things back into focus. It would be impossible to convey sheer remembrance. Anyone writing the memoirs of childhood can only hope to do so with the aid of the memory's powers of correction. To a writer, however, it is not memory but remembrance that is the essential source, because only remembrance has creative power. The thing Zikken tried to do, apparently aided by a weak memory, was to preserve remembrance as much as she possibly could. In other words, she was prepared to accept remembrance with all its inherent distortions in order to gain her literary ends. Zikken only needed her memory to select the essential elements and to keep her remembrance of things from becoming totally unintelligible. *The Atlas Butterfly* contains a segment that is both very telling on this score as well as characteristic of her style. Here her character Ferdie, who has to tell her a story, says: "You take everything into your hands, just for a moment, and quickly, the way a juggler does it, things flash right past your fingers. Every once in a while you grab something and then you hold that up to the light and imagine you have told a true story. So let's imagine just that. I'm starting all over again, then, and I'll do exactly as I please. I'll just have to forget about being honest because I couldn't talk if I didn't."

But anyone who writes wants to be understood. It is fair to say of Zikken that she has pushed her experiment with memory to the limit of comprehension. She has used the images she remembers of her youth to express a process of development and growth that we can follow from page to page. Following her information and her set arrangement, the reader proceeds and goes to work. We, the readers, are the ones who have to establish the connecting links with reality and who have to interpret the memories and retrace them to their source, to the little girl called Gembyr Egelie. As far as her odd-sounding names are concerned (besides those already mentioned, there are also Utari, Sari, Siranouche, and Syahaya), Zikken has said somewhere else that as a child she made a list of words like that. It was a wonderful game then, and later on it became a way for the author to keep reality at bay so as to preserve the memories intact.

The Atlas Butterfly is written around one central event. This is the arrival of a substitute teacher Mrs. Borneman with her little niece Utari (who is really her daughter) into the small European community of an Indies town in the interior, although just where in the interior does not seem to matter. There is a garrison stationed there, there is a captain, a doctor, a teacher, an engineer, and several other people who do not seem to matter much.

The teacher's arrival is announced by an Atlas butterfly. (This is the Attacus Atlas butterfly, largest known in the world with a possible wingspan of one foot.) With the onset of the rainy season, the butterfly has landed on the front veranda. The girl Gembyr is the first one to see it. Her mother is approaching. Breathlessly she looks at the brown and orange butterfly: "This means a momentous change, this means. . . ." She does not finish the sentence. And indeed, everything in the small community changes following the arrival of Mrs. Borneman and her "niece." Everything people had thus far been able to shore up now collapses. Everything that was potentially already there is now exposed, such as the inevitable rift between Gembyr and Ferdie, the tense relationship between Ferdie and his father, the doctor's loneliness, and the fragile relationship between Per and Manna. The presence of Mrs. Borneman causes commotion in the life of the doctor, who is a widower, and Mrs. Borneman also drives a wedge between Gembyr's parents, Per and Manna. Gembyr, who is about eleven or twelve years old, loses her friend Ferdie, the captain's son, on Utari's account. On Utari's account too a strong rivalry ensues between father and son.

They are all small dramas without solution. They do not reach any crisis but only appear briefly here and there and otherwise remain hidden. Everything and nothing happens, but everything is in disarray. Zikken succeeds very well in indicating without explaining all these human relationships, with a remarkable sense for the subtleties and slight shifts in human relationships.

For reasons of circumstance and her own natural inclination, the girl Gembyr finds herself living in a curiously peripheral situation. Her parents are Dutch-born, she is white and blond but she belongs neither to the *totok* nor to the Indies community. She is both between and outside of the two. "You are of pure stock," says the Indies lady Mrs. Borneman to her, "but your mind is mixed." She also feels more attracted by that which is dark than by things belonging to her own white world, and there is probably more than a touch of self-contempt here. As a result, this *totok* girl fits in soonest with the mixed Indies elements in her surroundings. Ferdie is a brown-colored boy and when he mentions his dead brother who was not only strong but blond also, Gembyr quickly tells him: "dark is much prettier."

Gembyr's situation is peripheral in yet another way. She is no longer a child but not yet an adult. Like any outsider, she is lonely. She has some contacts but no really deep relationships. She is left to her own devices and to her daydreams, which remove her even further from actual events and which cause her to undergo general hypertrophy. There is Ferdie, of course, who is several years older, but he now only comes over during vacations because he goes to school in the city. Still the rift does not take place until Utari arrives. Then Ferdie slips away for good and irevocably enters adulthood and another world. Upon discovering this, the girl Gembyr feels so hopeless that she makes a half-conscious attempt at suicide by allowing herself to drift out to sea on a raft. The description of this incident is perhaps one of the high points in the book, together with the chapter about the garden of the seven wonders. When she learns that Mrs. Borneman is to visit her parents, Gembyr imagines how she will show her through the garden of the seven wonders but it turns out that Mrs. Borneman tells her: "That's very nice of you, dear, I'd love to another time," and then continues to walk on with her parents.

The Atlas Butterfly is a book that reminds the reader of *Only Yesterday* in more than one respect. It is no less good, but different, especially on second thought. The events in the book are more disjointed and less integrated. They also merge frequently. This makes the book harder to read, especially in the beginning where allusions are made about what is to come later on. Only at the end does the reader realize their meaning because only then can one understand the relationship and meaning of those earlier references. *The Atlas Butterfly* is an exceptional book, one of the best among what we call "Indies belles-lettres."

Thereafter, Indonesia was absent from Zikken's novels and stories for a while till it appeared again in 1966 in a travel book called *Be Curious and Live Longer (Wees nieuwsgierig en leef langer)*. Israel and Portugal are its chief subjects, and the Indonesian memories were apparently added on. Even so, they are often quite charming. They are memories of her childhood, but unlike those in *The Atlas Butterfly*, these are not reminiscences dictated by her remembrance of things past. They are much more organized and the reader has a much easier time of it. There is nothing here to suggest the shadowy world of childhood. Rather, the child is shown leading its own life as observed by the author. A new element in these stories dealing with memories is the lighter tone which is only occasionally tempered by a consistent irony turned against the writer herself.

Its final story "Raméh" provides the link with the book that followed with the expanded and somewhat theatrical title *Raméh, Account of a Love (Raméh, verslag van een liefde, 1968)*. Fortunately, the story itself is anything but theatrical. Because Zikken uses the word "account" in her title, it is probably safe to assume that these memoirs written n the first-person singular deal with the "truth." In fact, the inside of the dust jacket makes mention of an autobiography. In some respect it can be regarded as a sequel to her previous book. The narrative tone is the same but the events are now centered around the theme of an adolescent love affair. When we come across some of the same happenings from *The Atlas Butterfly*, we realize the extent to which the material has been reworked. Again the plot deals with a boy-girl relationship. There are other friends as well but there is only one real friend and that is Raméh, a dark boy, as Ferdie was. Only it turns out that he is not really an officer's son but the child of a Hollander who walked off, leaving his Indonesian wife to take care of herself and his child. Together with Raméh, the narrator experiences the adventures of her youth, such as rescuing the dog and hiding it in a cave, and through Raméh she enters a racially mixed society. The book *Raméh* contains a number of stories which together still form a unit. They have been written with a good amount of self-mockery, and the fight with a girl friend is especially well done. The book is amusing and interesting but still lacks something *The Atlas Butterfly* has.

Although it is a totally different book, Zikken's *Yesterday is Never Over (Gisteren gaat niet voorbij,* 1976) does connect with *The Atlas Butterfly.* The book's subtitle reads: "A novel about Tempo Dulu," which is probably not her idea but her publisher's in its altogether too speculative emphasis on *tempo dulu,* the *good* old Indies days. Happily, the book does not suffer from this implied sort of nostalgia. As is really the case also in *The Atlas Butterfly,* it is first and foremost a return to childhood, in this instance to the confusing and turbulent high-school years which do indeed represent the yesteryears that are never entirely forgotten. The story concerns an Indies milieu and is situated in the Netherlands Indies because Zikken spent her youth there. Its autobiographical overtones have been disguised. Her childhood years for that matter do not give the least occasion to refer to them as the *good* old days. On the contrary, their interaction with the present must rather have been traumatic. Much more than a longing for *tempo dulu, Yesterday is Never Over* is really an attempt to penetrate a particular phase of childhood in order to recognize the existing trauma and to cure it by writing about it.

The story's design is a clever and ingenious find. During one of those many school reunions (most likely held in The Hague, that latter-day Batavia), which seems to fulfill a certain need in some people at set times, Janthe and Melissa get together. They are friends, although they are described as both "friends and enemies at the same time." The two young women meet a brown-colored young man with the somewhat Indonesian sounding name of Suukso. Janthe and Melissa are living in Holland with real Dutchmen for husbands who both shrug their shoulders at their stories about the Indies. The young women are a bit lonely, displaced, and estranged. Suukso's unexpected appearance creates a sudden change. Both are taken back to their childhood. Suukso stands out amidst the anonymity of the school reunion, and he is the one to put his hand in Janthe's.

He strikes her as familiar but she can not quite place him. The only thing his presence does is to create associations with other boys from a similar period. These associations in turn arouse feelings that have something (or everything) to do with eroticism, such as feelings about the attractiveness of a brown skin, an Asiatic shape of face, supple fingers and supple gestures, and an Indies accent. All of a sudden, she relives the kind of longing toward the unknown Suukso she knew in her youth, she now realizes, the longing for closeness and intimacy. Who is this Suukso? Was he that Indonesian boy on board their emigrant ship, or was he another perhaps or yet another?

Melissa has a similar experience. She too can not quite place Suukso and he also reminds her of various boys from her youth, all of them Indonesians, and part of an Indonesian setting too, she thinks. The similarity of their reactions is so nearly absolute that we begin to wonder if Janthe and Melissa are not really one and the same person, a split personality of some sort. But then again, this seems improbable in view of the fact that their relationship is real and marked by specific and personal, internal differences. The lively versus the subdued, the aggressive versus the defenseless, delight versus self-punishment are always present simultaneously. Confusion is the only constant element. That is why both of them are looking for the past in a mixture of reality and imagination, and as is the case with every powerful memory sometimes, it is both clear and hazy at the same time. Is this nostalgia perhaps? Aya Zikken provides her own answer: "Each person is born with his or her own longing and nostalgia and it does not make the least bit of difference whether this feeling is directed from time to time at something completely different, because it remains nostalgia just the same. Is it a longing for death or for life? Or is that the same?" This is what her book is all about.

7   Indonesia Revisited

The best word to describe the next literary and historical phase is not "Wiedersehen" with Indonesia, in the German and Dutch sense of the word, but "Indonesia Revisited," simply because the English word "revisited" implies a great deal more. It implies a confrontation, not just a "taking a look at the old place again," and it suggests also a re-viewing of it, as well as a reappraisal.

One may or may not dislike much about Sukarno, about his politics or his person, but we should credit him with realizing one thing very well. He understood that in his attempts to make Indonesia into a nation he could not sever the colonial ties without also getting rid of the Dutch. His so-called politics of confrontation during the conflict over western New Guinea provided him with that opportunity. The ties between the Netherlands and Indonesia were practically nonexistent for a period of almost ten years, with the telling result that the teaching of Dutch was cancelled in all schools.

In 1965, following the failed *kudeta* (coup d'état) in which Sukarno probably had a hand, and his gradual elimination, the *orde baru* was established. This new order allowed a different attitude toward the West, including the Netherlands, to come into being. It was a slow process and that may well be the reason why normalization of mutual ties between Indonesia and the Netherlands went as smoothly as it did. In any event, Indonesia had become accessible again, and it definitely became a country with which new friendly relations could be established. Only then did it appear that the personal ties had never been entirely broken, something Queen Juliana's visit to Indonesia in 1972 confirmed.

People from the Netherlands once again entered Indonesia in droves, either as entrepreneur, planter, international "expert," scientific researcher, or touring artist, but most of all as guest or tourist. An Indonesian wrote in July 1975 from Djokja: "The months of July and August are real tourist months. Dutch-speaking white people everywhere."

Only a relatively small number of them were visiting Indonesia for the first time. They had gone there simply because Indonesia means something different to the Dutch than do, for example, Singapore, Thailand, or Hong Kong. The influx may also have been the result of the "Come to Indonesia" campaign of the travel agencies with their familiar appeal of the "exotic," but, needless to say, this kind of tourist to Indonesia obviously misses the for-the-most-part indefinable but more profound relationship with a part of one's life. To this category of tourist belongs the contemporary novelist, Jan Wolkers, who went on an organized seventeen-day excursion tour with a group, the kind of trip calculated not to enable anyone to learn the least thing about Indonesia. Wolkers ended up seeing little more than what appealed to his masculinity and otherwise remained a stranger to the country. Neither of his two recent books, *The Loathing Bird (De walgvogel)* and *The Kiss (De kus)* are in the least concerned with Indonesia. *The Kiss*, for example, is about a personal drama between the main character and a friend. Although the story is fascinating in itself, it could have been situated most anywhere else and could have had any kind of background, tropical or nontropical.

However, the majority of those going to Indonesia had spent a part of their lives there. Many of them had not seen Indonesia in twenty years or so, and wondered what it would be like. Setting foot on Indonesian soil was already an experience in itself. They had been living those many years in the Netherlands. Some of them had valiantly tried to banish any thought of Indonesia from their minds (although always in vain), while others had been sitting out their time in a

Dutch apartment, feeling like exiles. Most of them had gradually become integrated into Dutch society but were never fully assimilated. They had continued to preserve their own spiritual and intellectual world (in which a belief in magic had always retained its place), had continued to follow their own social patterns, including entirely different toilet and eating habits, all the while with Indonesia on their horizon. They got together and made up Indies enclaves in the Netherlands, some of them extensive enough to put their stamp on certain city districts, as in The Hague, for instance. They had their own magazine *Tong Tong* (called *Monsoon [Moesson]* since January 1, 1978) which bound them together, its contributing writer Tjalie Robinson (died 1974) their symbol for preserving their own identity. They also organized their own annual fairs, such as the "Pasar Malam" in The Hague, and they held their own school reunions.

Remarkably little has been written about the lives of these Indies people in Holland. This absence is a curious phenomenon in itself. They felt themselves to be a community, albeit with fluid borders. They do not need to be told that they are a minority because they know they are. However, in contrast to other, more vociferous minorities in the Netherlands, it seems as if they are in the process of making themselves invisible. They have done so by adapting themselves (still something quite different from being assimilated) and by no longer asking to be understood. They have mostly resigned themselves to their situation, with some bitterness and with a latent nostalgia, but for the rest they have an attitude best expressed by *sudah*, "let it be," while they still have one another to lean on for the duration.

In 1978, the Indies "Moesson" series brought out a slight, sympathetic book written by an Indies man called Ralph Boekholt. He was born in Bandung in 1953 but had been entirely brought up in Holland. He is now living and studying in the Netherlands. There he belongs to the young generation of Indo-Europeans who really never knew either the Indies or Indonesia. He is quite different from the old Indiesman or Indo. As he says himself: "Old Indo is homesick, young Indo has adapted himself," even though he knows the old Indies person and his way of life. He keeps in frequent touch with his grannies, uncles, and aunts. He is not like them but he understands them and they soften his heart whenever he is around them because he is tied to them. The existence of all these Indies people who still continue to feel themselves a little ill at ease in the Netherlands puts him in a melancholy mood. He found a very telling title for his book by calling it *Mendung (Mendoeng)*, which means "not sunny," or overcast. This is the way their lives are also, and it is also the mood of his brief impressions in the book. For all its brevity, it is still something of a challenge to sociologists. Its meaningful and fine photographs both contrast and link Holland and Indonesia with one another.

To many of these "Indies Netherlanders," seeing Indonesia again became a profoundly moving experience. Their return affected both sides, in fact. Now the Dutch could be regarded as friends by an older generation of Indonesians who still spoke Dutch, and who no longer had to feel frustrated by the colonial situation. Younger Indonesians, unburdened by the problems of colonialism, approached them in the most natural way of all, as strangers but lacking all preconceived notions of whether they were either friend or foe. They proved as forthcoming as one human being can be toward another. The most remarkable experience was the realization that the former colonial relationship played practically no part in their mutual contact, neither to the Indonesians, nor to the people from the Netherlands. The reexamination of former prejudices, self-criticism, and the acceptance of an independent Indonesia had gone very smoothly. There had not really been any problems to speak of, not even emotional ones.

Or had there been some problems, after all? Some people, for instance, found it difficult to accept the fact, especially after seeing the country again, that Indonesia was no longer their country. They had been born there, it was the country where they grew up, the land of their mothers and grandmothers, their other fatherland, to be exact. They had been able to accept the changed political situation well enough but found it difficult to be foreigners, to be regarded as outsiders. No matter what, it was their country too, simply because their roots were there. They too bore the Indonesian *tjap,* meaning that they also bore the stamp of Indonesia. The Indonesians must also have thought that people who felt this close to their country could not be very bad. Only, it was not easy to express this ambivalent feeling and to communicate it. They talked and wrote about it, in *Tong Tong* magazine particularly, where they expected to be best understood, but there were those who expressed themselves in what we afterwards call literature.

An early phase in this emotional confrontation with Indonesia brought forth a short story called "House of Rain" ("Het regenhuis"). It appeared in 1963, when Indonesia was still closed to the Dutch, and it was published in *Guest Book of Singel 262 (Gastenboek van Singel 262)* and published by Querido publishers for private use. Its author was the totally unknown F. van den Bosch (born 1922), who had not previously published anything. It is a splendid story, and a restrained statement of loyalty to and affinity with the country he regards as his own, although fate has decided otherwise.

He came to the Indies with his parents when he was about four or five years old. Although he was born in Utrecht, he had an Indies childhood, which makes all the difference. He was about twenty when the Japanese arrived and took him prisoner, only to release him again into a concentration camp with thousands of other prisoners. This was the Kesilir prison camp for civilians in east Java, originally an agricultural colony established by the Indo-European Society. It was also the camp where Willem Walraven died.

"House of Rain" starts out with the main character walking through the landscape around Kesilir. The story represents the author's attempt to return to the country that seemed lost forever. For years, in fact, he had tried to erase it from his memory. His return is not without its difficulties and conflicts. The house of rain in this story becomes symbolic of his desire to return. He wishes to make this abandoned house, that stands "somewhere in a forgotten corner of human existence," into his own house and home. He wants to be taken in again and accepted by it as he was on the first day, he wants to return to the earth and to the elements of nature. "Here a man could sink away into the mud and become so defenseless a raindrop was enough to make him fall to pieces. It was all very familiar and all very good." The land does not surrender itself easily, however. He has to fight before he can hope to make the house his own. Using an atmosphere of hallucination, Van den Bosch has tried to give form to a process of painful searching and groping with every means available to him. "Just as my eyes and my tongue, so too are my feet instruments of love for the land as it was once created and as it was made by man in the course of many centuries."

It was not until 1978 that "House of Rain" appeared in a collection, together with three other stories entitled simply: *House of Rain and Other Stories*. The title story is pivotal to this collection, in more ways than one. It also takes up the central position. Two stories precede it, both of which are situated in the Indies. These are "Nom-de-Guerre" (stage name) and "Sarinah." The story that follows it is situated in Sweden, which strikes one as odd at first, but in retrospect its affinity with Indonesia does become apparent.

The story "Nom-de-Guerre" goes back to the (Indies) childhood of the author. It starts out with two boys who, playing in the ruins of an old fortress, find a brick with the name "Benson" stamped on it. This mysterious, magical sounding name leads to all sorts of identifications and transformations. Carefully crafted from childhood experiences, the story moves between reality and fantasy. The initial position of "Nom-de-Guerre" has meaning because it has potentially remained Van den Bosch's world, the reality that is perpetually transformed by the imagination. This holds true for all his stories, even for "Sarinah." Although the latter tale is based on the reality of camp Kesilir, there too its reality is shifted and compressed, if only through its rectilinear form, consisting almost exclusively of dialogue. In consequence, the tale seems immobile, and we get the feeling of walking around within an enclosed square amidst a small group of prisoners. Mutual tensions exist but each is dependent upon the other for reasons of self-preservation. No matter how heterogeneous the group is, all share the same fate, and all men have in common with one another the fact that they have to make do with a kind of life reduced to the performance of the most primitive needs, close to nature and the earth. Almost spontaneously, the system of *gotong-royong,* a way of rendering mutual assistance, has evolved within that community. This binding element has led to mutual understanding and even to the use of a language containing many Indonesian and a few Japanese-derived words. The title "Sarinah" comes from a well-known *kront jong* song of Indo-European origin, which one of the prisoners sings repeatedly as a Song without Words. It has become the theme song of a certain period and certain situation.

The final tale, "Disponent Andersson," is the account of a ramble through Lapland told by an unknown traveling companion on a train. It is told by one "Disponent Andersson" ("disponent" being the polite form of address), with whom the author has in fact scarcely exchanged a word. At first glance, there seem to be hardly any parallels between the rugged mountain landscape of northern Sweden and the mountain ranges in the tropics, but after awhile we come to realize that these parallels do in fact exist. They share the same impenetrable, stolid, and sometimes even hostile nature which taunts and which invites a careful, step-by-step conquest. Man can only maintain himself here if he knows and has fathomed nature's character and behavior. Man's only hope for survival lies in exercising the utmost in strength, understanding, and circumspection. It may sound odd, but Van den Bosch's description of the Swedish landscape reminds one irrepressibly of Junghuhn's descriptions of the volcanoes on Java. Lapland's inhospitable nature, the peaks, the high plains, the rock formations, all of them remind Van den Bosch of mountaineering trips he undertook on Java. Even the banks of peat moss remind him of the dykes around the rice fields, but he is not just reminded of a tropical landscape but also of past events and of people. On the very top of Linavare, of all places, he remembers faces from his childhood. "Whatever brought me to this place?" he asks himself. "Was it my long exile in Holland, the hidden force of my longing for Babu Suntjiani, for my friend Ted, for a girl from the past perhaps?" The memory of Indonesia is never to be banished and will always crop up again, and not just for Van den Bosch but for all of us who were born and raised and have lived there.

In 1969, shortly before the great stream of tourists gained momentum, Hella Haasse made her first trip back to Indonesia. She wrote a book about it which she called *Scratches on a Rock (Krassen op een rots)*. She got her title from Walraven's *Letters (Brieven)*. The passage from which she derived her title reads in full: "We, you and I, or those coming after us, are never going to make it here, but for these people nothing ever changes. Our influence here amounts to less than a scratch on a rock. . . ." And what indeed does Dutch influence amount to but a few scratches on a rock? It is no accident that Walraven's sentence gave her a shock of recognition because nothing whatever remains of her particular childhood.

Haasse has said somewhere in *Identity Card* that almost every book she writes is really a search of sorts that always leads to her own inner self. To her a trip is not just a trip, and she is not the kind of author to make a "sentimental journey" to Indonesia and serve it up in the papers or in a book. A journey to her is a means of discovering her identity. Therefore an ordinary travel account will not do for Haasse, because it would mean the purposeful isolation of something that she cannot isolate because it is bound up with her past, present, and future, with her own development. For that reason, her travel account about Indonesia is not a travel journal in the strict sense of the word, and certainly more than its subtitle "Notes of a Trip through Java" suggests. It is, in fact, a personal compendium, a synopsis of everything Indonesia means to her, has meant to her, and will continue to mean.

Anyone born and raised in Indonesia like Haasse who returns there after thirty years' absence cannot escape a comparison between past and present, between the former Netherlands Indies and Indonesia, and certainly not a comparison between Hella Haasse as a girl and the mature writer she now is. Seeing one's country of origin again involves a process where present and past, subject and object are continuously interacting. To clarify such a process was the task Haasse set herself. Two possibilities were open to her. One possibility was that she integrate and rewrite the experiences and images of her childhood in her travel account. This would have meant unavoidably "falsifying" her childhood because it would have to be seen from the perspective of the present. That is why she chose another method, which she had used earlier, although never in quite such a concentrated manner: she opted for a puzzle or collage procedure, which meant that she would not integrate her information but instead put it side by side in a particular arrangement. She had the advantage of already possessing the information. In the first place, she had kept a diary when a girl, and, furthermore, she had two unpublished stories, respectively written fifteen and twenty-three years earlier. Finally, there were the fragments that had already appeared in *Self-Portrait as Puzzle* and in *Identity Card*. She must have assumed that her authentic information would come across better than a new version of it rewritten to fit this new context. Making the book into something resembling a puzzle would also involve the reader more by providing him with the essential ingredients he could then work with. Arranging her book cannot have been easy but the method suits Haasse. She has a feeling for recognizing "patterns, structures, motifs, and themes," the same things that attract her in music, but the question remains how the reader reacts to her demand. This very much depends on the reader. He has to be a good reader and he has to have a feeling for patterns and structures, etc., himself. The critic Kees Fens is definitely one such reader but he still had some difficulty with her composition, especially with the setting of both stories. He must certainly have guessed too that they were meant to serve as contrasts, but they are contrasts that are too distantly placed from one another.

Scratches on a Rock not only interweaves childhood and present, but also alternates from one genre to the next. One may well object to her switching from essay to critical review, and from fact to fiction, just as one may object to her political and historical information, but *Scratches on a Rock* is a good book even so. It is nothing negative but something positive rather, to say that the book leaves an overall impression of confusion. This is the very reason why the book is an exact reflection of the feelings and thoughts that must have overwhelmed Haasse as she revisited Indonesia.

Not long thereafter, Johan Fabricius also went to the land of his birth, together with a small band of nine other nostalgic crusaders and a retired bookbinder from Amsterdam. No doubt they had a good as well as pleasant companion in Fabricius, with whom they could exchange reminiscences. He also turned out to be an excellent guide, better no doubt than their Dutch "hostess."

His book *Sentimental Journey*, which appeared in 1971, falls somewhere between a story with impressions of a trip and a travel guide with notes, things to see, and so on. It is not, as in Haasse's case, a search for one's own true self, nor a confrontation, but a friendly little book illustrated with photographs. Its third and revised 1973 printing is the one to buy under its new title *A Trip to the New Indonesia (Een reis door het nieuwe Indonesië)*, with the idea of a "sentimental journey" relegated to the subtitle. The things Fabricius has to say remain on the surface but the book does not pretend to be anything more than it is.

Fabricius's sometimes frightening productivity, and the fact that much of his work bears the traces of it, has been criticized ad nauseam, and not just by the author of *Mirror of the Indies* alone. Maybe the time has come to say something about its positive aspect too. Anyone who has the art of storytelling down as well as Fabricius has, and who writes as regularly as he does, is a master at the writer's trade, and that is nothing to belittle. But craftsmanship does not begin to function well unless it is also connected with what is under the writer's skin and begins to show signs of a certain vision, for example, or else reveals a certain tone or a distinct attitude toward the work at hand. Fabricius may well have gone easy on himself many times, but the connection between ability and vision is present in his epistolary novel *Dipanegara* (1977). The book takes its title from the name of the leader and inspirer of the resistance against the Dutch during the Java War, which lasted five years, from 1825 to 1830.

Fabricius informs us in his *Sentimental Journey* that as a boy he regarded Dipanegara as his romantic hero who suffered injustice at the hands of the Dutch and who declared a *perang sabil*, a holy war, against the infidel Christian dogs. In itself, this is something curious because the school texts about Dipanegara he must have read as a boy would certainly have portrayed him as a rebel and an overzealous and dangerous fanatic. Such at least was the image our patriotically slanted Dutch view of history managed to maintain for decades.

During his ultimate exile, Dipanegara wrote, in Javanese of course, a verse chronicle about the Java War called the *Babad Dipanegara*. As do all ballads, it contains a mixture of genealogical data, religious speculation, and transcendental representations. This work is of incalculable value to anyone desiring to know Javanese philosophy. W. Palmer van den Broek had translated the *Babad Dipanegara* in 1865 but his translation is no longer adequate. The historian and Javan scholar S. van Praag was the first to make the work generally accessible in his *Unrest on Java* (*Onrust op Java*, 1947) by quoting extensively from it, complete with needed notes and commentary. Van Praag had become fascinated by the figure of Dipanegara, who he thought "towered head and shoulders above his Dutch and Dutch-Indies contemporaries." This was a new angle altogether. Fabricius also gives the impression of having consulted the *Babad Dipanegara*, although he does not say anything about having done so. His book about Dipanegara is not a historical work, nor is it a biography, not even a romanticized one. It is definitely a novel, a novel of letters about the Java War in which the statements of Europeans are all the time paralleled and juxtaposed with statements from the *Babad Dipanegara*. It is a method that casts his story in relief, but we should not forget that Fabricius got most of his material from Western sources. He used the six-volume, almost overly detailed standard work on the Java War by P. J. F. Louw and E. S. de Klerck, both army officers, which appeared between 1894 and 1909. He also used a number of less important works. Fabricius does not quote directly from Dipanegara's *babad* but paraphrases whatever he can use for his novel.

Naturally, this is his prerogative as a novelist, just as it is fit for him to have the officers, soldiers, officials, and all others involved in the war write fictitious letters based on whatever historical materials he selected. As Fabricius smilingly describes this procedure, these letters were written "posthumously at the request of the author in order to help him shed light on the human aspects of the five-year drama." No historian need ask himself therefore if all the facts are correct or whether Fabricius has done a proper job in selecting his sources or whether indeed he has availed himself of every possibility to provide a clear picture of Dipanegara. Indeed, Fabricius has not. The materials he culled from his sources he recast totally, changing their language to contemporary Dutch, and arranging his facts on the basis of literary considerations. And rightly so, from his point of view. His epistolary novel has turned into a clever piece of work, written in a genre considered antiquated ever since the eighteenth century but of which Fabricius shows us the possibilities again. By using a difficult procedure, he has succeeded in writing a captivating book.

One possible objection is that the title *Dipanegara* does not quite describe the contents and hence creates the wrong impression.

His book is not really about Dipanegara but about the Java War, in which Dipanegara plays an active part. The book's emphasis is on the events surrounding the war. The conclusion of the book coincides therefore with the end of the war and with Dipanegara being sent into exile. We hear nothing further about what happened to Dipanegara from then on. The information from the *babad* is used in the first place to provide a contrast to the other facts given in the "private" letters, but it is not used to gauge or to portray the person of Dipanegara. Still, the discrepancy between title and subject should not influence one's evaluation of the book. What counts is that Fabricius has been altogether successful in his literary intention.

Van Praag's *Unrest on Java*, appearing shortly after World War II, was like so much handwriting on the wall and signaled a changed view of Dutch colonial history. Van Praag speaks of "Dipanegara's true greatness" and tries to make his readers appreciate it. His book appeared in 1947, the year the policing actions were about to start or had already begun. Van Praag was vehemently opposed to the war and held up the Java War as a warning to his compatriots: "Don't repeat the mistakes of the past, put a halt to every arrogant show of force. Try to understand what a guerilla war on Java would mean, as the years 1825–1830 prove to us in no uncertain terms." It is clear from this that as a historian and as a human being Van Praag belonged to the camp of the opposition.

And what about Fabricius, one wonders, where does he stand thirty years after those so-called policing actions, what is his view of the Java War and of Dipanegara? It is not that easy to say. There is not the slightest doubt about his respect for Dipanegara and, to use his own words, he no longer beats himself proudly on his colonial breast. Yet, there is a certain reservation in his attitude.

He has Captain Roeps write in his last letter to his wife that he does not believe that Dipanegara will enter history as "The Great Hero of Liberty." But this is exactly what did happen. By opposing the Dutch, Dipanegara, as a representative of the Javanese aristocracy and contemporary elite, succeeded in bringing about a mass movement and a complete revolution. Obviously, people in Indonesia have come to regard the Java War as a preamble to what was not completed until after World War II, and they regard Dipanegara as their first great revolutionary and fighter for freedom. He has been officially proclaimed a hero of the revolution. This may well be based on legend because he was more a Javanese mystic than anything else, but legends have a way of becoming reality, particularly where they fulfill the desire for self-esteem based on historical greatness. There is no doubt that Dipanegara was "a great man," all myth-making aside. Of course, he also relied on his strategic leaders, Sentot among them (the same who pronounces the "Malediction" on the Dutch in Roorda van Eysinga's poem, see p. 94), as well as on the aspirations and sentiments of the people.

His return to Indonesia and his fondness for the land of his birth and its people have also forced Fabricius into a confrontation of sorts, which has led him to have a different appreciation of an important phase in colonial Dutch and Indonesian history. For this reason too his novel could easily be discussed within the context of this chapter without our having to resort to any sleight of hand.

Even more relevant is his latest book, *The Screech of the White Cockatoo (De schreeuw van de witte kakatoe)*, which appeared early in 1978. The book's slightly more than eighty pages give an account of someone revisiting the land where he spent his early childhood, much the way Fabricius himself did. However, he has placed the

event in a different, historical context, making it a mixture of historical fact and fiction.

In 1817, on the island of Saparua in the Moluccas, a revolt broke out
against the Dutch government headed by the legendary hero Thomas
Matulesi, alias Pattimura. The rebels, who had been provoked by all
sorts of Dutch measures, orders, and sanctions, murdered the Dutch
resident, his wife, and two of their children hiding in Saparua's fortress. Their eldest son, six years old, was spared by a fluke and taken
care of by one Samuel Pattiwael. Following the surrender of the rebels, the child was returned to the Dutch. His family sent him to Holland to be cared for and educated. In his book, Fabricius has this surviving son return to the Moluccas when he is sixty years old. From
then on, Fabricius uses his literary discretion and gives his imagination free rein. The historical facts have been well integrated in the
story. The first half is clearly, soberly, and fascinatingly told, but the
further Fabricius strays from historical reality, the more he loses
sight of his own limits. Here the story runs away with itself and becomes altogether too obviously contrived. Love, of course, is not allowed to be absent either.

On page sixty-three of his book, Fabricius uses a phrase that might
well have served as a motto for *Mirror of the Indies*, because it does
not just apply to him but to nearly all the Dutch who have spent a
long time in the Indies/Indonesia, especially to those born and raised
there: "that strange period in my distant past always caused me to
feel an outsider in Holland."

Precisely this sentiment happens to be the pervasive theme in Willem Brandt's poetry. It is the theme of feeling a stranger here and over
there at the same time, the familiar ambivalence with its attendant
feeling of nostalgia. This is an unknown and incomprehensible feeling to many native Hollanders who tend to belittle it, even those who
have spent "some time" in Indonesia, and then mostly in an exclusively European milieu.

Brandt spent nearly thirty years in the Indies/Indonesia. The feeling of the homeless exile living in the Netherlands occurs rather frequently in his poetry, often in his best poems. In 1975, like so many
others, he made the almost obligatory trip to Indonesia. He wrote a
journal in verse about it, called *The Land of Return* (*Het land van
terugkomst*, 1976). One can easily follow his route in it. Apparently
the volume was popular with many who had lived in the Indies, and
in 1977 a second edition appeared. Brandt was already seventy years
old when he took this trip and he realized that this visit could very
well be his final farewell to Indonesia. Happily he appears not to be
too melancholy about the fact. When he returned to the Nether-

lands, he made a discovery which may or may not have surprised him but which was nonetheless curious and almost universal. He realized that he no longer felt like an exile:

> Again it's just the sea that keeps us far apart,
> But never do I go again cast out.
> Forever healed on your most generous heart,
> I'll meet you still on my autumnal route.

It is interesting that Brandt's nostalgia is mostly inspired and determined by the natural world, either with or without the trappings of towns, houses, or people. There is none of this in the work of Margaretha Ferguson. The world of nature is only sporadically represented there. Especially her more recent books show a very personal and almost obsessive concern with the problem of colonialism. Ferguson is perpetually aware of her position and gives the impression of being preoccupied with her intellectual responsibilities.

Her trip to Indonesia in 1974 stirred up a great deal in her and made her aware of problems that had really always occupied her. These were her anticolonial feelings and her colonial reactions which continued to assert themselves in her happy surprise at the changed racial relationships. She became aware of raw emotions within herself for which she had to find a solution, simply out of a need to rid herself of an inner ambivalence and a certain degree of anxiety that she must have sensed in herself.

During her trip she faithfully kept a journal, now and then forcing herself to find the time. It turned into quite a tome therefore, both personal and factual in content, but one that fails to hold our attention for any length of time. This is because of its overabundance of facts and impressions, and because her voice sounds too hurried and too strident. In an interview, Ferguson said she had the odd feeling her books were not meant for a contemporary but for a future audience, in the way of a time capsule. Looked at this way (and why indeed not?), we can accept the publication of her diary entitled *Other People Are Living There Now (Nu wonen daar andere mensen*, 1974).

The problem of Indonesia continued to occupy her without relief, even after her return to Holland. When she felt sufficiently recuperated from her impressions, she started work on a novel. What with domestic and social obligations, it took her two years to finish it. During the interview already referred to, Ferguson said that the intentions of that novel were "simply to present in a story a number of people, white, Indo-European and Indonesian, in their relationships to one another. I have tried, in addition, to find a synthesis between social involvement and individual experience, emphasizing the internal lives of the characters involved." This sound very much like an assignment or a program. The question is whether she has managed to render the program invisible in writing her story. In this respect she has been only partially successful. The plot of her novel *Elias in Batavia and Djakarta (Elias in Batavia en Djakarta,* 1977) is too transparent and her often long-winded dialogues are all too programmatic, lacking in spontaneity. It is difficult to escape the impression that her personal involvement has had a detrimental effect on her abilities as a novelist and that it has tempted her to utter generalities and simplifications, and those are the last things any real novel can support.

This is truly regrettable because Ferguson demands respect both as a person and on account of her consequential attitude, her frankness, and her steadfastness. Still, she ought to have chosen a different format to express her intense concerns, such as simply a personal statement. Her decision to choose the novel instead is doubly regrettable because she is a most capable writer. Her short stories have provided ample evidence of her ability. This recent work too has situations where her subtle directions can conjure up an atmosphere of relationships between people through her use of a gesture, through the movement of an eye, or with just a few casual thoughts. Limiting her scope would also have helped because only such self-limitation can force upon her the degree of concentration her book lacks. Her potential abilities continue to be best realized in the short story.

Youngest but not least among all these nostalgic pilgrims is Hans Vervoort, who was born in 1939 in Magelang (central Java) of European parents. It is obvious from just a few phrases that he knows how to write. At the onset of the Japanese occupation in 1942, his mother and her two small children were taken to a prison camp for women where his one-year-old brother died, an event that left deep scars. His father was forced to work as a POW, first on the Burma railroad and later in the Japanese mines. After the war, the family went to the Netherlands for a vacation, returning to Indonesia nine months later. When he was fourteen years old, Hans Vervoort went to the Netherlands for good and finished high school there. During his student days, he was an editor of *Propria Cures,* a magazine that has been the spawning ground for a remarkable number of Dutch literati, Vervoort among them. He is a marketing analyst now, and it is quite possible that making up lists of questions and writing reports has influenced his style. In any case, Vervoort is an exact writer of clear sentences and compact dialogues without difficult or fancy words.

In 1970, *Tiny Bits for Reading (Kleine stukjes om te lezen)* appeared, followed in 1973 by *Today Meat, Tomorrow You (Heden mosselen, morgen gij)*, presumably inspired by the funereal motto *Hodie Mihi Cras Tibi*, again a collection of short stories named after one of them. These are a bit longer than the stories in the first collection. Both collections have rather a lot of gruesome things happen in them and these hide quite a lot of general fear on the author's part. They are all about accidents, illness, death, eroticism, and such. Vervoort is a sober fellow who is just as suspicious of his sobriety as he is of all his other emotions. He is aware of the fact that one thing can drown out another. In between all this, he tries to keep his balance, and in the process he mocks himself ever so slightly with a grin. It is a process the reader can understand well enough.

A number of the stories have something to do with the Indies simply because that is where they took place and because the Indies make up a part of Vervoort's life that he could never quite rid himself of. The thing he probably least expected to happen to him did happen: the longing to see Indonesia again grew very strong. Its memories slowly surfaced and took on forms suspiciously resembling the outlines of nostalgia and homesickness. In any event, the urge grew in him, as the phrase goes, to return to the country of his childhood. "But not like just another tourist," he must have thought. Why could he not just go to Indonesia, and take a chance? He chose to go in his own peculiar way, much the same way young Dutch people like to travel down through France. He went, accompanied by his wife and two young children and a friend of theirs, another nostalgic crusader.

Anyone undertaking a trip of this kind, beyond the pale of tourism, in order to stay away three and a half months, must have really been seized by longing. Such a way of traveling, and with such a private retinue as his, has a way of leading to all sorts of obstacles. Nobody can say, however, that Vervoort was an indifferent traveler. He thought to be able to still his longing only by going, and so he went, probably without anticipating all the problems. Up to a point he must have been blissfully ignorant of all the changes that had taken place and he was, moreover, burdened by all sorts of Dutch habits (such as always looking for a cold beer), and by typically Dutch value judgments. This invariably leads to misunderstandings, but his travel account *Out in the Noonday Sun (Vanonder de koperen ploert,* 1975) with its frequent, small ups and downs has an irresistible and comical effect. Just like Springer, Vervoort is able to laugh at himself and he has the ability to recognize a "crazy" situation when he sees one, even when he is the victim of it. This certainly pleads well for him and it is precisely what makes his travel account so pleasant to read. He plays the part of a total stranger and outsider, although between the lines—and especially on account of what he leaves unsaid—he remains intimately involved with everything that transpires. Only he is not the kind of man to write preciously, and he definitely shuns all literary pretension. His book is one of sober and sobering reportage, but when it comes right down to it, it presents just as fierce a battle against nostalgia as the travel accounts of Haasse or Ferguson, not to mention Fabricius's *Sentimental Journey.*

Not everyone will be pleased with Vervoort's *Out in the Noonday Sun.* It will undoubtedly give rise to numerous misunderstandings, even mutual misunderstandings. For one thing, the Indies old-timers who have had no trouble exchanging the good old Dutch East Indies for modern Indonesia will get all in a huff about his desecration and lack of understanding. On the other hand, leftist pedants, for example, will vilify Vervoort because he nowhere mentions having encountered a police state. Instead, he tells us that he was free to go and to travel anywhere he wanted to. The reason he does not talk about Suharto's regime, for example, could well be that anything dictatorial transpiring in Indonesia would simply take place beyond the tourist's ken. What does strike Vervoort is the friendliness and openness of the people, something that does not exactly suggest that they are living under heavy pressure from above. All Vervoort wanted was to be an unbiased tourist. He could not and did not want to have any other point of view.

His book is not for those who already know what Indonesia is all about but for individualists such as Hans Vervoort himself who simply wish to travel through Indonesia as interested laymen the way he did, untrammeled and ignorant, if necessary. For the latter, Vervoort has added a number of sound suggestions, printed in italics. That way his book looks a bit like a travel guide.

His nostalgia will probably have been extinguished by his recent visit but chances are that he will sooner or later plan a new trip to Indonesia. This would seem to lie within the realm of expectations. The initially idealized image can be replaced by that of a more realistic Indonesia, ultimately still leaving one the memory of sun, nature, and friendly, hospitable people. In short, it would leave one a country to go back to, but a country to return to without nostalgia and better prepared, and all that would be pure gain for Hans Vervoort.

In 1977, his long novel *Black Rice (Zwarte Rijst)* appeared. Black rice is an Indonesian delicacy, the so-called *wadjik,* prepared from black, sticky rice. The black ingredient in the title also suggests something about the overall sadness of the entire story. It involves all sorts of sadness, really, which seem a bit too compacted here, such as lost illusions, a disaster, some sort of kidnapping, complete with murder and mayhem, and the realization of something irreparable, with a little extraneous eroticism and too much drinking in between. In contrast to the other stories, Indonesia is little more than a backdrop this time. The action is difficult to place exactly, and the Indies and Indonesia seem a bit mixed up, just as memory and reality are. Taken all in all, everything seems to come at once here, and maybe too many things have been concentrated into too small a scope. As one goes along, one is tempted to take the story apart because it contains unforgettable vignettes such as a child's drowning, an image from his memory, and the sudden wish to commit suicide at the waterfall, an experience that is also partly a memory.

Black Rice is not a "successful" novel but it is definitely so well written that we would not want to exchange it for many so-called well-written stories.

8   Rob Nieuwenhuys / E. Breton de Nijs

Inasmuch as Breton de Nijs and the author of this book are twins who crawl into each other's skin from time to time, it is not feasible to follow the same procedure as that in previous chapters. All told, there are three possible approaches. The first one would have R. Nieuwenhuys writing about Breton de Nijs in the third-person singular. The second approach would be to have a third person writing about both Breton de Nijs and Rob Nieuwenhuys. Finally, a third approach would be for R. Nieuwenhuys to write in the first person singular about Breton de Nijs, and about himself. Before we decide, however, we should ask ourselves what the point of all this would be. It might possibly help to establish a greater degree of "objectivity" and it might be a guarantee against too much "subjectivity." But really, even to *choose* the third person constitutes a subjective act in itself, and if we chose the third person, we would only be hiding the first-person singular behind it, and this would make little sense. For that reason I have opted to write in the first-person singular. In any case, in doing so I will feel a lot less constrained.

I was born in 1908 in Semarang. My father was born in the Netherlands, my mother in the Indies. I grew up in Batavia but spent my high-school years largely in Surabaja. I was nineteen when I went to Holland for the first time. It was a country I thought I knew from books but that turned out quite differently all the same. When I was twenty-six, I returned to Indonesia. Since July 1952, I have been living in Holland, and I have only seen the country of my birth once since then, for a two-month visit in October and November of 1971. The visit proved again how essential my Indies childhood was. A childhood spent there determines a certain cultural pattern and one's responses to it. It also means a relationship with Indonesia that is irreplaceable and that anyone coming to the country later in life will never attain, simply because he or she will lack certain experiences. I have tried several times to give a written account of my peculiar position of living between "two homelands." I have done so first as E. Breton de Nijs by writing the only novel I ever wrote, *Faded Portraits (Vergeelde portretten)*, as well as several short stories which have appeared in magazines and anthologies.

My first encounter with literature was in high school in Surabaja. I have written about it in the commemorative book of a teachers' society. My interest led me to study literature but not literature in the strict sense of the work, partly because the curriculum at Leiden University offered little chance of doing so. I did not get interested in writing until much later when I was back in Indonesia again. There I read everything by P. A. Daum I could get my hands on, and I wrote an article about him in *Greater Netherlands (Groot Nederland*, Sept. 1939). It was Daum who introduced me to *tempo dulu*, the period when my mother was still a young girl. In any case, Daum stirred something in me and I suspect that the inception of both my novel *Faded Portraits* (1954) and of my book of photographs *Tempo Dulu (Tempo Doeloe*, 1961) is due to his influence. I wrote these books under my pseudonym E. Breton de Nijs, a nom de plume that I have reserved for my most personal books.

Before the war, I was on the editorial staff of *The Torch (De Fakkel)*. There I was asked to do a special two-volume issue on Indonesia and was given carte blanche to do the job. I wrote away to a number of people and fairly quickly got a number of poems and novels together written by authors such as Resink, Vuyk, Walraven, and Suwarsih Djojopuspito. I took a chance myself and wrote a story that I also included. It was called "One of the Family" ("Een van de familie") and it contained essentially the material for my later novel. Greshoff and Walraven had similar reactions to it. Greshoff wrote me in a letter: "It's just like a Japanese toy, the kind you put into a glass of water and which then begins to open up and blossom, except that your story is too concentrated to open up." And Walraven wrote: "You are moving through your story with the speed of an express train, and I would want to expand and elaborate on nearly every sentence of it." I certainly took their criticism to heart. Just as obedient as Friedericy had been to Alberts, in prison camp I did what Greshoff and Walraven had suggested, and expanded my story. One of my problems was finding a format, writing a novel that did not have to conform to the novelistic tradition. I had tried earlier to write a "real" novel but had not gotten anywhere with it. I then solved my problem by casting it in the shape of a chronicle.

A critic, just one, in fact, wrote that my novel was little more than a number of unrelated stories, arbitrarily arranged. The very opposite is true. Its chapters are closely related, in fact. I have tried to write a story that only pretended to move forward, thinking of Proust perhaps, while in reality aiming for a clear composition. Another way of putting it is that I have purposely striven to bring about a particular arrangement. The first and the final chapter bracket the family history, putting it in between parentheses, as it were. I have obviously also used the flashback technique that struck me as very effective in a novel by James M. Cain, *The Postman Always Rings Twice.* My first chapter contains everything in a nutshell, such as Aunt Sophie's relationship to the girls, that of Uncle Alex to his sisters, as well as my own relationship to Aunt Sophie, which is mostly revealed by its tone. This chapter also introduces the book's most important characters and, again, the way they relate to each other, such as Uncle Alex to his children. The tragedy of Aunt Sophie's life is suggested by what I have Aunt Christien say: "Poor dear, . . . she has known so little happiness in her life." Uncle Tjen is the link between Aunt Sophie, her family, and my own mother. I describe him first in order to concentrate on the main character, Aunt Sophie, later on.

Although a great deal of it is made up, my novel is based on fact. However, memory or some other faculty of mine has altered the reality in my book, while at the same time charging it with a definite sentiment, with a feeling and atmosphere which that reality by itself never really possessed. Hence truths, half truths, and all kinds of truths have been combined to make one single image that takes the place of memory. I think anything remembered is really a thing reimagined, or imagined anew. I have to say that one of the dearest characters in my book, the girl Winny, who is composed of pure memory, is only vaguely outlined. Her outline is blurred by remembrance but all the more dear for that reason. That is the way these things are. If one wishes to use the awkward phrase "to create" at all, then I believe I have written not by using a creative imagination but by using a creative memory instead.

I have known all the people I write about, or rather this sort of people, so well that they have become a part of me. For years I lived among them, and to this day I consider myself an "Indies fellow" belonging to an "Indies group." I would not dream of denying what I still am. The notion that I might have treated my characters without sufficient affection or love is nonsense, of course. What is true, however, is that by the time I began the book, I had in many respects lost my feelings of solidarity with them. I found myself no longer capable of sharing their opinions, their judgments and prejudices. By then, the colonial ambiance no longer struck me as something natural. My meeting with a fellow Indonesian student, as related in the book, is authentic and it influenced me decisively. All of a sudden it made me look at the entire family in a totally different light. At the same time, however, I continued to feel strong ties to them, especially through the bond with my mother.

Taken all together, these people represented the colonial patriciate. Strictly speaking, I never belonged to it myself. As a stranger from Holland, my father was excluded from it, and on my mother's side too the patrician aspect had only come about by marriages into it. Aunt Sophie, of course, was very much a part of it, and she always spoke of the family and of all the others. They were a ruling class, accustomed to giving orders, accustomed to sitting in judgment of others and, if need be, to making use of someone else's freedom. Early in the twentieth century, a few of them still lived in the manner of landed gentry, while others had become merchants or officials. Yet each in his and her own right was a person who still had power. Even so, by the time they entered into my life via Aunt Sophie, their position was already in decline. Still, they continued to retain something I have remained sensitive to to this very day and that was a certain allure, a colonial allure if one prefers. They all still possessed a distinct style of life, but ... but maybe it is best to quote from my own book. There is no point in paraphrasing my own words and describing in different words my relationship with Aunt Sophie. She was the representative of this great clan, this dying class, even then already "plants without juices and without soil." I have been particularly obsessed, I think, with this decay and by the tragedy of this group of people who became uprooted and who was twice swept away by an avalanche. The first was the growth of capitalism and the subsequent Europeanization of society, the second was Indonesian nationalism. These people were torn away and swept along to be finally cast up on the shores of Holland, where their grandchildren are now in the process of developing themselves into a certain nuance of Dutch society.

Although Aunt Sophie is the main character in my book and I also write about other people, *Faded Portraits* is still an autobiography of sorts, even though it deals with different realities. For reasons of composition and so as not to detract from the unity of the story, I left out several figures who played an important part in my childhood. One of these is my younger brother, while another, my private *babu*, Nèneh Tidjah, is hardly present at all. All she does is walk around with a jar of *menjan* (incense) on *malam djumahat* (Thursday night), going through all the rooms muttering charms to ward off evil. She played a far more important role in my life. Nènèh Tidjah was with me during the first seven or eight years of my life, and spent more time with me than my mother did.

Whenever I reduce myself to a child again, Nènèh Tidjah is the first person I see. Only later, after her death, did my mother enter my life for good. I have made up some of this incompleteness in my book by writing about her and my relationship with her. Nènèh Tidjah introduced me to her Javanese world through her endless stories about gods and goddesses, about heavenly nymphs, demons, ghosts, petrified people, and the kind that could assume whatever shape they wished. Sometimes, she would recite entire dialogues and speak with two different voices, just a real storyteller or a *dalang* (the invisible narrator who shows the *wajang* puppets) does. Mountains have always meant a great deal more to me than mere overgrown protuberances in a landscape. They were inhabited by mountain spirits. Rain at night has always given me anxiety because I knew that then the *kuntianaks* would step down from the trees. A large circle around the moon would keep me in dread of some approaching cataclysm for days. Earthquakes and volcanic eruptions were echoes of supernatural battle and I knew that "up there" the great battle was being fought. The natural world of the Indies, thanks to Nènèh Tidjah, has always been more than a natural display that was either pretty or ugly, but always something alive and breathing, a world that was *angker*, alive with spirit and magic. This consciousness of things magical, to give it a name, has weakened in time and is no longer as acutely present. Although still active, it has gone underground, so to speak.

I realized this when I revisited my country of origin after twenty years' absence. The sense of magic was not there all the time, no more than once in a while and then only very briefly, but it was still there. Nènèh Tidjah bequeathed me an intimate relationship with Java's nature, one that I miss in the Netherlands, even though I admire, for example, the wide Frisian landscape with its clouds and its ever-moving water in lakes and rivers.

My second book, which appeared in 1959, was a collection of articles. The first two articles, "Tempo dulu ("Tempo doeloe") and "Maurits" (the pseudonym for P. A. Daum), had been written some twenty years earlier. I called the collection *Between Two Mother Countries* (*Tussen twee vaderlanden*, 1959; 2d ed., 1967). The title is not characteristic of the contents so much as of my own cultural position. I am typically someone living between two mother countries or fatherlands, and I am obviously not alone in that position. I am someone caught between the two worlds, someone who really has no country at all, although this is putting it too strongly. The situation would seem tragic somehow but it is not because this duality (another loaded term) actually is a good position from which to write. However, at times it seems as if I have two faces, one looking around here in Holland, with its own interests, and the other still facing the country that disappeared below the horizon. I am not really sure where I stand, and for that reason I am not quite sure who I really am. The search for my own roots as expressed in *Between Two Mother Countries* lacks the personal element that exists in my novel. Hence I have published it under my own name and not under my pseudonym. Whichever way one chooses to look at it, this collection of articles does not stress my personal life.

This is not quite the case where my book of and about photographs from the Indies is concerned. *Tempo doeloe* (the Indonesian spelling is tempo dulu), which literally means "times past," appeared in 1961 under my pseudonym E. Breton de Nijs. The book actually contains the illustrative material for my articles about *tempo dulu* and Daum, as well as for my novel *Faded Portraits*. But it is sufficiently personal, or rather it has such a personal meaning to me that I considered the use of my pseudonym justified. I should really have dedicated it to my mother because I kept meeting her throughout the book, either as a girl or as a young woman, since it deals with her world. Some people regard *Tempo doeloe* as nostalgic but the book deals with an era from long before my own time. It may well arouse a feeling of nostalgia in others, but as far as I am concerned, I think I am as ambivalent about *tempo dulu* as I am about my childhood.

The book emphasizes a period in the Indies that was coexistent with that of Napoleon III of France or the American Civil War, and maybe this arouses feelings of affection and romanticism in others. My criticism of Indies society of the past is shown clearly enough by the photographs from the Achin War and others, as well as from the accompanying text which I have kept as noncommittal and straightforward as possible. But I will admit that the pictures in the book have a way of getting to me also, especially the ones of avenues, trees, gardens, rivers, bathing spots, and particularly those of houses with people within and about. They have a way of reaching my heart—it is my past as well as that of my parents and grandparents (whom I never knew), of the extensive "great Indies family" that together we make up. But all of this is definitely a thing of the past. The people staring out at us from those photographs are dead now. They lie buried in one of those hundreds of abandoned and deteriorating European cemeteries. With good reason, I put my book of photographs together in such a way that it ends with a photograph showing just such a European graveyard. It is subject to weathering decay. The photograph in question is from long before the war.

After *Tempo doeloe*, I published a number of anthologies of Indies/Indonesian literature. The first was called *Parting of Ways* (*Bij het scheiden van de markt*, 1960 and 1965); the second anthology is called *Gossip and Literature* (*Van roddelpraat en litteratuur*, 1965), which goes back further in time. I also wrote two biographies under my own name, similar to the French series "Les écrivains de toujours," one about the linguist Van der Tuuk, the other about the great naturalist Franz Junghuhn.

Nicolaus de Graaff is no discovery of mine, for I already knew him through Du Perron, but Jacob Haafner is. He is a strongly motivated social writer about whom I would have liked to say more. Johannes Olivier too proved a happy find. His mockery of the moneyed aristocracy of Batavia did more than just amuse me. Still, the great discovery was Junghuhn. Running ahead of the completion of this book, I already wrote a short biography of him containing extensive excerpts from his writings called *Inexhaustible Nature* (*De onuitputtelijke natuur*, 1966). In Junghuhn's eyes, similar to my own, nature possessed an indwelling spirit too, albeit a totally different one. His pantheism, however, and his conviction that one can only hope to approach God through nature made a bond between him and nature which goes deeper and far beyond the "beauty and sweetness of the landscape." It is a bond that he too will never lose.

I have also made some other and smaller "discoveries" or "finds," such as recognizing the single, totally unknown story by its equally unknown author F. van den Bosch. I am singling out his "House of Rain" because I came upon it so totally unexpectedly, as in the similar case with Koelewijn's two stories. In addition to these, naturally there are those authors I was already acquainted with, and which I could not consider "discoveries" any longer but about whom I have been able to write with a different and a better kind of pen, I would like to think. My text should leave no doubt which ones they are.

Index

Abendanon, J. H., 157, 158, 161, 163
Achin Wars, 173, 180
Adams, Henry, xiv, xxii n
adat, x, xiii, 53, 152
Adiningrat family, 127
agrarian policies, 43, 48–49, 59
Alberts, A., xxiv, xxvi, 290–98, 324
Ambonese Herbal (Rumphius), 29, 31
Ambon's Museum of Curiosities (Rumphius), 29, 31
Angkatan '45, 208
angker. See magic and occult
Anwar, Chairil, 209
arts, 151, 182, 184

babu, xiv
Barentsz, Willem, 5
Batavian Commercial Daily, 96, 97
Batavian News (ed. P. A. Daum), 111, 127, 205
Batavian Society for Arts and Sciences, Royal, 34, 44, 45, 46, 50, 206
Baud, Elisabeth, 126
Baud, J. C., 59, 60, 61
Baudisch, A., 127
Beets, Nic. (pseud. L. A. Koelewijn), 232, 233, 245, 329
Bel, Ies van, 236
Beretty, D. W., xxviii
Berlage, H. P., 184
bersiap period, 237, 238, 239
besaran. See estates
Besnard, Albert, 226
Beyle, H., 191, 198
Binnerts, C., 227
Blume, C. L., 46, 56, 58

Boeka. *See* Hansen, P. C. C.
Boekholt, Ralph, 309
Bontekoe, Willem Ysbrantszoon, 3, 8–12
Boon, J. (pseud. Tjalie Robinson), 198, 301
Borel, Henri, 111, 137, 144, 161, 183
Bosch, F. van den, 310–13, 329
Bosch, Joh. van den, 59
botany, 28–31, 46, 67–76
Braak, Menno ter, 111, 112, 171, 191, 192, 199, 273
Brandt, Willem, 226, 228, 229, 240, 318–19
Brest van Kempen, J. J., 85
Brink, Jan ten, 90
Brom, Gerald, xv, xvi, xvii, xviii, xxii n, 24, 111, 189, 298
Brooshooft, P., 155, 157, 160
Brummund, J. F. G., 69
Bus de Gisignies, L. P. J. du, 55, 57, 58, 59
Busken Huet, Conrad, xxv, 1, 8, 24, 25, 90, 161
Buyskes, A. A., 43

Cain, James M., 325
Camphuis, Johannes, 27, 28, 32, 36
Capellen, G. A. G. Ph., Baron van der, 42–53 passim, 55, 57, 58, 60
Capellen, Robert Jasper van der, 60
Carleton, J., 38
Carpentier Alting, Rini, 299
Carrington, Charles, xxii n
Chailley-Bert, J., 134
Chasteleyn, Cornelis, 36
Chinese, 183, 239
Coen, Jan Pietersz., 12
Cohen, Alexander, xviii, 106–10

Cohen Stuart, A. B., 54
Company. *See* United East India Company
concentration camps. *See* prison camps
concubinage, 57, 120, 143, 146, 167, 201, 202, 217
conservative movement, 42, 178
corruption, 33–34, 104, 135
Cortenbach, A. Paul, 241
The Counselor (H. J. Friedericy), 284
Country of Origin (E. du Perron), xv, xxv, 189–93, 259
Couperus, Louis, xvii, xxix, 123–33, 134, 152, 160, 161, 184, 278
Courier dit Dubekart, A. M., 103–6
Creusesol. *See* Graafland, I. P. C.
Critique and Reconstruction, 204, 205, 206, 220
Cuijpers, Ed., 181
cultivation system *(cultuurstelsel)*, xi, 92, 98, 101

Daendels, Herman Willem, x, 41, 45
daily press, xxviii
The Dam, 178, 179
Damsté, H. T., 152, 175
Daum, P. A. (pseud. Maurits), xvi, xxiv, xxvii, xxviii, xxix, 111–22, 124, 137, 145, 219, 324, 327, 328
The Dawn, 69
"A Debt of Honor," *The Guide* (C. Th. van Deventer), 156
Defoe, Daniel, 15
Delft Academy, 61, 92, 102
De Nijs, E. Breton. *See* Nieuwenhuys, R.
Dermoût, Maria, xxv, xxvi, xxix, 255–67, 278
Deutel, Jan, 9
Deventer, C. Th. van, 156, 157, 161
Deventer, S. van Jszn., 79
Deyssel, L.van, 129, 137
Dipanegara (J. Fabricius), 97, 315
Diponegoro, 97, 315
Djajadiningrat, Roswitha, 246
Djajadiningrat family, 224
Djojohadikusomo, Margono, 224
Djojopuspito, Sugondo, 208, 209
Djojopuspito, Suwarsih, 207, 208, 209, 210–13, 324
Does, Frank van der, 6
Dokarim, 175
Domela Nieuwenhuis, F., 99, 108, 109

Doorn, J. A. A., 248
Douwes Dekker, E. (pseud. Multatuli), xvi, xvii, xxii n, xxv, xxvi, xxvii, xxix, 48, 52, 67, 77–93, 94, 95, 96, 98, 100, 101, 102, 103, 105, 106, 109, 116, 148, 164, 191, 203, 204, 218
Douwes Dekker, E. F. E., 221, 222
dukun, xiv
Dutch society, 21, 44–45, 97, 106, 113, 121, 140, 162, 173
Dutch women in the Indies, 138, 143, 144, 155, 167–70, 201, 225–39 passim, 255, 300
Duymaer van Twist, J. J., 85

East West Society, 183, 184
economics, 96, 114, 156
education, 46, 59, 159, 210
Eeden, F. van, 160, 161, 186
Eggink, Jan, 227
Eighties Movement, 118, 139, 150
Eijkelboom, Jan, 244
Elias, E. R. Duncan, 240, 241
Elias, W. H. J., 241
Elout, C. Th., 43
Elsschot, Willem, 111, 250
enforced labor. *See* cultivation system
epistolary genre, 80, 98, 100, 213, 214, 220, 315
estates, 117, 195, 255
ethical movement, xi, 129, 154–63, 179, 207, 283
Eurasians, social position of, 18, 60, 61, 113, 124, 130, 135, 139, 145, 148, 150, 151, 168, 173, 221, 272–79 passim, 308–10, 325–26
European attitudes, 53, 54–55, 57, 61, 136, 144, 145, 147, 152–53, 154, 157, 184, 203, 217
European society in Indonesia, 20, 21, 22, 36, 47, 49, 59, 146, 300
Eysinga, van. *See* Roorda van Eysinga
Eysselsteijn, Ben van, 188, 279

Fabricius, Johan, 10, 241, 278–82, 314–18, 322
Faded Portraits (R. Nieuwenhuys), xiv, xx, xxiii n, 227, 324, 325, 326, 328
fascism, 198, 203, 205, 206
The Fatherland, 200, 286
Faulkner, William, xii
Fens, Kees, 280

Ferguson, Margaretha, 237, 299, 319–20, 322
Fock, D., 178
Focquenbroch, Willem Godschalk, 19
Forum, 199, 209
Free Netherlands, 207, 279
Friedericy, H. J., xxvi, xxix, 227, 282–90, 324
Furnivall, J. S., 157

Galen Last, H. van, 222, 223, 224
Gandhi, Mahatma, 187
Goens, Rijklof van, 7
Gomes, P., 238, 241
Gomperts, H. A., 198, 199
Gonggrijp, G., 145
Gonggrijp, G. L., 189
Gooyer, A. C. de, 242
gossip. *See* oral tradition
government, 114, 129, 148, 203
government structure in the Netherlands Indies, 84
Graaff, H. J. van de, 44, 46, 47, 48, 58
Graaff, Nicolaus de, xxix, 2, 16–19, 20, 21, 22, 36, 329
Graafland, I. P. C. (pseud. Creusesol), 124, 141–45, 155
Graeff, A. C. D., 178, 179
's-Gravesande, H., 165
Greater Netherlands, 112, 324
Great Mutiny, 97
Greshoff, Jan, xxvi, 163, 190, 196, 199, 279, 302, 324
Groneman, Isaäc, 76
The Guide, 52, 87, 91, 111, 156, 290

Haafner, Jacob, 21, 329
Haan, F. de, xxv, 6, 7, 19, 24, 25, 44
Haasse, Hella, 298–301, 313–14, 322
Haghe, Adolf ter. *See* Koch, J. A.
Hakluyt, Richard, 5
Hakluyt Society, 2, 3
Hansen, P. C. C. (pseud. Boeka), 146, 155
Hatta, Mohammed, 181, 186, 207
health, 16, 34, 35, 46, 66–76 passim, 168, 201
Heekeren, C. van, 230, 231, 232
Heemskerk, Jacob van, 5
Hendrix, W. J., 248
The Hidden Force (L. Couperus), 126–32, 134, 145
Hien, H. A. van, 258

Hoëvell, W. R., Baron van, xxvii, xxix, 24, 59–66, 67, 78, 83, 90, 91
Hofhout, Johannes, 7
Hofland family, 117
Hofwijk, J.W., 242
Hogendorp, C. S. W., 42, 46, 51, 52, 55, 57, 58
Hogendorp, Dirk van, 33, 36, 37–42, 204
Hogendorp, Gijsbert Karel van, 33, 39, 40, 42
Hogendorp, Willem van, xvi, 33–36, 37
Hoogewerff, G. J., 8
Hoogte, Albert van der, 243, 244
housekeeper. *See* concubinage
Houtman, Cornelis de, 5, 8
Hucht, Willem van der, 80
Huet, Conrad Busken. *See* Busken Huet, Conrad
Hueting, J. E., 247, 248
Hulswit, M. J., 181
hypocrisy, 22, 49, 66

Idenburg, A. W. F., 156
The Indies Fatherland (ed. P. A. Daum), 111, 113, 115
The Indies Guide, 147
The Indies Home, Past and Present, 181, 184
Indies Weekly, 149
Indo-Europeans. *See* Eurasians
Institute for the Tropics, Royal (Colonial Institute), 181
The Islands (A. Alberts), 290–93, 294, 295
Israëls, Isaäc, 184
Itinerario (J. H. van Linschoten), 3, 4, 5

Jagt, M. B. van der, 146, 179, 180
Jarrell, Randall, xviii, xxii n
Jasper, J. E., 149–51, 152, 155
Java Courant (ed. Jszn. S. van Deventer), 79
Java Courier, 142, 171, 203, 222
Java War, 97, 316, 317
John Company (A. van Schendel), 163–65
Jonge, B. C. de, 179
Junghuhn, Franz Wilhelm, xvi, xviii, xix, xxiii n, xxiv, xxix, 67–76, 329
Justice for All, 99, 108, 109

Kaempfer, Engelhard, 31
Kalff, G., 10
Kalff, S. (critic), 105

Kartini, Raden Adjeng, 158
Kartodirdjo, Sartono, 84
Kat Angelino, A. D. A. de, 178, 179
Kawi-Balinese language, 102
Kempetai, 187
Kerckhoven, Simon van, 15
Keyzer, S., 23
Kipling, Rudyard, xiv, xxii n
Kleian, J., 172, 173
Knaap, Otto, 139, 140, 182
Koch, D. M. G., 205, 206, 220
Koch, J. A. (pseud. Adolf ter Haghe), 222
Koelewijn, L. A. See Beets, Nic.
Koets, P. J., 206, 208
Kol, H. H. van, 157
Koloniaal Tijdschrift, 146
Koopman, M., 138
Koster, Paul J., 137
Kraemer, H., 178
Kruseman, A. C., 77, 83

landscape, descriptions of, xxiv–xxv, 4, 6, 7, 8
Larbaud, Valéry, 191, 200
The Last House in the World (B. Vuyk), 267, 268, 274
Léautaud, Paul, 200; cited, xxiv
Lebak Affair, 84, 85–87, 88, 106, 204
Leendertz, C. J., 259
Leffelaar, H. L., 229
Lelyveld, Th. B. van, 184
Lennep, Jacob van, 86, 87, 90
Leur, J. van, 206
Library of the Indies, xix
Limburg Stirum, J. P. van, 156, 178, 179
linguistics, 54, 100–3
Linschoten, Jan Huygen van, 3, 4, 5, 19
Linschoten Vereeniging (Society), 2, 3, 8, 17
The Locomotive, 178

MacGillavry, Annemie, 237, 238, 241
magic and occult, xiv, 117, 124, 125, 126–32, 153, 174, 257, 258, 263, 265, 267, 299, 327
Mahieu, Vincent, xxvi
Manders, J., 173, 227, 228, 241
Mangku Negoro, 186
Mangunkusomo, Sujitno, 206, 208, 209, 210, 213
Mangunkusomo, Tjipto, 207
manors. See estates

Marsman, H., 199, 268, 269
Matulesi, Thomas (Pattimura), 318
Maurik, H. van, 242
Maurik, Justus van, 134, 135, 141
Maurits. See P. A. Daum
Max Havelaar (E. Douwes Dekker), xvi, xxvi, xxvii, 48, 56, 77, 78, 79, 82, 83, 84, 85, 86, 87, 88–90, 91, 92, 93, 95, 97, 105, 106, 108, 160, 191
May Movement of 1848, 61–62, 66
Meylan, G. F., 46, 47
Mercure de France, 110
Merlijn, H. J. See Friedericy, H. J.
Mirror of the Indies (N. de Graaff), xxix, 17, 18
Mirror of the Indies (R. Nieuwenhuys), xvii, xix, xx, xxii n, 208, 315, 318
Monsoon, 309
Moojen, P. A. J., 183
Mook, H. J. van, 178, 271
Motley, John Lothrop, viii
Muljono, Joke, 246
Multatuli. See Douwes Dekker
Muntinghe, H. W., 43, 46, 50, 52, 58

Nagel, G. H., 46, 52, 56, 57, 58
Nasution, Ida, 209
nationalism, 178, 180, 183, 185, 206, 221–24, 270–72
national socialism. See fascism
Neck, Jakob van, 6, 7, 8
Nederburgh, S. C., 39
Nènèh Tidjah. See Tidjah, Nènèh
Netherlands Indies Magazine (ed. W. R. van Hoëvell), 66, 70, 73, 77, 78
Netherlands Indies, Past and Present, 184
The Netherlands Lion, 123
Netherlands Trading Company, 88
Nieuwenhuys, Rob (pseud. E. Breton de Nijs), xiii, xiv, xvii, xviii, xix, xx, xxi n, xxii n, xxiii n, xxvi, 227, 299, 315, 323–29
Nieuwenkamp, W. O. J., 184
njai. See concubinage
Norsfield, 46
Noto Suroto, 184–88, 281
Nuis, Aad, 252
Nusantara, 206

O'Connor, Flannery, xii
Oedaja (ed. Noto Suroto), 185, 186

Oldenbarneveldt, Johan van, ix
Olivier, Johannes, xxv, xxvii, 46, 47, 49, 50, 52–54, 55, 56, 57, 58, 60, 329
oral tradition, xxvii–xxix, 257, 259, 260, 264, 284
The Oriental (ed. J. Olivier), 53
Orientation, 208, 246, 275, 301
Overbeke, Aernout, 19, 20

Paku Alam family, 186
Parr, Charles McKew, 4
Pattimura, 318
Perron, E. du, xv, xvi, xvii, xviii, xxii n, xxv, xxvi, xxix, 18, 40, 41, 111, 112, 189–213 passim, 220, 259, 272, 273, 298, 299, 329
Philip II, viii, ix
Pirngadi, Mas, 151
Plancius, P., 4, 5
policing actions, 239, 240, 241, 242, 244, 245, 246–48. *See also bersiap* period
Poortenaar, J., 184
population, increase of, 155, 201
Potgieter, E. J. 9, 10, 52
Praag, S. van, 315, 316
prijaji, xi
Pringgodigdo, Nining, 207
Prins, Jan, 183
prison camps: Dutch, 207, 231, 232; Japanese, xxii n, 151, 215, 221, 225–39 passim, 241, 274, 285, 286, 290, 311–12, 320, 324
Pudjangga Baru, 209, 210

racial views, 21, 60, 61, 142, 144, 145, 147, 149, 154, 157, 166, 196, 197, 217, 272–73, 319
Raffles, Thomas Stamford, x, 42, 43, 45, 50, 51, 60
Ransom, John Crowe, xii
regent. *See* government structure
Regteren, Seyger van, 12
Reinwardt, C. G. C., 46
resident. *See* government structure
Resink, G. J., 178, 324
revolution. *See bersiap* period; policing actions
Ridder, André de, 123
Ridjali, 26
Ritter, W. L., xxv
Robbers, Herman, 171
Robinson, Tjalie. *See* Boon, J.

Rochussen, H., 70, 76
Rochussen, J. J. (minister of colonies), 73, 86, 87
Roorda, Taco, 102
Roorda van Eysinga, Ph. P. 46, 52, 54–55, 57, 58, 60, 317
Roorda van Eysinga, S. E. W., 94–100
Rouffaer, G. P., xxv, xxvii, 92, 145, 146
Rumphius, Georg Everard, xvii, xxv, xxix, 24, 26, 28–31, 32, 261
Ruyter, J. de, 83
Ruzius, J. B., 139

Samkalden, H., 206
Schendel, Arthur van, 163–66, 285
Schilt, Jan, 247
Schimmelpenninck, Rutger Jan, 41
Schmidt, Max C. P., 70
Schneider, C. J. (pseud. F. Springer), 249–52, 321
Schneiders, A. J., 245
Scholte, Lin, 241, 299
Schouten, Wouter, 13, 19
Sentot, 97, 317
Sevenhoven, J. I. van, 46, 50, 52
Sikap, 207
Situmorang, Sitor, 209
Sjahrir, Soetan, 196, 207, 208, 209, 210
Skeat, W. W., 265
slavery, 22, 35–38, 64
Snouck Hurgronje, Ch., 157
Sontag, Susan, xx, xxiii n
Sötemann, A. L., 88, 191
Sprang, Alfred van, 240
Springer, F. *See* Schneider, C. J.
Stavorinus, J. S., 20, 21, 44
Stendhal, 191, 198
Stokram, Andries, 14, 15
Stokvis, J. E., 157, 178
Subardjo, Achmad, 206
Suharto, 322
Sujitno. *See* Mangunkusomo, Sujitno
Sukarno, xi, 206, 207, 212, 213, 222, 223, 307, 308
Sumohardjo, Urip, 224
Surabaja Courant, 104, 141
Sytzen, Job, 243, 247
Székely-Lulofs, M. H., 170–76, 222

Tacitus, 5
Tagore, Rabindranath, 185, 187
Tempo dulu, xii, 197, 202, 324, 328

Teuku Umar, 175
Thomas (journalist), xxviii
Thorbecke, J. R., 63
Thorn, W.. 45
Tidjah, Nènèh, xiv, xxi n, xxii, 327
Tirade, 16
Toba-Batak language, 102
The Torch, 220, 221, 324
totok, xiii
The Transcriber, 77, 78
travel, yearning for, 3, 16, 104, 152, 194, 216, 217, 238, 243, 273, 278, 301, 308, 322
Tuuk, H. N. van der, xvii, xviii, xxiii n, xxiv, xxix, 100–3, 146, 329

Udaya (ed. Noto Suroto), 188
Umar, Teuku, 175
United East India Company, ix, 41, 44, 163–66
urban expansion, 181, 201

Valentijn, François, xvii, xxix, 22–24, 25, 26, 27, 32, 36
Valette, G. J. P. de la, 126
Varenne, Jan, 247, 248
Veenstra, J. H. W., 195, 203, 204
Veer, Gerrit de, 5
Veer, Paul van 't, 41, 65
Vermeulen, G. J., 242
Versteegh, Caroline, 77, 78, 79, 81
Vervoort, Hans, 320–23
Verwey, Albert, 105
Vestdijk, S., 190
Veth, Bas, xxviii, 134–40, 154, 160, 182
Veth, P. J., 24, 65, 66, 87, 91

Vinne, J. van der, 46
Vitalis, L., 92
Vleuten, L. C. van, 137, 138, 141
VOC. See United East India Company
Vollenhoven, C. van, xiii, 157
Vroman, Leo, 226
Vuyk, Beb (E. de Willigen-Vuyk), xxix, 124, 208, 210, 267–78, 324

Wadman, Anne, 279, 281
Wal, S. L. van der, 59
Walraven, Willem, xvii, xxiv, xxvi, xxviii, xxix, 197, 202, 213–21 passim, 311, 313, 324
Warnsinck, J. C. M., 17, 18
Warren, Robert Penn, xii
Weitzel, A. W. P., 99
Wertheim, W. F., 96
Wessem, Constant van, 272, 273
Westenek, L. C., 151, 152, 155
Wielenga, D. K., 280, 281
Wijnbergen, Everdine (Tine) van, 80, 81, 86, 88
Wilson, Edmund, xvii
Woensel, Pieter van, 16
Wolkers, Jan, 308
women, influx of Dutch, 167
Woude, Johan van der, 265
Wybrands, Karel, xxviii

Zaalberg, F. H. K., 119
Zentgraaff, H. C., xxviii, 203, 205
Zikken, Aya, 298, 301–7
Zola, Emile, 114, 115, 116
Zwaan, J., 247